Migration into ar

MANCHESTER
1824

Manchester University Press

rethinking **art's** histories

SERIES EDITORS
Amelia G. Jones, Marsha Meskimmon

Rethinking Art's Histories aims to open out art history from its most basic structures by foregrounding work that challenges the conventional periodisation and geographical subfields of traditional art history, and addressing a wide range of visual cultural forms from the early modern period to the present.

These books will acknowledge the impact of recent scholarship on our understanding of the complex temporalities and cartographies that have emerged through centuries of world-wide trade, political colonisation and the diasporic movement of people and ideas across national and continental borders.

Also available in the series

Performance art in Eastern Europe since 1960 Amy Bryzgel

Art, museums and touch Fiona Candlin

The 'do-it-yourself' artwork: Participation from fluxus to relational aesthetics Anna Dezeuze (ed.)

Fleshing out surfaces: Skin in French art and medicine, 1650–1850 Mechthild Fend

The political aesthetics of the Armenian avant-garde: The journey of the 'painterly real', 1987–2004 Angela Harutyunyan

The matter of miracles: Neapolitan baroque sanctity and architecture Helen Hills

The face of medicine: Visualising medical masculinities in late nineteenth-century Paris Mary Hunter

Glorious catastrophe: Jack Smith, performance and visual culture Dominic Johnson

Otherwise: Imagining queer feminist art histories Amelia Jones and Erin Silver (eds)

Photography and documentary film in the making of modern Brazil Luciana Martins

After the event: New perspectives in art history Charles Merewether and John Potts (eds)

Women, the arts and globalization: Eccentric experience Marsha Meskimmon and Dorothy Rowe (eds)

Flesh cinema: The corporeal turn in American avant-garde film Ara Osterweil

After-affects|after-images: Trauma and aesthetic transformation in the virtual Feminist museum Griselda Pollock

Vertiginous mirrors: The animation of the visual image and early modern travel Rose Marie San Juan

The synthetic proposition: Conceptualism and the political referent in contemporary art Nizan Shaked

The paradox of body, building and motion in seventeenth-century England Kimberley Skelton

The newspaper clipping: A modern paper object Anke Te Heesen, translated by Lori Lantz

Screen/space: The projected image in contemporary art Tamara Trodd (ed.)

Art and human rights: Contemporary Asian contexts Caroline Turner and Jen Webb

Timed out: Art and the transnational Caribbean Leon Wainwright

Performative monuments: Performance, photography, and the rematerialisation of public art Mechtild Widrich

Migration into art

Transcultural identities and art-making in a globalised world

Anne Ring Petersen

Manchester University Press

Published by Manchester University Press
Altrincham Street, Manchester M1 7JA

www.manchesteruniversitypress.co.uk

British Library Cataloguing-in-Publication Data
A catalogue record for this book is available from the British Library

ISBN 978 1 5261 2190 5 hardback
ISBN 978 1 5261 2192 9 paperback

First published 2017

Typeset by
Servis Filmsetting Ltd, Stockport, Cheshire
Printed in Great Britain
by TJ International Ltd, Padstow

Contents

Illustrations

Plates

Figures

Tables

Acknowledgements

I began researching the topic of this book – how contemporary art and culture have been, and are still being, transformed by intensified migration and globalisation – in the autumn of 2009. A couple of months on sabbatical and the benefit of a modest sum for buying the most essential books, many of which later became central to this study, provided me with the necessary resources to do some groundwork. For this opportunity, I am deeply grateful to Peter Madsen, at the time Professor, and now Professor Emeritus, in the Department of Arts and Cultural Studies at the University of Copenhagen. Without his support, this book might never have been written.

Over the next five years, parts of the book slowly emerged in the form of articles. In this phase the key driver of the project, which was not yet defined as such, or as a book, were my activities as leader of the national/international research network 'Network for Migration and Culture' (NMC) (funded by the Danish Council for Independent Research from 2011 to 2014). An important source of inspiration has been the many keynote addresses and papers given at the international conferences and seminars organised by the network, not forgetting the extended and lively discussions that developed as an integral part of these events. I would like to credit all the participants in the NMC seminars and conferences – no one is mentioned specifically, but no one is forgotten – for the various and numerous insights gleaned from these events. Special thanks goes to Stine Høholt, chief curator at Arken Museum of Modern Art, Ishøj, Denmark, for inviting me to speak at an international seminar organised in connection with the museum's marvellous exhibition of contemporary art from India, *India: Art Now*, in the fall 2012. The inspirational power of the works in this exhibition and the scholars and curators who spoke at the seminar (documented in *Arken Bulletin*, 'Migration – Contemporary Art from India', 2013) can be traced directly in the prominent role played by artists from India in this book. In connection with the exhibition at Arken, I met art historian and critic Zehra Jumabhoy. Zehra generously shared her impressive expertise on contemporary art from India with me and has opened my eyes to new aspects of it through her eagerness to discuss this rich field. For the knowledge and understanding resulting from this exchange, I am especially grateful.

My greatest debt undoubtedly lies with the members of the NMC coordination group: Mads Anders Baggesgaard, Mirjam Gebauer, Eva Jørholt, Frauke Wiegand, and with Sten Pultz Moslund and Moritz Schramm in particular. The interdisciplinary sparring offered by this group of peers – with discussions leading to clarification and valuable insights into how 'migration' is studied in other fields – has helped me to think through the connections between the arts, society and politics as well as the interrelations of migration, culture and the arts.

I would also like to acknowledge my friends and colleagues in the Department of Arts and Cultural Studies at the University of Copenhagen. First and foremost, I would like to thank Gunhild Borggreen for attentive reading of an earlier draft of the manuscript and for valuable comments and suggestions for how to strengthen the book. As anyone who has taught in a university will know, supervising MA and PhD students on their theses is a process based on exchange and inspiration that goes both ways. I would, therefore, like to thank former PhD fellows Sabine Dahl Nielsen, Sidsel Nelund and Martin Glaz Serup for the many enriching conversations that resulted from the privilege I had of supervising them on their explorative research projects on contemporary art and literature. Apart from specific events and people, the development of one's ideas and arguments is stimulated by the daily grind of university life in contingent and unpredictable ways. Students on my courses, and MA students I have supervised for their theses on related topics, have also been active participants in the developments of many ideas and themes.

I would also like to thank Nicola Gray and Susan Womersley for excellent linguistic assistance in the preparation of the manuscript, and the staff at Manchester University Press, especially Editorial Director and Commissioning Editor Emma Brennan, for their enthusiasm and enduring support. They have been ideal copy editors and publishers, respectively, and made the preparation of the manuscript an instructive and rewarding process. In addition, I have benefited from the constructive comments and advice of the anonymous reviewers and the series editors Marsha Meskimmon and Amelia Jones.

Finally, yet importantly, I would like to add sincere thanks to Beckett-Fonden and The Novo Nordisk Foundation's Committee on Art History Research (ref. no. NNF16OC0018844) for their support of the research that led to this book and its publication.

Some of the chapters include and reconfigure previously published articles. The author and the publisher would like to thank the relevant editors, journals and publishers for their kind permissions to use copyrighted material. Chapter 2 is based on Chapter 12,'Identity Politics in the "Global Art World"', in *Challenging Identities: Individual – Collective – Politics*, edited by Peter Madsen and published by Routledge in 2016 (Reproduced by permission of Taylor and Francis Group, LLC, a division of Informa plc). Chapter 3 was developed from the essay 'The Artist as a Migrant Worker? Framing Art in an Age of Intensified Globalization and Migration' published in *Arken Bulletin* in 2013 in the themed issue 'Migration – Contemporary Art from India', edited by Christian Gether, Stine Høholt and Camma Juel Jepsen. The analysis of Fred Wilson's and Yinka Shonibare's works in Chapter 4 expands on Chapter 9, 'Mining the Museum in an Age of Migration', in *The Postcolonial Museum: The Arts of Memory and the Pressures of History*, edited by Iain Chambers, Alessandra De Angelis, Celeste Ianniciello, Mariangela Orabona and Michaela Quadraro, and published by Ashgate in 2014. My analysis of Isaac Julien's *Western Union: Small Boats* included in Chapter 6 was published as Chapter 11,'Migratory Aesthetics and the Politics of Irregular Migration: A Case Study of Isaac Julien's *Western Union: Small Boats*', in the 2015 anthology *The Culture of Migration: Politics, Aesthetics and Histories*, edited by Sten Pultz Moslund, Moritz Schramm and the author. It is included here with the kind permission of the publisher, I.B. Tauris.

Translations: All quotations from French, German and Danish sources have been translated by the author. When quoting from a published translation, the translation is cited.

Introduction

This study is based on the premise that in an increasingly globalised world, mobility and cultural contacts are both common aspects of everyday life and complicating factors with respect to national, regional, cultural and communal identities and notions of belonging. Millions of people are migrating, and even those who have never left their homeland are affected by the restlessness of our contemporary world.[1] Paul Virilio has pinpointed the urgency and enormous consequences of recent migration:

> A billion people moving over half a century – that's never been seen before. All this calls into question – what? Sedentariness, the city, the fact of being here and not elsewhere, the fact of being settled in a region, in a nation … So the question for us is: how will we cope with this perpetual motion, the perpetual motion of history in motion?[2]

Migration, understood as the movement of people and cultures, gives impetus to globalisation and the transculturation processes that the interaction between people and cultures entails. Important facilitators of transcultural connectivity throughout the world are, of course, the media – broadly understood here as diverse modes of communication across time and space by technological and other means, one of them being contemporary art, the subject matter under discussion here. This book explores the transformative impact of migration and transculturation through the lens of contemporary art and the distinctive perspective it can provide on how notions of identity, belonging and community change with migration and globalisation.

These processes also affect the politics and aesthetics of art itself. The days are gone when the art world could be conceived of as a closed system endowed with an integrity that enabled works of art to function as autonomous objects within, yet at the same time independent of, the social, economic, political and media systems of the societies that encompass it. Today, art should be seen, rather, as an open system, increasingly entangled in global 'financescapes' and 'mediascapes'[3] – in the former, given art's role as a crucial sphere of capital investment and 'a vector for the flight of global capital';[4] and in the latter through art's growing visibility on the Internet, and the contribution that has been made to the general aestheticisation of everyday life and lifestyles through design, spectacle, staged events and cultural tourism, etc. Yet, the art world still constitutes a particular field, a virtual space of discursive and sociological separation produced by a generalised community of artists, curators, collectors, critics, scholars and associated institutions and professionals.[5] Despite this relative separateness, representations of migrants and migrancy have become common, to some extent, in contemporary art, while the art world's modes of production, distribution, reception and institutionalisation have themselves been transformed by the increased mobility of people, goods, information, images – and works of art. Thus, the causes of the art world's transformation should also be sought 'outside' the art field, and an appropriate place to start is in the social sciences.

In the 1990s, a so-called 'mobility turn' began in the social sciences in response to the realisation of the historical and contemporary importance of movement to individuals and societies. Historically, the conceptualisation of place and movement in the social sciences has been dominated by a dichotomisation between sendentarism and deterritorialisation, i.e. the tendency to perceive human beings as either static, and dwelling in a specific place, or as placeless nomads – and to take the locational stability of sendentarism to be the norm. The mobility turn opposes this dichotomy and testifies to the ongoing attempt to chart and understand how international migration and other mobilities – such as tourism and travel mobilities, for example – have profoundly reforged societies and politics in recent decades, and how the transporting of people and the communication of information and images increasingly converge and overlap through the recent digitisation and extension of wireless infrastructures.[6]

In acknowledging that after the Second World War cardinal events around the world have increasingly involved international migration, sociologist Stephen Castles and political scientist Mark J. Miller famously called their leading book on the subject *The Age of Migration: International Population Movements in the Modern World*.[7] The phrase 'the age of migration' does not imply that migration is something new, as human beings have always migrated. However, the character of migration changed with the beginnings of European colonial expansion in the sixteenth century. This reached a peak between the mid-nineteenth century and the First World War with the mass migrations from Europe to North America. While this period was mainly one of transatlantic migration, the movements of people that began after the Second World War, and which have increased dramatically from the 1980s onwards, have involved all regions of the world. In this phase, political and cultural changes, as well as the spread of new transport and communication technologies, have made migration easier, and international migration has, in turn, become 'a central dynamic within globalization' and an issue of major importance in domestic and international politics.[8] The increased frequency of travel also contributed to eroding the old dichotomy between migrant-sending and migrant-receiving states, as more and more countries experienced both emigration and immigration (although one or the other often prevails). At the same time, some nations have taken on a crucial role as transit zones for migrants, including the irregular (also known as undocumented or illegal) migrants whose numbers, according to Castles and Miller, have probably never been greater than today.[9] This development puts new pressures on the sovereignty of nation-states, especially on their ability to regulate the movements of people across their borders, while the ensuing enforcement of borders and 'gates' regulating movement also creates immobilities and social exclusions as well as jeopardising the lives of migrants. The horrific number of migrants drowning by the thousands in the Mediterranean Sea over the years this book was being written is a tragic reminder of the fatal consequences of European border and asylum politics, which have reflected a global tendency among affluent nations to fortify their borders against the destitute displaced from their homeland by war, persecution, climate change or other disasters.

In addition, 'transnationalism' poses cultural and political challenges to nation-states. As migration becomes technically easier and travelling quicker, many migrants, and their descendants, develop vital and durable relationships in two or more societies. The ties can be social and cultural, political or economic, or all of these. Transnational ties are often believed to undermine the undivided loyalty traditionally perceived to be paramount to sovereign nation-states that are also concerned about irregular migration. Thus, for decades, 'immigration' has been one of the most contested issues in the political debates of Western societies, and has provoked a range of critical responses. Scholars from the social sciences and philosophy, from the more specialised fields of study of migration, diaspora, postcoloniality and transnational citizenship, and from cultural and literary studies, have launched trenchant critiques of the bounded categories of nation, ethnicity, community, place and state that have dominated political debates. Instead, they have foregrounded displacement, disjuncture, dialogism, hybridisation and belonging as basic conditions of migrant subjectivity. By highlighting acts of 'homing',[10] 'regrounding'[11] and 'togetherness-in-difference',[12] writers such as cultural studies scholar Ien Ang and sociologists Avtar Brah and Mimi Sheller have made a convincing case for the complex and dynamic interplay between 'travel and dwelling, home and not-home'.[13]

Global art

Concurrently with this increase in and broadening of scholarly interest, the issue of migration has also sparked the imagination and critical engagement of contemporary artists and attracted the attention of professionals from 'the art world'. The mobility turn in the neighbouring social science disciplines has also been brought to bear in a number of significant ways on the material, social, intellectual and institutional practices belonging to the visual arts[14] – from works of art that are preoccupied conceptually with geographical movement and transnational issues, to the creation of hybrid aesthetics and the debates on the globe-trotting that artists and their works participate in. Globalisation and the intensified multi-directional migration of recent decades have also profoundly changed the structures and practices of the art world. As Pamela M. Lee has pointed out:

> the art world is itself both object *and* agent of globalization, both on structural grounds (its organization and distribution) and in workaday practice. Indeed, in responding to the geopolitical and transnational preoccupations of the work of many contemporary artists, the art world enlarges at once its geographically overdetermined borders and its conventionally Eurocentric self-definitions in the process.[15]

The most telling sign of how profoundly the mobility turn has affected the visual arts is perhaps the spread of the term *global art* in the discourses on art, where it is often used as a synonym for internationally circulating contemporary art. The notion of a global production of contemporary art gained ground in connection with the 1989 exhibition *Magiciens de la terre* at the Centre Georges Pompidou and the Grande Halle at the Parc de la Villette in Paris. The exhibition's curator Jean-Hubert Martin sought to go beyond the ethnocentric and hierarchical division between 'the West' and 'the rest', between artists and artisans, and Western 'international' art and non-Western ethnographic artefacts or 'primitive' art, which had until then structured the discourses on modern and contemporary art.[16] The inclusive designation of the participants as 'magicians' of the Earth was chosen for the Paris exhibition to avoid protests by Western art critics. The show was the target of some severe criticism, but it was also praised as the first truly global exhibition of contemporary art. Since 1989, the interest has largely centred on the question of 'how to deal with the fact that modern international art had lost its geographical frontiers, or home base, and had now ended up in *global art*'.[17] Ethnicity had always been a concern in ethnographic discourses, but not in the Western discourses on modern art. Around 1989–90, it became an integral part of a new concern with identity politics and 'difference', even among those who presented themselves as 'post-ethnic' (e.g. as artists from India, instead of 'Indian' artists). As Hans Belting has pointed out, *Magiciens de la terre* functioned as a rite of passage, a transitory and profoundly transformative event:

> The project would have been impossible before, and was no longer possible afterwards when globalization had opened up a new territory of art ... The *Magiciens* project led into no man's land where we still are and where we navigate with the help of provisional terminology ... It now seemed that *inter-national* art, an art between nations, thought to be sure Western nations, had been an affair of the modern age and that the term no longer covered a polycentric map where cultures took over the former distinctions of nations.[18]

The emergence of new art regions with a transnational character, such as the Asian region, or Latin-America or the Middle East, testifies to the formation of specific regional art worlds where art encounters different conditions and cultural traditions.[19] The clearest example of this is the Asian region. In recent years, it has seen transnational forums and discourses involving art schools, universities, museums and art exhibitions, in particular the biennials and triennials that have proliferated in the region and which have contributed significantly to the development of a distinct focus on art from Asia. Australian art historians Caroline Turner and Jen Webb have pointed out that while the major cultures of India, China and Japan, along with Western colonialism, have exerted a significant historical influence, there are also cross-cultural interconnections between the Asian nations in the modern era which have been numerous and complex.[20] For centuries, Europeans regarded Asia as an 'imitative' periphery whose artists were destined to follow the lead of Western artists if they were to become truly *modern* artists. As Asia is now well on its way to becoming the global centre of economic and artistic activities in the twenty-first century, there has been a significant shift in the nature and reception of Asian contemporary art. As a result, critical thinkers have begun to reposition the art of this region, leading to the emergence of the distinct field of art historical enquiry called Asian contemporary art.[21]

It is important to keep in mind that the notion of global art is far from a modernist conception of international art, just a broader and larger one. In its own definition, global art is contemporary and 'in spirit postcolonial' in that it seeks to replace the centre and periphery scheme of a hegemonic Western modernity with a notion of coexisting regional art worlds that interact as well as compete within the framework of an overall global art system and late capitalist globalisation.[22]

People on the move

The term 'migration' captures the dual nature of the migrant experience: every immigrant who arrives as a newcomer from the point of view of the receiving country is, at the same time, an emigrant from the perspective of those who stayed behind in the home country. Notwithstanding its advantage of relative impartiality and dual reference to im- and emigration, the term 'migrant' is simply too broad to allow for sufficient analytical precision. There is a whole family of terms for people on the move and for those who reside temporarily or permanently as an immigrant in a country other than that where they hold citizenship: tourists, migrant workers, asylum seekers, expatriates, terrorists, business people, refugees, exiles and members of other diasporas, or of the armed forces, etc. Not all of them allow for voluntary migration and self-willed acts of becoming (within the limits set by social, economic and historical determinants), and not all are relevant and heuristically useful to this study.

I will turn to T. J. Demos's *The Migrant Image: The Art and Politics of Documentary During Global Crisis* for a typology that not only enables me to make the necessary distinctions between major types of migration but also makes it possible to map a shift in priorities in the visual arts and some historical differences in the manner in which artists have addressed migration. As Demos observes, recent decades have seen a movement in the visual arts away from the category of 'exile' and its associations with empires, tragic banishments, severe penal sentences and predicaments of unbelonging and yearning for a lost 'homeland'. In most of the twentieth century, the figure of the exiled has also served as a model or metaphor of the alienated individual, engulfed in 'the psychic disequilibrium of traumatic *unheimlichkeit*' and suffering from what philosopher György Lukács diagnosed as 'transcendental homelessness'.[23] Kobena Mercer noted that modern uses of the term 'exile' have often imbued it with 'an aura of dissidence and opposition to oppressive regimes'.[24] Nowhere is this truer than in the spheres of art and politics. Demos argues that a shift of historical perspective from modern to contemporary art presupposes a terminological move away from 'exile' to the cluster of concepts associated with 'migration', among which Demos selects three concepts common in the humanities as well as the social sciences: *diaspora* (referring to a geographical dispersal in the collective sense); *refugees* (referring to victims of persecution, disasters or forced displacement); and *nomadism* (which Demos uses with specific reference to 'artistic nomadism' and the representation of unbounded movement in art). In his introduction to *The Migrant Image*, Demos discusses these categories in relation to different decades – the diasporic art of the 1980s, the nomadic practices of the 1990s, and the heightened attention to forced migration, refugees and camps since the 2000s. Demos insists that the shifts of emphasis are not clear-cut, nor is his chronological periodisation definitive. As the categories often overlap, they should be treated therefore rather as genealogical categories.[25] However, the growing concern about forced migration should also be seen as a response to a historical moment of crisis. It reflects the fact that (civil) wars and political, religious and ethnic persecution, particularly in Africa and the Middle East, have resulted in the greatest number of refugees and the deepest humanitarian crisis since the Second World War. Thus, the United Nations High Commission for Refugees' (UNHCR's) annual global report from 20 June 2016 registered the highest level of worldwide displacement ever recorded, with a total of 65.3 million people forcibly displaced at the end of 2015 compared to 59.5 million a year earlier and 37.5 million a decade ago.[26] In addition, in 2015 only 201,400 refugees[27] were able to return to their home countries.

In *The Migrant Image*, Demos focuses primarily, although not exclusively, on artistic representations of forced migration and refugees. In contrast, this present book explores diasporic and nomadic migration, in addition to forced migration, as some of the forms in which geographical mobility can manifest itself under the pressures of globalisation and neo-liberal capitalism. As interconnected forms in the same historical time-space, these different types of migration are juxtaposed in a reflection on some of the differences emerging as a result of migration, and on migration itself as plural and riven by inequalities. On a more utopian note, I hope that by drawing on art's ability to put things in a different perspective and its sensitivity to the complexities of human relations, this book may contribute to the development of a more empathic, respectful and reciprocal understanding of the conditions of migrants in receiving countries, and help expand our knowledge of how migration contributes to profound and often conflictual transformations of society, as well as to its overall plurality and cultural richness.

Politics and the political

> There is not first the thought and then the image. The image is itself a modality of thinking. It does not represent, but rather proposes, thought … This is the unhomely insistence of the artwork, its critical cut, its interruptive force.[28]

Taking my cue from postcolonial scholar Iain Chambers' remark on the 'critical cut' of art, I would like to propose that what has emerged in the first decades of the twentieth-first century is not merely a remarkable proliferation of representations of migration and migrants – that is to say, a consolidation of a new theme in art (although it is also that). Nor is it a new 'art of migration' or 'diasporic art', both problematic terms suggesting a definable, coherent aesthetics historically belonging to 'the age of migration'. What does, in effect, seem to be happening is that a significant number of contemporary artists have invested their creativity in transforming artistic practices into *critical modalities of thinking about migration* in order to question – or, as Chambers would have it, 'interrupt'– orthodoxies about migration and propose alternative and often unsettling perspectives on the workings of migration and the conditions of migrating in a globalised world. This formulation does not define art solely as an object, i.e. a representation or 'a work' of art, but also as a *politically charged action*. It suggests that art should be understood as a performative process of engagement and critical reflection which is undertaken by artists and audiences alike. Thus, the incorporation of the problematics of migration into the visual arts includes the invention of new ways of visualising and theorising the decisive role of international migration and mobilities 'in constellations of power, the creation of identities and the micro-geographies of everyday life'.[29] With regard to the critical gesture of art, political theorist Chantal Mouffe is even more radical than Iain Chambers as she defines critical art as an art that instigates dissensus by making visible what hegemonic discourses obscure, and by 'giving a voice to all those who are silenced within the framework of the existing hegemony'.[30] Mouffe's insistence on art's ability to give a voice to the excluded is pertinent to the topic of this book, as is the underlying conflation of art and politics.

Linking migration to politics and the political in the context of art and aesthetics, as this book does, necessitates some clarifying distinctions. Firstly, that between 'politics' and 'the political': here, I turn to political theorist Yannis Stavrakakis's useful distinction between *politics*, as a separate sphere of activities, structures, ideologies and institutions, and *the political*, as 'the ontological moment, the ontological horizon, of every shaping/ordering of social relations, of every social topography'.[31] Stavrakakis's understanding of the political in art is based on discourse theory and Chantal Mouffe's understanding of every social order as fundamentally political, which also implies that the fields of art and politics mutually constitute each other. As Mouffe has explained, there is an aesthetic dimension in the political, as well as a political dimension in art. Hence, the real issue is not whether art is political or not, but concerns the possible forms of *critical* art, i.e. the various ways in which artistic practices can contribute to challenging the dominant consensus and bring to light what it tends to obliterate.[32] If art is intertwined with political discourses, as Mouffe argues, one cannot take for granted that an artwork is necessarily more enlightening, trustworthy or politically neutral than, for example, a political speech or a news broadcast. It is important to bear this in mind when studying artworks related to a vexed issue such as migration. Works of art may also reproduce ethnic stereotypes and binary oppositions between 'us' and 'them', stigmatise migrants or nourish the fear of strangers. As Stravrakakis notes, 'As a complex articulation of truth and untruth, conservatism and radicalism, artistic practices, in their constitutive impurity, can intervene in the public space in a variety of different and conflicting ways, both hegemonic and counter-hegemonic.'[33]

Secondly, it is important to differentiate between migration and the politics of migration. *Migration* is, among other things, about the experience of geographical movement, emotional attachments, living hybridities and what sociologist Nira Yuval-Davis has called 'a mode of relational state of emotion and mind'.[34] It involves a multi-layered and multi-territorial process of losing one's sense of feeling 'at home' in one place and, in most cases, regaining a sense of personal, social and political belonging elsewhere through an ongoing process of 'regrounding'[35] or '*getting-back-into place*'.[36] Broadly speaking, *the politics of migration* comprise political projects aimed at defending or denying the rights of the freedom of movement and negotiating the position, recognition, identity and representation of migrants in society. As W. J. T. Mitchell has noted, on the level of politics, the issue of migration is thus 'structurally and necessarily bound up with that of images'. Not only do images move from one environment to another, making the 'migration of images' fundamental to the ontology of images and visual cultures as such; images also 'go before' the immigrant and the first encounter with the receiving country: 'before the immigrant arrives, his or her image comes first in the form of stereotypes, search templates, tables of classification and patterns of recognition'.[37]

Accordingly, it is helpful to introduce a third analytical distinction between two of the typical ways in which 'mobility' can manifest itself in works of art. Reflecting on the connections between images and migration, Mitchell has distinguished between *migration as a thematic in the visual arts* and *the migratory nature of the visual forms themselves*, i.e. 'images themselves as moving from one environment to another, sometimes taking root, sometimes infecting entire populations, sometimes moving onwards as rootless nomads'.[38] The latter is fundamental to the life of images, the way they are used, the meanings they produce and the effects they have on people. It is almost impossible to define the nature of images without attributing to them the capacity for migration, circulation, reproduction, relocation and cross-cultural translation. Later in this introduction, Danh Vo's art project *We, The People (Detail)* (2011–13) will make it clear that the two modes of mobility can intersect in art in many ways, meaning that artworks often require a consideration of both aspects.

In summary, there are two basic dimensions always to be considered when exploring migration through art and aesthetics. On the one hand, the life-changing experience of migration tends to become internalised, in that the act of migration is usually followed by some kind of everyday life in another place where the migrant experience becomes an integral part of everyday practices and the social life and identity of the subject. In this sense, migration and artistic representations of migrants' lives unfold within the encompassing socio-cultural framework of *the political*. On the other hand, when migration becomes an object of *politics*, it becomes an issue in some way – whether in national legislative and administrative immigration policies; in the ideological debates about multiculturalism and the recognition of minorities; in the image politics of news broadcasts about immigrants; or the strategies of cultural institutions vis-à-vis artists with a migrant background. Recognising the deep entanglement of these two dimensions, politics and the political, this study will address aspects of both the representation of the experience of migration and the politics of migration in contemporary art.

Migration into art

The title of this book cannibalises the title of Kenneth Clark's classic study *Landscape into Art* about the history of the landscape motif in art, first published in 1949.[39] Although my study does not map the rise and historical development of a genre, as Clark's does, it shares its ambition to explore how artistic representations contribute to shaping structures of knowledge. In *Landscape into Art*, Clark examined how art has contributed to and changed ideas of 'nature' through the centuries; *Migration into Art: Transcultural Identities and Art-making in a Globalised World* explores how artistic imagination is currently contributing to shaping ideas of migration and the closely related notions of belonging and identity. Like Clark's *Landscape into Art*, this book is based on the premise that art is about the world, and that art marks the changes in our conception of the world and the ways in which human beings position themselves in it. In Clark's understanding, it was not until the seventeenth century that artists began to cultivate landscape painting for its own sake and tried to systematise the rules of the genre. Only then did landscape come 'into art' as a dominant genre of Western art with a new aesthetics 'of its own'.[40] I wish to propose that in recent decades, and under different historical circumstances, migration has come 'into art' as a thematic and a condition that many artists are engaging with. Their attempts to articulate 'migration' as a topic and experience have sparked a diversity of aesthetic responses that cannot be contained within the boundaries of genre such as Clark's 'landscape'. In a discussion of what the distinguishing features of black British art in the 1980s might be, Kobena Mercer has suggested that 'British blackness' should be placed in 'the bigger picture of diaspora aesthetics in twentieth century art as a whole'.[41] This formulation not only invokes the breadth of 'diaspora aesthetics', or 'migratory aesthetics';[42] it also makes it clear that the category of genre cannot encompass it. As the overarching topic of this book, 'migration' must thus be understood broadly, but to ensure precision it is necessary, in the book's chapters, to distinguish between different kinds of migrants and between varying conditions of migration and transculturation.

This study aims to contribute towards a more nuanced debate about art's entanglement and critical engagement with processes of migration and globalisation; the resulting art provides a key source of improving our understanding of how these processes transform identities, cultures, institutions and geopolitics. Its contribution to the debate can be found where the complexities of contemporary art and cultural identities meet the paradoxes of globalisation and the transcultural experience of migration as structured by mobility and settlement, longing and belonging, identification and disidentification.

Migration into Art: Transcultural Identities and Art-making in a Globalised World centres on three interwoven concerns that run as connecting threads through the chapters. Firstly, it is concerned with *identity* and *belonging*. This thematic relates to the artist's own identifications and sense of belonging, as well as identity and belonging as a topic in art. Identity is a key issue here because migration unsettles and challenges the identities of the people who migrate, but also of those who stay behind, and indeed of the communities where migrants settle. It thus involves a complex set of questions regarding identification, estrangement, in- and exclusion, decolonisation (in a broad sense), recognition, and more. What does it mean, for instance, to 'belong'? And how do experiences of globalisation, transculturality and transnationality shape belonging? How important is cultural and national identity for an artist's self-understanding and the reception of the artist's work? (See Chapters 2, 3, 4 and 5.)

I bring in the idea of transculturality, most notably developed by philosopher Wolfgang Welsch as a necessary cosmopolitan corrective to ethnocentrism and xenophobia.[43] Transculturality indicates a certain quality (of an idea, an object, a self-perception or way of living) which joins a variety of elements indistinguishable as separate sources. The prefix *trans* signals a turning away from the essentialist definition of 'cultures' as homogeneous ethnic, religious or national entities. As an analytical perspective, transculturality permits a more dynamic designation of culture as constituted by boundary-transgressing mobility and ongoing processes of transformation.[44] While traditional notions of acculturation and homogenisation stress uniformisation and adaptation to a dominant culture or majority, a transcultural perspective allows an examination of local and non-conforming modes and protagonists of cultural (ex)change, thus sharpening our awareness of the intermixing processes and heterogeneity of the cultural phenomenon in question, and bringing our attention to its local as well as its cosmopolitan affiliations.

The first set of issues invariably leads to the second, which revolves around *visibility* and *recognition*. Here, I am concerned with the potential of art to highlight migration-related issues and 'represent' particular groups of migrants, but also with the visibility and recognition of migrant artists. What impact do increased mobility and migration have on the art world and the careers and works of artists? As the structures of the art world have been profoundly transformed by globalisation and migration, a book on art and migration must also be attentive to how the discursive, institutional, economic and structural changes have paved the way for the 'global art' paradigm and undermined the art world's 'geographically overdetermined borders'.[45] In other words, it must reflect on how artists with a migrant background can be made institutionally visible as an expression of society's recognition of migrants' art and transcultural practices. However, in the discourses on art and art institutional policies, categorising an artist as 'migrant' is a double-edged sword. It can be a precondition for recognition and for the inclusion of cutting-edge artists from formerly marginalised minorities and peripheries; but it can also become a straitjacket that leads to the exclusion of some artists from being recognised 'on equal terms' by reducing them to 'ethnic artists'. A study of connections between art, artists and migration must also consider this compelling dilemma (see Chapters 1, 2 and 4).

Thirdly, this study is concerned with the more encompassing question of the interrelations between *aesthetics* and *politics*. The issue of the intertwinement of aesthetics and politics in contemporary works of art is a contentious one and has already generated much debate. Any study that explores artistic engagement with a politicised topic such as 'migration' needs to consider how the political issues are articulated. 'Aesthetics and politics' must, therefore, be a component in this book, but it does not seek to fully explore the relationship between aesthetics and politics as a theoretical problem. Instead, it engages with the notions of politics and the political on an analytical level, using specific discourses and works of art as entry points (see Chapters 1, 4 and 6).

The topic of migration is permeated not only with political but also with ethical urgencies. Thus, it requires sensitive handling and involves dilemmas of representation. In Chapter 6, this has led to considering the meta-question of how to triangulate and balance aesthetics, politics and ethics when creating or writing about artistic representations of migration, especially forced migration. Queries as to the political effects of artworks open up the question of the social field that the work constructs and of which it is also a part. This has to do with the possibilities of reception that the work engenders, which the discourse of ethics can help unpack. As philosopher Alain Badiou writes, for the ancient Greek philosophers ethics concerned the search for a good way of being and a wise course of action.[46] Today, the word is often used in a non-distinctive way and designates 'a principle that governs how we relate to "what is going on", a vague way of regulating our commentary on historical situations (the ethics of human rights), technico-scientific situations (medical ethics, bio-ethics), "social" situations (the ethics of being together), media situations (the ethics of communication), and so on'.[47] Ethics thus provides a perspective that may enable us to explore how artists seek to 'move' audiences, and thereby operate directly upon the world in which the work is situated.[48] An ethical perspective is not premised on representation but enacts a shift from a hermeneutic approach, which emphasises decoding, to a consideration of the means by which the work creates certain conditions of reception; or, as artist and writer Walead Beshty explains:

> The central concern of an ethical analysis is not whether the work can be evaluated positively or negatively in ethical terms, but instead resides in the more complex question of the aesthetic manifestation of the ethical dimension of the work of art, i.e. its proposal of a modification to the social contract, with the artwork acting as the signification of this modification. So, if an artwork is understood as affecting or generating relations among viewers, how is this negotiation with the ethical dimensions of an artwork manifested in aesthetic terms (i.e. how are these aspects of its social existence manifest in the appearance of the work itself)?[49]

This study adopts Beshty's definition of ethical analysis. Accordingly, I am not concerned with the present attempts to engender normative ethico-political responsibilities and outlooks among artists and scholars.[50] Rather, I wish to investigate the ways contemporary artists have represented migration as a world-transforming force, because, as Marsha Meskimmon has argued, 'as a mode of ethical agency, art's potential is particular, not general and overarching'.[51] It is my contention that close readings of artistic representations of migration and migrant identities can help us understand and develop adequate ways of responding to some of the challenges arising from the complex experience of entanglement and 'togetherness-in-difference'[52] which has become a general condition of living in twenty-first century societies.

Migration of ideas through art

I would like to substantiate this claim that contemporary art can provide us with deep insights into the many ways in which intensified migration and globalisation have changed lives, cultures and societies in recent decades by way of three instructive examples that also indicate the transnational scope of this book's empirical field of study. As regards its three interwoven concerns, the first work to be considered, by Danh Vo, relates to all three, while the second, by Thukral & Tagra, and the third, by Emily Jacir, primarily engage with the first set of issues, i.e. identity and belonging, although it should be emphasised that Jacir does so in a highly political manner. In the case of Danh Vo, the kind of belonging and identification at stake is primarily the national self-identification as a 'we', or 'the people', whereas the works of Emily Jacir and

Thukral & Tagra are more concerned with attachments to an ethnic group or a homeland and with what 'belonging' might mean, or what it might become, in the diaspora.

Danh Vo was born in 1975 and spent his early childhood in Vietnam before his family fled the country in the wake of the war between North Vietnam and the US. Eventually, he came with his family to Denmark where he grew up and later enrolled at the Royal Academy of Fine Arts in Copenhagen. He left this institution to finish his studies at the Städelschule in Frankfurt, and then settled in Berlin. A profound interest in issues of cultural identity, displacement and exchange pervades his work and figures prominently in a number of sculptural works that involve the transposition of artefacts from one context into another. Some include objects relating to his own personal or familial narratives, others to the political history with which his own story is interlinked.[53] He often chooses symbolically charged objects that he then deconstructs conceptually (as well as physically), thereby creating complex poetic systems of meaning which are meant to bring silenced or wilfully forgotten aspects of political history to light.

In *We the People (Detail)* (2011–13) (see figure 0.1), Vo adopted this conceptual and deconstructivist approach with the French sculptor Frédéric Auguste Bartholdi's *Statue of Liberty*. The project is quite explicit with respect to art's role as an integral part of the transactions and ideologies that produce political behaviour. *We the People (Detail)* effectively refutes the common assumption that art is separated from the social sphere, or, at best, merely reflective of it.[54] Given in 1876 as a gift from the French people to the US to mark the anniversary of the latter's independence, the *Statue of Liberty* became for generations the ultimate symbol of freedom and democracy, as well as a part of the iconography of American identity and power. It was intended as a tribute to the two countries' contributions to the republican principles of equality and democracy and as a commemoration of American independence. Since it was dedicated in 1886, the *Statue of Liberty*, standing 45 metres tall on Liberty Island in New York Harbour, has also symbolised the hopes of a better life for the refugees and new immigrants arriving in New York. For millions of people, Lady Liberty has been a welcoming symbol of the 'golden door' to the land of opportunities and the 'American Dream' of geographical and social mobility, prosperity and the freedom of individual independence. In *We the People (Detail)*, Danh Vo has appropriated this key emblem of Western political ideals, which has also provided him with a textbook example of art's ability to furnish political ideologies with cognitive and emotional resonance. The artist produced a full-scale replica of the statue, but abstracted it by *not* assembling the approximately 250 sculptural parts into one piece. Instead, the replica remains split into fragments that are not immediately identifiable as pieces of the *Statue of Liberty*. The artist thus

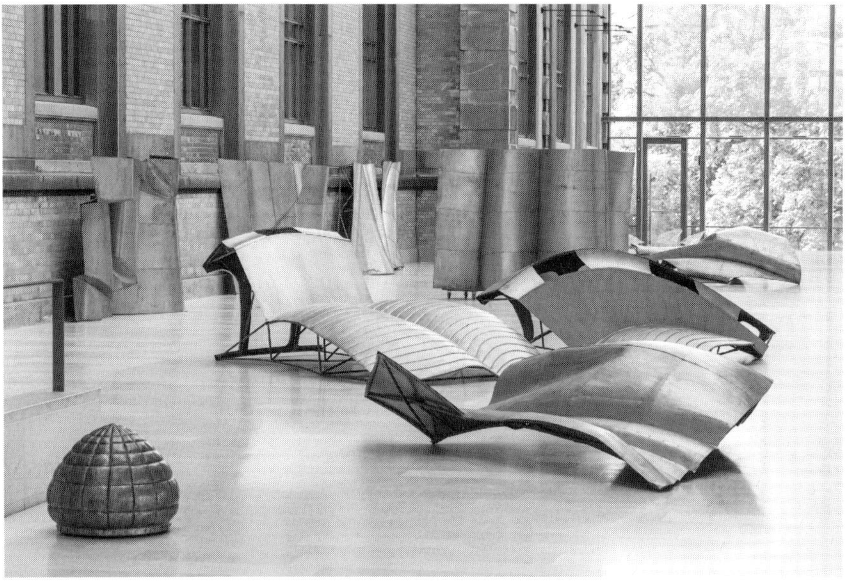

Danh Vo, *We The People (Detail)*, 2011–13. Installation view from the exhibition at Statens Museum for Kunst (the National Gallery of Denmark), 2013. Copper, dimensions variable. Recreation on a 1:1 scale of Frédéric Auguste Bartholdi's Statue of Liberty's copper exterior, produced in approximately 250 individual pieces near Shanghai, China, and meant to be exhibited individually or in small groupings. © Danh Vo. Photograph: Anders Sune Berg, courtesy of the artist. **0.1**

visually and metaphorically dismembered the figurative sculpture of *Libertas*, the ancient Roman goddess of freedom. Since 2011, the individual elements have been shown in changing constellations and circulated in exhibitions across the world. When Kunsthalle Fridericianum in Kassel put on the first exhibition of elements from the project in October 2011, Vo named it *JULY, IV, MDCCLXXVI*.[55] The title refers to 4 July 1776, the date of the signing of the US Declaration of Independence from Great Britain. Vo took the writing in Roman numerals from the tablet that the figure of New York's *Statue of Liberty* is holding in her left hand. Accordingly, the exhibition title highlighted the issue of political independence and democracy.

When the National Gallery of Denmark exhibited approximately 100 elements from the project in 2013, they were displayed under the title *We the People (Detail)* that has since become the title of the work. This title caused a subtle shift in emphasis to issues of nationhood and peoplehood. Throughout the period of the exhibition, new parts of the sculpture were added regularly while other parts were moved around or sent to other destinations.[56] Nonchalantly distributed in the spacious indoor 'Sculpture Street', some rested on dollies or wooden pallets, reminding visitors of a warehouse with goods ready to be shipped abroad. By choosing to show *Libertas* dismembered and scattered on the floor, Vo created what could be read as an impressive metaphor for the failure of the world's state leaders to actualise the high political ideals symbolised by the statue, whose original title was *Liberty Enlightening the World*. *We the People (Detail)* also reflects on the dramatic shift in the economic power structure of the world. Like the original, Vo's replica was fashioned out of copper sheets, but the gigantic sculpture was not produced in Europe but in China, in collaboration with a team from Basel's Kunstgiesserei. As curator Mirjam Varadinis has noted: 'In view of the questionable financial and legal situation of workers as well as the political regime in China, this relocation of production is extremely ambivalent and, in fact, almost cynical when coupled with the "freedom" symbolized by the *Statue of Liberty*. On the other hand, it might be read as unabashed honesty in exposing economic dependencies.'[57]

Contrary to the 'sedentary' statue on Liberty Island, Vo's exhibitions were characterised by a constant flux of the replica's *disjecta membra*, which were really only passing through the respective venues. The artist was, thus, deliberately highlighting *circulation* – of goods (including artworks), of images, political ideologies and people – as a feature of today's globalised world. The work's very mode of being became a telling index of how the forces of globalised capitalism radically transform the conditions of producing and distributing artworks. Despite the huge weight of the copper fragments, the whole project was geared towards mobility, and consequently also towards highlighting the migratory nature of art and images. As Vo declared: 'Let her travel, let her be spread around. Let it just be this fluid mass that travels and becomes something very different from what the one in New York is.'[58] The physical scale of the work will never be fully visible, due to the geographical distribution of the separate elements across many exhibition venues, nor will the distances involved in its widespread reach ever be known. Yet, precisely because of their weight and greater than human scale, the elements of *We the People (Detail)* conjure up an imaginative space that invites viewers to recognise what would otherwise remain invisible to the eye: the ungraspable scale of global circulation and the potentially worldwide reach and impact of migratory images and ideas.

Although the artist contrasts the immobility of the *Statue of Liberty* at Liberty Island with the mobility of his own work (and with this repeats the outworn sociological dichotomisation between sedentarism and deterritorialisation), *We the People (Detail)* can be read as an allegory of the mobility of the *Statue of Liberty* in New York *as image*. This highly symbolically charged image has travelled all over the world and been subjected to various kinds of local appropriation and contestation. Issues of globalisation, migration and dislocation are thus critical to *We the People (Detail)*, but it would be misleading to conclude that it is only or primarily about the migration of people and images. *We the People (Detail)* is, I contend, first and foremost a work about the migration of a particular set of Western political ideas: political freedom, democracy, nation-state and peoplehood.

'We, the people' are the first three words of the Preamble of The United States Constitution from 1787,[59] a phrase that articulates the national ethos of the US which is rooted in the 1776 Declaration of Independence and its proclamation that 'all men are created equal' and 'endowed by their creator with certain inalienable Rights' including 'Life, Liberty and the pursuit of Happiness'.[60] By appropriating the famous opening words of The United States Constitution as the title of his fragmented, circulating and internationally distributed copy of the *Statue of Liberty* (that was made in China), Danh Vo spotlights how the 'nation-state' has itself become a circulating cultural form adapted worldwide to different kinds of societies. Anthropologist Arjun Appadurai has explained how the accelerated speed and spread of the Internet and the parallel growth in travel, cross-cultural media, global advertising and the outsourcing of work have resulted in a significant increase in the global flows of cultural forms: 'this current period – approximately from the nineteen seventies to the present – is characterised by the flows not just of cultural substances, but also of cultural forms, such as the novel, the ballet, the political constitution, and divorce, to pick just a few examples'.[61]

Appadurai argues that what is appropriated is primarily a matter of forms, idioms and techniques rather than specific, substantive content. Circulating cultural forms generate diverse interpretations in different local contexts. The local is, therefore, never merely a mirror image of the global. To Appadurai, the nation understood as an 'imagined community', with strong bonds of identity and claims to statehood and territorial belonging, is a particularly useful reminder of these mechanisms of cultural appropriation: 'Thus the nation form represents a more vital circulating ingredient than any specific ideology of nationalism … The idea of "the people" is more important than any specific populist ideology. The idea of a foundational legal document for a national polity outweighs this or that particular constitution.'[62]

By invoking the Preamble of The United States Constitution in a context of global circulation, *We the People (Detail)* points out the document's status as a generic symbol of the voice of the people and the constitutionalised national polity. As philosopher Benjamin Lee has observed, the global cultural economy of colonialism has been transformed into a system of nation-states by what he, referencing Appadurai, describes as new 'cultures of circulation'.[63] According to Lee, cultures of circulation are produced by the forms that circulate through them, and which also provide the 'building blocks' needed for the creation of the new social imaginaries that are so vital to the development of modernity. Social imaginaries are ways of imagining the social which themselves mediate collective life. For an example of cultures of circulation, Lee refers to historian and political scientist Benedict Anderson's influential historical analysis of how nationalism emerged as a product of interactions between certain cultural forms, such as novels and newspapers, and their circulation enabled by a globalised print capitalism. According to Anderson, this resulted in a new social imaginary and cultural formation centred on the idea of a constitutionalised peoplehood.[64] An important example of the cultural performativity of circulation is, in effect, the creation of a new form of 'we' identity, that of 'the people' which is at the core of many modern social imaginaries.[65] The printed textuality of The United States Constitution allows it to be perceived as springing from the people in general and not from any particular individual, group or state legislature, argues Lee. 'We, the people' is a 'form of self-creating collective agency', a rhetorical figure that gives voice to 'the people' of both nationalism and identity politics.[66] In other words, it functions as a performative utterance, creating what it names:

> Each reading of a 'nationalist' text creates a token instance of a *we* that subsumes the narrator/character/reader in a collective agency that creates itself in every act of reading. These token *we's*, when aggregated across acts of reading, become the basis for the imagined community of we-ness at the heart of nationalism … Anderson's imagined community of nationalism is created through narratives that embrace the narrated-about characters as referents, the author/narrator as the sender of the narrative event, and the readers as the narrated-to addressees.[67]

According to Benjamin Lee, 'We, the people' is thus a product of large circulatory processes and, at the same time, a constitutive agent of these processes. As a performative utterance, the rhetorical figure articulates the 'we-ness' of 'the people', thereby creating a semiotic space for nationalistic forms of collective agency. Bearing Lee's argument in mind, it is easier to see just how ambiguous Danh Vo's *We, the People (Detail)* actually is. From one perspective, it serves as a reminder that, in a political context, art can function as a floating signifier into which political groups can read whatever serves their interests and beliefs.[68] The fragmented statue functions not only as a symbol of the downfall of Western notions of freedom and democracy, as Mirjam Varadinis has suggested.[69] The scattering of the elements across spaces, institutions and borders can also be read as a metaphor for the dissemination, cultural translation and resulting transmutation of the very same ideals of democracy and notions of nationhood and peoplehood to which the rhetorical figure 'We, the people' is foundational. In this context, it is also noteworthy that Vo has chosen to cite the constitution of a country that perceives itself as a multicultural nation and officially celebrates and recognises the historical influence of immigrants of all backgrounds. Coinciding with the exhibitions of Danh Vo's *We the People (Detail)* across the world in 2013, President Barack Obama confirmed this perception of the US as a proud nation of immigrants in his annual presidential declaration on Constitution Day and Citizenship Day:

> America's Constitution has inspired nations to demand control of their own destinies. It has called multitudes to seek freedom and prosperity on our shores. We are a proud Nation of immigrants, home to a long line of aspiring citizens who contributed to their communities, founded businesses, or sacrificed their livelihoods so they could pass a brighter future on to their children. Each year on Citizenship Day, we welcome the newest members of the American family as they pledge allegiance to our Constitution and join us in writing the next chapter of our national story.[70]

Recapitulating W. J. T. Mitchell's distinction between migration as a thematic in the visual arts and the migratory nature of the visual forms themselves, one might infer that *We, the People (Detail)* combines a consideration of migration as a multi-layered and politicised thematic with an exploration of the migratory nature of images and ideas, in which sculptural elements – the fractured replica of a static monument – are deliberately staged as being on the move and circulating, like transnationally distributed luxury goods in an exclusive art circuit. As Mitchell remarks, it is important to differentiate between the neutral notion of images in *circulation*, i.e. moving freely 'basically without consequences', and the notion of *migration*, which is 'fraught with contradiction, difficulty, friction and opposition' – but, one might add, also invested with agency, hope, dreams and a genuine potential for transformation. Danh Vo's project demonstrates that images can be migrants, too, arriving from elsewhere whether bidden or unbidden. Fraught with 'contradiction, difficulty, friction and opposition', they may seem alien and can sometimes have alienating effects, as for example when, like Vo's *We the People (Detail)*, the image becomes a 'returning migrant': the work returns (from China), a key symbol of (primarily) Western ideals, (primarily) to the West, where it appears utterly strange in its new shape(s), familiar yet completely alien.

Dreams and inequities of mobility

The following juxtaposition of the Indian artist duo Thukral & Tagra's installation *THE ESCAPE! Resume/Reset* (2012) and Palestinian-American artist Emily Jacir's project *Where We Come From* (2001–3) is deliberately contrastive and is intended to gesture towards the impressive breadth of contemporary artistic approaches to migration as a thematic. Migration, as a topic, is too wide-ranging to be described empirically here within the constraints of a single volume. Yet, as a thematic, in particular the actual act of migrating, it can be said that it exists in a field of tension between a receiving country and a home country and between memory and imagination. It also frequently entails a tension between, on the one hand, migration as involving expectations of gain and change, and, on the other, as tied to an experience of loss, although the positive and negative experiences are not necessarily linked to the different countries of attachment in any straightforward manner.

Thukral & Tagra's coupling of pop art and social messaging is often thought to embody the spirit and voice of Indian youth and the way young Indians reshape their identity and dreams under the pressure of hyper-commercialisation and globalisation. Jiten Thukral and Sumir Tagra are both of Punjabi origin; they live and work in Gurgaon, a swish suburb of Delhi with gigantic shopping malls and large houses built in an eclectic style known as Punjabi Baroque, and consumerism and hyperbolical eclecticism feature prominently in their works. Travelling abroad several months of the year for their art projects, Thukral & Tagra are also fascinated by the phenomenon of the emigration and eventual repatriation of Punjabis in India, the subject of several of their works. *Artificial Strawberry Flavour* (2008), for example, couples capitalism and migration: it is composed of a swarm of recycled ketchup and chocolate syrup bottles decorated with hand-painted miniature portraits of young Sikhs from Punjab in streetwear – a human product to be shipped abroad. Thukral & Tagra are more concerned with the ways in which the imaginary shapes emigration than the facts of migrants' living conditions. In their works, the imaginary is articulated in two ways: in the escapist form of their fantastic, eclectic and multi-coloured universe; and in their preoccupation with the aspirations of migrant and socially mobile Indian youth.[71]

The duo's large installation *THE ESCAPE! Resume/Reset* (2012) (see plate 1) was realised at Arken Museum of Modern Art in Denmark. The installation revolves around the emigrant's imagined idea of a better life elsewhere and comments on today's migratory world society.[72] Thus, it can be read as a reflection on the dream of creating a new identity for oneself, of becoming another kind of person belonging to a different kind of world. In this polymorphous interactive installation, Thukral & Tagra cross the boundaries between graphic and interior design and between painting, video, sculpture and installation. They deploy a flexible nomadic aesthetic that ignores the rules and limits of the particular media involved, 'focusing on content as it flutters between contexts'.[73] On an overall level, the installation reflects a perception of India in the first decade of the twenty-first century as what Mumbai curator, writer and gallerist Peter Nagy has called 'an over-stimulated place, over-whelmed by its multiple pasts and possible futures'.[74] Even before entering *THE ESCAPE! Resume/Reset*, the synthetic beeps from the classic Super Mario video game can be heard. Once inside what turns out to be an aircraft cabin, living room and games arcade in one, the visitor discovers that the aural backdrop is matched by a bewildering amalgam of visual elements competing for the visitor's attention: the walls are papered in a pattern of aeroplane-window ovals, casino chips and stylised drips of colour. The *Artificial Strawberry Flavour* work is also included in the installation: the bottles with their miniature portraits of fortune seekers who have emigrated are scattered across the wall like family portraits, enhancing the spurious homely atmosphere created by the thick carpet and the Indian airline seats upholstered in a range of cosy-looking cotton print fabrics, and the two kitsch angels in sneakers holding a crystal chandelier adorned with sports trophies. Yet sensations of homeliness flit through this hybrid space, which is dominated by seats arranged to mimic an airline cabin in flight, with hand luggage scattered everywhere and shirts and saris draped over some of the seats. The ambiguity of this ambience unsettles the classical dichotomy between the sedentary and the migratory as it suggests a more complex interrelationship between travel and dwelling, and between feelings of freedom and belonging. Using anthropologist James Clifford's evocative formulation, the installation evokes a sense of 'traveling-in-dwelling, dwelling-in-traveling'.[75]

Despite the allusions to domesticity and dwelling, a sense of precariousness pervades the room. On the wall with the iconic portraits, a sign made of Indian lamps spells out 'O': Save Our Souls. On the opposite wall, a series of eight paintings with detailed representations of subjects from classic pinball games addresses the question of life opportunities from the perspective of gaming, loudly backed up by the sound of the Super Mario video game. Within the overall narrative of the installation, the pinball game functions as a metaphor for migration as a kind of gambling for a better life, in which the subject is thrown hither and thither by life-changing circumstances, the imperatives of consumer culture and blind chance. But it also refers to the 'disoriented and fluid life conditions of Indian youth' as well as 'the artists' own childhood, when India still constituted a closed economic system'.[76] In the pockets on the seat backs, one can find a pamphlet with short stories about travelling as well as a boarding pass with gaming coupons printed on the back that read 'Limited time – unlimited chances', strengthening the work's association of the migrant's journey with gambling. Several of the seat backs have iPads mounted in them, with an app featuring Indian music videos and documentaries. There are also short stories about people who had recently migrated to Canada or the Middle East, perhaps, or who dreamt of doing so. Each story is presented next to a portrait designed as a playing card. The visitor, now seated as a fellow traveller, can swipe the upper or lower part of the card to piece together a new story and portrait, different from the previous one, but expressing a similar desire to go abroad. The latent movements that this interactive installation suggests could only be triggered, in some instances, by the active and self-reflective participation of the visitors, while other elements function like traditional pictorial representations. Although the pinball game paintings are framed by blinking lights, their imagery is fairly traditional, often centring on a symbolic representation of home as a floating hot-air balloon, trailing clotheslines like moorings for temporary anchorage. Despite the heterogeneous character of the material presented in *THE ESCAPE! Resume/Reset*, the installation clearly centres on the young generation's desire to emigrate to fulfil their optimistic dreams of education, a successful career and a wealthy lifestyle. However, its disturbing amalgam of the transit space of an aeroplane, a living room and a commercial gambling venue also suggests that there is a dark side to migratory life: 'to escape' through emigration also means to be exposed to precariousness and confronting the difficulties of developing a new sense of belonging and anchorage elsewhere.

Emily Jacir's neo-conceptual project *Where We Come From* (2001–3) (see figure 0.2) also deals with uprooting and belonging, but seen through the lens of exile and homesickness.[77] Using her ability to move relatively freely within Israel with her American passport, Jacir promised to fulfil some of the wishes of Palestinians living in exile or who are either forbidden entry into their homeland or have their movements in it restricted by the Israeli authorities. Crucially important to the project was that, at the time, more than half of the participants were living and working either in Israel or inside Palestine – in the West Bank, Jerusalem and Gaza. The actions that her work documents were based on the following question: 'If I could do anything for you, anywhere in Palestine, what would it be?' The artist thus exploited her own freedom of movement (still not devoid of danger) to realise the desires of exiles, as far as it was in her hands to do so. The project comprises a series of texts written in plain black lettering on white panels that describe the various requests in Arabic and English. Colour photographs presented next to the framed texts testify to Jacir's fulfilment of them. Most of the wishes are humble and relate to family ties and everyday life: 'Go to Haifa and play soccer with the first Palestinian boy you see on the street', reads one plea. Another says 'Drink the water in my parents' village', while another asks Jacir to 'Do something on a normal day in Haifa, something I might do if I was living there now.' In her documentation of the wishes and the fate or status of the people who expressed them, Emily Jacir also adds a note on what she did in order to fulfil each wish.

A man named Munir expresses the wish: 'Go to my mother's grave in Jerusalem on her birthday and put flowers and pray.' The text tells the viewer that Munir lives only a few kilometres away in Bethlehem, but the Israeli authorities have denied him access to Jerusalem so he cannot visit his mother's grave on the anniversary of her death. The accompanying photograph shows Jacir's shadow cast over the tombstone as she carries out the task.

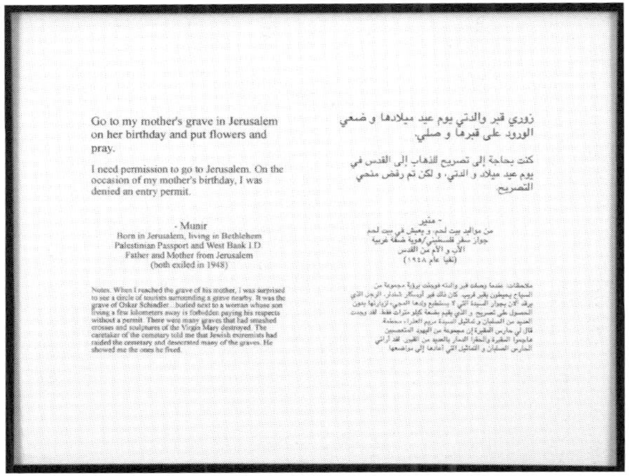
Go to my mother's grave in Jerusalem on her birthday and put flowers and pray.

I need permission to go to Jerusalem. On the occasion of my mother's birthday, I was denied an entry permit.

- Munir
Born in Jerusalem, living in Bethlehem
Palestinian Passport and West Bank I.D
Father and Mother from Jerusalem
(both exiled in 1948)

Notes. When I reached the grave of his mother, I was surprised to see a circle of tourists surrounding a grave nearby. It was the grave of Oskar Schindler…buried next to a woman whose son living a few kilometers away is forbidden paying his respects without a permit. There were many graves that had smashed crosses and sculptures of the Virgin Mary destroyed. The caretaker of the cemetary told me that Jewish extremists had raided the cemetary and desecrated many of the graves. He showed me the ones he fixed.

زوري قبر والدتي يوم عيد ميلادها و ضعي الورود على قبرها و صلي.

كنت بحاجة إلى تصريح للذهاب إلى القدس في يوم عيد ميلاد و الدتي، و لكن تم رفض منحي التصريح

- منير
من مواليد بيت لحم، و يعيش في بيت لحم
جواز سفر فلسطيني/هوية ضفة غربية
الأب و الأم من القدس
(نفيا عام ١٩٤٨)

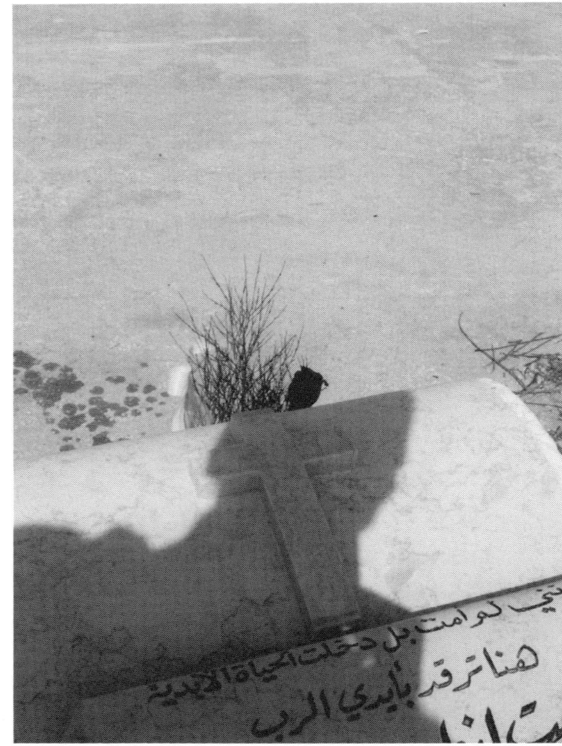

Emily Jacir, *Where We Come From*, 2001–3, detail (*Munir*). American passport, 30 texts, 32 c-prints and 1 video. © Emily Jacir. Photograph: Bill Orcutt, courtesy of Alexander and Bonin, New York. **0.2**

The image is cropped so tightly that it conveys only minimal information: a relief of a Christian cross and a fragment of the engraving in Arabic on the tombstone identifies the graveyard culturally. A bit of barren, sun-drenched soil is all we get to see of the Middle Eastern environment. Chromatically, the photo is reduced to a ghostly greyscale. Approximating a monochrome, the documentary photograph evokes an acute sense of absence that is amplified rather than mitigated by the artist's shadow. As T. J. Demos has observed in his perceptive analysis of Jacir's work, she exposes the visual absences of the Palestinians who responded to her query, those who were either forced out, or are prohibited from moving around within the Occupied Territories. She also exposes the deprived political status of the Palestinians, dictated as it is by Israeli law and enforced by means of militarised borders, walls and checkpoints.[78]

For the viewer, the transition from text to image, which are placed in proximity to each other, seems easy: a mere shift of the eyes is enough. Mentally, it will also not be difficult for most people. Visiting family, friends and the place where one grew up are activities usually taken for granted, but for those caught up in the Israeli–Palestinian conflict, which has driven many Palestinians into exile since 1948, the gap between the wish expressed in the text and the photo's actualisation of the wish cannot be overcome.[79] According to Demos, Jacir's text-image pieces operate by fulfilling three different kinds of desire. Jacir meets the exile's request, thereby also revealing 'the privations exiles suffer over things that most of us take for granted'. By enacting the requests, Jacir also seems to fulfil her own desire 'to reassemble the splinters of diaspora into a single place, into some form of narrative continuity, into an interconnected history'.[80] Moreover, since *Where We Come From* does not act as a substitute for the basic rights of access denied to those in exile, it also makes plain 'the absences that Jacir's service *cannot* fill'. As viewers read their way through the stories, *Where We Come From* inculcates viewers with a yearning for some sort of resolution or answer to the inequities of movement outside of the work.[81] Experiencing the work, it could be said, also creates a strong sense of the tenacity and emotional power of feelings of belonging.

In many ways, these two works mark opposite ends of the spectrum of contemporary migratory aesthetics: Thukral & Tagra's installation seems to celebrate an ideal of universal freedom of movement, whereas Jacir draws critical attention to the real inequalities of mobility and the injustices they entail. The Indian duo focus on migration imagined as gain and fulfilment of a dream of a better future with open opportunities of a glorious homecoming. Jacir, on the other hand, engages with migration, or more precisely exile, experienced as a loss, fraught with painful memories of a homeland whose borders are closed and can no longer be crossed. Thukral & Tagra's work is an immersive installation that literally bombards the visitor with visual, auditive and tactile impressions. By contrast, Jacir's work consciously exploits conceptual art's aesthetic of sensory restraint, bordering on deprivation. *Where We Come From* is basically a documentary work and thus oriented towards history and reality. Thukral & Tagra's work is phantasmagorical and transports the viewer to a world of fantasies about what life could become through mobility. Jacir voices a critique of the forced displacement of the Palestinian people and makes an indirect plea for a solution to the Israeli–Palestinian conflict. On a more general level, her piece is concerned with what Jacir calls '(im)mobility': the inequality between those who can and cannot enjoy the rights of moving freely across borders.[82] Among the requests, there are also those pleas that reveal a strong desire for a return to Palestinian land, figured as a connection to the land, to family and to memories of cherished places. Yet, Jacir's work does not suggest an imaginary or utopian escape from the oppression and restrictions of occupation.[83] This point should be stressed, because today there are multiple reasons why it would not be possible to make *Where We Come From*: Gaza has been sealed off, so that it is no longer possible to access the area in either direction; Palestinian towns in the West Bank have been surrounded by multiple walls, effectively isolating them from each other; and the 'freedom of movement' that made this project possible is no longer granted to American and European passport holders, such as Jacir.[84]

Thukral & Tagra's installation, on the other hand, envelops the visitor in an intoxicating escapist fantasy. Their installation presents itself as a homage to unrestricted social and geographical mobility and a set of ideals historically associated with the American Dream. Just as Danh Vo staged the return of the dream of liberty and democracy (embodied by the *Statue of Liberty* returning in fragments from China) to art institutions primarily in Europe and the US, so Thukral & Tagra staged (in a European art museum) the return of the American Dream, reconfigured and hybridised by an Indian migrant perspective. Despite their different perspectives on migration, these three examples show significant similarities. They are about the historical world and invite their audience to reflect on how they resonate with contemporary political issues; they also uncover how deeply patterns of life, cultural forms, political and legal systems, and so on, have been affected by various kinds of migration since the mid-twentieth century.

Migration's entry into art discourses

Such concerns with the transformative power of 'movement' (in terms of transnational travel and migration) and with cultural translation and hybridisation have also filtered through to academic discourses on art. What follows is a summary literary review that aims to show how the growing attention to the thematics of migration in art discourses since the 1980s has produced significant, if rather scattered, groundwork of relevance for this study. The remainder of the Introduction accounts for how I am positioned in this field, as well as the theoretical underpinnings and chapter structure of the book.

Since Arjun Appadurai and the sociologist and cultural theorist Nikos Papastergiadis, at the new millennium, distanced themselves from existing research on migration in the social sciences by stressing the importance of the *cultural* dimension,[85] there has been a growing interest in examining the connections between globalisation, migration and culture as well as the impact of this nexus on the formation of identities. Important contributions have also come out of cultural studies, particularly since the 1990s.[86] Another important innovative strand that also gathered momentum in the 1990s proceeds from postcolonial studies.[87] These partially overlapping fields have contributed considerably to the critical discourse on migration and culture by shedding light on power relations in cultural encounters and multicultural societies, on marginalisation and racialisation, identity politics and the confluential and conflicted nature of transculturation. Nevertheless, sociological and anthropological perspectives have dominated the cultural studies approach – as well as the postcolonial one – to cultural analysis, and, more often than not, these have given prominence to political agendas. As Mikkel Bolt has pointed out, the new kind of 'culture-oriented' (post)Marxist theory developing with critical theory, French structuralism, cultural studies and postcolonial studies after the Second World War redefined and expanded the Marxist notion of the political by 'culturalising' it, thereby paving the way for new ways of theorising the political.[88] The critical discourses on 'migration and culture' and 'art and migration' spring primarily from these theoretical traditions and have contributed to 'culturalising' the political.

As a critical response to the tendency of these to evade aesthetics, affectivity and the significance of the formal aspects of cultural artefacts, some of the more recent studies in the visual arts have reintroduced formal analysis as the foundation of the interpretation of the artefact's social, historical *and* political meaning. I will return later to this resurgence of interest in 'aesthetics' which has helped the topic of art and migration take centre stage.

In the field of comparative literature, it has been common since the 1980s to refer to 'migrant literature' as a literary category with a related field of specialised research into the historical, political, semiotic and linguistic issues related to writings by and about migrants, including the contestation of the category of migrant literature itself. The fields of art history and visual culture have no such broadly accepted descriptor, nor is there a defined and named field dedicated to researching art and migration. A possible advantage of this might be that categorisations may not be so deeply ingrained, but the downside is that the absence of a common category or descriptor has made it difficult to delimit studies in art and migration as a field, and led to it being almost impossible to make questions of the methodological and theoretical foundation of such studies a common concern. Yet, the nexus between art, migration and globalisation has begun to attract the attention of a growing number of art historians and other scholars.[89] Unlike the social sciences, cultural studies, postcolonial studies and literary studies, art history has only recently begun to contribute substantially to the interdisciplinary field of migration studies. This is quite surprising because ever since the waves of refugees provoked in the aftermath of the Second World War, migration has had a crucial impact on the visual arts, both as a catalyst of artistic transformations and as a theme in art.

The rise of the Nazis in 1933 caused the unprecedented forced migration of hundreds of artists within and, in many cases, away from Europe. Books such as Serge Guilbaut's *How New York Stole the Idea of Modern Art*,[90] and especially the exhibition and catalogue *Exiles* + Émigrés*: The Flight of European Artists from Hitler*,[91] have long since established how vital the influx of artists and intellectuals fleeing from war and persecution in Europe was to the development and ensuing temporary 'world leadership' of the American art scene. However, the art world has been slow to recognise the importance of the influx of artists to Europe from former colonies in the wake of decolonisation after the Second World War. Particularly in the early days of identity politics in the art world, in the 1980s and early 1990s, recognition came with considerable reluctance. In the second half of the 2000s and the early 2010s, a number of books on the interrelations between contemporary art, migration and globalisation have been published. Taken together, they might not represent a proper 'turn', but the fact that this nexus has now become the topic of book-length art historical studies certainly testifies to the beginning of a new phase in the formation of a critical discourse on art and migration and its discourse-transforming impact on the wider debates on art. For better and for worse, the art system and the hegemonic discourses on art are gradually assimilating the discourse on art and migration – a process subjected to closer examination in Chapters 1 and 2. This change evidently includes both the risk of domestication, i.e. that the discourse on art and migration loses its 'critical cut' (Chambers), and the lure of profoundly changing the art system and its dominant discourses from within.

Among the single-authored books, T. J. Demos's *The Migrant Image: The Art and Politics of Documentary during Global Crisis* stands out because it is as much a cultural critique as a study of the ways in which contemporary artists have transformed documentary practices in their representations of refugees, migrants, the stateless and other mobile lives. Cultural critique is also at the heart of Nikos Papastergiadis's *Cosmopolitanism and Culture*, in which he explores how a new cosmopolitan imaginary is developing in the arts under the impact of global processes, first and foremost migration, and what roles artists can play in reclaiming conditions of hospitality and imaginative engagement with 'the other' in the cultural climate of 'ambient fears' which has spread in the West after 9/11.[92] Marsha Meskimmon, in *Contemporary Art and the Cosmopolitan Imagination*, also pursues the idea that art shares in the discourses on cosmopolitanism, globalisation and locational identity. It is particularly relevant to the present study because most of her examples are artworks that engage with questions of migration, identity, belonging and 'homing'. In the overall scheme of things, it seems that, outside of the US, it is in Britain that the transformation of the multicultural art scene through migration has attracted the most sustained scholarly attention. This impression is substantiated by the publication in the 2010s of Leon Wainwright's *Timed out: Art and the Transnational Caribbean*[93] and artist and writer Eddie Chambers' *Black Artists in British Art: A History since the 1950s*.[94] There are also monographs on transculturation resulting from other histories of exchange, such as Siobhán Shilton's study of contemporary art from a Francophone space, *Transcultural Encounters: Gender and Genre in Franco-Maghrebi Art*,[95] and Caroline Turner and Jen Webb's monograph *Art and Human Rights: Contemporary Asian Contexts*. The latter explores how the interplay between local and global forces has changed the art scene in Asia, and how artists from this region have engaged with human rights issues and the plight of refugees and immigrants as part of the artists' endeavours to help build more equitable societies and develop cross-cultural approaches to world-making and making art. A specific focus on refugees is found in *Counter-Memorial Aesthetics: Refugee Histories and the Politics of Contemporary Art* by Veronica Tello, who explores how artists have taken part in the production of images and narratives of refugee experiences and histories. Through close readings of selected works, Tello traces the emergence of 'counter-memorial aesthetics' characterised by a conjunction of heterogeneous signifiers and voices and images from many times and places.

The social, economic and institutional effects of globalisation on the whole art system are by now well documented by some essential publications, such as Charlotte Bydler's *The Global Art World Inc.: On the Globalization of Contemporary Art*,[96] Lotte Philipsen's *Globalizing Contemporary Art*[97] and Pamela M. Lee's *Forgetting the Art World*. Substantial empirical research and further critical discussions have been added by, among others, *The Global Contemporary and the Rise of New Art Worlds*. Co-edited by art historian Hans Belting, curator Andrea Buddensieg and artist, curator and media theorist Peter Weibel, this comprehensive volume (which accompanied the exhibition *The Global Contemporary: Art Worlds after 1984*) reaps the fruits of the research project GMA (Global Art and the Museum), which was initiated by the Center for Art and Media Karlsruhe, Germany, and concludes a series of anthologies.[98]

A number of significant anthologies and co-authored works have also added fresh perspectives to the discourse on contemporary art and migration. *Exiles, Diasporas and Strangers* is the last anthology in the groundbreaking four-volume series of historical studies, 'Annotating Art's Histories', edited by Kobena Mercer. It combines postcolonial and art historical approaches to shed new light on the role of estrangement and displacement in late twentieth-century art and to foreground the multi-directional patterns of cross-appropriation shaping the century's artistic practices.[99] Another anthology that should be mentioned is art historian Burcu Dogramaci's *Migration und künstlerische Produktion. Aktuelle Perspektiven* ('Migration and Artistic Production: Current Perspectives'),[100] which reflects the latest stage of research into migration and the arts in German art history and cultural, media, literary and urban studies in the 2000s. A rethink on art history's largely Eurocentric framework has been undertaken in Jill H. Casid and Aruna D'Souza's edited volume *Art History in the Wake of the Global Turn.*[101] Coming from various disciplinary and theoretical backgrounds, the contributors propose ways to reorient the field and rewrite some of its basic narratives. Like Casid and D'Souza's anthology, Saloni Mathur's edited volume *The Migrant's Time: Rethinking Art History and Diaspora*[102] is based on a conference at the Sterling and Francine Clark Art Institute and published in the series 'Clark Studies in the Visual Arts'.

With its focus on the theme of migration as a rising subject matter in art and a factor shaping the conditions of art, the aims of this present publication are more in line with Mathur's anthology, which has served as an important source of inspiration and provided me with valuable insights as well as models of how to approach the topic. At the same time, I am indebted to the publications resulting from a European collaborative research project on the interrelations of migration and the arts for giving me a sense of direction in the early phase of conceptualising this book. Chapter 1 will return to this project that was spearheaded by the feminist art historian Griselda Pollock and cultural theorist and video artist Mieke Bal, who also coined the project's core concept of migratory aesthetics. The publications resulting from this project have not only provided me with a critical theoretical concept but also set a standard for how to balance my dual interests in the aesthetic and the political aspects of art's relation to migration.

Situating this book

A remark on the situated perspective that structures the way this book frames the exploration of art and migration is needed. My perspective is inevitably shaped by the fact that I am a white woman scholar from Scandinavia who trained as an art historian, has been dedicated to studying the impact of migration on contemporary art since 2009 and doing interdisciplinary work in the interstices between art history and the wider field of cultural studies for even longer. In recent decades, my home country Denmark has experienced a significant increase in immigration from non-Western countries. As in other affluent Scandinavian and European countries undergoing similar transformations, this has unsettled the hegemonic monocultural notion of national identity. It has challenged the whiteness of Danish culture and created a whole range of struggles over minority rights, identity politics and racism as well as nourishing fears about immigrants, especially from Muslim majority countries. It has resulted in a repeated tightening of the rules on immigration and integration and fuelled hostile anti-immigrant, nationalist discourses. But civic counter-movements have also come into being, such as *Venligboerne* – a network of local groups of volunteers to help newly arrived asylum seekers settle in, which, in the wake of the rising numbers of asylum seekers since 2014, has spread to more than a hundred Danish cities.[103] So, even if this book is not about art from Denmark, the local circumstances and need to develop a more empathic and appreciative understanding of migrants and migratory culture has had some bearing on this author's perspective and exploration of a wider world.

Although Scandinavia is part of 'the West', the Scandinavian countries have historically been assigned an ambiguous position on the margins of the global art world. The regional art world of Scandinavia is not in 'the centre' of the Western art world, but neither is it peripheral to the Western metropolitan centres in the same sense as many art scenes in Africa, South America and other 'Southern' regions. I would like to propose that this ambiguous position and the perspectives it enables could best be described as *semi-peripheral*.[104] Like all perspectives, a semi-peripheral perspective is partial, which means that it has certain limitations, but also certain potentialities. Scandinavian scholars are at one and the same time positioned as privileged Western insiders and marginalised outsiders to the cultural and art institutional hubs of the Western art world. We are thus offered a historical opportunity to use this ambiguous position heuristically to develop the kind of double perspective that is needed when examining the interrelations of art and migration in the context of a globalised art world. In my understanding, the semi-peripheral perspective on contemporary art is related to the 'stereoscopic vision' attributed to migrants by Salman Rushdie, because migrants are at the same time insiders and outsiders in society.[105] When a semi-peripheral perspective is coupled with empathy, an ethical move from 'speaking about' to 'speaking nearby' becomes possible. According to the originator of this expression – filmmaker, writer and scholar Trinh T. Minh-ha – 'speaking nearby' is a way of speaking that does not represent the object as if it were distant from the speaking subject but reflects on itself and 'can come very close to a subject without, however, seizing or claiming it'.[106]

My situated perspective is broadened by the theories used to underpin the three principal concerns of this book. The first was subsumed under the categories of *identity* and *belonging*. My concern with the representation of migrants' identities and belonging has led me to the writings of Stuart Hall and Amelia Jones to find adequate redefinitions of the concept of identity as a performative process centred upon *identification* and *representation*. In Chapter 5, I follow Hall and Jones in their endeavours to move beyond the binary Western models of self and other, transmitted through neo-Hegelian philosophy to discourses on the visual arts.[107] As envisioned by Hall, it would be better to leave behind the notion that identity is 'an already accomplished fact, which the new cultural practices then represent' and think instead of 'identity as a "production" which is never complete, always in process, and always constituted within, not outside, representation'.[108] For Hall, such a rethink on the concept of identity would also entail a reconsideration of the cultural producer/artist as a historical and situated subject; a reconsideration that rejects the post-structuralist proclamation of the 'death of the author', i.e. the idea that the author, together with the intent and the biography of the author, is insignificant because he or she does not structure and control the production of the meaning of the work, which is supposedly generated by the reader's response.[109] This reconsideration would involve addressing questions such as: from which position of enunciation does the cultural producer/artist speak? How is this position articulated in the artist's works? And which historical, cultural and discursive contexts frame the position from which they speak?[110]

The term 'identification' contains a dual reference. According to the *Oxford English Dictionary*, identification refers to'The determination of identity; the action or process of determining what a thing is or who a person is; discovery and recognition'. It can also refer to an instance or result of this, e.g. an image – typically a portrait of some kind, or a documentary means of proving one's identity such as a passport or other signs that can be used to establish who one is. However, the term not only refers to identification of *others* and signs of their identity, but also to *self*-identification, or, as defined by the dictionary, 'The state of being or feeling oneself to be closely associated with a person, group, etc., in emotions, interests, or actions; the process of becoming associated in this way'.[111] Thus, in psychology, identification can refer to the frequently unconscious adaptation of one's ideas and behaviour to accord with those of a person or group seen as a model.

In any case, identification and self-identification need a medium to materialise; they come into existence through various discourses and modes of representation – bodily, visual, textual, oral, etc. In a world saturated with images, *visual* media play a critical role in enabling representations of identity and according public visibility to individuals and groups. Thus, in a basic sense, the visual arts are intimately connected to the idea of identification as a generative process, a performative act. As Amelia Jones puts it, 'art is always already *about* identity or, as I will call it, identification in the first place'.[112] This means that art is already entangled in identity politics, either explicitly or indirectly, and that viewers are involved, too, since their ideas of identity condition their individual encounters with works of art. Moreover, the artists are also 'identified' through their works as it were. A work of art may activate prejudice about the 'other', but it may also counter and challenge fixed stereotypes, thereby potentially opening up a more sophisticated understanding of identity not as a stable essence but as something that undergoes lifelong transitions and is shaped and reshaped by changing, intersecting identifications and intersubjective encounters with others.

Belonging is central to the question of the formation, and transition, of identities. In the arts, discussions on migrant identity formation have formerly tended to focus on the problems arising out of the experience of displacement and the loss of home. Displacement has often been linked to either the nostalgic longing for a lost homeland, or, in extension to that, the 'task of re-placing' oneself in the receiving country.[113] Instead of seeing the different forms of belonging as pre-given conditions and unchangeable affiliations, it is widely accepted today that they are the result of ongoing renegotiations.[114] Studying the works and lives of artists can help us develop a complex and translocal understanding of contemporary forms of belonging. Here, it is productive to turn to cultural geography. In their introduction to *Translocal Geographies: Spaces, Places, Connections*, geographers Katherine Brickell and Ayona Datta explain how the increasing interest in the notion of translocality has led to a stronger emphasis on local–local connections, situatedness and 'groundedness' during transnational migration, albeit often with a predominant focus on national boundaries. To depart from the national framework, they introduce the notion of *translocal geographies* to draw attention to the interconnectedness of places with a variety of other locales, thereby enabling the examination of migration across different spaces and scales, such as rural–urban, inter-urban, trans-regional and transnational.[115] When addressing the question of how people connect to places and interact with new environments, Brickell and Datta thus propose a 'place-based' instead of a 'place-bound' notion of the local to underscore that 'as people become more mobile, so too do locales become stretched and transformed'.[116]

This change of terminology applies particularly to migrants who often have to negotiate what Appadurai has called 'disjunct registers of affiliation',[117] but its scope is much wider because it accommodates a need for change in our general understanding of belonging and 'emplacement'. Western political and media discourses on migration tend to define minority groups in terms of their ethnic background. These discourses perpetuate a problematic and no longer tenable distinction between the cultural figures of the migrant and the sedentary; between cultures of dwelling and cultures of migrancy, or *diaspora*; and between 'new' and 'old' members of society, those who 'belong' and those who do not 'belong', as if such 'we' and 'they' groups could be easily identified and separated. We are living in a world where migration influences everybody's lives, whether directly or indirectly, and where the possibilities of transnational travel and communication have increased significantly, despite the flagrant inequalities of access. As a result, the interconnectedness of people with different backgrounds and origins has become a common experience. This condition is not only a determining factor for those members of society who have first-hand experience of migration or who are descendants of migrants; it is, in varying degrees, part of the everyday experience of all those living in societies that are shaped by past and current migration. Hence the need to reconsider issues of translocal belonging and transnational and transcultural identity, as well as the visibility and recognition of migrants, along with the aesthetics and politics of representation.

My second concern was signalled by the keywords *visibility* and *recognition*. Several of the scholars mentioned above for their work on the topic of art and migration have underscored the artwork's potential to question the dominant orders of visibility and invisibility in order to 'transform the visual field of politics', to borrow T. J. Demos's succinct words.[118] Chapters 4 and 6 in the present volume explore how this potential may be activated to challenge or transform the existing politics of representing migrants and migratory culture. Demos uses Jacques Rancière's theory of the politics of aesthetics as support for his analysis of Steve McQueen's film *Gravesend* (2007) about the victims of globalisation who are usually not represented in the media and political discourses, and are thereby excluded from 'globalization's imaginary' and rendered invisible.[119] He refers to Rancière's thoughts on the partitioning of the sensible to show probable cause that art can destabilise the discursively defined border between visibility and invisibility, and that some artists may well have a unique potential to instigate such a disruption because of their professional ability to 'creatively recalibrate representational conditions'.[120] Demos's and Rancière's understanding that it is the current sensory and discursive regime that determines how and where the borderline between the visible and the invisible is drawn is highly pertinent to my exploration in Chapters 4 and 6 of artists' interventions in museums and some representations of clandestine migration, since they all seek to challenge the dominant order of visibility and invisibility.

According to Rancière, 'the distribution of the sensible' operates as an implicit algorithm governing the sensible order that parcels out forms, places and access to participation in our common world. Rancière understands aesthetics to be a system of forms which determines what presents itself to sense experience and establishes the modes of perception within which sense experience is inscribed. Accordingly, he asserts that aesthetics constitutes the political by partitioning the sensible, meaning that it discriminates between who can say, hear, make and do what, where and when. Aesthetics 'is a delimitation of spaces and times, of the visible and the invisible, or speech and noise, that simultaneously determines the place and the stakes of politics as a form of experience'.[121] Aesthetics defines the modes of representation that structure the individual art forms, but aesthetics also transcends the sphere of art because it partitions the sensible within everyday life and in the realm of politics. Aesthetics defines the character of the political in art by determining how the political is articulated with sensory and artistic means, and these means are used differently in different art forms. In 'the aesthetic regime', Rancière's polemical term for the modern art system, the sensible can evade and transgress its common and normative forms. When artworks parcel out the sensible in ways that deviate from the dominant representational codes by proposing another distribution of the sensible, they can be seen as 'political interventions'. According to Rancière, they become political by drawing on their potential to disrupt the conventional ways of understanding the world and bring the previously marginalised, unspeakable or invisible into the sphere of representation.[122] However, as Mieke Bal and Miguel Hernández-Navarro have pointed out, 'the invisible' may also be what has become so 'normal' as to become non-visible.[123] Artworks can draw the viewer's attention to that which is taken for granted or regarded as a self-evident, or naturalised, truth. Making visible people and phenomena willingly or unwillingly overlooked – such as, for instance, refugee camps and irregular migrants or *sans papiérs* in detainment centres – can be a powerful instrument to raise political consciousness and inspire politically and ethically motivated action, even if the work itself does not appear to be overtly political. As W. J. T. Mitchell has observed: 'The most salient fact about migration in our time is the way it has become, not a transitional passage from one place to another, but a permanent condition in which people may live out their lives in a limbo of illigalized immigration, perpetual confinement in a refugee camp, or a perpetual motion and rootlessness, driven from place to place.'[124]

Rancière's understanding of the political role of aesthetics as a distribution of the sensible brings us to the third concern of this book: the conundrum of reconciling an interest in *politics* with an interest in *aesthetics*, a consideration of 'content' with a consideration of 'form'. The branches of migration studies that explore migratory cultures have close links to cultural studies and postcolonial studies, and share their penchant for prioritising the political. As literary scholars Elleke Boehmer and Sten Pultz Moslund have contended, in these fields it may seem like an unaffordable indulgence, or even a provocation 'to speak of aesthetic approaches to those kinds of art that respond to political and ethical urgencies, or to histories of violence and suffering. In the eyes of the critics, this would imply a withdrawal from the real world into a depoliticised realm of beauty, harmony, disinterested contemplation and artworks reduced to matters of "pure form".'[125]

However, if one turns away from the traditional Kantian and modernist notions of aesthetic judgement and transcendental art, which often underlie such reservations, and instead adopt Jacques Rancière's and Chantal Mouffe's understanding that politics and aesthetics are interdependent, the notion of aesthetics can help us gain insight into the particularity of art's contribution to the discourses on migration and culture. As already indicated above, I have found theoretical support in the writings of Rancière and Mouffe, both philosophers who have exerted a great impact on contemporary discussions on politicised art and the politics of aesthetics.

On the level of analysis, Rancière's understanding of aesthetics and political art is complemented by Elleke Boehmer's definition of the term 'aesthetic' as referring to an interest in form as a determinant part of a work's content. In Boehmer's understanding, the term implies attention to the generic and formal aspects of the work and its connotative language, but also a concern not to relate that work only to historical, social and political contexts. Although Boehmer does not refer to Rancière, her approach is in tune with Rancière's observations on the double effect of political art.

Rancière insists that political art thrives on an inherent paradox that also generates its peculiar double effect. It must ensure the 'readability of a political signification' to communicate its political claims on an intellectual, reflective level; at the same time it must produce an aesthetic or perceptual shock caused by 'that which resists signification' to move the audience on an affective, sensory and bodily level. Rancière explains that 'In fact, this ideal effect is always the object of a negotiation between opposites, between the readability of the message that threatens to destroy the sensible form of art and the radical uncanniness that threatens to destroy all political meaning.'[126] Contemporary artistic imagination often endows the representation of migration, particularly forced migration, with urgent political signification. Yet, the message is communicated with artistic means, i.e. in an affective, non-verbal, equivocal and often unsettling – or, with Rancière, uncanny – manner. In other words, artists have to walk on a razor's edge to avoid two pitfalls and balance the effects, or reception, their work may produce in an ethically responsible way. One the one hand, they have to steer clear of the untimely aestheticisation of politics and of turning the dispossessed into a merely pleasurable spectacle; on the other, they have to avoid the temptation to communicate an unequivocal political message, thereby destroying the 'radical uncanniness' that makes the work artistically interesting and evocative.

An overview

As these theoretical considerations suggest, the three core concerns of this book cannot be separated but will run through the book like interwoven threads rather than constitute thematic divisions between its chapters. Instead, a movement from the general to the particular structures the order of chapters: from discourses on art, to the art institutional structures that determine artistic careers and the status of artefacts, to specific works of art.

Chapter 1 seeks to establish a historical and theoretical framework by relating this study to the current discourses on the relations between globalisation, migration and contemporary art. It gives an account of how 'globalisation' and 'migration' have been articulated in distinct ways in Western discussions of contemporary art since the 1990s, and how the two discourses differ and intersect. It supplements the introduction by mapping the two main discourses that connect the publications mentioned in the literature review to a wider range of texts and ties the texts together as a field of research centring on some common concerns. The unifying aim of Chapters 2 through 6 is twofold: firstly, to examine how contemporary art implicitly or explicitly interacts with socio-cultural, historical and political contexts related to migration; and secondly, to use close readings of selected works and texts to show how, at the same time, art transcends cultural and political determinations. In this book, artists will thus appear in three different roles: as professional labour migrants, as presumed spokespersons for particular groups of migrants, and as individual artists who articulate subjective perspectives on the world by means of aesthetics.

Since the question of how individual and cultural identities are shaped in migration is at the heart of this book, half of its chapters (Chapters 2, 3 and 5) are concerned with the discourse on identity politics in the art world or how artworks can articulate experiences of multiple attachments and evoke a sense of (cultural) belonging. Chapter 2 gives a critical review of the previous debates on identity politics and art institutional multiculturalism, emphasising the dichotomies ingrained in the discussions and the ambiguous way institutional multiculturalism has regulated the mechanisms of inclusion and exclusion. Chapter 3 seeks to move beyond the binaries structuring these debates, exploring how increased mobility has changed the work patterns of many artists and equipped them with dual or plural cultural and national attachments. The chapter concentrates on artists as professional labour migrants and considers the impact of migration and globalisation on artists' career patterns and the conditions of being an artist. It examines the changing role of the artist from the perspective of migration studies and seeks to characterise the social and institutional conditions under which highly mobile contemporary artists live and create their works. In short, Chapter 3 is concerned with a growing artistic nomadism, and its perspective is primarily institutional and socio-cultural. It seeks to provide a basis for understanding why so many artists are deeply involved in issues of migration on both a personal and professional level by examining a new role for artists which has become more and more common in recent decades: the artist as a migrant worker.

Lurking in the shadows of this topic is the risk of idealising borderless travel while overlooking the barriers and restrictions to the movements of the less privileged. Accordingly, Chapters 4 and 6 shift the focus from artists with a considerable amount of freedom to move socially and geographically, to artistic representations of less privileged migrants – be it clandestine migrants, confronted with the harsh realities of contemporary transnational measures to 'secure' nation-state borders, or those who have been 'integrated' in Western societies, perhaps for generations, but who have been marginalised and have remained literally invisible in Western cultural institutions. Chapter 4 is founded in a political concern with the recognition and visibility of migrants and their histories in museums, and the need for change in institutional practices, curatorial perspectives and the writing of history emerging with intensified transnational migration. Accordingly, Chapter 4 takes an overall perspective on museums as gatekeepers of history and also touches upon the general issue of the interrelations between aesthetics and politics. More specifically, it seeks to uncover some of the inequalities of mobility and reflects on how artists' interventions in museums can be deployed strategically to make colonial exploitation and patterns of thought that otherwise have remained invisible, visible. It is important to discuss the (in)visibility of migrant histories in museums, because museums play an important part in shaping the public image of 'who we are' and 'where we come from' as a society. Through the stories they tell with the exhibits selected for display, and in the way they are displayed, museums and galleries contribute to defining a society's cultural identity and memory. However, since the encounter with works of art evolves as a reciprocal process between embodied viewers and sensate images, art can also encourage identification on a more subjective level and enable individuals to discover new or other ways of being in the world. Accordingly, Chapter 5 explores how art can be deployed to develop dynamic transcultural models of identity, examining the work of three artists who probe colonial and postcolonial archives of histories and use the 'hidden histories' they uncover for an imaginative reconfiguration of traditional models of identity. Like Chapter 3, Chapter 5 aims to overcome dichotomic thinking, but instead of focusing on the artists, it deploys the feminist concept of intersectionality to account for how works of art can act as agents and articulate a complex understanding of identity as intersectional, transcultural and dynamic.

Chapter 6 returns to the issue of aesthetics and politics. It expands on the question of the interrelations between migration politics and aesthetics by bringing ethics into the equation. At the same time, it shifts the focus from the representation of migrant culture as part of national culture and identity to that of the clandestine migrants who are excluded from the nation-state and denied participation in the public sphere altogether. The underlying issue of Chapter 6 is the politics of representation, and particularly the question of how aesthetics, politics and ethics can be triangulated and balanced when artists seek to make visible the conditions of irregular, or clandestine, migration – and when scholars analyse the solutions the artists produce.

Writing *about* and writing *with* art

In *Contemporary Art and the Cosmopolitan Imagination*, Marsha Meskimmon has aptly described her textual method as coupling close reading with what she calls 'writing *with* [art]'.[127] Meskimmon is admirably consistent and radical in her application of this method, and as such, her book constitutes a category of its own. Yet, her general shorthand description 'writing *with*' could fit a number of recent interdisciplinary studies of contemporary art, including Amelia Jones's *Seeing Differently: A History and Theory of Identification and the Visual Arts*, T. J. Demos's *The Migrant Image*, Nikos Papastergiadis's *Spatial Aesthetics: Art, Place and the Everyday*[128] and Mieke Bal's writings on migratory aesthetics,[129] as well as the work of many scholars who, like this author, have taken their cue from these leading figures. Close reading is vital to most art historical research, which draws from the specific materials and practices studied. Traditionalist art historians have often contented themselves with this *modus operandi*, writing *about* art within the borders of art history. Writing *with*, on the other hand, uses close analysis of selected artworks to transgress these disciplinary borders. Here, close analysis is used as a bridgehead to developing concepts, interpretations, perspectives and discussions related to wider historical and political issues in a generative interchange with knowledge, perspectives and modes of thoughts that have originated in other academic fields. As regards the present study, discourse analysis, postcolonial studies and migration studies have been particularly useful.

All the artists whose work is discussed in this volume can be characterised as belonging to 'the global contemporary' or 'global art', because their practices unfold on terms dictated by an art world ruled by globalisation and neo-liberal capitalism, and they show their works around the world. Moreover, they all have a migrant background and/or have developed a nomadic career pattern. The transnational and transcultural expansiveness of this book is, in some ways, an outcome of its consideration of mobility, but it also reflects an underlying wish to contribute to the broader trend of opening up the discourse on art to artists and art scenes outside the West. The principle guiding the selection has therefore been the issues addressed in the respective chapters. The selection criteria have been that the selected works should address the issue in question and be representative of a larger body of works in which the chosen artist deals with migration-related issues. This study will not pretend to settle the confusion resulting from the proliferation of concepts associated with various kinds of migration and cultural encounters; nor does it aspire to delineate a supposedly coherent aesthetic or a definable genre produced by cultural hybridisation – a 'migrant art', to match the descriptor 'migrant literature'. It seeks instead to avoid the pitfall of such restrictive categorisations. At the same time, it takes seriously the need to think through how the so-called 'mobility turn' and the growing awareness of the transforming power of migration have made it necessary to reconfigure our understanding of the many practices belonging to the visual arts, not only in today's world but since the beginning of history. This must be done with care and foresight because the revision of the visual arts, the art world and the vocabulary and methodologies of art history is only in its infancy. This is why *Migration into Art* examines selected model examples through close readings instead of striving for encyclopaedic coverage. This is why the book cannot merely present writings *about* art; it must aspire to writing *with*.

Notes

1 Nikos Papastergiadis, *The Turbulence of Migration: Globalization, Deterritorialization and Hybridity* (Cambridge: Polity Press, 2000), p. 2.
2 Paul Virilio, 'Foreword', in Paul Virilio *et al.* (eds), *Native Land: Stop Eject* (Paris: Fondation Cartier pour l'art contemporain, 2009), pp. 7–8.
3 Arjun Appadurai, *Modernity at Large: Cultural Dimensions of Globalisation* (Minneapolis, London: University of Minnesota Press, 2000), pp. 33ff.
4 Pamela M. Lee, *Forgetting the Art World* (Cambridge, Mass., London: The MIT Press, 2012), p. 22.
5 *Ibid.*, p. 17.
6 Mimi Sheller and John Urry, 'The new mobilities paradigm', *Environment and Planning A*, 38 (2006), 207–26, 212.
7 Stephen Castles and Mark Miller, *The Age of Migration: International Population Movements in the Modern World.* 4th Edition (Basingstoke: Palgrave Macmillan, 2009).
8 *Ibid.*, p. 3.
9 *Ibid.*, pp. 3, 7–8.
10 Avtar Brah, *Cartographies of Diaspora: Contesting Identities* (London, New York: Routledge, 1996).
11 Sara Ahmed *et al.*, 'Introduction: Uprootings/Regroundings: Questions of Home and Migration', in Sara Ahmed *et al.* (eds), *Uprootings/Regroundings: Questions of Home and Migration* (Oxford, New York: Berg, 2003), pp. 1–22.
12 Ien Ang, *On Not Speaking Chinese: Living between Asia and the West* (London, New York: Routledge, 2001), p. 17.

13 Sheller and Urry, 'The new mobilities paradigm', 211.
14 Saloni Mathur, 'Introduction', in Saloni Mathur (ed.), *The Migrant's Time: Rethinking Art History and Diaspora* (Williamstown, Mass.: Sterling and Francine Clark Art Institute, 2011), pp. vii–xix, p. viii.
15 Lee, *Forgetting the Art World*, pp. 4–5.
16 For a historical overview of the reception of this much debated exhibition, see: Lucy Steeds *et al.*, *Making Art Global (Part 2): 'Magiciens de la Terre' 1989* (London: Afterall, 2013).
17 Hans Belting, 'From World Art to Global Art: View on a New Panorama', in Hans Belting, Andrea Buddensieg and Peter Weibel (eds), *The Global Contemporary and the Rise of New Art Worlds* (Karlsruhe: ZKM Center for Art and Media Karlsruhe, 2013), pp. 178–85, p. 181.
18 *Ibid.*, p. 182.
19 Hans Belting and Andrea Buddensieg, 'From Art World to Art Worlds', *ibid.*, pp. 28–31, p. 28.
20 Caroline Turner and Jen Webb, *Art and Human Rights: Contemporary Asian Contexts* (Manchester: Manchester University Press, 2016), pp. 3–4.
21 Melissa Chui and Benjamin Genocchio, 'What Is Asian Contemporary Art? Mapping an Evolving Discourse', in Melissa Chiu and Benjamin Genocchio (eds), *Contemporary Art in Asia: A Critical Reader* (Cambridge, Mass., London: The MIT Press, 2011), pp. 1–14, p. 5.
22 Belting, 'From World Art to Global Art: View on a New Panorama', p. 178.
23 T. J. Demos, *The Migrant Image: The Art and Politics of Documentary during Global Crisis* (Durham, N.C., London: Duke University Press, 2013), pp. 1–2. Demos quotes Lukács' *The Theory of the Novel: A Historico-philosophical Essay on the Forms of Great Epic Literature* (London: Merlin Press, 1971), p. 41.
24 Kobena Mercer, 'Introduction', in Kobena Mercer (ed.), *Exiles, Diasporas and Strangers* (Cambridge, Mass., London: inIVA and The MIT Press, 2008), pp. 6–27, p. 19.
25 Demos, *The Migrant Image*, pp. 4, 12.
26 UNHCR, 'Worldwide Displacement Hits All-Time High as War and Persecution Increase' (18 June 2015), unpaginated, www.unhcr.org/558193896.html (accessed 16 November 2016); Adrian Edwards, 'Global Forced Displacement Hits Record High' (20 June 2016), unpaginated, www.unhcr.org/news/latest/2016/6/5763b65a4/global-forced-displacement-hits-record-high.html (accessed 16 November 2016).
27 UNHCR, 'Global Trends: Forced Displacement in 2015' (20 June 2016), www.unhcr.org/global-trends-2015.html (accessed 16 November 2016).
28 Iain Chambers, 'Adrift and Exposed', in Isaac Julien (ed.), *Isaac Julien – Western Union: Small Boats* (Warszawa: Centre for Contemporary Art Ujazdowski Castle, 2009), pp. 8–13, p. 10.
29 Tim Cresswell, 'Mobilities I: catching up', *Progress in Human Geography*, 35:4 (2011), 550–8, 551.
30 Chantal Mouffe, 'Artistic activism and agonistic spaces', *Art & Research: A Journal of Ideas, Contexts and Methods*, 1:2 (2007), 1–5, 5.

31 Yannis Stavrakakis, 'Challenges of re-politicisation: Mouffe's agonism and artistic practices', *Third Text*, 26:5 (2012), 551–65, 552.
32 Mouffe, 'Artistic activism and agonistic spaces', 4–5.
33 Stavrakakis, 'Challenges of re-politicisation', 554.
34 Nira Yuval-Davis, *The Politics of Belonging: Intersectional Contestations* (London: Sage, 2011), p. 200.
35 Ahmed *et al.*, 'Introduction: Uprootings/Regroundings'.
36 Sten Pultz Moslund, 'A Migrant Aesthetics through the Phenomenality of Place', in Sten Pultz Moslund, Anne Ring Petersen and Moritz Schramm (eds), *The Culture of Migration: Politics, Aesthetics and Histories* (London, New York: I.B. Tauris, 2015), pp. 223–39, p. 230.
37 W. J. T. Mitchell, *Seeing through Race* (Boston, Mass.: Harvard University Press, 2012), p. 127.
38 *Ibid.*, p. 126.
39 Kenneth Clark, *Landscape into Art* (London: John Murray, 1976).
40 *Ibid.*, p. 229.
41 Kobena Mercer, '"Diaspora Didn't Happen in a Day": Reflections on Aesthetics and Time', in R. Victoria Arana (ed.), *'Black' British Aesthetics Today* (Newcastle: Cambridge Scholars Publishing, 2007), pp. 66–78, p. 74.
42 Mieke Bal, 'Lost in Space, Lost in the Library', in Sam Durrant and Catherine M. Lord (eds), *Essays in Migratory Aesthetics: Cultural Practices between Migration and Art-making* (Amsterdam, New York: Rodopi, 2007), pp. 23–36.
43 Wolfgang Welsch, 'Transculturality: The Puzzling Form of Cultures Today', in Mike Featherstone and Scott Lash (eds), *Spaces of Culture: City, Nation, World* (London: Sage, 1999), pp. 194–213. For a critical discussion of Welsch's concept of transculturality, see Monica Juneja and Michael Falser, 'Kulturerbe – Denkmalpflege: transkulturell. Eine Einleitung', in Monica Juneja and Michael Falser (eds), *Kulturerbe und Denkmalpflege transkulturell. Grenzgänge zwischen Theorie und Praxis* (Bielefeld: transcript, 2013), pp. 17–34.
44 *Ibid.*, p. 17.
45 Lee, *Forgetting the Art World*, pp. 4–5.
46 Alain Badiou, *Ethics: An Essay on the Understanding of Evil* (London, New York: Verso, 2001), p. 1.
47 *Ibid.*, p. 2.
48 Walead Beshty, 'Introduction: Toward an Aesthetic of Ethics', in Walead Beshty (ed.), *Ethics* (London, New York: Whitechapel Gallery and The MIT Press, 2015), pp. 12–23, p. 19.
49 *Ibid.*, p. 20.
50 For important and inspiring contributions, see Demos, *The Migrant Image*; Marsha Meskimmon, *Contemporary Art and the Cosmopolitan Imagination* (London, New York: Routledge, 2011); Nikos Papastergiadis, *Cosmopolitanism and Culture* (Cambridge, Malden: Polity Press, 2012); Joanna Zylinska, *The Ethics of Cultural Studies* (London, New York: Continuum, 2005).
51 Marsha Meskimmon, 'Making worlds, making subjects: contemporary art and the affective dimension of global ethics', *World Art*, 1:2 (2011), 189–96, 192.

52 Ang, *On Not Speaking Chinese*.
53 Mark Sladen, 'Monuments and Follies', in Mark Sladen and Eamonn Maxwell (eds), *Monuments* (Lismore: Lismore Castle Arts and Mousse Publishing, 2013), pp. 11–21, p. 20.
54 Murray Edelman, *From Art to Politics: How Artistic Creations Shape Political Conceptions* (Chicago, London: The University of Chicago Press, 1995), p. 2.
55 See: http://archiv2.fridericianum-kassel.de/ausstellungen/rckblick/v001/ (accessed November 2016). Danh Vo's assistant Marta Lusena has confirmed the number of parts and that (part of) the work was exhibited for the first time in Kassel in 2011. Email from Marta Lusena to the author, 19 May 2014.
56 In November 2013, the following venues were marked on a Google map on the museum's website: Miro Foundation, Barcelona, Spain; Kunsthalle Fridericianum, Kassel, Germany; Jardin des Tuileries, Paris, France; New Museum, New York, US; Bangkok Art and Culture Centre, Bangkok, Thailand; Kunstraum Innsbruch, Austria; Center for Curatorial Studies, Hessel Museum of Art, Bard College in Annandale-on-Hudson, New York, US; SMAK, Gent, Belgium; OCT Contemporary Art Terminal, He Xianging Art Museum in Shenzen, China; The Renaissance Society at The University of Chicago, Chicago, US; Sammlung Boros Bunker, Berlin, Germany. In addition, the project was also included in Lismore Castle Arts' 2013 exhibition *Monuments*, curated by Mark Sladen. See: https://maps.google.dk/maps/ms?msid=204376734234379506011.0004be7d81d520039403e&msa=0 (accessed November 2013).
57 Mirjam Varadinis, 'Shattered freedom', *Parkett*, no. 90 (2012), 210–16, 211.
58 Danh Vo in an interview, in English, aired on German TV in the ZDF cultural programme *Der Marker* (2011). Quoted *ibid.*, 214–15.
59 The United States Constitution, see: www.usconstitution.net/const.html (accessed 16 November 2016).
60 The Declaration of Independence, see: www.ushistory.org/declaration/document/ (accessed 16 November 2016).
61 Arjun Appadurai, 'How histories make geographies: circulation and context in a global perspective', *Transcultural Studies*, 1:1 (2010), 4–13, https://journals.ub.uni-heidelberg.de/index.php/transcultural/article/view/6129/1760 (accessed November 2016), 7.
62 *Ibid.*, 10–11.
63 Benjamin Lee, 'The Subjects of Circulation', in Ulf Hedetoft and Mette Hjort (eds), *The Postnational Self: Belonging and Identity* (Minneapolis and London: University of Minnesota Press, 2002), pp. 233–49, pp. 234–7.
64 *Ibid.*, p. 235.
65 *Ibid.*, p. 238.
66 *Ibid.*, pp. 239–41.
67 *Ibid.*, pp. 239–40.
68 Edelman, *From Art to Politics*, p. 9.
69 Varadinis, 'Shattered freedom', 210.
70 Barack Obama, 'Presidental Declaration – Constitution Day, Citizenship Day, and Constitution Week, 2013', 16 September 2013, www.whitehouse.gov/

the-press-office/2013/09/16/presidential-proclamation-constitution-day-citizenship-day-and-constitut (accessed 16 November 2016).

71 Samira Rahmatullah, 'Thukral & Tagra', in *The Matter Within: New Contemporary Art of India* (San Francisco: Yerba Buena Center for the Arts, 2012), p. 46.

72 The installation was made for an exhibition of contemporary art from India, *India: Art Now,* shown in 2012 at Arken Museum of Modern Art, Denmark. I will refer to this particular version of the installation and build on Dorthe Juul Rugaard and Christina Papsø Weber's close analysis of the work in Dorthe Juul Rugaard and Christina Papsø Weber, 'Performing in transit: identities and spaces of agency in *the Escape! Resume/Reset*', *Arken Bulletin*, special issue 'Migration – Contemporary Art from India', no. 6 (2013), 71–9.

73 Peter Nagy, 'Thukral & Tagra: The Alluring Snare of Deceptive Scenographies', in *Thukral & Tagra* (New Delhi, New York: Nature Morte and Bose Pacia, 2007), pp. 5–13, p. 5.

74 *Ibid.*, p. 6.

75 James Clifford, 'Travelling Cultures', in Lawrence Grossberg, Cary Nelson and Paula A. Treichler (eds), *Cultural Studies* (New York, London: Routledge, 1992), pp. 96–112, p. 108.

76 Rugaard and Weber, 'Performing in transit', 71.

77 For illustrations of Jacir's series *Where We Come From*, see: Pat Binder and Gerhard Haupt, 'Emily Jacir: Where we come from', *Nafas Art Magazine*, October (2013), unpaginated, http://u-in-u.com/nafas/articles/2003/emily-jacir/ (accessed February 2017).

78 Demos, *The Migrant Image*, p. 104.

79 T. J. Demos, 'Desire in diaspora: Emily Jacir', *Art Journal*, 62:4 (2003), 68–78, 70.

80 *Ibid.*

81 *Ibid.*, 78.

82 Demos, *The Migrant Image*, p. 104.

83 *Ibid.*, pp. 112, 116.

84 I am indebted to Theodore Bonin from the artist's gallery, Alexander and Bonin, for providing me with this information and the perspective it gives on Emily Jacir's work.

85 See Papastergiadis, *The Turbulence of Migration*; Appadurai, *Modernity at Large*.

86 These include Paul Gilroy's seminal study *The Black Atlantic: Modernity and Double-Consciousness* (Cambridge, Mass.: Harvard University Press, 1993) as well as Kobena Mercer, *Welcome to the Jungle: New Positions in Black Cultural Studies* (London, New York: Routledge, 1994); and Jan Nederveen Pieterse, 'Globalisation as hybridisation', *International Sociology*, 9:2 (1994), 161–84.

87 Important contributions include Edward Said, *Orientalism* (London: Routledge, 1978); Said, *Reflections on Exile and Other Literary and Cultural Essays* (London: Granta Books, 2001); Homi K. Bhabha, *The Location of Culture* (London, New York: Routledge, 1994); Stuart Hall, 'Introduction: Who Needs "Identity"?', in Stuart Hall and Paul du Gay (eds), *Questions of Cultural Identity* (London, Thousand Oaks, Calif., New Delhi: Sage Publications, 1996), pp. 1–17; Hall, 'Creolization, Diaspora, and Hybridity in the Context of Globalisation', in

Okwui Enwezor (ed.), *Créolité and Creolization* (Ostfildern-Ruit: Hatje Cantz, 2003), pp. 185–98; Rasheed Araeen, Sean Cubitt and Ziauddin Sardar (eds), *The Third Text Reader on Art, Culture and Theory* (London, New York : Continuum, 2005 (2002)); Gilroy, *The Black Atlantic: Modernity and Double-Consciousness*.

88 Mikkel Bolt, 'På råbeafstand af marxismen. Et bidrag til kritik af kritikken af kritikken (Latour, Foucault, Marx)', *Kultur & Klasse: Kulturkritik nu*, no. 122 (themed issue on 'Culture Critique Now') (2016), 141–77, 168–70.

89 Veronica Tello's book from 2016 also outlines the contours of an emergent field of writings on migration and aesthetics. Her mapping is brief, though, as her primary concern is art historical memory studies and the reception of Michel Foucault's concept of counter-memory. See Veronica Tello, *Counter-Memorial Aesthetics: Refugee Histories and the Politics of Contemporary Art* (London: Bloomsbury Academic, 2016), pp. 13–14, 23–5, 30–3.

90 Serge Guilbaut, *How New York Stole the Idea of Modern Art: Abstract Expressionism, Freedom and the Cold War* (Chicago: University of Chicago Press, 1985).

91 Stephanie Barron and Sabine Eckmann (eds), *Exiles + Emigrés: The Flight of European Artists from Hitler* (Los Angeles: Los Angeles County Museum of Art; Montreal: Montreal Museum of Fine Arts; Berlin: Neue Nationalgalerie, 1997).

92 Papastergiadis, *Cosmopolitanism and Culture*, pp. 19–35.

93 Leon Wainwright, *Timed Out: Art and the Transnational Caribbean* (Manchester, New York: Manchester University Press, 2011).

94 Eddie Chambers, *Black Artists in British Art: A History since the 1950s* (London, New York: I.B. Tauris, 2014).

95 Siobhán Shilton, *Transcultural Encounters: Gender and Genre in Franco-Maghrebi Art* (Manchester, New York: Manchester University Press, 2013).

96 Charlotte Bydler, *The Global Art World, Inc.: On the Globalisation of Contemporary Art* (Uppsala: Acta Universitatis Upsaliensis, 2004).

97 Lotte Philipsen, *Globalizing Contemporary Art: The Art World's New Internationalism* (Aarhus: Aarhus University Press, 2010).

98 Hans Belting, Andrea Buddensieg and Peter Weibel (eds), *The Global Contemporary and the Rise of New Art Worlds* (Karlsruhe: ZKM Center for Art and Media Karlsruhe, 2013). The preceding anthologies are Hans Belting *et al.* (eds), *Global Studies: Mapping Contemporary Art and Culture* (Ostfildern: Hatje Cantz Verlag, 2011); Hans Belting and Andrea Buddensieg (eds), *The Global Artworld: Audiences, Markets and Museums* (Ostfildern: Hatje Cantz Verlag, 2009); Peter Weibel and Andrea Buddensieg (eds), *Contemporary Art and the Museum: A Global Perspective* (Ostfildern: Hatje Cantz Verlag in association with ZKM, Karlsruhe, 2007).

99 Kobena Mercer (ed.), *Exiles, Diasporas and Strangers*, Annotating Art's Histories (Cambridge, Mass., London: inIVA and The MIT Press, 2008).

100 Burcu Dogramaci, *Migration und künstlerische Produktion. Aktuelle Perspektiven* (Bielefeld: transcript, 2013).

101 Jill H. Casid and Aruna D'Souza (eds), *Art History in the Wake of the Global Turn* (Williamstown, Mass.: Sterling and Francine Clark Art Institute, 2014).

102 Saloni Mathur (ed.), *The Migrant's Time: Rethinking Art History and Diaspora* (Williamstown, Mass.: Sterling and Francine Clark Art Institute, 2011).
103 www.eazyintegration.dk/index.php/historien-om-venligboerne (accessed 20 May, 2016). *Venligboerne* refers to the kind and helpful spirit of neighbourliness. It is a contraction of the words *venlig* (friendly) and *nabo* (neighbour).
104 Anne Ring Petersen, 'Global art history: a view from the North', *Journal of Aesthetics & Culture*, 7 (2015), www.aestheticsandculture.net/index.php/jac/article/view/28154 (accessed 16 November 2016).
105 Salman Rushdie, 'Imaginary Homelands', in Salman Rushdie (ed.), *Imaginary Homelands: Essays and Criticism 1981–1991* (London: Granta Books, 1991), pp. 9–21, p. 19.
106 Nancy N. Chen, '"Speaking Nearby": a conversation with Trinh T. Minh-Ha', *Visual Anthropology Review*, 8:1 (1992), 82–91, 87.
107 Amelia Jones, *Seeing Differently: A History and Theory of Identification and the Visual Arts* (Abingdon, New York: Routledge, 2012).
108 Stuart Hall, 'Cultural Identity and Diaspora', in Nicholas Mirzoeff (ed.), *Diaspora and Visual Culture* (London, New York: Routledge, 2000), pp. 21–33, p. 21.
109 Roland Barthes, 'The Death of the Author', in Stephen Heath (ed.), *Roland Barthes: Image, Music, Text* (New York: Hill and Wang, 1977), pp. 142–8.
110 Hall, 'Cultural Identity and Diaspora', p. 21.
111 'Identification' in *Oxford English Dictionary*, online-dictionary, www.oed.com (accessed 14 August 2015).
112 Jones, *Seeing Differently*, pp. 2–3.
113 Ien Ang, 'Unsettling the National: Heritage and Diaspora', in Helmut Anheier and Yudhishthir Raj Isar (eds), *Heritage, Memory and Identity* (London, Thousand Oaks, Calif., Singapore: Sage, 2011), pp. 82–94, p. 86.
114 See Ruth Lister, *Citizenship: Feminist Perspectives.* 2nd Edition (New York: Palgrave Macmillan, 2003); Marsha Meskimmon, 'As a Woman, My Country Is … On Imag(in)ed Communities and the Heresy of the Becoming-Denizen', in Marsha Meskimmon and Marion Arnold (eds), *Home/Land: Women, Citizenship, Photographies* (Liverpool: Liverpool University Press, 2016), pp. 253–68.
115 Katherine Brickell and Ayona Datta, 'Introduction: Translocal Geographies', in Katherine Brickell and Ayona Datta (eds), *Translocal Geographies: Spaces, Places, Connections* (Farnham: Ashgate, 2011), pp. 3–20, pp. 3–4.
116 *Ibid.*, p. 6.
117 Appadurai, quoted *ibid.*, p. 13.
118 Demos, *The Migrant Image*, p. 31.
119 *Ibid.*, p. 28.
120 *Ibid.*, p. 31.
121 Jacques Rancière, *The Politics of Aesthetics: The Distribution of the Sensible* (London, New York: Continuum, 2004), p. 13.
122 *Ibid.*, p. 19.
123 Mieke Bal and Miguel Hernández-Navarro (eds), *Art and Visibility in Migratory Culture: Conflict, Resistance and Agency* (Amsterdam: Rodopi, 2012), p. 14.

124 Mitchell, *Seeing through Race*, p. 132.
125 Elleke Boehmer, 'A Postcolonial Aesthetic: Repeating Upon the Present', in Janet Wilson, Christina Sandru and Sarah Lawson Welsh (eds), *Rerouting the Postcolonial* (London, New York: Routledge, 2010), pp. 170–81, pp. 172–3. See also: Moslund, 'A Migrant Aesthetics through the Phenomenality of Place'.
126 Rancière, *The Politics of Aesthetics*, p. 63.
127 Meskimmon, *Contemporary Art and the Cosmopolitan Imagination*, p. 10.
128 Nikos Papapastergiadis, *Spatial Aesthetics: Art, Place and the Everyday* (London, Sydney, Chicago: River Oram Press, 2006).
129 Bal, 'Lost in Space, Lost in the Library'; Bal, 'Double Movement', in Mieke Bal and Miguel Hernández-Navarro (eds), *2 Move: Double Movement, Migratory Aesthetics* (Murcia: Bancaja, Enkhuizen: Zuiderzeemuseum: 2007), exhibition catalogue, CD-ROM, unpaginated; Bal, 'Heterochrony in the Act: The Migratory Politics of Time', in Mieke Bal and Miguel Hernández-Navarro (eds), *Art and Visibility in Migratory Culture: Conflict, Resistance and Agency* (Amsterdam: Rodopi, 2012), pp. 211–38.

1 Globalisation-from-above and globalisation-from-below

The relationship between globalisation and migration is complex, in terms of both history and theory; so also are the interrelations between the discourses on globalisation and migration and the artistic phenomena that the Introduction subsumed under the categories of global art and migratory aesthetics. This chapter seeks to draw up an outline of how 'globalisation' and 'migration' have been articulated in Western discussions of contemporary art since the 1990s, and how the two discourses intersect. The discourse on 'art and globalisation' is more encompassing than that on 'art and migration', so I will take the former as my starting point. Migration is one of the causes and vehicles of economic, political and cultural globalisation, as well as one of the effects of globalisation, and can thus be seen as an aspect of it, in terms of conceptualisation. In a discussion of globalisation, migration and transculturation, Stuart Hall introduced a distinction between two vectors in the globalisation processes that I will use to structure the discourse analysis that follows. Hall describes migration as a disruptive *cultural* force that acts as 'the joker in the globalization pack'.[1] The complex and multi-directional character of contemporary migratory movements disrupts governmentality, or the business of governing, in unpredictable ways as it intersects with the overall pattern of the division between the overdeveloped 'North' and the underdeveloped 'South'. This means that migrants have 'an ambiguous position' in contemporary globalisation. Hall explains:

> Driven hither and thither by the push-pull of a global system they do not dominate, they are a subaltern element in the process of *globalization-from-above*. At the same time, seeking by whatever means – legal or illegal – to evade the consequences of globalization, they move along uncharted routes, and exploit their lateral connections in order to negotiate or subvert the borders, barriers, legal constraints, and regulative regimes metropolitan powers put in place – a sort of deregulated *globalization-from-below*. Since the rules and the climate surrounding migration within the West (Europe, North America, Australasia) are constantly shifting, they are all potentially 'sans papiers' – Empire's 'multitudes'.[2]

Using Hall's distinction, I contend that the discourse on art and globalisation primarily revolves around issues concerning globalisation-from-above, whereas the discourse on art and migration mainly revolves around problematics related to globalisation-from-below.

Globalisation-from-above

Since the 1990s, terms such as 'global art', 'the global contemporary' and 'the global art world' have become a staple of mainstream art discourses. Thus, Jonathan Harris begins his introduction to the anthology *Globalization and Contemporary Art* by comparing 'globalisation' to the well-established terms 'modernism' and 'renaissance', which not only are specialised terms in art history but also refer to the organisation of society beyond art and the historical processes and systems that shape society.[3] As the globalisation and global art terminology is broad and vague, some preliminary clarification is needed. For this purpose, I will turn to Lotte Philipsen's structural distinction between three dimensions in the globalisation of the art world.[4] Firstly, there is art *institutional* globalisation. Secondly, there is the *discursive* globalisation that concerns the selection and the written and curatorial representation of art from different parts of the world; for instance, the discourse on the so-called New Internationalism in the 1990s has played a major part in the development of 'global perspectives' on contemporary art. The New Internationalism has also been of fundamental importance to the more sustained studies in the impact of migration on art which have gained ground since 2005. Thirdly, there is the curatorial *ideal* of a contemporary art that is global in itself, which underpins curatorial practices, particularly in connection with the large international events like biennials (see Chapter 2).

As regards the institutional globalisation, philosopher Noël Carroll has described this process as the development of 'a single, integrated, cosmopolitan institution of art, organised transnationally', i.e. a worldwide institutional apparatus with an operationally reliable repertoire of themes and meaning-producing curatorial strategies which can be mobilised on any of the world's largest art scenes. The fact that participants from everywhere may now share converging traditions and practices, and that art from anywhere can now be distributed and exhibited in transnationally coordinated venues, is something 'substantially unprecedented', suggests Carroll.[5]

This leads us to the celebratory discourses on art itself as a global, or worldwide, phenomenon. As Hans Belting has noted, two different concepts of 'art from the whole world' are circulating: *world art* and *global art*. The term global art refers to the global production of art as a more recent phenomenon, while world art refers to the history of art and is based on an older notion of world art as the top of the hierarchy of world art heritage. However, in older and popular art historical accounts the term world art is also used about the top of *Western* art heritage.[6] In the German discussion of discursive globalisation, this exclusionary use of the term world art is sometimes conveyed by playing on the linguistic similarity between the words *Weltkunst* ('world art') and *Westkunst* ('Western art'). As Peter Weibel has phrased it, *Weltkunst* in the older, traditionalist sense of the term is often defined as *Westkunst*, and *Westkunst* is defined as '*weisse Kunst*', or white art.[7] There is no consensus regarding the use of the terms global art and world art, which thus seem to function as floating signifiers in today's historiographical and curatorial discussions. Due to the emergence of the so-called world art studies as a revisionist, comparative and interdisciplinary offshoot of art history, the term world art has, in fact, recently been imbued with positive 'global' connotations.

While 'world art', in the meaning of 'world art heritage', is typically a museum item, or is acknowledged as (protected) cultural heritage, so-called 'global art' is sometimes at odds with the art museum as a hegemonic, Western type of institution. According to Belting, the cause of this misalignment is that many non-Western artists resist being associated with the traditional categories of artistic heritage, whether the ethnic traditions of their country or the modernist traditions as they have historically been defined in Western art history. In this respect, they take a *post-ethnic* and *post-historical* stance.[8] Even though the Western art world sees itself as 'globalised', not many art institutions in the West have begun systematically to include non-Western art in their collections. The fact that the kind of recognition that comes from being not only (temporarily) exhibited but also (permanently) collected by museums has been a long time coming is not merely a result of Western prejudice and disdain; it also has to do with the ways in which much non-Western art positions itself ambiguously between Western modernist and non-Western ethnic traditions. Rejecting both, as well as the traditional dualism between (Western) art and (ethnic or popular) artefact, such art is often left to operate in an institutional borderland, and vacuum, between the ethnographic museum and the museum of art.[9]

Regarding discursive globalisation – i.e. the written, spoken and curatorial articulations of contemporary art as including artists from all over the world, the discussion about New Internationalism has been an important catalyst for change in art institutional practices. For that reason, Lotte Philipsen has defined New Internationalism as a discourse in its own right with a distinctive aesthetic and political agenda. Chapter 2 will expand on the issues of inclusion and recognition at stake in New Internationalism. Here, I wish to focus on how discursive globalisation has affected the discipline of art history by considering the question: has art history been globalised too?

In his introduction to the anthology *Is Art History Global?*, James Elkins has suggested that there are several indications that the discipline of art history has been globalised, in the sense that a set of purposes, methods, narrative forms, critical concepts and key texts originating primarily in Western traditions of art history have been disseminated as a basic knowledge for critics and art historians around the world. Notwithstanding any postcolonial critique of Westernisation, a fair amount of 'global' consensus about the discipline's methodology has been established, even if its empirical field of study has become more heterogeneous than ever before, and the subject matter changes with its location. Elkins's point of view is interesting because it does not stand alone. It not only tallies with that of Noël Carroll, as quoted above; more importantly, Elkins distils his perspective from the contributions to the anthology, which include a roundtable about the globalisation of art history, with six participants and twenty-eight 'assessments' and an 'afterword' written by geographically scattered peers whose brief was to reflect on the discussion from a distance. Taken together, the contributions indicate how art history is practised in various countries, and whether or not approaches and methods have become standardised. On this evidence, Elkins concludes that art history is in the process of becoming 'a global enterprise':[10] 'A worldwide set of practices identifiable as art history poses a fascinating challenge. No one can read everything, but a worldwide endeavor, especially one whose coherence is contested and problematic, requires worldwide reading. For me, that obligation is one of the principal reasons this subject is so interesting.'[11]

This apparent globalisation of the discipline is an important precondition for the emergence of *world art studies*. As Elkins remarks, no one can read everything. Therefore, the formation of world-encompassing studies in art will require the participation of and exchange between scholars from all regions of the world. In 2008, art historians Kitty Zijlmans and Wilfried van Damme published the first comprehensive volume about the field, the anthology *World Art Studies: Exploring Concepts and Approaches*. It was John Onians, a specialist in 'neuroarthistory' and a bridge-builder between art history and neurobiology, who first proposed the idea of world art studies in the early 1990s.[12] In contradistinction to the discussions on global art, which centre on contemporary art and also include the deconstruction and expansion of Western notions of modernism, world art studies centre on historical studies, and, accordingly, give pride of place to archaeology and anthropology in their broad, multidisciplinary spectrum of methods. As van Damme writes in the introduction, world art studies aspires 'to approach its subject matter from a global perspective across time and place and to study it from all relevant disciplinary viewpoints imaginable, ranging from evolutionary biology to analytic philosophy'.[13] Thus, it seems reasonable to infer that world art studies are, in effect, a product of globalisation that could not have emerged without intensified transnational connections and exchange between scholars across the world. However, the pervasive effects of globalisation should not lead to the assumption that there could be a genuine global arts culture founded in a common reservoir of memories and histories, because cultural signifiers and identities always rely on local contexts and resonance as well.

Intersections between globalisation and migration discourses

I will conclude my examination of the discourse on 'contemporary art and globalisation' by considering the role of the globalisation concept in the literature on 'contemporary art and migration' where the concept appears to have two functions. The first is to act as the target of a somewhat unfocused but often relentless critique of society and capitalism. Armed with Marxist and neo-Marxist critical theory and anti-capitalist arguments from, among others, Michael Hardt and Antonio Negri in their seminal study *Empire* (2000), this type of argument attacks the allegedly homogenising effects of globalisation on culture as well as neo-liberal forms of economic imperialism. In this line of reasoning, globalisation is synonymous with globalisation-from-above.[14] A recurrent problem in this type of globalisation critique is that it frequently adopts the macro-theories of globalisation, which the social sciences have developed to account for the global effects of the underlying economic systems and societal mechanisms. As a result, they often move to a high level of abstraction where the relations between the global and the local are only considered in very generalising terms. The problem is that even when a picture (e.g. a reproduction of an artwork) is circulated globally by mass media and the Internet to become what Caroline A. Jones has called a 'global icon', the dialectic between the global and the local is vital, because the production and the reception of the image will always take place locally. Both the production and the reception of images and artworks are *located* in a specific place, or distributed among a plurality of specific places. Thus, a strange negligence of 'place' underlies the idea that art has been globalised merely because it can be distributed globally through exhibitions and other media. As opposed to verbal expressions that require linguistic translation, the visual can pass relatively unhindered across the borders between linguistic communities, yet the local is the only place where the visual can be observed and understood. As Caroline A. Jones points out, we need two different levels of examination to analyse such travelling objects of visual culture: 'One is local and detailed; the second is extensive and dispersed'. Even when visual culture and art are global in their distribution, the recipients are situated and 'experience their readings as specific'. As Jones concludes, 'they *re-localize* the object in each new context of reception'.[15]

Macro-theoretical generalisation is one of the reasons why social science concepts of globalisation often prove unproductive when applied to studies of visual cultures as material cultures. Unlike the concept of globalisation, which can accommodate local specificities only with some difficulty, the concept of migration has the potential to frame the discussion of 'the glocal' in fruitful ways because it allows a transcultural focus on the specific intersections involved in a particular cultural encounter. The migration concept can thus accommodate the interaction between the different cultures and scales (local, regional, global) that are at work in migration-related art. However, in studies of art and culture, the social science use of the term migration, as it refers to emigration and immigration, must be coupled with a set of humanistic concepts with which to investigate the cultural and artistic processes, effects and representations of migration – concepts such as translation, transculturation, hybridisation and aesthetics. It is important to remember that this is not a question of choosing between mutually exclusive perspectives – that is to say, of examining either 'globalisation' or 'migration' as a problematic. Globalisation is important to contemporary artistic practices, not least when the origin of the work is lost in what could be termed the global mainstream, or when the expression and content of a work turns out to be so hybridised and polycultural that it is not possible to give an account of its provenance. In other words, globalisation influences cultural and artistic practices, and the concept cannot just be substituted with migration as if the two terms were synonyms.

We have thus come around to the second and, in my opinion, more productive function of the globalisation concept. It can be a useful and necessary instrument when examining the social, political, economic, discursive and institutional structures and mechanisms of the art world, particularly how the so-called 'biennial boom' since the 1980s has gradually transformed the world map of exhibitions and enabled artists from all continents to circulate worldwide. Charlotte Bydler's study *The Global Art World, Inc.* and Lotte Philipsen's *Globalizing Contemporary Art* are good examples of this use of the globalisation concept to substantiate the supposition that art *institutional* globalisation-from-above has been increasingly tangible since the 1980s and 1990s. Philipsen examines how the mechanisms of 'globality' have affected the art world since the 1990s. Bydler considers the nomadic career patterns of artists and cultural workers, as well as how the historical relations between former colonies and colonisers still act as a determining factor in the geopolitics of the art world. In addition, she examines how transnational mobility, i.e. moving from the periphery to a centre, can further an artist's career. However, neither of these authors is committed to exploring how migration shapes artistic expressions and projects, which this book aims to do.

Globalisation-from-below

As opposed to the emphasis on globalisation-from-above in the discourse on contemporary art and globalisation, globalisation-from-below takes centre stage in the discourse on contemporary art and migration. Here, nodal points such as migration, diaspora, exile, refugeedom, displacement, precarity, subalternity, cosmopolitanism, cultural translation, creolisation and migratory aesthetics push globalisation into the background. Often drawing on postcolonial and decolonial studies and theories, the writers contributing to this discourse typically place themselves in the classical position of the critical, leftist intellectual – as exemplified in some of the writings that have been influential for this author by, for example, Rasheed Araeen, T. J. Demos, Okwui Enwezor, Mieke Bal, Griselda Pollock, Nikos Papastergiadis, Leon Wainwright and Nicolas Bourriaud.[16]

Although the authors themselves may not necessarily distinguish between different kinds of migration, and although sharp distinctions cannot be drawn, a particular distinction should be made between 'forced' and 'voluntary' migration. On the one hand, there are exiles and refugees/asylum seekers, i.e. individuals or groups of people who have been forced to leave their home country because of political conflict, persecution, destitution or for environmental reasons. On the other, there are those who move for economic reasons, education and work, and who are frequently described as labour migrants. Yet, the fact that people who are driven to migrate by extreme poverty are often considered economic migrants indicates that the distinction is not clear-cut. Migration, as an umbrella term, covers this broad range of migratory movements, which can be motivated by different and complex economic, work-related and personal circumstances as well as the pressures of decolonisation, forced displacement, and natural and man-made disasters.[17] That migration in this broad sense of the word is actually a causal factor in the globalisation of the art world is evident when the issues under discussion relate to the labour migration of artists or to the postcolonial critique of the exclusion of non-Western artists from Western art institutions. Moreover, a concern with refugees and undocumented migrants, often linked to philosopher Giorgio Agamben's figure of bare life, has permeated the imagination, aesthetics and discourses of contemporary art.[18] A key example of this is Veronica Tello's study of artworks in which the documentation of singular events related to refugee experience is embedded in complex image networks. Tello identifies a particular paradigm in contemporary art, which she names 'counter-memorial aesthetics' with reference to the artists' dedication to generate aesthetic counter-memorialisations of refugeedom. Counter-memorial aesthetics is characterised by the use of various montage techniques to preserve the otherwise vanishing images and voices of refugees and to represent refugee experiences as heterogeneous in a double meaning of the word, contends Tello. First of all, they are in excess of allegedly homogeneous national bodies and narratives, and, secondly, they are part of the countless flows and interconnected events that structure the globalised world of the twenty-first century. By stressing the heterogeneous montage character of counter-memorial aesthetics, Tello demonstrates how artists such as Isaac Julien, Tania Bruguera and Hito Steyerl seek to counter the conventional understanding of counter-memory as structured by a binary antagonism between victors and vanquished, and 'a battle between us and them – "us" being the hospitable benevolent people and "them" the xenophobic public'.[19]

In texts concerned specifically with forced migration and exile in relation to art, authors often communicate their critical political stance more directly as the topic is usually artists in war-related exile, or artists affected by the forced displacements of peoples such as the Jewish, Palestinian and African diasporas.[20] Even in the discourse on forced migration and exile, the terms 'exile' and 'diaspora' are sometimes applied to artists who have roots in countries where persecution has taken place, but who have not been compelled to migrate as a result of any such persecution, or because of war or oppression of ethnic, sexual or religious minorities, and have rather done so for educational and career reasons. In this extended use, 'exile' and 'diaspora' may place the artist in the position of a spokesperson for the suppressed and displaced. The problem here is not so much that the artist's 'project' may not convincingly substantiate such a radically critical and political reading, but that the artist may be represented as a political victim with limited agency, and that their works may be forced into a singular and reductive political frame of interpretation.

The term 'diaspora' needs a special mention. Traditionally, it has been used to refer to the exodus of the Jews following the destruction of the Second Temple in 586 BC. It has also been applied to enslaved Africans and to the Armenians who fled the massacre perpetrated by the Ottoman Empire during and immediately after the First World War. In this classical use, diaspora refers to 'large-scale involuntary displacements and an inability to return home, coupled with a great yearning to do so'.[21] However, since its more recent revival it has been used flexibly – too flexibly, according to some critics – about almost any migrant group in any situation, as is seen in political scientist Gabriel Sheffer's definition of 'modern diasporas' as 'ethnic minority groups of migrant origins residing and acting in host countries but maintaining a strong sentimental and material link with their countries of origin – their homelands'.[22] In art discourses, too, the term diaspora has developed into a floating signifier that is sometimes used about forced displacements, and about (artists from) ethnic minority communities – such as, for example, the Indian diaspora in the UK, which has constituted a well-established minority community for several generations.

Turning to the broader discourse on migration and contemporary art, I wish to stress that the discussions on art related to migration, diaspora and exile are closely connected, and that the terms therefore tend to bleed into each other. The discourse on migration and contemporary art is obviously not a fixed entity, as there are many different and shifting perspectives on the interrelationship between art and movement. Nevertheless, it is possible to identify two recurrent theoretical positions in the art and migration discourse since the 1990s, which I will call *the postcolonial position* and *the migratory aesthetics position*. They should not be seen as firm standpoints but, rather, as two distinct *perspectives on* and *approaches to* the thematics of art and migration. They are frequently combined, but usually one tends to dominate the other. When domination is conspicuous, it is possible to identify them as positions. The postcolonial position, which applies a postcolonial lens to issues of art and migration, has primarily been articulated and shaped by the influential British journal *Third Text* (1987–), in particular by its editors and regular contributors, both on the pages of the journal and in their other writings. A glance at the editorial group in the early years is illuminating in itself. In 1991, the Editor (and founding editor) was Rasheed Araeen, Jean Fisher was Associate Editor and Nikos Papastergiadis was an Editorial Assistant – all of whom have remained leading voices in shaping the international postcolonial debate on art and migration. The journal's Advisory Committee included the artist Mona Hatoum and Gilane Tawadros, a curator, critic and founding director of inIVA (Institute of International Visual Arts, London). The journal's International Council comprised some of the principal protagonists of postcolonial theory and art history: Homi K. Bhabha, Geeta Kapur, Sarat Maharaj, Partha Mitter, Edward W. Said, Gayatri C. Spivak, as well as Stuart Hall and the African-American artist Howardena Pindell.[23] As I will elaborate in Chapter 2, *Third Text* became an important channel for the international dissemination of postcolonial theory, as well as for postcolonial perspectives on art and visual culture. The journal also contributed significantly to the critique of the institutional exclusion of migrant artists and the institutionalised attempts at multiculturalism that tended to categorise non-Western artists separately as 'ethnic artists', a critique central to the postcolonial discourse on art and migration. Another important aspect of this discourse is the demand for recognition of modernist movements outside the West, and the accompanying idea that the traditional Western understanding of modernism must be revised to accommodate the heterochronous and variegated unfolding of different modernisms in other parts of the world.

The interest in the modern features of non-Western art has been steadily increasing since the 2000s. This has stimulated research into the epistemological, aesthetic and formal aspects of modern and contemporary art, which, in the 1990s and early 2000s, were overshadowed by postcolonial identity politics, i.e. a political concern with the recognition of the artist's cultural identity and a sometimes heavy-handed focus on the connections between ethnicity and the institutional mechanisms of exclusion.[24] While those who adopt the postcolonial position basically endorse a political project, fighting exclusion and seeking recognition of minority and migrant cultures and identities, the supporters of the migratory aesthetics position pursue epistemological and aesthetic objectives first and political objectives second. The latter position is founded on an understanding of how migrants, either partly or wholly separated from the places, language and social forms of their home country, have to straddle two cultures that put each other in perspective, often in tensional and illuminating ways. It thus revolves around a wish to explore how a migrant identity and existence can become a rich soil for artistic activity, aesthetic experimentation and innovative perspectives. I have used Mieke Bal's neologism *migratory aesthetics* to designate the second position because it appears to be the theoretical concept that is most frequently used to mark this position. It is also the concept that, so far, has been subjected to the most thorough theoretical clarification and discussion. The most viable alternative term is probably 'diasporic aesthetics' used by Kobena Mercer as a general descriptor for art by individuals with a migrant background when advocating that more attention should be given to 'questions of aesthetics in the actual experience of works of art'.[25] It is this position that constitutes the foundation of his work as editor of and contributor to the 'Annotating Art's Histories' series of topic-based historical studies of non-Western modernisms.[26]

As mentioned in the Introduction, the term 'migratory aesthetics' was coined and developed in connection with a transnational collaborative research project on the topic led by Mieke Bal and Griselda Pollock. Since the term was introduced around 2005, it has spread in scholarly discourses on culture and the arts.[27] The contributors to the project broke new ground by developing innovative frames for understanding the epistemological and aesthetic *as well as* the semiotic and political dimensions of art and culture created by individuals with a migrant background, or by individuals exploring the topic of migration without having a migrant background themselves. The results were collected in Sam Durrant and Catherine M. Lord's co-edited volume *Essays in Migratory Aesthetics: Cultural Practices between Migration and Art-making*[28] and Mieke Bal and Miguel Hernández-Navarro's anthology *Art and Visibility in Migratory Culture: Conflict, Resistance and Agency.*[29] In addition, Griselda Pollock curated and wrote a catalogue essay for the group exhibition *Migratory Aesthetics*, and Bal and Hernández-Navarro co-authored the exhibition catalogue *2 Move: Double Movement, Migratory Aesthetics*,[30] in which they presented some of their foundational work on migratory aesthetics. Mieke Bal's contribution to the leading concept of the collaborative research project has been particularly valuable. She conceived of migratory aesthetics as a kind of placeholder to stimulate discussions, i.e. as an open concept that the participants could define, each in their own way. As demonstrated by the aforementioned publications, the concept is heuristically productive as it helps to focus discussions on the nexus of art and migration in a way that balances reflections on art's political content and ethical engagement with a consideration of its aesthetic dimensions, in a cultural atmosphere where issues of immigration, asylum-seeking and cultural diversity are high on both serious and populist political agendas. Griselda Pollock's interpretation of the term is worth quoting because it makes explicit its political character as well as the question mark at the core of the term, which signals its openness to further interpretation and discussion:

> So what does this term mean? Does *migratory aesthetics* suggest an aesthetic dimension to the social and cultural experience of migration? Yes. Does it suggest that aesthetics as ways of living and making sense of the world migrate? Yes. Does it suggest migration involves an aesthetic of being and transformation of the self? Yes. Does it imply a re-evaluation of an often negative, paranoid and anxiety-ridden response to incoming 'others' by exploring both what migration feels like from within and how societies are animated – painfully as well as creatively – by the challenge of differences we should celebrate rather than fear or resist? Yes.[31]

Pollock's terminological clarification also led her to answer the classic sceptical question: why study art when society urgently needs solutions to real political crisis and social challenges? This question is rooted in a common belief that aesthetics is only about art secure in its ivory tower of beauty and pleasurable contemplation, safely removed from the troubles and injustices of the world. As Pollock points out, this idealising separation of art from life, which discredits art and aesthetics in the context of societal discourses, is simply not valid any more:

> In post-twentieth century culture, the aesthetic addresses ways of experiencing, knowing and representing the worlds we live in, crossing emotion and thought, sensation and idea, offering ways into complex experience and difficult concepts through its own affective, affecting and embodied visual, literary, filmic and musical rhetoric ... The aesthetic is not, therefore, about abstracted beauty freed from daily social realities; in post-Auschwitz and post-colonial times, the aesthetic as a singular articulation that interrupts the massified clichés of media culture, as ways of speaking, showing and representing from a specific experience and place, open lines of inter-subjective encounter and potential communication that allows for *singularity*.[32]

Overall, the writings resulting from this research project do not express the same strong political commitment and institutional critique as those written from a radical postcolonial position, since the former are more committed to developing analytical concepts and in-depth analyses of works of art. Nevertheless, the project's ethical and political perspectives were informed by postcolonial thinking and concepts, among others. Those who prioritise the epistemological and aesthetic perspectives also seek institutional recognition of artists with migrant backgrounds, but, unlike those who apply a distinct postcolonial perspective, they usually try to pave the way for recognition by analysing, theorising and endorsing the *aesthetic* potential and characteristics of migratory artworks. Hence, the discourse on migratory aesthetics is not so much concerned with the recognition of the artist's cultural identity and difference, but, rather, with demonstrating the topicality and significance of the work's content and aesthetic. While the postcolonial position's concepts and frames for understanding have primarily been developed deductively by adopting concepts and perspectives from postcolonial theory, scholars who explore migratory aesthetics tend to develop their key analytical concepts inductively by testing them in close readings of exemplary artworks, literary texts, films or exhibitions.[33]

As 'migratory aesthetics' was coined as the key concept of a collaborative project, Bal's intention must have been strategic: to start a discussion about the interrelations between migration and aesthetics. Thus, it seems to be a deliberate decision on her part to keep the concept open and fluid by introducing it as:

> *a non-concept*, a ground for experimentation that *opens up possible relations with 'the migratory'*, rather than pinpointing such relations. As a provisional circumscription of the modifier, let me call it a feature, or a quality of the world in which mobility is not the exception but on its way to becoming the standard, the means rather than the minority.[34]

Introduced as a 'non-concept', migratory aesthetics has initiated what I would describe as a series of performative speech acts, which, through repetition and displacement of the concept's meaning, have worked against consensus in favour of a uniform definition and imbued the concept with a plural semantics, thus enabling its productive adaptation to various strands of cultural analysis. As Jill Bennett has noted, migratory aesthetics is 'a strategy: a transitional politics'.[35] Importantly, this strategy is based on aesthetic analysis. For the contributors to the two anthologies and two exhibitions that resulted from the research project, the term migratory aesthetics does not refer to a thematic art, an art *about* migration, but primarily to an art that is fundamentally *shaped by* the effects of migration. It is an art characterised by instability, signs of continuous movement (as in video art) or double movements. As an analytical perspective, migratory aesthetics represents a politics different from that of the usual documentary accounts of specific migrations or mixed identities. In Jill Bennett's words, it offers 'a politics of contemporary culture as "migrant"; that is, a culture transformed by migration but emphatically not a separable minority culture. In this arena, pressing concerns (the refugee issue, 'multicultural' politics and contemporary divisions, as well as fundamental issues of democratic participation) emerge *through* the aesthetic analysis, as it were.'[36]

Considering this inclusive political and aesthetic agenda, the choice of the term migratory aesthetics – and not migrant art, or migrant fine arts – presents itself as a deliberate one. The concept of art is rooted in Western thinking and thus tainted with Eurocentric perspectives, hierarchies and exclusions. Although the concept of aesthetics is also of Western origin, as it derives from the Greek word *aesthesis*, its meaning is not limited to artworks or artistic activity defined in terms of media, such as painting or sculpture. Up to the time of Immanuel Kant and his influential philosophy of aesthetics, *aesthesis* meant, rather, the transmission and communication of sense and feeling through bodily perception and cognition. Thus, it can encompass a broader range of phenomena instead of restricting the field of study to what the fine arts system recognises as 'art'. On the downside, the fairly open definition of migratory aesthetics can also lead one into a minefield, because it assigns a dual role to 'migration' as both a useful analytical concept and a dynamic, ongoing socio-historical process. Therefore it requires careful balancing: if one disengages too much from the actual social and historical circumstances in order to accommodate 'aesthetics', one risks losing sight of the socio-historical process. In this case, the always localised processes of transculturation involved in migration may become reduced to a very general cosmopolitan outlook on the world. But the neglect of the aesthetic dimensions in postcolonial identity politics and the dissociation from Western traditions often leaves unanswered the crucial question of how migrant artists contribute not only to changing institutional structures but also to renewing artistic and cultural expressions.

The challenge for all those who wish to use the concept of migratory aesthetics as a catalyst for an analysis of cultural change related to migration, and to the kinds of mobile individuals that these changes both create and are created by, consists in avoiding two pitfalls. On the one hand, there is the risk of overemphasising aesthetics and turning the representation of specific migrant experiences into a general, apolitical aesthetics of migration to be celebrated as an almost universalised multicultural or cosmopolitan ideal. On the other, neglect of the significance of the aesthetic dimensions of art and culture may lead to a situation where the migrant is denied any kind of agency and active participation in the *cultural* transformation of society, and it will, in any event, make it difficult to pinpoint what the contributions of the artists are.[37] The contributors to the collaboration on migratory aesthetics have sought to avoid both pitfalls. They have also found ways to deal with the innate tension of the very concept of migratory aesthetics: the tension between the desire to develop a deeper understanding of the processes of migration and transculturation, and a desire to renounce all this complicated socio-cultural knowledge and start with the groundwork – the attentive observation of the work of art itself.

Notes

1 Hall, 'Creolization, Diaspora, and Hybridity in the Context of Globalisation', p. 195.

2 *Ibid.*, pp. 195–6, emphasis added.

3 Jonathan Harris, 'Introduction. Globalization and Contemporary Art: A Convergence of Peoples and Ideas', in Jonathan Harris (ed.), *Globalization and Contemporary Art* (Chichester: Wiley-Blackwell, 2011), pp. 1–15, p. 1.

4 Lotte Philipsen, 'The Globalisation of Contemporary Art: Interests, Articulations, and Impact of the Discourse of New Internationalism in the Visual Arts' (PhD dissertation, Aarhus University, 2008), 17.

5 Noël Carroll, 'Art and globalization: then and now', *Journal of Aesthetics & Art Criticism*, 65:1 (2007), 131–43, 136.

6 Hans Belting, 'Contemporary Art and the Museum in the Global Age', in Peter Weibel and Andrea Buddensieg (eds), *Contemporary Art and the Museum: A Global Perspective* (Ostfildern: Hatje Cantz Verlag in association with ZKM, Karlsruhe, 2007), pp. 16–38, 33–4.

7 Peter Weibel, 'Jenseits des weissen Würfels. Kunst zwischen Kolonialismus und Kosmopolitismus', in Peter Weibel (ed.), *Inklusion: Eksklusion. Versuch einer neuen Kartografie Der Kunst im Zeitalter von Postkolonialismus und globaler Migration* (Köln: DuMont, 1997), pp. 8–36, p. 11.

8 Belting, 'Contemporary Art and the Museum in the Global Age', p. 34.

9 See *ibid.*, pp. 19–20.

10 James Elkins, 'Art History as a Global Discipline', in James Elkins (ed.), *Is Art History Global?* (New York, London: Routledge, 2007), pp. 3–23, p. 21. Elkins's essay in the anthology *World Art Studies* also contains further reflections on what to conclude from the contributions to *Is Art History Global?* See Elkins, 'Can We Invent a World Art Studies?', in Kitty Zijlmans and Wilfried van Damme (eds), *World Art Studies: Exploring Concepts and Approaches* (Amsterdam: Valiz, 2008), pp. 107–18.

11 Elkins, 'Art History as a Global Discipline', pp. 22–3.

12 Wilfried van Damme, 'Introducing World Art Studies', in Zijlmans and van Damme (eds), *World Art Studies: Exploring Concepts and Approaches*, pp. 23–61, pp. 54–7.

13 *Ibid.*, p. 27.

14 Sean Cubitt, 'Citizens, Consumers and Migrants', in Scott McQuire and Nikos Papastergiadis (eds), *Empires, Ruins + Networks: The Transcultural Agenda in Art* (London, Chicago: Rivers Oram Press, 2005), pp. 304–17; T. J. Demos, 'On the Diasporic Public Sphere', in Hans-Jörg Heussert and Kornelia Imesch (eds), *Visions of a Future: Art and Art History in Changing Contexts* (Zürich: Swiss Institute for Art Research, 2004), pp. 103–16; Caroline A. Jones, 'Is International Modernism National? Is Global Postmodernism Local? Questions for Art History', in Heussert and Imesch (eds), *Visions of a Future*, pp. 117–28.

15 Jones, 'Is International Modernism National?', p. 119.

16 Rasheed Araeen, 'The other immigrant: the experience and achievements of

Afroasian artists in the metropolis', *Third Text*, 5:15 (1991), 17–28; Araeen, 'Our Bauhaus others' mudhouse', *Third Text*, 3:6 (1989), 3–16; Araeen, 'Re-thinking history and some other things', *Third Text*, 15:54 (2001), 93–100; Bal, 'Double Movement'; Bal, 'Lost in Space, Lost in the Library'; Bal, 'Heterochrony in the Act'; Nicolas Bourriaud, 'Altermodern', in Nicolas Bourriaud (ed.), *Altermodern: Tate Triennial* (London: Tate Publishing, 2009), pp. 11–24; T. J. Demos, 'The Ends of Exile: Towards a Coming Universality?', in Bourriaud (ed.), *Altermodern: Tate Triennial*, pp. 73–88; Demos, *The Migrant Image*; Okwui Enwezor, 'Modernity and Postcolonial Ambivalence', in Bourriaud (ed.), *Altermodern: Tate Triennial*, pp. 27–40; Nikos Papastergiadis, 'From the Edges of Exile to the Limits of Translation', in Diana Nemiroff (ed.), *Crossings* (Ottawa: National Gallery of Canada, 1998); Papastergiadis, 'The South in the North', *Third Text*, 5:14 (1991), 43–52; Papastergiadis, 'Hybridity and ambivalence: places and flows in contemporary art and culture', *Theory, Culture & Society*, 22:4 (2005), 39–64; Wainwright, *Timed Out*; Griselda Pollock, *Migratory Aesthetics* (Leeds: AHRC CentreCATH, University of Leeds, 2006).

17 Khalid Koser, *International Migration: A Very Short Introduction* (Oxford, New York: Oxford University Press, 2007), pp. 16–19.

18 Giorgio Agamben, *Homo Sacer: Sovereign Power and Bare Life* (Stanford: Stanford University Press, 1998).

19 Tello, *Counter-Memorial Aesthetics*, p. 2.

20 The principal example is Barron and Eckmann (eds), *Exiles + Emigrés*. See also Nicholas Mirzoeff (ed.), *Diaspora and Visual Culture: Representing Africans and Jews* (London, New York: Routledge, 2000). It is in the writings of T. J. Demos that we find the topics of exile and diaspora treated most thoroughly. In *The Exiles of Marcel Duchamp*, Demos examines how Duchamp visualised, defined and used the conditions of exile in periods during the First and Second World Wars when he went into exile in New York and Buenos Aires. See T. J. Demos, *The Exiles of Marcel Duchamp* (Cambridge, Mass., London: The MIT Press, 2007). In continuation thereof, Demos has interrogated similar problematics in contemporary art in *The Migrant Image*.

21 Koser, *International Migration*, p. 25.

22 Gabriel Scheffer, *Modern Diasporas in International Politics*, Croom Helm 1986, p. 3. Quoted from Koser, *International Migration*, p. 25.

23 This information is taken from the imprint page of *Third Text*, 5:15, 1991 – a special issue on 'British Art in a Century of Immigration'.

24 The clearest sign of this interest in non-Western modernisms and expressions of 'modernity' is the significant art historical accounts that have been published about this subject, including Partha Mitter, *The Triumph of Modernism: India's Artists and the Avant-Garde, 1922–47* (London: Reaction Books, 2007) and Kobena Mercer (ed.), *Cosmopolitan Modernisms*, Annotating Art's Histories (Cambridge, Mass., London: inIVA and The MIT Press, 2005); Mercer (ed.), *Discrepant Abstraction*, Annotating Art's Histories (Cambridge, Mass., London: inIVA and The MIT Press, 2006). In addition, the importance of non-Western modernisms is underscored in a range of studies in contemporary art, including

Gerardo Mosquera and Jean Fisher (eds), *Over Here: International Perspectives on Art and Culture* (Cambridge, Mass.: The MIT Press, 2004); Enwezor, 'Modernity and Postcolonial Ambivalence'; Nicolas Bourriaud, *The Radicant* (New York: Lukas & Sternberg, 2009); Mercer (ed.), *Exiles, Diasporas and Strangers*; Terry Smith, 'Rethinking modernism and modernity now', *Filozofski vestnik*, 35:2 (2014), 271–319; Smith, *Contemporary Art: World Currents* (London: Laurence King, 2011).

25 Mercer, '"Diaspora Didn't Happen in a Day": Reflections on Aesthetics and Time', p. 76.

26 *Cosmopolitan Modernisms*; *Discrepant Abstraction*; *Exiles, Diasporas & Strangers*; *Pop Art and Vernacular Cultures*, Annotating Art's Histories (Cambridge, Mass., London: inIVA and The MIT Press, 2007).

27 The research project began in 2004–5 with a collaboration between the doctoral school Amsterdam School of Cultural Analysis (ASCA) at the University of Amsterdam, headed by Mieke Bal, and the Centre for Cultural Analysis, Theory and History (Centre CATH) at the University of Leeds, led by Griselda Pollock. The project began with two workshops and developed into an international collaboration between a changing group of scholars, primarily from the fields of cultural studies, comparative literature and art history, and mostly from Spain, the Netherlands and the UK. The earliest public use of the term seems to be the exhibition *Migratory Aesthetics*, curated by Griselda Pollock and held at the University Gallery at the University of Leeds. In the press release of 11 January 2006, Pollock explained that the collaboration on the topic of migratory aesthetics involved a network of thirty scholars and artists. The subsequent dissemination of the term beyond the network is manifest in several of the contributions in Sten Pultz Moslund, Anne Ring Petersen and Moritz Schramm (eds), *The Culture of Migration: Politics, Aesthetics and Histories* (London, New York: I.B. Tauris, 2015). See also Marsha Meskimmon and Dorothy Rowe, 'Editorial Introduction: Ec/centric Affinities: Locations, Aesthetics, Experiences', in Marsh Meskimmon and Dorothy Rowe (eds), *Women, the Arts and Globalization: Eccentric Experience* (Manchester, New York: Manchester University Press, 2013), pp. 1–14; Emma-Lucy O'Brien, 'Migratory aesthetics: an email exchange', *Irish Review*, 39:1 (2008), 93–100; Ofra Amihay, 'Immigwriting: Photographs as Migratory Aesthetics in the Modern Hebrew Novel', in Ofra Amihay and Lauren Walsh (eds), *Future of Text and Image: Collected Essays on Literary and Visual Conjunctures* (Newcastle upon Tyne: Cambridge Scholars Publishing, 2012), pp. 131–66; Kass Banning, 'The nine muses: recalibrating migratory aesthetics', *Black Camera*, 6:2 (2015), 135–46; Amna Malik, 'Migratory Aesthetics: (Dis)Placing the Black Maternal Subject in Martine Attille's *Dreaming Rivers* (1988)', in R. Victoria Arana (ed.), *'Black' British Aesthetics Today* (Newcastle upon Tyne: Cambridge Scholars Publishing, 2007), pp. 243–61.

28 Sam Durrant and Catherine M. Lord (eds), *Essays in Migratory Aesthetics: Cultural Practices between Migration and Art-making* (Amsterdam, New York: Rodopi, 2007).

29 Bal and Hernández-Navarro (eds), *Art and Visibility in Migratory Culture.*

30 Pollock, *Migratory Aesthetics*; Bal and Hernández-Navarro (eds), *2 Move: Double Movement, Migratory Aesthetics*.
31 Pollock, *Migratory Aesthetics*, p. 27.
32 *Ibid.*, p. 28.
33 Instructive examples are 'heterochrony', adopted from biology and developed into an analytical term for art history by Mieke Bal in'Lost in Space, Lost in the Library' and 'Heterochrony in the Act', as well as the artist Lily Markiewicz's adaptation of Heidegger's and Edmond Jabès's concepts of dwelling and Sigmund Freud's concept of the uncanny to her own work, in 'No Place – Like Home', in Durrant and Lord (eds), *Essays in Migratory Aesthetics*, pp. 37–48.
34 Bal, 'Lost in Space, Lost in the Library', p. 23; emphasis added.
35 Jill Bennett, 'Migratory Aesthetics: Art and Politics Beyond Identity', in Bal and Hernández-Navarro (eds), *Art and Visibility in Migratory Culture*, pp. 109–26, p. 124.
36 *Ibid.*, p. 120.
37 For a discussion of the potential pitfalls and the connection between migratory aesthetics and postcolonial theory, see Sam Durrant and Catherine M. Lord, 'Introduction: Essays in Migratory Aesthetics', in Durrant and Lord (eds), *Essays in Migratory Aesthetics*, pp. 11–19; Graham Huggan, 'Unsettled Settlers: Postcolonialism, Travelling Theory and the New Migrant Aesthetics', in Durrant and Lord (eds), *Essays in Migratory Aesthetics*, pp. 129–44.

2 The politics of identity and recognition in the 'global art world'

Identity politics informed by postcolonial critique dominated the discourses on the interrelations of globalisation, migration and contemporary art in the 1990s and the early 2000s. The previous chapter characterised the position from which the struggle for recognition of non-Western artists was launched, designating it the postcolonial position, in contradistinction to the migratory aesthetics position that gathered momentum in the 2000s. This second chapter examines the historical role and impact of the postcolonial position in greater detail, firstly by analysing its underlying notion of cultural identity as well as its institutional critique, and, secondly, by tracing how this critique has paved the way for greater recognition of artists from non-Western diasporas in an increasingly globalised art world.

One of the aims of this chapter is to work through the binarisms and simplifying categorisations of classic identity politics in the visual arts. This critical revision provides a basis for the attempt to move away from dichotomous ways of thinking about identity and belonging in Chapter 5, which returns to the question of identity at the level of the artwork. However, as Amelia Jones has argued, there is no way around the reiteration of the binaries of some of the labels, even when one seeks to complicate them and avoid homogenisation with respect to easily stereotyped categories such as culture, gender and race. The binary distinction between 'Western' and 'non-Western', for example, is unavoidable in the discourse analysis that follows, because it is a widely circulated and thus culturally and historically relevant distinction, which evidently carries different connotations depending on who is using it.[1] In this book, I follow Jones in using the term non-Western to indicate a Euro-American perspective and its projection of what it is 'not', i.e. its embedded notion of the non-Western 'other' that has been shaped historically by the still active logic of colonialism, but which has also been challenged by postcolonial critique. This is in accord with Jones's observation that even a reflective usage of shorthand binary terms such as 'Western' and 'non-Western' does not solve the basic problem of language, which tends to reiterate what the text seeks to critique or at least analyse. Still, such shorthand expressions are necessary in the face of the complexities of the discourses on identity under discussion.[2]

In the face of the problems with these terminologies, I wish to introduce the idea of a cluster of concepts as a useful instrument for mapping notions of identity at work in the discourses on identity and recognition.[3] For my purposes, a cluster of concepts is a group of loosely connected concepts that are linked to each other in a relational way. A conceptual cluster bears some resemblance to what discourse analysts term signifying chains, in particular to chains of equivalence. Whereas a chain of equivalence equates particular signifiers of a single text, thereby providing a temporary fixation or *closure* of the signs, the concepts in a cluster are scattered across numerous texts by different authors, and each of them can be linked to a sub-cluster of concepts and signifiers with a narrower meaning. In other words, a conceptual cluster constitutes a conceptual landscape that generates the particular notion of a phenomenon at work in a specific, historical context – in this case, the notion of identity developed in Western art discourses of the 1990s and 2000s. Like a cultural landscape, which is not a natural phenomenon but modified over time by the effects of human activity, a cluster is a construct that bears the traces and strata of its shaping over time.

I deploy this understanding of a cluster of concepts to examine the changing identity politics of the contemporary art world. In this context, I use the term *identity politics* to refer to political and ideological arguments that focus on the self-interest and perspectives of artists and groups of artists that have hitherto been marginalised in the West, and especially in Europe, on the basis of their cultural identity and non-Western origin. Obviously, not all artists from any given minority are professionally involved in identity politics. However, this is of minor relevance to the argument developed here, as the focus of this chapter is not the identity of individual artists but a *discourse* on cultural identity in which artists are seen as representatives of specific cultural or ethnic groups. Accordingly, I will adopt a discursive approach that sees 'identity' as a construction. This not only offers an alternative to the traditional art historical celebration of subjectivity in the individual artist as the locus of authenticity and originality, even genius; it also provides a means to circumvent the idealising notion of the artist as a superior being, the embodiment of visionary creativity, so that we can instead focus on the differences and hierarchies that determine the ranking and careers of contemporary artists and the reception of their work. As Stuart Hall has pointed out, a discursive approach must be aware of the mechanisms of exclusion that the process of subjectification entails. In other words, it must reflect on the question of *identification* and how (self-)identifications come into existence through discourse. In Stuart Hall's wording, identification is 'a process of articulation … And since as a process it operates across difference, it entails discursive work, the binding and marking of symbolic boundaries, the production of "frontier-effects". It requires what is left outside, its constitutive outside, to consolidate the process.'[4]

The concept of identity adopted here relates primarily to the cultural aspects of identity, and the focus will be on the question of how 'identity' becomes associated with notions of cultural difference, ethnicity, migration and, more generally, globalisation in the discourses on contemporary art. It is not possible to draw clear lines of demarcation between a person's psychic, social and cultural identity, and any attempt to draw such lines runs the risk of reductionism. In any event, I will use the term *cultural identity*, not to reduce the complexity of 'identity' to a single dimension or to signal that there is a stable, ethnic, religious, communal and socio-cultural core of the self, but simply to stress that it is the collective, i.e. socio-cultural and ethnic, dimensions of 'identity' that come to the fore in this chapter.

The concept of cultural identity has played a seminal role in the discourses on contemporary art since the 1980s. Armed with arguments from postcolonial theory and supported by the very real and transformative forces of globalisation and migration, discussions about identity politics in the art world have fundamentally transformed the dominant Western conception of the 'international art world' as an exclusive club for Westerners only. Such discussions paved the way for an institutional multiculturalism that has changed the mechanisms of inclusion and exclusion of non-Western and migrant artists in the art institutional system of the West. To illustrate this transformation, I will use a telling survey by Lotte Philipsen of the number of Western and non-Western participants at selected Documenta exhibitions between 1955 and 2007. Since 1955, Documenta has taken place every five years in Kassel, Germany, and is still generally considered to be one of the most important international art events in the Northern hemisphere. Historically, it has served as an example that countries all over the world have looked to, and sometimes consciously rejected, when developing the conceptual and organisational framework for their own art biennials. The number of biennials around the world has now reached an estimated 100 to 200 biennials and they fulfil a wide array of functions, the most important being as '"hegemonic machines", which link the local to the global within the field of symbolic struggles for legitimation'.[5] However, as the philosopher Oliver Marchart has convincingly argued, Documenta's leading position no longer goes unchallenged, since anti- and postcolonial biennials have contributed significantly to the development of the biennial format, particularly since the 1989 Havana Biennial.[6] As Marchart has explained:

> The idea that an exhibition should create some form of interaction with the city where it takes place (and not to simply descend like a UFO); all of the current

> negotiations around 'participation'; the renewed interest in strategies in art education within the context of the educational turn, which was incidentally already anticipated at the third Havana Biennial and did not arrive in the centre [of the Western art system] until 'D11' and 'd12' – the oh-so-critical, discursive and politically savvy West cannot claim a patent for any of this.[7]

The list of participating countries in the catalogue for the first Documenta in 1955 contained only Western nations. This suggests that, although eight of the 148 participating artists (5 per cent) were born outside the West, it was very difficult for the art institutional system of the 1950s to 'imagine anything non-Western as belonging to the discursive formation of modern art'.[8] The figures in Philipsen's survey showed that, since 2002, the number of artists born outside the West featured in Documenta has increased to the point that about half of the participants have a non-Western background. Moreover, an increasing number of the participants work in non-Western parts of the world. Of the 116 participating artists at *documenta 11* (2002), fifty were born outside the West, i.e. 43 per cent of the total number of participants, and twenty-six of the fifty artists lived outside the West. Of the 113 artists in *documenta 12* (2007), sixty-four, i.e. 56 per cent of the total number of participants, were born outside the West, and fifty-three of those sixty-four non-Western artists lived outside the West.[9] Employing Philipsen's distinction between Western and non-Western artists, I have made a count of artists in *dOCUMENTA (13)*. The figures for *dOCUMENTA (13)* in 2012 suggest a decreasing percentage of non-Western participants, but, interestingly, it also shows that some Western-born artists are now based outside the West, thereby contributing to the general '*decentralization of the West*'.[10] Of the 202 participating artists, eighty, i.e. 40 per cent, were born outside the West, and fifty-six of those eighty non-Western artists were living outside the West (either permanently or periodically), as were seven of the Western-born artists. Significantly, thirty-five artists were described as living between two or more cities, e.g. Dutch-born Gabriel Lester between Amsterdam and Shanghai, Italian-born Giuseppe Penone between Turin and Paris, Singaporean Simryn Gill between Sydney and Port Dickson in Malaysia, Venezuelan Javier Téllez between New York and Berlin, and so on. A few had even chosen to be presented as itinerant. Emily Jacir was described as living 'around the Mediterranean', Egyptian-born Anna Boghiguian as living 'in this world' and the Lebanese Tarek Atoui as 'nomadic'. When artists are described as living between named cities, they are basically presented as what the Indian-born, New York-based writer Suketu Mehta has termed 'inter-locals', i.e. migrant city dwellers who do not remain 'uprooted' and 'nomadic' but are moving between and develop attachments and allegiances to several specific locations.[11] The figures from *dOCUMENTA (13)* not only testify to a new integrationist or multicultural institutional policy but also to the globalisation of the art world. They tell us that the institutional infrastructure of artistic practices – academies and art schools, exhibition galleries, museums, biennials, dealers, buyers, collectors, etc. – has spread across the globe.[12] In the context of such encompassing cross-fertilisation at all levels of art production and circulation, it seems almost old-fashioned to attempt to slot artists into categories based on their place of birth or place of residence, even if these socio-cultural 'sites' might be in the foreground of their artistic practices.

However, although multiculturalism represents a more egalitarian and inclusive institutional policy, it has also produced new and more sophisticated forms of exclusion masquerading as inclusion. This leaves the problem of the 'true' recognition of non-Western artists unsolved. What follows is a case study of the rise and fall of institutional multiculturalism in the art world. The purpose is to examine the discourse on cultural identity in the art world since the 1980s in order to bring to light the dilemmas of multicultural policies and the ways in which globalisation unsettles and transforms the established structures, discourses and self-understanding of European cultural institutions. My analysis focuses on the societal microcosm of the art world, not the 'multi-cultural question' in society at large.[13] The conclusion drawn from this examination will lead to the proposition that, in order to transcend the negative effects of institutional multiculturalism, such as the tendency to overemphasise the ethnic categorisation of artists, we do not need an even stronger emphasis on identity politics. As the proponents of the migratory aesthetics position have suggested, we should, rather, reconsider and acknowledge the works of art themselves as aesthetically, cognitively and politically significant and moving articulations of the artist's subjective perspective on the world.

The art world: a global village?

Since the mid-1990s, the term *global art* has gained currency in discourses on the visual arts, where it is used about contemporary art. In 2011–12, a five-year research project on global art and the globalisation of the art world culminated in the huge exhibition *The Global Contemporary: Art Worlds after 1989* at ZKM, the Center for Arts and Media Karlsruhe, Germany. The exhibition, and the series of scholarly publications leading up to it and accompanying it, not only consolidated 'global art' as *the* nodal point of the discourses on contemporary art but they also reflected how concerned European cultural institutions seek to revise the understanding of art and cultural identity historically ingrained in their institutional practices in the light of the 'global turn'. As Peter Weibel, the director of ZKM and co-curator of the exhibition, has remarked, for the West globalisation means that Western artists are increasingly subjected to the same mechanisms of inclusion and exclusion as non-Western artists. The rise of art from Asia, Africa and South America in the globalised exhibition system and art market breaks up the Western monopoly on defining what counts as 'art' and 'culture', and, consequently, who and what should be excluded.[14]

Unlike the 'verbal', the 'visual' can move rather flexibly across linguistic borders. Although they are not outside the realm of translation and interpretation, works of art can be in highly diverse exhibition contexts in different parts of the world and still make some sense to local visitors. This nourishes the notion of globalised art. And yet, as was suggested in Chapter 1, the term 'global art' is problematic. Strictly speaking, there is no such thing as global art, because that would mean an art from everywhere and nowhere. The making of art is a material practice; and, like all material practices, it takes place in and is determined by a local context. Correspondingly, a work of art is always received and interpreted locally.[15] Nevertheless, the *popularity* of the term 'global art' is historically significant. It testifies to the profound impact of globalisation on the entire art system. With increased contact and exchange between different parts of the world, certain artistic practices and media, curatorial methods and exhibition formats (the biennial, above all), and critical concepts and narrative forms have been disseminated around the world as a kind of default option for local art scenes. Moreover, in the parlance of curators and art critics, 'global art' implies that non-Western art is included as opposed to the older Western notion of the international as something confined exclusively to the West with its self-allotted patent on values such as 'modernity', 'progress' and the 'avant-garde'. Thus, it is not the individual works of art that are global. It is the institutional, economic, and discursive systems that sustain their production, distribution and reception which have become globalised. We can, in effect, speak of a *global art world* in the sociological sense of the word.

Charlotte Bydler has mapped the transformations of the institutional, economic and social structures of the art world in her book *The Global Art World, Inc.* Bydler observes that the globalisation of the art world communities has resulted in a segregation in which international contemporary art and local contemporary art still fall away from each other as separate art practices for different forums and audiences.[16] Drawing on American sociologist Immanuel Wallerstein's world-systems analysis, which is sensitive to the historical changes in the hierarchies and respective influence of the 'cores', 'semiperipheries' and 'peripheries' of an interconnected world, Bydler maps the spheres of influence of the various 'cores' or centres of the global art world and considers how their hegemonic positions affect the appreciation of art and the recognition of artists.[17] In other words, the scope of an artist's professional and economic success depends on the artist's geographical location in the art world: a legitimating hierarchy has been established that classifies works of art by assessing their value as being at a 'local', 'regional' or 'universal' level. As Gerardo Mosquera has pointed out, 'It goes without saying that if they [artists] are successful in New York they will immediately be universal. The elitary production of the centres is automatically considered "international" and "universal", and one can only gain access to these categories when one can make it there.'[18]

Globalisation means that the major art communities of large cities have plugged into the international urban circuit of the 'global art world'. Borrowing a term from Marshall McLuhan, Bydler describes this circuit as a global village because it is structured like a transnational network. The inhabitants of the global village of the arts are connected by a novel sense of being members of a world community, whose knowledge and references are shaped by the Internet – the telecommunication technology that enables members to keep in touch with art events worldwide.[19] In the 1990s and 2000s, an increasing number of art scenes outside the West became connected to this circuit, too; a development that nourished the assumption that contemporary art has become global. However, the widespread usage of the term 'global art', or the mere ascertainment that the contemporary art scene is globalised, does not always reflect the underlying conditions and inequalities of this situation.[20]

As regards the structural conditions, Bydler has pointed out that the 'global art world' is structured like an international labour market, in which artists, curators and other migrating cultural workers on short-term contracts have developed precarious transnational and cosmopolitan career patterns. By using anthropological and sociological methods to analyse this flexible labour market, Bydler has pinpointed the economic and institutional causes for why so many contemporary artists have become 'urban *nomad artists*' with a migratory frame of mind.[21] The relevance of Bydler's study to the topic of cultural identity is made all the more pertinent because she demonstrates that transnational migration and labour migration are the primary causes of art communities becoming globalised, and that the notions of what counts as ground-breaking art and leading art scenes have changed.

As Nikos Papastergiadis has observed, artists are not only among the most mobile members of society, 'they are often the outriders of the transformations between the local and the global'.[22] Owing to migration – in particular, migration in the wake of decolonisation – many non-Western artists have emigrated from the liberated colonies to their former European 'mother countries', driven by the desire to be at the centre of events and the dream of making an international career. This means that migration patterns are still, to some extent, formed by the history of colonialism. Even if the spectrum of sender countries has expanded considerably, there is still a geopolitics of migration in the art world.[23] On top of this, making a career as an artist often includes adopting a migratory lifestyle. Chapter 3 will expand on this by examining how living and working as a migrant has reconfigured the conditions of production as well as the reception of many artists' work.

The discourse on cultural identity

This is not the place to trace the long and complicated history of the obstacles and discrimination encountered by non-Western artists in the West and their gradual recognition, but let it be said that until the 1980s it was just as difficult for non-Western artists to gain recognition for their work and make a career in the West as it had been for women artists before the 1960s. Yet, although the art world has gradually become more egalitarian, especially in the 2000s, obstacles still remain– for non-Western as well as for women artists. The tide did begin to turn in the 1980s, however. At that time, the joint forces of migration and globalisation had intensified to the point that the institutional system could no longer ignore the critique of its discrimination against artists of non-Western origin. Two opposing developments characterise the 1980s: on the one hand, there was critical debate on institutional policies and attitudes towards artists of non-Western origin, with accusations that the system was institutionally racist, while, on the other, art institutions and curators began gradually to adopt more multicultural policies.[24] Thus, cultural identity became an issue in the discourses on contemporary art and curatorial practices – and it has remained so until today.

In the discourse on cultural identity in relation to contemporary art, the most frequently used term is not 'cultural identity', although cultural identity and identity politics are clearly the issue. The debates are structured and regulated by a whole cluster of interrelated terms with obvious ideological and political implications. In table 2.1, I have tried to sketch the conceptual landscape in which this discourse has unfolded in the 1990s and 2000s. 'Cultural identity' is inserted at the top to indicate its status as the real issue of the current debates. Immediately below are inserted the principal nodal points in this cluster of concepts: 'culture', 'ethnicity', 'migration', 'globalisation' and 'multiculturalism'. Beneath this line follow the conceptual contexts of these nodal points, their sub-clusters, so to speak, or chains of equivalence. When 'cultural identity' is discussed in relation to 'culture', it is often done with a reference to the dichotomy between Western and non-Western culture, which tends to activate other binaries as well: the trope of modernity versus tradition, or the 'national' versus the 'foreign', which are so central to discussions of cultural 'heritage', museum collections included. As for the nodal point of ethnicity, it is closely associated with concepts of race and accusations of racism, as well as (non-Western) otherness, authenticity, ancestry and 'roots'. In the critical discourse on the cultural identity of 'ethnic' artists

Table 2.1 *The cluster of concepts that informs the discourses on contemporary art and cultural identity in the 'global art world' of the 1990s and the 2000s.*

cultural identity

culture	ethnicity	migration	global-isation	multi-culturalism
Western/ non-Western	non-Western	forced & voluntary migration	decoloni-sation & recolonisation	identity politics
modernity/ tradition	race & racism	turbulence & rupture	hybridisation as cultural translation	difference & outside/ inside position
national/ foreign	otherness	postcolonial, diasporic etc. experiences of migration	commodifica-tion of ethnic & racial difference	cultural diversity
'the art world'	authenticy	transnational connections	cosmo-politanism	'New Internationa-lism' & 'global art'
heritage	ancestry 'roots'	nomadism 'routes'	cultural crossings	recognition

with a migrant background, Western expectations of ethnic 'authenticity' and 'roots' in exotic 'other' traditions tend to carry negative associations and to be keenly contested. Migration and globalisation also function as nodal points, connecting the discourses on contemporary art to discourses on social and political issues in society at large. In table 2.1, the concept of migration functions as an umbrella term for more specialised terms such as forced and voluntary migration, transnational connections, postcolonial and diasporic experiences of migration, and nomadism and 'routes' (as a shorthand for identities and a sense of belonging shaped by migratory movements). The same goes for globalisation; it is associated with concepts such as decolonisation and (economic and cultural) recolonisation, cultural crossings, hybridisation (understood as a process of cultural translation and transculturation), the commercial exploitation of ethnic and racial difference, and, last but not least, 'cosmopolitanism' – an ideology and way of life that is sometimes contested but more often than not is celebrated in the global art world.[25] In discourses on art, multiculturalism is seldom referred to as a political ideology. The term is mostly used about the institutional policies that regulate who and what is exhibited or included in the collections of public museums and galleries as part of the national heritage. It also refers to the identity politics and struggle for recognition of groups of minority artists, and to the carefully constructed 'cultural diversity' so characteristic of many group exhibitions of contemporary art – particularly the biennials. Thus, notions of institutional multiculturalism also act as the driving force behind the promotion of 'global art'. Moreover, in the art world, considerations of multiculturalism also include an insistence on the positive value of 'difference' and an awareness of the ambiguous outside/inside position of migrant and non-Western artists living and working in the West.

The diagram in table 2.1 is not exhaustive, and its sub-clusters could be structured in other ways. Its primary function is to serve a heuristic purpose and provide an idea of the overall picture. It emphasises certain elements common to many of the contributions to the discourse on contemporary art and cultural identity, so that we can see them in a more systematic way. It demonstrates that the discourse on cultural identity in the 'global art world' is informed by a very *complex network* of entangled, intersecting and antagonistic concepts, reflecting the variety of agendas and positions articulated in this discourse. It also indicates that the discourse is permeated by *binary thinking*. Even today, the fulcrum of the discourse is the opposition between 'the West' and 'the Rest', or 'the North' and 'the South'. Thus, as table 2.2 demonstrates, a series of recurrent binaries could easily be extracted from it. Oppositions such as power/powerless, modern/indigenous, centre/periphery, insider/outsider, white/ethnic, etc., continue to structure the critical assessments of the art institutional system. This is particularly noticeable in the writings by

Table 2.2 *Recurrent dichotomies in the discourse on cultural identity in the 'global art world'*

Western	Non-Western
International (Western hegemony)	Global (the 'global art world')
Modern	Indigenous
Colonial	Postcolonial
Power	Powerless
Self	Other
Roots	Routes
National culture	Foreign culture
Insider	Outsider
White	Ethnic
Art	Culture
Center	Periphery
Innovation	Tradition
Avant-Garde	Followers
Majority	Minorities

one of the most prominent advocates of equality in the art world, the British-Pakistani artist, writer and editor Rasheed Araeen. In a critical attack on the alleged complicity of some protagonists in postcolonial theory, Araeen likens the situation to an ideological war. Either you can side with a Western institutional power still underpinned by colonial structures, or you can side with its subaltern critics: 'There is no in-between space to hide. You have to be on one side or the other.'[26]

The struggle for recognition

In Europe, London has been the epicentre for the debates on cultural identity. These debates have by no means been confined to the London art community, but the critique of Eurocentrism in the contemporary art world has, to a large extent, been articulated and disseminated by two influential transcultural organisations based in London: the scholarly journal *Third Text*, founded in 1987 by Rasheed Araeen, and the Institute of International Visual Arts (InIVA), founded four years later in 1991 but which did not have an actual physical location until 1994. Since then, InIVA has published a whole range of influential anthologies dealing with issues of cultural identity and recognition, cross-cultural perspectives, and transcultural exchange in relation to contemporary and modern art. Like *Third Text*, these publications have circulated internationally, and they have been instrumental in bringing about global perspectives in the discourses on contemporary art.

Of special importance is the 1994 anthology *Global Visions: Towards a New Internationalism in the Visual Arts*, co-published by Kala Press, *Third Text*'s publishing arm, and InIVA, and containing the proceedings from the symposium 'A New Internationalism' held at London's Tate Gallery in April 1994. The speakers were artists, scholars and curators from Europe, North and Latin America, Asia, Africa and Australia, invited to present divergent views on the emerging phenomenon that the symposium labelled 'New Internationalism'. Considering the global mix of speakers, it is not surprising that there was no concluding consensus on the character and aims of New Internationalism. As Philipsen remarks in her thorough analysis of *Global Visions*, New Internationalism was not a well-defined concept but, rather, a heterogeneous discursive formation, structured, it could be added, by a whole cluster of concepts. Nevertheless, it is possible to identify three issues of concern that link the diverse contributions and which add up to a common approach with regard to the question of cultural identity in the international art world. First of all, there was *deconstruction* in the form of a critical analysis of Western art institutions and art history with a view to disclosing their ethnocentric and racist structures and practices; secondly, there was a call for more focus on *art* as significant in itself, not just as a vehicle for identity politics or for cultural and anthropological concerns; and, thirdly, there was an emphasis on *cultural difference* as inherently complex and valuable.[27] There is a fundamental conflict underlying these three issues, however. The first articulates a demand for revolutionary changes in the practices and structures of Western art institutions from a position in postcolonial theory and multicultural identity politics. In contrast to this, the second evokes a fundamentally Western ideal of autonomous art. The political demand for recognising the cultural identities of non-Western artists and the aesthetic demand for recognising the autonomy of their art (i.e. its independence from the politics of multiculturalism and the particularity of the individual artist's work and contribution to 'global art') often intersect in conflicting and contradictory ways in the discourse on cultural identity in the 'global art world'. Or, to put it in another way: the political demand that institutions recognise formerly excluded ethnic and cultural groups – i.e. recognise group identities – sometimes runs counter to the individual's need for an appreciation of her or his unique particularity as a professional artist and a subject situated in a specific historical, cultural and social context.[28]

The term New Internationalism was only used for a few years. From the mid-1990s, the discourse on New Internationalism faded as it became apparent that the changes it called for were actually happening. Meanwhile, the aforementioned label 'global art' gained currency, and the label 'international art' was reintroduced but now with a new set of global connotations.[29] However, the ideology and aims underlying the discourse on New Internationalism lived on in the discourse on 'global art'.

In the 1990s, the most important vehicle for articulating these discourses was the journal *Third Text*. Theoretically and ideologically, *Third Text* was mainly founded in postcolonial theory, but it also engaged with and was informed by feminism and the Black Arts Movement, which were instrumental in the politicisation of issues regarding the practice and legitimation of art in Britain in the 1980s.[30] The issues and forces that were behind *Third Text* at that time demonstrate that the new international discourse emerged from an environment inside a Western *geography* that did not consider itself as truly and solely belonging to the *cultural space* of the West.[31] Hence, *Third Text* used postcolonial theory as a platform for its fight for the cultural recognition of diasporic artists and for institutional equality in the Western art world. As the sociologist Jan Nederveen Pieterse remarked in 2001, '*Third Text* has been one of the vehicles through which "postcolonial theory" has been internationally disseminated, a medium of transcultural communication in the world of arts, in effect internationalizing a trans-Atlantic critical discourse.'[32]

The founding editor of *Third Text*, Rasheed Araeen, has been one of the most salient critics of Western art institutions and art history. In the first editorial of *Third Text* from 1987, Araeen declared that the aim of the journal was to provide 'a critical forum for Third World perspectives on the visual arts', which represented nothing less than 'a historical shift away from the centre of the dominant culture to its periphery in order to consider the centre critically. This does not imply a fixed distance. The movement can be repeated or reversed as long as a critical relationship with the dominant discourses is maintained.'[33] In 2002, *Third Text* took stock of its previous efforts in *The Third Text Reader on Art, Culture and Theory*. One of the regular contributors to the journal, Sean Cubitt, drew attention to the fact that there had been a fundamental change in *Third Text*'s struggle for recognition when an increasing number of non-Western artists, many of them with a migrant background, began to make successful careers in the 'global art world'. In its first decade, *Third Text* concentrated on disclosing 'the institutional closures of the art world' and how artists with African, Caribbean and Asian backgrounds were systematically excluded. The second decade began 'the enquiry into the new phenomenon … of the assimilation of the exotic Other into the new world art'. As Cubitt concluded, 'the nature of the art institutions has changed over these years, and the critique must evolve with it'.[34]

Far beyond the *Third Text* circle, the focus of the critique has shifted away from the institutional mechanisms of exclusion towards the ambiguous strategy of inclusion and the 'integrationist discourse' developed by Western art institutions,[35] especially in countries such as the US and the UK, Canada and Australia, where many cultural institutions have embraced multiculturalism as a policy. According to some critics, institutional multiculturalism is a regulatory instrument appropriated and deployed by the West to continue to sustain its cultural hegemony. It segregates white artists from non-white artists by categorising art by the latter as 'ethnic art'.[36] As a result, the identity politics of institutional multiculturalism is blamed for being a severe obstacle to 'true' recognition of the individual artist because it perpetuates a hierarchy in which Western artists obtain recognition on the basis of their individual artistic merits, whereas non-Western artists are only recognised as representatives of the ethnic community and local culture to which they or their ancestors belong. Jean Fisher, another prominent advocate of a global perspective on art, identified the problem as early as 1994: '"Multiculturalism" remains stained above all by the West's failure to engage in a dialogue of equality with its neighbours and to relinquish its control over meaning production. The West, in short, never ceases in its attempts to re-centre itself as the privileged subject of knowledge.'[37] Rasheed Araeen has also made a shrewd analysis of how British art institutions exercise 'control over meaning production'. He regards the institutional policies of cultural diversity as the very cause of the current over-attentiveness to artists' cultural identity and ancestry, which, to his regret, has also affected the way the artists themselves self-identify through their choice of topics and aesthetics:

> Many AfroAsian artists are now trapped within this institutionalised space which is exclusively reserved for them, particularly when this space is the only space available to them to fulfil their ambitions for successful careers. It is therefore understandable why most of the work of the young generation of AfroAsian artists today is so concerned with their own culture or cultural identities, oscillating between the so-called periphery and the centre.[38]

Araeen made this critical observation in 2001. Today, institutional policies of cultural diversity are still highly contested in the world of the arts. In the course of the last two decades, words such as 'multiculturalism', 'ethnicity', 'difference' and 'hybridisation' have become so overused and burdened with diverse meanings that one hesitates to use them. Institutional multiculturalism has surely contributed to this exhaustion, and if this is a sign of its success in influencing mainstream perceptions then the dilution of these key words is part of the price of collective transformation.[39] In 2009, T. J. Demos took stock of the damaging effects of institutional multiculturalism when he stated that it had resulted in 'the fixing of cultural, racial and sexual signs within the discourse of political correctness, which correlated in the 1990s both to the social divisiveness of identity politics and to the commodification of ethnic and racial difference within neo-liberal globalization'.[40]

This chapter has emphasised the transformative effects of the critique of institutional policies and identity politics in the Western art world, transformations that are important and worth celebrating. However, the critical discourse on cultural identity has also had some questionable effects, apart from those identified by Demos above. It has, to a certain extent, perpetuated and strengthened the kind of binary thinking in which the West is associated with uniformity and universality, whereas the rest of the world is associated with multiplicity and difference. As a result, dichotomies and segregations have become deeply ingrained in the discourse on cultural identity in relation to contemporary art. As mentioned above, the critical discourse is itself structured around a series of recurrent binary oppositions that are used to mark symbolic boundaries and create 'frontier-effects' (see table 2.2). Thus, it is not only non-Western and migrant artists who are trapped in stereotypical frameworks. The critique of Eurocentrism and multiculturalism abounds in inverted stereotypes that trivialise the concept of 'Western art' and 'Western Modernism'. To take an example, Rasheed Araeen's article 'A new beginning: beyond postcolonial cultural theory and identity politics' leaves the impression that all Western artists are white males, steeped in the universalising project of modernism – like his historical models, Picasso, Mondrian and Brancusi – and that all these male artists are successfully working in the metropolitan centres of Paris, London and New York, where they participate in an imaginary unified Western modernism.[41] In effect, when the cultural identity of Western artists is produced within the discursive formation of 'New Internationalism' and 'global art', there seems to be no space for the recognition of differences internal to the West.

The critical discourse on Westernism and multicultural identity politics often ignores several factors. It disregards the fact that the European and American art worlds have 'internal peripheries' – such as the former Eastern European countries and Scandinavia – and the fact that there are multiple 'modernisms' and 'avant-gardes' in Europe and the US, some of which have *also* been overlooked. To shed some light on this issue, I wish to turn to Taiwanese art historian Chin-tao Wu. In 'Biennials without borders?', Wu examines artistic representation at major international gatherings such as biennials by analysing the national statistics that underpin the marketing of biennials as transnational, for example when the 2006 Singapore Biennial boasted of '95 artists from over 38 countries'.[42] Like Philipsen, Wu chooses Documenta as her primary object of investigation, focusing on the nine Documenta exhibitions held between 1968 and 2007. She maps the overall patterns of the artists' origin by using typical regional categories: North America, Latin America, Asia, Africa and Oceania. Of special interest is the fact that Wu divides Europe into two. Despite the enlargement of the European Union, Wu observes, there are still two Europes in contemporary art practice. One comprises the UK, Germany, Italy, France, Switzerland, Austria, and, to a lesser degree, The Netherlands, Belgium and Spain. These countries supply the majority of European art figures, and, thus, constitute what Wu terms 'Europe A'. The remaining countries, whose artists appear only sporadically at international exhibitions, form what Wu calls 'Europe B'.[43] Wu, in so doing, describes the *internal* hegemony and mechanisms of inclusion and exclusion that structure European contemporary art. She articulates the existence of a peripheral West and points to a powerful hierarchy that is often disregarded in the universalising postcolonial critiques of Eurocentrism in the Western art world: artists living and working in 'Europe B' do not automatically hold a position of advantage and privilege which secures access to the magic circle of recognition, distinctions, fame and art historical canonisation. The tendency to designate artistic 'peripheries' as places whose artistic activity is less important than that of the presumed centres for artistic production and trade in art remains formative to the internal structure of the European art world to this day. In the twenty-first century, there are still barriers, especially for artists from 'Europe B', and the new valorisation of non-Western art in the international exhibition system – as seen, for instance, in the craze for art from India and China – could reinforce the tendency to leave the histories and productions of already outlying areas in even stronger disregard.

The second aspect that the critical discourse on Westernism tends to ignore is the fact that Western cultures are diverse and heterogeneous in themselves. An image tends to be disseminated of a monolithic 'Western modernism' that leaves divergent artistic activities in the 'peripheries' out of the picture, thus repeating the notion of a normative modernism coined by its Western proponents which reproduces the very same mechanisms of exclusion that it criticises.[44] In fact, one could consider whether the old Westernism has simply given way to a new 'global' centrism: a *metrocentrism*.

The critique of Western ethnocentrism also often turns a blind eye to the fact that the 'global art world' has several centres of power, and that economic and cultural power relations are rapidly changing. One of the key features of the art market today is that trading is increasingly global, with the most important markets for contemporary art now outside Europe. In 2010, China overtook London to become the second largest art market; in 2011, China outstripped New York to become the largest worldwide.[45] In addition, talented Chinese, Indian and Japanese artists increasingly draw the attention of the 'global art world' towards the East. So, is it not about time to drop the old binary trope of Western versus non-Western art? Surely, if Westernisation is an issue, so is Easternisation.[46] My point is, that power relations in the art world today are much too complex to be captured by binary thinking. There are several cores, many semi-peripheries and numerous local peripheries.[47]

The pitfalls of cultural identity

The blind spots in the critique of Westernism remind us of the need for more complexity-sensitive methods and theories in the field of art history and art criticism. However, the development of such a conceptual apparatus would be beyond the scope of this study, as would the task of reconciling the dual demand for equality and difference, which is 'the dilemma, the conundrum – the multi-cultural question – at the heart of the multi-cultural's transruptive and reconfigurative impact'.[48] Since one of the purposes of this chapter is to establish a critical frame of reference for the discussion of identity as identification in Chapter 5, I will conclude with some remarks on a possible way to escape the pitfalls of 'cultural identity'. What needs to be done first is to disentangle the understanding of the artist's cultural identity from the emphasis on ethnic, national and civilisational identity at work in the current political discourses in the West and in institutional multiculturalism. Otherwise, we risk nourishing the kind of divisive understanding of the world's multiple cultures so persuasively formulated by Samuel Huntington when he proposed his political theory of the 'clash of civilizations':

> Civilizations are differentiated from each other by history, language, culture, tradition and, most important, religion. The people of different civilizations have different views on the relations between God and man, the individual and the group, the citizens and the state, parents and children, husband and wife, as well as differing views on the relative importance of rights and responsibilities, liberty and authority, equality and hierarchy. These differences are products of centuries. They will not soon disappear. They are far more fundamental than differences among political ideologies and political regimes.[49]

One of the problems with Huntingtonian isolationism and cultural relativism is that it disregards the mass migration in evidence today, and the fact that, in diasporic conditions, people are often obliged to adopt shifting and multiple positions of identification. According to Stuart Hall, migrants and those from minority communities 'are all negotiating culturally somewhere along the spectrum of *différence*, in which disjunctures of time, generation, spatialisation and dissemination refuse to be neatly aligned'.[50] We should also try to avoid the 'biographical' pitfall of regarding the artist's life story as the essential content of the artist's work – the master narrative that generates all the other possible interpretations and contextualisations of the work, which are then treated as subordinate aspects of the biographical master narrative. Among artists themselves, identification with artists from other cultures, even other centuries, can be more crucial to the form, meaning and cultural significance of their work than their own personal ancestry and life story, whether their own biography is based on stable 'roots' or migratory 'routes'. When artists identify with other artists they seldom identify with their indigenous cultural identity or 'civilisation' but primarily with their artistic projects. As performance and queer studies scholar José Esteban Muñoz has pointed out, the structures of cross-identification have often been particularly conspicuous in the work of queer artists, such as the Cuban-born Felix Gonzalez-Torres. Eschewing the role of Latino artist, and the notion of the 'ethnic artist', Gonzalez-Torres articulated his own understanding of the complexities of identity formation in the following way: 'Who is going to define my culture? It's not just Borges and García Marquez, but also Gertrude Stein and Freud and Guy Debord – they are all part of my formation.'[51] Deliberately countering the expectation that his work should be shaped by a strong identification with the Latin American masters, Gonzalez-Torres stresses his influences from such diverse figures as a queer Anglo-American modernist, an Austrian father of psychoanalysis and a French situationist and theorist of the spectacle.[52]

To conclude, what is needed in critical discourses on art is not *more* identity politics, but, rather, a reconsideration of the work of art that takes the work seriously as art without lapsing into old-fashioned modernist aestheticism. We need a reconsideration of the work of art as an articulation of the artist's situated experience of and perspective on the world, an exploration of the artwork that is equally attentive to its sensory, affective, cognitive, political and historical strata. As scholars and critics, we need to move beyond the notion of identity as something fixed and put more emphasis on identification as a multi-directional process, i.e. as a performative act of self-representation in which cultural differences are continually negotiated, and where elective affinities and voluntary acts of identification with the projects of other artists and cultural producers may be of greater significance than ancestry and ethnicity. In short, we need to find ways to deconstruct the misconception that the artist's 'authentic' ethnic roots and cultural identity are always the prime sources of the work's meaning. Only then can we get beyond the deadlock of the critical discourse on institutional multiculturalism.

In Chapter 5, I will attempt to unpack this line of thought, theoretically and analytically, and argue that a dynamic notion of identification may provide us with a way to break the impasse of binary identity politics, the essentialist biographical perception of migrant artists as 'ethnic artists' and the somewhat simplifying dichotomisation that structure the discourses on transnationalism, in which movement is generally seen as operating between two distinct national formations: the 'here' of a receiving country and a 'there' of a sending country. By drawing on the understanding of identification proposed by Stuart Hall, and developed and deepened by Amelia Jones and José Esteban Muñoz, I hope to enter the borderlands of a more complex understanding of belonging and identity.

However, more immediately, the next chapter will address an issue more directly related to the institutional transformation of the art world explored in this one – namely, how globalisation and migration have also changed the role and work of artists, as these processes have provided many artists with new conditions of possibility for developing cross-cultural artistic practices.

Notes

1 Jones, *Seeing Differently*, p. xviii.
2 *Ibid.*, p. xix.
3 This chapter reconfigures previously published material by expanding on the transformative impact of migration on cultural and institutional structures and on identity politics in the art world. See Anne Ring Petersen, 'Identity Politics in "the Global Art World"', in Peter Madsen (ed.), *Challenging Identities: Individual – Collective – Politics*, Routledge Advances in Sociology (New York, London: Routledge, 2017), pp. 222–38. The core ideas were first presented in a short essay: Petersen, 'Identity politics, institutional multiculturalism, and the global art-world', *Third Text*, 26:2 (2012), 195–204.
4 Hall, 'Introduction: Who Needs "Identity"?', p. 3.
5 Oliver Marchart, 'The globalization of art and the "biennials of resistance": a history of the biennials from the periphery', *World Art*, 4:2 (2014), 263–76, 264.
6 *Ibid.*, 267–9, 273–4.
7 *Ibid.*, 273.
8 Philipsen, 'The Globalisation of Contemporary Art', 123. Philipsen's dissertation was published two years later in 2010 in an edited form: *Globalizing Contemporary Art*.
9 In Philipsen's survey, the category 'non-Western' includes artists from Africa, Latin America, Asia (including Japan but excluding Australia), the Middle East, and Eastern European countries that were formerly part of the USSR. See 'The Globalisation of Contemporary Art', 120.
10 Marchart, 'The globalization of art and the "biennials of resistance"', 263.
11 Suketu Mehta in Piali Roy, 'In Conversation with Suketu Mehta: The City Speaks', *Cities of Migration* (2011), unpaginated, http://citiesofmigration.ca/ezine_stories/in-conversation-with-suketu-mehta/ (accessed 16 November 2016). My only deviation from Philipsen's distinction between Western and non-Western artists is that I have counted Indigenous Australian artists as non-Western. As regards artists' groups and collaborative projects with named members, the members have been counted individually. The count is based on Katrin Sauerländer (ed.), *Das Begleitbuch/the Guidebook*, Vol. 3/3 of the Documenta (13) Catalogue (Ostfildern: Hatje Cantz Verlag, 2012).
12 Philipsen, 'The Globalisation of Contemporary Art', 120–2.
13 Stuart Hall, 'Conclusion: The Multi-Cultural Question', in Barnor Hesse (ed.), *Un/Settled Multiculturalisms: Diaspora, Entanglements, 'Transruptions'* (London, New York: Zed Books, 2000), pp. 209–41.
14 Peter Weibel, 'Preface', in Jens Lutz *et al.* (eds), *The Global Contemporary: Art Worlds after 1989*. Exhibition Brochure (Karlsruhe: ZKM Museum of Contemporary Art, 2011), pp. 4–5. See www.global-contemporary.de (accessed 16 November 2016).
15 Bal, 'Lost in Space, Lost in the Library', p. 25; Jones, 'Is International Modernism National?', p. 119.
16 Bydler, *The Global Art World, Inc.*, p. 156.

17 *Ibid.*, pp. 33–6.
18 Gerardo Mosquera, quoted in Joaquín Barriendos Rodríquez, 'Global Art and Politics of Mobility: (Trans)Cultural Shifts in the International Contemporary Art-System', in Bal and Hernández-Navarro (eds), *Art and Visibility in Migratory Culture*, pp. 313–34, p. 327.
19 Bydler, *The Global Art World, Inc.*, p. 14.
20 Philipsen, 'The Globalisation of Contemporary Art', 229–30.
21 Bydler, *The Global Art World, Inc.*, p. 14.
22 Papastergiadis, *The Turbulence of Migration*, p. 11.
23 Bydler, *The Global Art World, Inc.*, p. 218.
24 Rasheed Araeen, 'A new beginning: beyond postcolonial cultural theory and identity politics', *Third Text*, 14:50 (2000), 3–20, 3.
25 For an in-depth analysis of how globalisation, collaborative work and new platforms for sharing knowledge have stimulated the development of cosmopolitanism and a 'cosmopolitan imaginary' in the global art world, see Papastergiadis, *Cosmopolitanism and Culture*.
26 Araeen, 'A new beginning', 15.
27 Philipsen, 'The Globalisation of Contemporary Art', 24–5.
28 Axel Honneth, *The Struggle for Recognition: The Moral Grammar of Social Conflicts* (Cambridge: Polity Press, 1995), pp. 99–130 *passim*.
29 Philipsen, 'The Globalisation of Contemporary Art', 2.
30 Araeen, 'A new beginning', 12.
31 Philipsen, 'The Globalisation of Contemporary Art', 71.
32 Jan Nederveen Pieterse, 'Changing definitions', *Third Text*, 14:53 (2001), 91–2, 92.
33 Rasheed Araeen, 'Why Third Text?', *Third Text*, 1:1 (1987), 3–5, 5. See also 'A new beginning', 19–20.
34 Sean Cubitt, 'In the Beginning: Third Text and the Politics of Art', in Rasheed Araeen, Sean Cubitt and Ziauddin Sardar (eds), *The Third Text Reader on Art, Culture and Theory* (London, New York: Continuum, 2005 (2002)), pp. 1–7, p. 3.
35 Nikos Papastergiadis, 'Restless Hybrids', *ibid.*, pp. 166–75, p. 167.
36 The idea of 'ethnic art' was first introduced by Naseem Kahn in her book *The Arts Britain Ignores* (1976). In 1982, it was officially recognised by the Arts Council of Great Britain, and since then it has become integral to multiculturalism, or cultural diversity, in the UK as well as elsewhere. See Araeen, 'A new beginning', 13.
37 Jean Fisher, 'Editor's Note', in Jean Fisher (ed.), *Global Visions: Towards a New Internationalism in the Visual Arts* (London: Kala Press and The Institute of International Visual Arts, 1994), pp. x–xiv, pp. x–xi.
38 Araeen, 'Re-thinking history and some other things', 98.
39 Pieterse, 'Changing definitions', 91.
40 Demos, 'The Ends of Exile', p. 79.
41 Araeen, 'A new beginning', 11.
42 Chin-Tao Wu, 'Biennials without borders?', *New Left Review*, no. 57 (2009), 107–15, 109.
43 *Ibid.*, 110.
44 The four-volume book project *The Cultural History of the Avant-Garde in the*

Nordic Countries (2013–) is an exemplary project that seeks to pluralise and add nuances to the existing, shallow image of the 'peripheral' Western avant-gardes of the twentieth century. See Tania Ørum and Jesper Olsson (eds), *A Cultural History of the Avant-Garde in the Nordic Countries 1950–1975* (Amsterdam, New York: Brill – Rodopi, 2016); Hubert van den Berg *et al.* (eds), *A Cultural History of the Avant-Garde in the Nordic Countries 1900–1925* (Amsterdam, New York: Brill – Rodopi, 2012).

45 Hans Belting, 'The Art Market: Hans Belting in Conversation with Clare McAndrew', in Belting, Buddensieg and Weibel (eds), *The Global Contemporary and the Rise of New Art Worlds*, pp. 261–6, p. 263; (unnamed) 'Globalization Data', *ibid.* pp. 131–8.

46 For a perceptive analysis of the cultural dominance exerted by the Chinese art institutional system over Taiwanese artists, see Chin-Tao Wu, 'Occupation by absence, preoccupation with presence: a worm's-eye view of art biennals', *Journal of Visual Culture*, 6:3 (2007), 379–86.

47 For a discussion of the particularity of the view from the Nordic 'semi-periphery', see Petersen, 'Global art history'. For summary mappings of the polycentric global art world, see Bydler, *The Global Art World, Inc.*, pp. 150–7; Hans Belting and Sara Giannini, 'Mapping: The Biennials and New Art Regions', in Belting, Buddensieg and Weibel (eds), *The Global Contemporary and the Rise of New Art Worlds*, pp. 100–28.

48 Hall, 'Conclusion: The Multi-Cultural Question', p. 235.

49 Samuel Huntington, 'The clash of civilizations?', *Foreign Affairs*, 72:3 (1993), 22–49, 25.

50 Hall, 'Conclusion: The Multi-Cultural Question', p. 227.

51 Felix Gonzalez-Torres, in Tim Rollings, 'Interview with Felix Gonzalez-Torres', in William S. Bartman (ed.), *Felix Gonzalez-Torres* (New York: A.R.T. Press 1993), p. 19. Quoted from José Esteban Muñoz, *Disidentifications: Queers of Color and the Performance of Politics* (Minneapolis, London: University of Minnesota Press, 1999), p. 166.

52 *Ibid.*

The artist as migrant worker 3

The burgeoning of contemporary art, and ideas about art, from non-Western countries is altering previous expectations of art created outside Western-dominated art scenes, and with the increasing prominence of non-Western art comes the need for profound changes in the Western-dominated methodologies and perspectives of curators, critics and art historians.[1] Art today is on the move, and so are the perspectives on it. Or they should be if we are to develop decolonising and 'de-Westernising' art historical approaches, which not only acknowledge the historical impact of Western models but also supersede them by developing better ways of mapping and examining the relativities and complexities of interacting local and global forces.[2]

According to Terry Smith, a key characteristic of art in the late twentieth and the twenty-first century is 'its becoming contemporary with itself'.[3] According to Smith, a worldwide shift from *modern* to *contemporary* art was prefigured in the major movements in the late modern art of the 1950s and 1960s in Europe and America, and became explicit in Western art discourse during the 1970s and 1980s. Smith sees postmodernist practices as an important signal of a worldwide change; and regards postmodern and post-structuralist theory as the first analysis of this change. When contemporary art became a market phenomenon in the major metropolitan centres during the 1990s, it was expanded, but also, at the same time, divided, by an influx of art from other regions of the world.[4] This major change does not initiate in and is not spreading from a dominant centre, or set of centres, Smith contends, but is happening at different times and is configured in distinctive ways by the specific conditions and histories of each art-producing locality. Thus, he acknowledges that the hegemonic notions of what it is for art to be 'con-temporary' (i.e. with time, meaning up to date, modern and vanguard) are determined by temporal and geographical differences. Moreover, these differences constitute a classificatory framework within which some forms of art are recognised as 'contemporary' while others are dismissed (as belated, provincial or 'minor').[5] In Smith's understanding, 'the widespread art of contemporaneity'[6] is 'a worldwide phenomenon' and it defies Western universals precisely because it encompasses multifarious ways of being in time and space:

> it grows not only from local 'modernisms' (whatever they may be), but, more precisely, from the specifics of the negotiations between traditionalisms, indigeneities, and modernizations in that place, those that occurred not only in art circles but at every level of personal and collective life. Recently, these negotiations take place in unprecedented awareness of the proximity of various other contemporaries everywhere, and in the context of the decline from dominance of Western narratives of art's historical development.[7]

With the growing awareness and visibility of art from non-Western regions, 'the narrative of multiple modernities' has become a paradigm within much art historical, curatorial and critical thinking concerned with modern and contemporary art,[8] but is also accompanied by discussions of its pitfalls.[9] Important theoretical and critical components for the new narratives have already been provided by postcolonial art historians and scholars engaged in world art studies, as well as by the critical discourse on the position of non-Western artists in the West as discussed in Chapter 2. Nonetheless, there is still a long way to go before scholars have developed appropriate methods and tools for analysing art that represents a migrant subjectivity, and art that relates simultaneously to local and global aesthetics and circumstances. As we shall see, these two cross-cultural aspects of art often turn out to be two sides of the same coin. Chapter 2 analysed the critical discourses on identity politics and institutional multiculturalism in an increasingly globalised Western art world. Here in Chapter 3, the perspective shifts from the institutional and discursive transformations to the question of how these transformations have altered the careers and work patterns of many artists, and, as a result, undermined the nineteenth-century conception of the artist as an autonomous, self-governing creator of rarefied objects in pursuit of her/his own individual vision and signature style. In Johanna Drucker's words, 'We jettisoned the idea of originality a long time ago. But, oddly, we remain attached to the concept of the individual talent.'[10] This traditional model continues to structure the way artists are marketed and presented in many exhibitions, galleries and auction houses today; and there is nothing to suggest that the marketable concept of the autonomous creator is going to go out of use in the foreseeable future. Nevertheless, we need new conceptual models because we cannot account for the extent to which contemporary artistic practices and careers are structured by migratory experience without developing a conception of the artist as a relational and transculturally interconnected subject.

Indian art and artists on the move

A case in point is the so-called 'new art' from India, i.e. art created by Indian artists after the economic reforms of the 1990s initiated by the then Finance Minister Manmohan Singh,[11] reforms which introduced an Indian version of neo-liberal capitalism and opened India's doors to globalisation and the West. In less than two decades, the economic transformation of India, in tandem with an aesthetic re-evaluation of twentieth-century Indian art, has created art stars such as Nalini Malani, Subodh Gupta, Jitish Kallat, Shilpa Gupta, Atul Dodiya and Bharti Kher.[12] This has been accompanied by soaring prices for work by Indian artists,[13] the enthusiasm of biennials to include Indian artists and a flood of ambitious, nationally framed surveys of 'contemporary Indian art' in museums of modern and contemporary art in London, Vienna, Berlin, New York, Paris, Turin, Brussels and Lille.[14] The exhibition *India: Art Now* at Arken Museum of Modern Art, south of Copenhagen,[15] and the 2010 visit of the travelling exhibition *Indian Highway* at HEART, the Herning Art Museum,[16] are merely local Danish reverberations of a much more encompassing turn of the tide, the semi-peripheral aftershock of an epistemological and structural quake in the epicentre of the Western art world.

As Mukti Khaire and R. Daniel Wadhwani have substantiated, the international emergence of Indian art did not result solely from the economic reforms that transformed Indian art into a commodity. It also required the efforts of art historians, critics and curators who, between 1995 and 2007, reclassified Indian twentieth-century art from being judged as 'provincial' or 'decorative' to recognising in it a variety of 'modernism', thereby ensuring Indian art a central place in the increasingly powerful discourse on multiple modernities. According to Khaire and Wadhwani, this new categorial understanding was adopted, not only by art critics and institutions, but also by auction houses, which began to apply the same criteria that were used to assess Western modernisms to Indian works.[17] It was the shared discourse and intersubjective understanding and expectations among the auction houses, the collectors, the investors, and the museums, galleries, scholars and critics, i.e. the professional 'audience' for Indian art, which acted to institutionalise modern Indian art as a distinct market category within the classification schemes used in the international fine art market.[18] Khaire and Wadhwani underscore the important role played by auction house texts in translating aesthetic value into economic value, but also how other art world professionals had laid out the preconditions:

> the influence of auction texts on audience perceptions of the category was contingent on the interpretive work of other actors. It was through the texts produced by journalists, museums, and critics that the set of value constructs that

> appeared in the auction catalogs became structural in character … as they were adopted in the interpretations of other high profile actors in the field and became the criteria by which broader audiences learned to judge the art.[19]

Contemporary artists profited from this institutionalisation of Indian modernism at the time of entering the art market[20] and soon acquired international career trajectories, a factor that further increased the economic value of and demand for their work.[21] However, being in the international spotlight means that the big names are no longer based full-time in India. Many of these artists have developed what the curator, cultural theorist and poet Ranjit Hoskote has described as an amphibian practice: they schedule exhibitions back in the subcontinent while also being included in international survey shows as protagonists of the 'New Indian Art'.[22] It is thus difficult to pinpoint exactly what makes an artist 'Indian'.[23] An amphibian career pattern and a local–global practice enable Indian artists to be anchored in a local scene and context, to varying degrees, while simultaneously working on temporary, looser assignments at different locations and in a global context. According to Hoskote, this amphibian practice has created a 'multi-track' consciousness among many Indian artists.[24] Others might call this consciousness hybrid, cosmopolitan or transnational, but beyond the differences of terminology is a general issue with wider aesthetic, social and economic ramifications: that an amphibian practice is not a local Indian exception; rather, it seems to be the rule in what Charlotte Bydler has dubbed 'the global art world, inc.'

In her introduction to the anthology *The Migrant's Time: Rethinking Art History and Diaspora*, Saloni Mathur underscores the need to take seriously how the 'mobility turn' in the social sciences has impacted visual art practices and discourses. The notion of migration that is so central to this turn signals a broad range of intellectual concerns with respect to the precarious condition and transformative potential of human displacement.[25] Accordingly, the mobility turn should also have a bearing on how we conceptualise 'the global art world'. As mentioned in Chapter 2, Charlotte Bydler has analysed how the art world is structured like an international labour market, where artists, curators and other cultural workers on short-term contracts have developed transnational and cosmopolitan career patterns.[26] This means that artists often have to adopt a migratory lifestyle, supporting themselves for years in residency programmes and ceaselessly circulating in group exhibitions and biennials around the world. Such artists, who have their home in one country, work for extended periods in a second and third country, and exhibit in yet other countries, make traditional notions of location, origin and authenticity seem obsolete and in urgent need of reconsideration.

In the following, I will unpack the issue of artists on the move today and consider the questions that the title of this chapter implies: have artists in demand on the global exhibition circuit become a kind of migrant worker in the international labour market of the global art world? And, if so, what kind of migrants are they? And what kind of artists? Furthermore, if artists *have* become migrant workers, what consequences does this have for the study of artworks that feed on the hybridisation processes resulting from the cross-cultural entanglements caused by migration and globalisation?

The traffic in art

It is important to remember that the workings of the global art world affect not only artists from non-Western countries but those in Western countries with a well-functioning art-institutional infrastructure as well. In other words, artists from the peripheries of the West are also subject to the pull of the dominant art centres. As the Indian art critic Zeenat Nagree has contended, the increasing frequency of travel also changes the manner in which audiences have the opportunity to observe the evolution of an artist's work and thus to understand the individual works in the larger context of the artist's *oeuvre*. Artists with an international career often show major works abroad that audiences in the artist's home country will only see at a later date. Nagree makes it clear that she does not want to uphold the nativist idea that artists need to show works primarily in their places of origin, but, conversely, seeks to draw attention to a general change in the temporal constitution of consumption patterns and local scenes for contemporary art, which eventually transforms art itself: 'this *interrupted viewerly environment* is symptomatic of a larger shift in what one might call the consumption pattern of contemporary art – this incontrovertibly shapes the status and substance of the art even as the traffic of artists and their artworks in and out determines the altering complexion of the Indian art world'.[27]

The comings and goings of local artists, as well as of artists from abroad, seem to put local art scenes in a state of flux and discontinuity as the established temporal reception patterns are thus fragmented. Nagree uses the Indian art world as a vivid example of how migration and globalisation have transformed artworks, art scenes and reception forms in recent decades, but her observations are indicative of transformations in 'peripheral' and 'semi-peripheral' art scenes around the globe. An example from Scandinavia is the young Danish artist Augusta Atla, who has made migration an integral part of her self-presentation by carefully recording her own restless movements on her website – the favoured means for making an artist immediately and globally visible to potential audiences and collectors. Between the years 2003 and 2012, Atla lived and worked in London, New York, Venice, Rome, Athens, Paris and Copenhagen. From 2011 to 2012, she mapped her own itinerary as a professional artist in a kind of web-calendar which allowed people to track her movements and exhibitions as she followed 'the thread of the "art of opportunities"' that is now the regime of artists with international reputations or ambitions.[28] After the web-calendar was taken down, Atla substituted it with an artwork blog where she profiled herself as a globe-trotting cosmopolitan: 'Between 2003 [and] 2015 Augusta Atla has lived in London, NYC, Milan, Venice, Rome, Copenhagen, Athens and Paris.' In her own perception, she has become not a rootless nomad but, rather, what Suketu Mehta has called an *inter-local* who 'lives and works between the European cities: Copenhagen and Athens, and currently has her atelier in Athens, Greece'. In 2016, the blog was linked to the artist's website, informing visitors that she was presently living in Copenhagen.[29] Like Augusta Atla, artists from India are also object lessons in how contemporary artists navigate between local and global opportunities, circumstances and power structure. I focus on some of them below.

The relatively short stays involved in setting up exhibitions outside one's own country of residence result in some nomadic movement, but deeper transitional ties often develop for those artists who actually relocate to one of the world hubs of artistic activity. Sometimes settling in such places for years, even decades, they enrol in the art academies and strive to gain access to the leading art institutions and the magic circle of success. This kind of long-term encounter and engagement with another country and culture often has a formative influence on an artist's work and their way of perceiving the world.[30]

To use the phraseology of the literary scholar Sudesh Mishra, the socio-cultural condition of a migrant can be seen as a 'scene of dual territory', where home and host territories function as the privileged and stable, but also tensional, coordinates of a chasm of identity and belonging: one is living without belonging in one territory, while belonging without living in the other. However, Stuart Hall, Paul Gilroy, James Clifford, Kobena Mercer and Mishra himself have all taken issue with this idea of bounded terrains and the tensional split between 'here and there' as constitutive of diasporic subjectivity. The migrant condition should, rather, be seen as what Mishra calls a 'scene of situational laterality'. In this 'situational laterality', the emphasis falls on how the migrant's identity and subjectivity are linked to an active and situation-specific *becoming* or *hybridisation*, and how this process forms part of a strategic *positioning* that is constitutive of identity.[31] Of these two fundamentally different notions of transnational attachments – dual territory and situational laterality, it is the latter that seems to provide us with the better basis for understanding the socio-cultural conditions of migrant artists. The lateral and situation-specific character of transnational attachments has been eloquently described by the artist, writer and art historian Marion Arnold, who grew up in Zimbabwe (then Rhodesia) and studied and taught in South Africa before settling in England in 2000:

> While external, strategic processes of adjustment and survival occur, and feelings of loss and alienation are processed, individuals may also exist in the space in-between where they are cognizant of an immediate reality and, simultaneously, are suffused by memories. Thus observed images of the here-and-now (the look of the street where one lives or the appearance of the corner-shop owner) jostle with visual memory flashes of 'home'. 'There' and 'here' intermingle as a stream of consciousness in the inner eye.[32]

> If you are from 'there' and living 'here' then the space in-between is filled with memories colliding with new realities. For artists this can be productive territory. As an outsider or onlooker you notice things, see sharply, observe what others take for granted. And, looking back through the lens of memory, you negotiate with the past so that it becomes a resonant presence not a belligerent bully. The past and present, here and there, can meet in the imagination in the space in-between.[33]

The Taiwanese artist Chu YinHua, who lives and works in her hometown of Taipei, has made similar observations. In her partly visual, partly textual essay 'Staging Memories', she reflects on how distance and intimacy, familiarity and estrangement structure her relationship to the Asian and European cities in which she has lived and worked over the years. She describes her position in Taipei as an insider, in Tokyo and Singapore as an outsider-insider because of the relative affinity between the cultures in Eastern and Southern Asia, in Paris as a tourist and outsider, and in London, where she did her PhD, as an insider-outsider. Through the medium of photography, she has examined how a migrant individual like herself can develop a sense of belonging when moving between the Western and the Eastern hemispheres. By using staged photography as well as snapshots from urban spaces, and by drawing on her personal experience of specific locations, she has explored the migrant's variable attachments to different urban geographies and cultures, and sought to pinpoint how basic human mechanisms of orientation structure the perception of unfamiliar urban cultures. Memories of places 'there' are as vital to Chu's orientation 'here' as they are to Marion Arnold. In a statement related to her photographic series *Tracing Memories* (2010), which explores how memories of familiar cities can function as an instrument of orientation, Chu describes her memories of places as 'guiding templates, translating and interpreting what is "foreign" in the current physical environment'.[34] *Tracing Memories* aligns in vertical columns a snapshot from a place in London with a snapshot of a reminiscent place in Taipei and a detail from a city map of London or Taipei. By juxtaposing visual details from the urban landscapes that she has traversed, Chu creates a visual metaphor of how memories can serve as an instrument to translate what is foreign in a new environment into something that is recognisable, comprehensible and navigable. Like Chinese artist Yin Xiuzhen's *Portable Cities* (2008–ongoing), a series of scaled-down cityscapes mounted in suitcases and portraying iconic buildings of cities where Yin has stayed, Chu's *Tracing Memories* demonstrates how contemporary women artists can make themselves 'at home everywhere'[35] even as they keep a critical distance from their 'homing desire'[36] in their artistic practice.

Circular migration and cross-cultural borrowing

As the lists of participants in large international exhibitions like *documenta 11, 12* and *13* reveal, the growing interest of the global art world in artists not based in Western metropolises has increased the opportunities for artists to develop an amphibian practice. It is my contention that the migratory pattern of artists, who have chosen to be based in their home country but must live as globetrotters and engage with many different cultures and places in order to pursue international careers, could best be described as *circular migration*. Circular migration is a type of migratory flow that migration researchers have observed only in recent years. It captures a significant change in the routes of migrant workers. In 2006 migration expert John Salt identified a new type of flow among Algerian workers in Europe. According to Salt, the migration of labour from Algeria into France has been replaced by forms of circulation in which many migrant workers work as suitcase traders throughout the Mediterranean region, often serving tourist markets. Instead of settling in a particular city, 'their moves take place within family networks which allow them to seize trading opportunities in whichever city they are presented'.[37] What Salt observes is a growing tendency among migrant workers to return home for a short period and then migrate again, enabled by the fast and relatively cheap means of transportation available today.

This pattern seems quite similar to the migrational flows of the global art world. Circular migration and long-term transnational migration are, of course, not mutually exclusive and certainly not where artists are concerned.[38] Neither is circular migration a new phenomenon. As the social anthropologist Stephen Vertovec has noted, it represents an age-old pattern of mobility, whether rural-to-urban or cross-border. What does seem to be specific to the present phase of globalisation is that a considerable proportion of migrants are no longer 'first movers' but have made multiple trips within their home country and abroad, and that the frequency of travel has increased considerably. In addition, the new interest among policymakers in circular migration reflects a growing recognition of the ways in which long-lasting transnational ties condition migration processes and migrant existence.[39]

The larger question for the issues under consideration here is, what impact a migratory lifestyle might have on the way artists work and on the content and aesthetic of their work. There will inevitably be different impacts on different artists – that is understood, so one should be careful not to generalise. I would like to suggest, however, that curators and art historians need to discuss these matters on a general methodological level, as well as at the level of particular case studies, if we are to develop the necessary analytical tools. In short, we are in want of a multi-sited methodology for art history, i.e. a parallel to what anthropologist George E. Marcus has called multi-sited ethnography. According to Marcus, multi-sited ethnography is a revival of comparative study in anthropology, where the comparative dimensions evolve as a function of the discontinuous movement among different sites: 'The object of study is ultimately mobile and multiply situated, so any ethnography of such an object will have a comparative dimension that is integral to it, in the form of juxtapositions of phenomena that conventionally have appeared to be (or conceptually have been kept) "worlds apart".'[40]

A multi-sited study of art would be complicated by the fact that it is not only people that move, material artworks do so as well, as do, in a wider sense, cultural forms. The migratory nature of visual forms can manifest itself in multifarious ways – as intangible flows of inspiration across cultural territories, for example; as explicit appropriation of artistic methods or imagery, in the form of artworks travelling to exhibitions and in exhibitions; or as de- and recontextualisation of particular images. Visual forms and images are themselves migrating phenomena, and, to some extent, always have been.[41] Studies in modern art have often examined the impact of art from one culture on that of other cultures, but, typically, from a Eurocentric perspective that sees cultural transactions as a one-way street where the standards are dictated by a hegemonic, modernised Western centre, and 'backward' peripheries remain recipients of influence. As Kobena Mercer has noted, art history has seldom been attentive to 'the *interactive dialectics* of cross-cultural borrowing – the give-and-take of expropriation and appropriation as a *back-and-forth* process that constitutes one of the basic conditions of modernity in the visual arts'.[42]

Anthropologising the artist

A prominent exception to this failure to consider the implications of cross-cultural interaction is Hal Foster's seminal article 'The Artist as Ethnographer', first printed in George E. Marcus and Fred R. Myer's 1995 anthology *The Traffic in Culture: Refiguring Art and Anthropology*. A year later Foster published an expanded version in his book, *The Return of the Real*, and it has remained central to the discourse on the ethics of artists' fieldwork and quasi-anthropological engagement with 'the other' ever since. Walter Benjamin's 1934 lecture 'The author as producer' is the springboard for Foster's critique of the ideological investments that Western artists and intellectuals on the left have made in subcultural and ethnic communities since identity politics took centre stage in the cultural debates of the 1980s. Foster's discussion of 'the ethnographic paradigm' that has shaped many leftist artistic practices and social outreach projects since the 1980s revolves around Benjamin's distinction between two ways in which artists and intellectuals can side with the working class. On the one hand, the artist can enact 'ideological patronage', which tends to assign a passive position to the other. In this case, the supportive artist assumes a place 'beside' the marginalised or disempowered group that the artist seeks to represent by proxy, so to speak. On the other, the artist can intervene in the very apparatus of traditional culture and media, and adapt it to the aims of a social revolution, argues Benjamin.[43] In this case, the artist, or the intellectual, becomes a producer, and solidarity is acted out through material practices that can actively involve the group in question and change the modes and means of production and representation; this type of engagement is not limited to the representation of a political issue or standpoint.[44]

Foster asserts that the recent ethnographic paradigm is 'structurally similar' to Benjamin's model of the author as producer, although 'the subject of association' has changed from a subject defined in terms of economic relations to one defined in terms of cultural identity. Thus, it is no longer the worker but 'the cultural and/or ethnic other', be it a minority community, the underclass or people otherwise stigmatised, underprivileged or disempowered.[45] Foster's critique of the ethnographic paradigm is relevant to the four Indian artists under scrutiny in this chapter, although none of them draw on anthropological methods or the participant-observer approach to 'fieldwork' so valued among contemporary ethnographer-artists. Anthropological methods offer a dialectical position between experience and interpretation on the condition that self-critique of its dual nature is made an integral part of the way it is practised. The problem here is that the conspicuous and explicit references to Indian culture in the work of Bharti Kher, Rina Banerjee, Ravinder Reddy, for example, and, to some extent, Anish Kapoor, may lead to a kind of self-anthropologisation. Without the necessary self-critique, artists might activate what Foster calls the *realist assumption* that 'the other' (in this case the postcolonial artist her/himself) is somehow *in* reality. This danger lurks particularly in Western and other foreign contexts where the artists are often presented as culturally 'other', and this fallacy can occur when the anthropological separation between the role of the indigenous informant/participant and the role of the ethnographer/observer somehow collapses. When artists study their 'own' culture in an 'ethnic' perspective, they assume the dual role of informant and ethnographer. If an artist does not articulate her or his observing distance clearly enough, the artist may be perceived as a representational figure instead of an investigator. In such cases, markets and audiences may too easily associate the artist's works with indigeneity and authenticity rather than criticality and reflexivity. Or, in Foster's phrasing, 'As the artist stands *in* the identity of a sited community, he or she may be asked to stand *for* this identity, to represent it institutionally. In this case the artist is primitivized, indeed anthropologized.'[46] This mechanism governs many of the representations of Indian art outside Asia, especially exhibitions based on a 'nationalist' approach to the selection of the artworks. Taken together, the selected works are expected to communicate a sort of national narrative. As Gunhild Borggreen has noted, this approach often leads to the more or less explicit assumption that the relatively small sample of artworks represents 'wider anthropological perspectives of the particular nation in question'.[47]

Foster's aim is primarily an ideological critique of artists' working methods, not to develop a new methodology for art history. Nevertheless, he does point to the need to rethink the existing theoretical notions of 'the other' in light of the complex interpenetration brought about by globalisation on all levels: 'Then there is the problem of the *politics* of this outside-other. Today in our global economy the assumption of a pure outside is almost impossible. This is not to totalize our world system prematurely, but to specify both resistance and innovation as immanent relations rather than transcendental events.'[48]

Foster's model of the artist as ethnographer captures the way artists have typically engaged in identity politics through identification with the cultural or ethnic 'other' as an uncompromised outsider, which they tend to idealise as the privileged 'outside-other' of cultural innovation and political transformation. The model of the artist as migrant worker proposed here suggests not so much an act of free will (i.e. the political agency, critical acts and egalitarian solidarity of an idealist artist) as a pragmatic adaptation to the predicament of purely immanent relations in the globalised art world and a tactical interaction with its transnational institutional and economic power structures. However, the migrant worker model *also* reflects the fact that the subjectivity and existence of a large number of contemporary artists are profoundly shaped by transnational migration, or circular migration, and the accompanying experience of being insiders and outsiders to several cultures and societies at the same time. Thus, in a broader historiographical perspective, the model calls for the development of innovative approaches to art history and curating that are sensitive to transcultural connectivity, amphibian practices and the accelerated circulation of people and cultural forms. This description of contemporary artists as engaged in transnational and/or circular migration leads us to the second key question of this chapter: what kind of artists has migration made them?

Radicant and nodal artists

Considering the highly diverse and unequal configurations of artistic careers, it is probably only possible to give speculative answers to the question above. I will attempt to do this by way of two suggestive metaphors coined by the art theorist and curator Nicolas Bourriaud and the visual theorist Johanna Drucker. After putting in circulation his concepts of relational aesthetics (1998) and post-production (2003), Nicolas Bourriaud published a volume of theoretical and critical essays where he introduced the terms 'altermodern' and 'altermodernity' to distinguish the twenty-first century's globalised and transcultural forms of the 'modern' and 'modernity' from the twentieth century's allegedly purely Western versions of modernity and postmodernity.[49] In Bourriaud's understanding, the cultural condition of altermodernity is characterised by a ceaseless movement and exchange that puts people, cultural material and significations in perpetual flux. Not surprisingly, Bourriaud points to migration, travel and 'cultural translation' as the primary causes. He singles out the exile, the tourist, the urban wanderer and, above all, the immigrant as the dominant conceptual figures of his understanding of altermodern culture,[50] in the same manner as his model Walter Benjamin singled out the *flâneur* and the film director as personifications of the experience of modernity.[51] In the context under consideration here, the most interesting aspect of Bourriaud's argument is not his concept of altermodernity but his reconsideration of the concept of the artist as signalled by the title of his book, *The Radicant*. With its play on the word 'radical', this evokes the twentieth-century notion of the radical avant-garde as a foil to the idea of the migrant artist as the paradigmatic figure of contemporary culture.

Bourriaud uses a metaphor borrowed from the Latin vocabulary of botany to describe the migrant's way of forming affiliations. *Radicans* (of *radico*, to grow roots) – in English, *radicant* – denotes a family of plants that grow by spreading above ground root suckers as they advance, such as strawberry plants and ivy for example. The plant can thus spread out in different directions, like ivy attaching multiple hooks to whatever surfaces present themselves, while strawberry plants send out runners that root in the ground and form new plants. This ability to form secondary root systems separates them from the botanical type Bourriaud calls *radical* (of *radix*, root), which grows out from one root and thus remains rooted in its original habitat. Bourriaud's twin concept of the radical and the radicant clearly repeats and reformulates that of the migrant and the sedentary, a staple of migration studies. Yet, the metaphor of the artist as a radicant individual may offer a way out of the binary logic of multiculturalist identity politics, which tends to overemphasise ethnic origin:

> The radicant develops in accord with its host soil. It conforms to the latter's twists and turns and adapts to its surfaces and geological features. It translates itself into the terms of the space in which it moves. With its at once dynamic and dialogical signification, the adjective 'radicant' captures this contemporary subject, caught between the need for a connection with its environment and the

> forces of uprooting, between globalisation and singularity, between identity and opening to the other. It defines the subject as an object of negotiation.[52]

While twentieth-century modernist artists were radical in their search for roots and the origin, or *der Ursprung*, from which art could be invented anew, the radicant artists of the twenty-first century spread their roots and let them gradually multiply as they grow, posits Bourriaud, thereby establishing a sharp distinction between modern and altermodern art and artists. For Bourriaud, to be radicant is to have one's roots in heterogeneous contexts and formats, continually pulling up old roots and generating new ones and attachments, and, in general, engaging in various kinds of translating activities: translating ideas, re-encoding or transcoding images, changing behaviour and outlook. For Bourriaud, cultural translation thus becomes the overriding ethical imperative for the 'semionauts' he considers radicant contemporary artists to be.[53]

For Johanna Drucker, connections, appropriation and exchange are also at the core of contemporary artistic practices. While Bourriaud's formulation revolves around the notion of *cultural translation*, Drucker's conception of the networked artwork and artist revolves around the idea of *circulation*. In Bourriaud's terminology, the contemporary migrant artist is a radicant; for Drucker, the prototypical artist is a *nodal artist*, a product of intersections in a network of social, artistic, technical and material connections. Drucker singles out German artist Sigmar Polke as the quintessential embodiment of the nodally networked artist who is acutely aware of the ramified system in which he is embedded. By using silkscreen, painting, textiles, cartoon images, photographs and icons of mass culture, Polke created works that incorporated the circulatory principles of images moving through different media. His practice was based on the explicit appropriation and recirculation of ideas, images and techniques, juggling them around to create new intersections between histories, images and aesthetic modes of expression. Although he has mostly been treated as 'an individual talent' and 'the resistant, the oppositional, the critical individual', Polke is actually, rather, 'a linkage apparatus', argues Drucker: 'Nothing derives, *sui generis*, from his conceptual practice, or graphical vocabulary. Quite the contrary: the brilliance, the strength and genius of his work is its play of connections and with connections. The thought experiment of rethinking fine art as a fully *social* practice finds its demonstration model in Polke.'[54]

Bourriaud's radicant artist and Drucker's idea of the nodal artist both break with the modern perception of the artist as an original creator and the way this is distinguished from – and, at the same time, linked to – the concept of the work of art as an individualised product of an original mind that leaves a unique imprint on it. As with the genre of the artist biography, which was similarly born in Renaissance Italy, such an understanding of the work of art has cemented approaches to art that focus on the singularity of the individual artist.[55] Conversely, Drucker and Bourriaud use the connectedness of the artist with other practitioners and actors in shifting geographical, sociocultural and artistic environments as a springboard for reconceptualising the figure of the artist as fundamentally intersubjective, social and networked. But if relationality is taken to be the defining condition of artistic practices, where does that leave the old notion of the artist as rooted in a national culture? Again, Indian artists provide us with a test case for a more common pattern in the way artists relate to national culture and identity.

Four Indian artists: a test case

As global studies scholar Manuela Ciotti has observed, Western actors have promoted Indian art in the global market and exhibition circuit, but Indian-owned capital, at home and in the diaspora, has been a decisive factor in the rise of Indian modern and contemporary art to a prominent position in the global art world.[56] Ciotti explains:

> The epicentre of this market is not Europe and the US – despite the 'west' still playing a major role in this story. At the same time, this is not a fully Indian story either; it is in fact a truly global one made up of galleries, auction houses, art fairs, business enterprises, buyers and artists operating at several geographical nodal points. In addition to prominent galleries in locations such as New Delhi, Mumbai, London and New York, among others, Indian art is shown at international fairs such as Art Dubai, Art Basel, Art Hong Kong, Art Basel Miami, while the growing popularity of the India Art Fair (previously Art Summit), held in New Delhi since 2008, testifies to art's appeal at home.[57]

Although many Indian diasporic artists are included in the survey exhibitions and travelling exhibitions of 'Indian contemporary art', according to Manuela Ciotti most of the works are, in fact, produced in India, just as India is very often, but not always, foregrounded as a cultural reference in the works. Not surprisingly, catalogue essays and reviews about art from India tend to revolve around the question of the artist's cultural identity and 'Indianness'. Sometimes this question is posed in a meta-reflective way, which underscores the generality and urgency of the problematic. In Zehra Jumabhoy's phrasing: 'What constitutes a "diaspora artist" for instance? Or, to put it another way, what makes someone "Indian"? Is it based on ethnicity, nationality, what someone decides to call themselves or just where they choose to be based? Is the globe-trotting Bandra boy Jitish Kallat more "Indian" than British Zarina Bhimji?'[58]

Let me suggest a partial answer to these questions. The artist's identity as 'Indian' often seems to be generated at the intersection between several factors: her/his Indian citizenship or membership of the Indian diaspora; the artist's wish to be included in the national category, for career or identity construction purposes; her/his engagement in representing India, or Indian diasporic experiences; and the curator's choice of a national framing of the exhibition in question. On second thoughts, the question to pose, therefore, is not only what makes an artist 'Indian', thereby suggesting that it is all about external socio-cultural factors and not the artist's agency and identification; it is also, how do artists consciously position themselves as 'Indian' through their use of particular artistic means of expression, their public statements and their choice of subject matter and/or an aesthetic that viewers, curators, scholars and art dealers may associate with 'Indianness'; choices which can involve the risk of self-exoticisation?

Reception is clearly an important factor here. For example, when curator Nicholas Baume interviewed London-based Anish Kapoor prior to his solo exhibition at the Institute of Contemporary Art in Boston in 2008, he began with two questions – one on the significance of the intersection between British and Indian culture, the other on the extent to which India had influenced the artist's work. Kapoor answered obliquely:

> I use red a lot. I've gone so far as to title a work *My Red Homeland*. It's true that in Indian culture red is a powerful thing; it is the color a bride wears; it is associated with the matriarchal, which is central to Indian psychology. So I can see what leads me there culturally, but there's more to it … Red has a very powerful blackness. This overt color, this open and visually beckoning color, also associates itself with a dark interior world. And that's the real reason I'm interested in it. Is that Indian? I don't know that it matters.[59]
>
> […]
>
> Could one do an analysis of my form in terms of Indian aesthetics? I expect one could. I'm drawn to form that seems to have multilayered interpretive possibility. Yet I'm not interested in overtly readable symbols. As much as I love Brancusi, a bird in space is too obvious for me – I think we've moved somewhere else.[60]

Kapoor clearly acknowledges the formative influence of his native country but also subtly suggests that a reading of his work in terms of ethnicity and nationality would be reductive because his works open 'multilayered' possibilities of interpretation.[61] However, other artists may be more keen than Kapoor to identify with India and use 'Indianness' as a marker of self and difference which can act as a spur to their work and career.

Bharti Kher (1969–) was born in London to Indian parents and educated in Britain, but 'returned' to live and work in Delhi where she now ranks as one of the most celebrated Indian artists. The question of how biographical circumstances bleed into the thematics and aesthetic of her works will be explored more fully in Chapter 5. With regard to the general questions of how migration, and the ensuing transculturation, impacts the connection routinely made between the artist's identity and nationality, the minimal biographical information provided here will suffice to make it clear that she represents a different aspect of the postcolonial positions developed in India and the Indian diaspora than that of Anish Kapoor, Rina Banerjee and Ravinder Reddy. In 2012, Kher installed a monumental minimalist cube of obsolete radiators, which she had bought from the US and shipped to India, at her solo show at the New York gallery Hauser & Wirth (see Chapter 5 for an analysis of this work). The title *The hot winds that blow from the West* (see figure 3.1) is an ironic statement in itself and its critical cut is supported by Kher's own statement on this major work of hers. It has often been quoted as a token not only of her keen awareness of her own cultural and geopolitical location in the world but also of her strong identification with India and an 'Eastern' perspective, and of a self-confidence founded in the rapidly growing political and economic power of the Asian region: 'From where I sit, the winds blowing nowadays from the West – from the places that were the seats of power and authority throughout the 20th century – are no longer as strong or reliable as

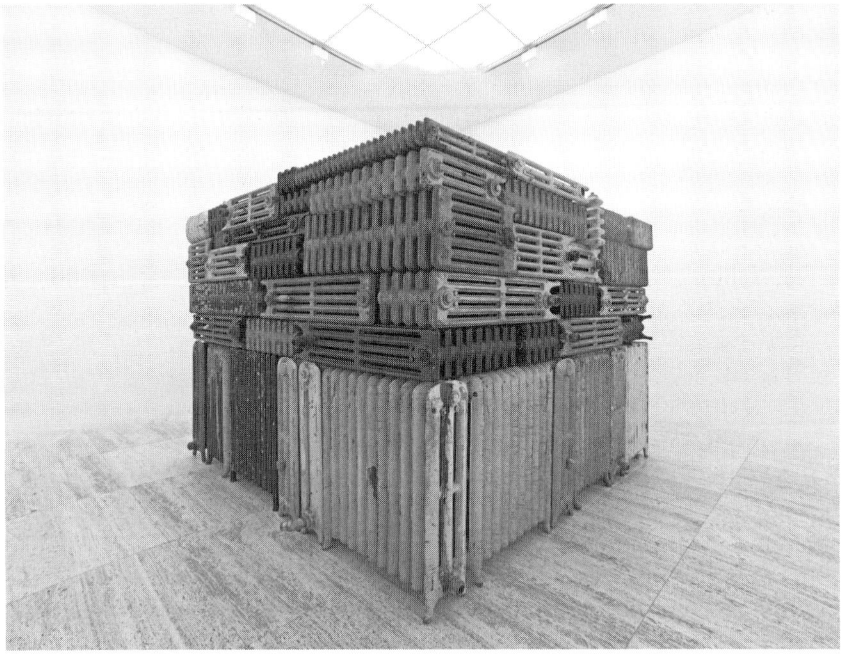

3.1 Bharti Kher, *The hot winds that blow from the West*, 2011. 131 old radiators. 195 x 264 x 254 cm. Installation view, Hauser & Wirth, New York, 2012. © Bharti Kher. Photograph: Genevieve Hanson, courtesy of the artist and Hauser & Wirth.

they were ... I suppose I am sending them [the radiators] back to the West as messenger and, perhaps, as warnings.'[62]

New York-based Rina Banerjee (1963–) was born in Kolkata (then Calcutta), but her family emigrated when she was three years old, first to London and then to Cleveland, Ohio. She finished a degree in polymer engineering at Case Western Reserve University in Ohio, in 1993, and then moved on to graduate studies in art at Yale School of Art, eventually settling in New York. Ravinder Reddy (1956–), on the other hand, was born in Suryapet, Andhra Pradesh, India, studied for a BA and MA in sculpture at the Maharaja Sayajirao University of Baroda between 1975 and 1982, and moved to London to study sculpture at Goldsmiths' College and ceramics at the Royal College of Art from 1982 until 1984, after which he returned to India, eventually basing himself in Visakhapatnam.

As several critics have observed, much modern and contemporary art from India is characterised by a hybridising fusion of 'local' Indian elements with elements and techniques of internationally disseminated Western art of the twentieth century, such as abstract expressionism, surrealism, pop art, minimalism, conceptual art, etc. Contemporary artistic practices in India thus draw on what Stine Høholt has aptly described as 'the "cannibalistic" work methods of the new global artists'.[63] The artists cannibalise, i.e. critically select and process elements and techniques from Western art scenes and symbolic systems, and combine them with elements of other origins to pursue different agendas. The straightforwardness with which this method is often employed is evident in the way Ravinder Reddy's freestanding colossal heads of wide-eyed women borrow from both Western and Eastern traditions: religious sculpture, pop art and industrial manufacture. Spectacular and emblematic, these heads constructed of painted polyester resin fibreglass seem to reference the ancient civilisations of Ancient Egypt, classical Greece, and, especially, monumental Hindu sculpture (see figure 3.2). The distant gaze of their bulging lotus-petal eyes, reminiscent of those of wooden temple sculptures in southern India, suggests that they embody 'some mysterious, mystical life' or are 'vessels made for religious rituals'.[64] At the same time, they also evoke contemporary urban types of women with lipstick-smeared lips and elaborate hairstyles with voluminous buns secured by plastic bands, ribbons and hairslides. Professor of Indian art Ajay J. Sinha has called them 'urban deities' to capture the ambiguous amalgamation of the sacred and the profane that constitutes a distinctive feature of Reddy's iconic and parodic spectacles.[65] Holland Cotter, the art critic for the *New York Times*, also noted the hybrid character of Reddy's earlier sculptures when he reviewed his first solo show in New York in 2001: 'monumental in size but uncertain as to identity, they would be equally at home at an amusement park or a temple ... The result is a hybrid, with roots in the past but also in the pop cultural present.'[66] Given that

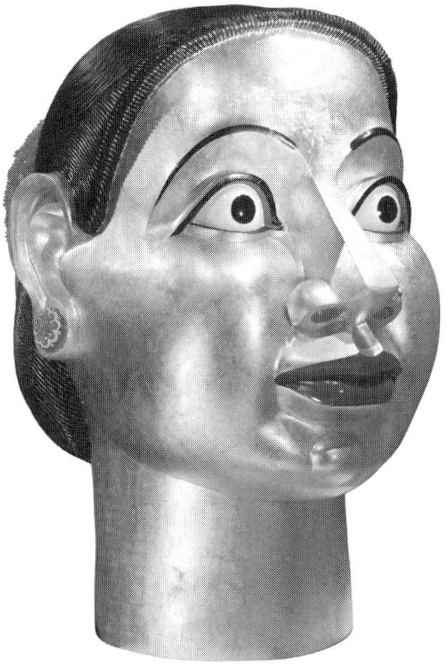

3.2 Ravinder Reddy, *Tara*, 2004. Polyester resin fibreglass, gold leaf. 183 x 124 x 173 cm. © Ravinder Reddy. Photograph: Chris Meerdo, courtesy of the artist and Walsh Gallery.

the distinctive hairstyles and Hindu references lend a distinctly 'ethnic' look to Reddy's cultural hybrids, it is not surprising that his works are frequently read anthropologically, i.e. as an expression of national traits or 'Indiannness'.

Rina Banerjee's sculptures are another textbook example of a cannibalistic working method. Her works are sophisticated poetic assemblages made of diverse artefacts from all over the world. Often suspended as if floating in the air, her sculptures evoke a dreamlike atmosphere and stage a distinctly artificial otherness. As curator Samira Rahmatullah has observed, 'Banerjee's mutant-like sculptures … are almost frighteningly extraterrestrial, yet at the same time inviting and seductive – a personification in many ways of the Other in the colonial and postcolonial mindset.'[67] Banerjee engages with the colonial past as well as the multifaceted diasporic present, and is sensitive to how the two are woven together. Incorporating objects from the colonial era, organic materials, textiles with local connotations, cowrie beads, feathers, tassels, horns, etc., Banerjee's works strike a delicate balance between the orientalist, the surreal and a critical postcolonial consciousness, which is often subtly conveyed by beguiling wordy titles, such as *The world as burnt fruit – When empires feuded for populations and plantations, buried in colonial and ancient currency a Gharial appeared from an inky melon – hot with blossom, sprang forth to swallow the world not yet all as burnt fruit* (2011) (see plates 3 and 4, and figure 4.2). Considering the historical connection between colonialism and capitalism, as well as the current state of globalised neo-liberal capitalism, it is not surprising that it is commerce that features behind Banerjee's artistic materials, which she sources 'from the world's great markets, from bazaars in Calcutta to New York's Garment District, from Wal-Mart to eBay'.[68] Moreover, as kinds of auto-orientalist fetishes that appropriate cultural stereotypes for critical purposes as well as self-profiling, her works invoke a centuries-old tradition among global travellers of bringing home exotic items, which when taken anywhere else in the world come to represent a specific 'other' culture.[69] In this case, though, the 'Indian culture' conjured by Banerjee's hybridising diasporic aesthetic is impossible to anchor in any particular place. By contrast, her anti-categorial assemblages disturb expectations of 'authenticity' and undermine the dominant Western notions of Indianness that are based on popular stereotypes of colonial origin.

According to Høholt, artists from India who use a cannibalistic method 'devour', absorb or reuse Indian cultural heritage and everyday culture, but often at one remove from India and its historical development. Among the 'distancing factors' can be the condition of living in the diaspora, as with Rina Banerjee and Anish Kapoor, but also a partial acculturation into the art forms and institutions of the West and, increasingly, the global art world, as seems to be the case with India-based Ravinder Reddy and Bharti Kher. In all instances, distancing effects may also be ascribed to the wide-ranging dislocations caused by globalisation, including the history of colonisation and decolonisation as well as the globalisation of the exhibition circuit. The works chosen for display abroad are often those that can translate into widespread and often stereotypical notions of a particular culture or nation, whereas those that are more closely tied to the local issues of a specific cultural and historical context can be difficult to make relevant to broader international audiences.[70] In fact, the artists' statements quoted in this chapter reveal an acute awareness of how the artists' relationship to the 'heritage' of their country of birth is configured by various distancing factors. Bharti Kher's statement about *The hot winds that blow from the West* is clearly meant to position her outside the West, as an 'Eastern' critic of Western culture and imperialism. For Rina Banerjee, on the other hand, it is imperative that her works reflect how a diaspora artist is positioned differently from a 'native' Indian artist as regards identification with homeland and heritage:

> Growing up abroad (as we called it) was a strange experience in the 1960s; there were so few Indians in the West. My parents saw themselves as international citizens. Maybe they imagined a future that we are just beginning to glimpse. I dream of this willingness to close the gaps between cultures, communities, and places. I think of identity as inherently foreign; of heritage as something

that leaks away from the concept of home – as happens when one first migrates … Where you live impacts who you are. I am a Non-Resident Indian, living in New York. I think it is important to ask what this means.[71]

Many artists from Asia are, in fact, transnational, living as members of a diaspora, or in their home country as belonging to one cultural group among many. Therefore, the experience and discourse of diaspora and racialised positions are important issues to these artists,[72] and many do engage with their culture of origin. As Høholt infers, the cannibalism at play in the works of 'the new global artists' can be seen as a kind of 'reverse cannibalism', that is to say, a cannibalism of the self rather than the other. It should not be confused with a casual eclecticism that merely toys with cultural material and signs: 'for most of these artists it is a question of a total existential process that may concern cultural figures, but in a certain sense brings the whole identity and existence of the artists into play'.[73] However, it is important to remember that it is also a hybridising cross-cultural cannibalism, which may draw on art forms and concepts of art that originated in the West, as well as a host of other cultural and artistic sources. Rina Banerjee's works, for instance, collapse ancient and colonial objects, symbols of her native India and of American culture, and Western and Asian cultures in a more broad sense, into the contemporary. Her works may mimic exotica, but if anything, the exuberant exoticism of her works functions as a hyperbole that maintains a reflective distance from the idea of an authentic or essential Indianness by gesturing towards the syncretism and complexity of cultural forms and symbols.

Anish Kapoor (1954–) travelled in the opposite direction to Bharti Kher. Born in Mumbai (then Bombay), Kapoor migrated to the UK where he has been based in London for many years. The question of how national identities are constructed by and for artists is put in an interesting historical perspective by looking at the reception history of Anish Kapoor, as he represents an older generation of British diaspora artists. In contrast to the three artists discussed above, Kapoor did not position himself and was not primarily identified as an 'Indian' artist when he first acheived success in the 1980s. At that time, his name was closely associated with the group known as the New British Sculptors, which included Tony Cragg, Bill Woodrow, Richard Deacon, Edward Allington and Julian Opie. All six artists were represented by the Lisson Gallery in London and were among the top ten artists who received the most coverage in art journals between 1975 and 1990.[74] This media exposure led to the notion of a 1980s generation of New British Sculptors, which was consolidated by public sector curators who organised a series of exhibitions in the UK and abroad. A large body of literature has also helped to secure critical recognition and establish the group's existence as an art historical 'fact', while the repeated stress on their 'Britishness' served to associate them with the grand tradition of modern British sculptors such as Henry Moore and Anthony Caro, as Nick Baker has observed.[75] Anish Kapoor, however, as Niru Ratman has noted, 'went to extreme lengths to play down any connection between his cultural identity and the work he produced'. Kapoor declined to participate, for example, in Rasheed Araeen's 1989 exhibition *The Other Story*, which showcased the works of black and Asian British artists at the Hayward Gallery in London.[76] Notably, when Kapoor created his installation *Descent into Limbo* for *documenta IX* in 1992, the exhibition guide only mentioned Kapoor's birthplace. No references were made to the artist's 'Indianness'; the focus was on his interest in organic forms and monochromatic colour effects. Nor was his work viewed in an 'anthropological' or 'orientalising' perspective as representing Indian culture. For this reason alone, the text from the Documenta guide is worth quoting here in full in support of Kapoor's previously quoted explanation that his works are really about multi-layered meaning and philosophical issues, not the ethnic particularities of 'Indianness'.

> Anish Kapoor was born in Bombay in 1954 and now lives in London. His sculptures derive from the basic stereometric forms of cone and sphere. The forms are often reminiscent of gigantic fruit and seed capsules, but the impression made by these biomorphic forms is frustrated by their colouring. Kapoor drenches his work with glowing pigments so that their surface absorbs a great deal of light, and they seem surrounded by an intense aura of colour. Kapoor has altered the three-dimensional constants of his work for documenta. A large round hole leads to a spherical underground space partly filled with pure colour pigment. From above, you look into infinite depths of purest blue. As in his stereometric standing sculptures, Kapoor creates an electric tension by his use of colour and form. The viewer's gaze looks in vain for a resting place. The feeling of dizziness evoked by Kapoor intensifies to a sense of stillness that seems beyond any concrete sensory experience.[77]

The New British Sculptors did not have a shared ideology; in fact, most of them rejected being lumped together as a unified generational group. Yet, they were sufficiently pragmatic and career-minded to recognise that the label was an efficient way of attracting the attention of international audiences. As Richard Deacon observed, 'as a package you are much more attractive as a group than you are individually at early stages'.[78] Perhaps a similar logic applies to the promotion of previously unknown Indian artists in the West, the unifying factor here being the broader anthropological category of 'Indianness', since neither 'medium' nor 'generation' can serve as common denominators.

Although Kapoor's name was primarily associated in the early years of his career with this 1980s generation of British sculptors, references to Indian culture and religion have been recognised as integral to Kapoor's non-figurative art since this time. Accordingly, in the entries on Kapoor's early work *As if to Celebrate, I Discovered a Mountain Blooming with Red Flowers* (1981) in the Tate Gallery's catalogue of acquisitions (1986) and illustrated companion (1991), India is ranked equally with Jungian psychoanalysis and archetypal images as enduring sources of inspiration for Kapoor. 'Then, in 1979 he made a visit to India which reacquainted him with early cultural memories which were to inform his subsequent work', the companion explains. The catalogue entry develops this further by making a causal connection between Kapoor's journey to his native country and his choice of coloured pigment as a signature material: 'On his return he made his first works out of coloured pigment. The use of powder, for which there is a precedent in Indian daily life and ritual, he also equates with the deliberate choice of 'poor' materials in the tradition of Arte Povera.'[79] Thus, it appears that it is only in the wake of the 'multiculturalism' that 'Indianness' has come to play a key role in Kapoor's public image and the reception of the artist – particularly when his works are presented to an Indian audience.

In 2010–11, Kapoor presented his *Shooting Into the Corner* (2008–9) (see figure 3.3) in a former Bollywood film studio in Mumbai. In this extraordinary work, a pneumatic compressor enabled a cannon, which Kapoor had developed with a team of engineers, to shoot heavy balls of red wax across the room and into the corner where the balls smashed against the wall, leaving imprints of wax trailing down the white surface of the wall to build a growing heap of the lumpy material reminiscent of blood clots. Installed at this particular site, *Shooting into the Corner* evoked gruesome cinematic evocations of murderous battles as well as India's violent past under British colonial rule. In the context of this exhibition, Kapoor expressed his personal view of nation and addressed the delicate question of the relationship between art and cultural identity, subtly pointing to the need to delink artworks from nationality when they circulate across state borders: 'My India has found a voice in my art', Kapoor declared; 'I'm Indian, my sensibility is Indian. And I welcome that, rejoice in that, but the great battle nowadays is to occupy an aesthetic territory that isn't linked to nationality.'[80] At the same time, he used the opportunity of his twin exhibitions in 2010–11, at the Bollywood film studio and New Delhi's National Gallery of Modern Art (his first exhibitions in India), to present himself as an Indian artist to local audiences. When interviewed by *India Real Time* in connection with the opening of the retrospective in Delhi, he described the exhibitions as his 'coming home', a remark picked up by the reporter who compared the event to 'the return of an extremely successful prodigal son'.[81] Kapoor even went so far as to suggest an 'Indian' reading of his works, explaining that his pigment-based sculptures, for instance, are likely to remind his audience in India of the bright piles of pigment stacked up on roadside stands for Holi, the festival of colours. Such an example shows how migrant artists can strategically play down or give more emphasis to their ethnic origin, and

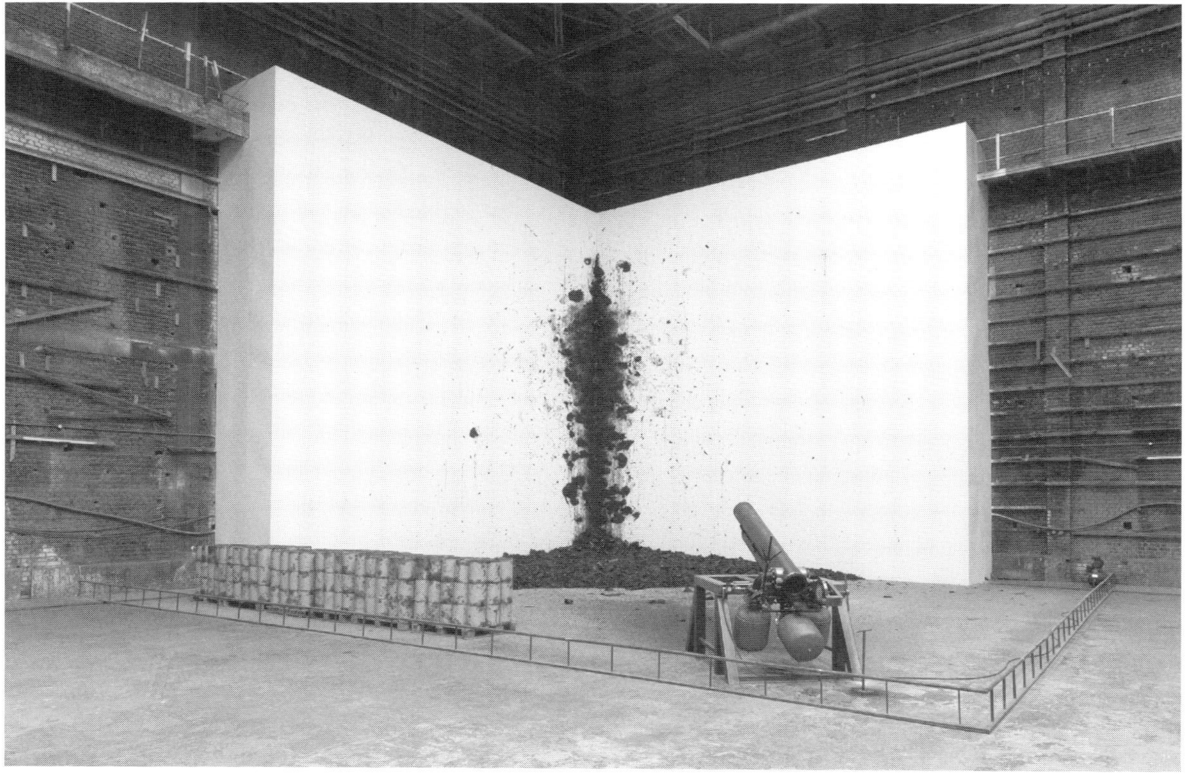

3.3

Anish Kapoor, *Shooting Into the Corner*, 2008–9. Mixed media, dimensions variable. Installation view from Mehboob Studios, Mumbai, 2010–11. © Anish Kapoor/copydanbilleder.dk. All rights reserved, DACS 2017. Photograph: Dave Morgan.

how identifications and disidentifications can result in permutations as artists adapt, *radicantly*, to different circumstances and cultural environments.

An artist's location – whether in India or abroad, 'in diaspora' – does not seem to be decisive in determining whether an artist is included in 'national'-themed exhibitions and promoted as an 'Indian' artist or not. However, location and origin *do* matter, as is demonstrated by Rina Banerjee's hybrid works and profound reflections on her own position in the world as a Non-Resident Indian (NRI). The works of diasporic artists like Banerjee may reflect the artist's place of residence and feeling of belonging in subtle ways that undermine not only traditional notions of 'Indian art' but also, and more importantly, the essentialist notion of 'whole' cultures and 'pure' national and cultural identities.

> I am so often asked, 'do you feel your work is Indian?' and almost always it is a person who is of Anglo or European Tradition who is doing this asking and never someone Indian. Living in India as an Indian is different than living somewhere else as an Indian and this difference is very crucial to how I see myself and the work produced by all Indians in the world. I live in New York City experiencing relationships with other non Indians, non Europeans … I am also aware that had I grown up in India I would have had [a] dramatically more dominant status in India. My awareness of these two coexisting identities for Indians and many others, presents a complex perspective on my Indianness, my familiarity with these other cultures impacts, alters how I express, orchestrates my Indianness while managing the constraints as well as privileges shaped by a dominant culture.[82]

Exhibiting across the world as well as in their countries of residence, Banerjee, Kapoor, Kher and Reddy have all developed what Ranjit Hoskote describes as amphibian practices. Despite the significant differences in their work patterns and the way they are positioned in the world, they all belong, in one way or another, to the class of migrating professionals in the global art world who are, so to speak, living in translation. Their artistic practices and their works are all transcultural and deal with the condition of crossing cultures. The traditional concept of the autonomous artist in pursuit of an original vision and aesthetic does not really fit any of them. It cannot account for the hybrid character of their works and the complex ways in which they filter materials, forms and symbols easily associated with India through their globalised aesthetic vocabularies, thus translating 'India' and 'diaspora' culturally for a diversified international audience. Other models of the artist's role are needed to describe them. While Banerjee, Kapoor and Kher can all be said to be *radicant* artists, in Bourriaud's sense, Drucker's concept of the nodal artist seems a more apt description of Reddy as he has remained in his country of origin for most, although not all, of his life.

This chapter's characterisation of the artist as a migrant worker is merely a germ of 'The thought experiment of rethinking fine art as a fully *social* practice' that Johanna Drucker has called for. Yet, without eliminating the singularity of artists' work, or the particularity of their methods and the distinctiveness of artistic perspectives, this model shifts the emphasis from the artist as a solitary and sedentary figure to an understanding of the artist as networked and migratory. It also turns away from an isolationist understanding of artistic practices towards a relational understanding of them as negotiations unfolding through material practices and subjected to the interconnected global and local forces that structure contemporary societies. The notion of the artist as a migrant worker proposed here does not posit a dichotomous distinction between boundedness and mobility, but stimulates reflection on how they interact and structure the artist's sense of belonging, nor does it exclude critical reflections on how the artist in question is positioned in relation to the grave inequalities between different sorts of migrants – from 'green card' workers and tourists, to undocumented migrants, asylum seekers and refugees.[83] Instead of cementing the myth of the artist as a detached creator, it invites a more profound exploration of how the artist's role has been reconfigured as that of a translator, mediator and bridge-builder between people and cultures.

Notes

1 The general argument presented in the first part of Chapter 3 expands on an earlier study; see Anne Ring Petersen, 'The artist as migrant worker? Framing art in an age of intensified globalisation and migration', *Arken Bulletin*, special issue 'Migration – Contemporary Art from India', no. 6 (2013), 42–9.

2 Smith, 'Rethinking modernism and modernity now', 295.

3 *Ibid.*, 286.

4 *Ibid.*, 314–15.

5 *Ibid.*, 286, 315.

6 *Ibid.*, 317.

7 *Ibid.*, 286.

8 *Ibid.*, 291.

9 *Ibid.*, 290ff.; Wainwright, *Timed Out*, pp. 9–10.

10 Johanna Drucker, 'After after', *The White Review*, no. 12 (2014), unpaginated, www.thewhitereview.org/art/after-after-2/ (accessed November 2016).

11 *Manmohan Singh* went on to be Prime Minister of India from 2004 to 2014.

12 Zehra Jumabhoy, 'Introduction', in *The Empire Strikes Back* (London: The Saatchi Gallery, and Jonathan Cape, 2009), pp. 17–79, p. 17.

13 Mukti Khaire and R. Daniel Wadhwani, 'Changing landscapes: the construction of meaning and value in a new market category – modern Indian art', *Academy of Management Journal*, 53:6 (2010), 1,281–304.

14 For a list and chronology of exhibitions of contemporary Indian art, see Brigitte Ulmer, 'Late Arrival: An Exhibition Chronology of Contemporary Indian Art', in

Kunstmuseum Bern (ed.), *Horn Please: Narratives in Contemporary Indian Art* (Ostfildern: Hatje Cantz Verlag, 2008), pp. 59–77.

15 Christian Gether *et al.* (eds), *India: Art Now* (Ostfildern: Arken Museum of Modern Art and Hatje Cantz, 2012).

16 Kathleen Madden and Thierry Prat (eds), *Indian Highway* (London: The Serpentine Gallery and Koenig Books, 2011).

17 Today, the term 'modern Indian art' refers to works produced between the early twentieth century and the 1980s. Khaire and Wadhwani, 'Changing landscapes', 1,289.

18 *Ibid.*, 1,282, 1,295.

19 *Ibid.*, 1,294.

20 Manuela Ciotti, 'Post-colonial renaissance: "Indianness", contemporary art and the market in the age of neoliberal capital', *Third World Quarterly*, 33:4 (2012), 637–55, 643.

21 Khaire and Wadhwani, 'Changing landscapes', 1,293.

22 Ranjit Hoskote, 'Kaleidoscopic Propositions: The Evolving Contexts of Contemporary Indian Art', in Gether *et al.* (eds), *India: Art Now*, pp. 54–62, p. 61.

23 Jumabhoy, 'Introduction', p. 64.

24 Hoskote, 'Kaleidoscopic Propositions', p. 61.

25 Mathur, 'Introduction', pp. vii–viii.

26 Bydler, *The Global Art World, Inc.*, p. 14.

27 Zeenat Nagree, 'Outside in & inside out', *Art India*, XVII: III (2013), 44–8, 46.

28 Patricia Falguières, 'Archipelago, 2007', in Claire Doherty (ed.), *Situation* (Cambridge, Mass., London: Whitechapel Gallery and The MIT Press, 2009), pp. 180–4, p. 180.

29 Augusta Atla's web-calendar no longer exists (accessed September 2012). Augusta Atla's artwork blog, https://augustaatla.wordpress.com/ (accessed May 2015) now links to her homepage http://augustaatla.com/cv.html (accessed November 2016). The web-calendar was more of a record of her whereabouts and a documentation of her itinerant life as an artist than a work of art.

30 For a close reading of the impact of American art on the Danish-born artist Thomas Bang, for example, who spent the formative years of his career in the US, see Anne Ring Petersen, 'American connections: the early works of Thomas Bang', *RIHA Journal*, article no. 0128 (2015), www.riha-journal.org/articles/2015/-jul-sep/ring-american-connections (accessed November 2016).

31 Sudesh Mishra, *Diaspora Criticsm* (Edinburgh: Edinburgh University Press, 2006), pp. 16–17; Ang, 'Unsettling the National', p. 86.

32 Marion Arnold, 'Here, There and in-Between: South African Women and the Diasporic Condition', in Meskimmon and Rowe (eds), *Women, the Arts and Globalization*, pp. 121–44, p. 126.

33 *Ibid.*, p. 139.

34 YinHua Chu, 'Staging Memories', in Moslund, Petersen and Schramm (eds), *The Culture of Migration: Politics, Aesthetics and Histories*, pp. 271–87, p. 281.

35 Meskimmon, *Contemporary Art and the Cosmopolitan Imagination*, p. 13.

36 Brah, *Cartographies of Diaspora: Contesting Identities*, pp. 180–2, 93.

37 John Salt, 'Current Trends in International Migration in Europe' (The Council of Europe, 2006), www.coe.int/t/dg3/migration/archives/documentation/Migration%20management/2005_Salt_report_en.pdf (accessed November 2016).
38 There is, of course, also the troublesome issue of what kinds of migrants and nationalities are permitted to pass which national borders, but this is an issue for border studies that I will leave aside, even though the issue has often surfaced in discussions of art, migration and politics; see, for example, Iain Chambers, 'Adrift and Exposed', in Lene Burkard (ed.), *Border Crossing* (Odense: Kunsthallen Brandts, 2012), pp. 72–7.
39 Stephen Vertovec, 'Circular migration: the way forward in global policy?', *International Migration Institute. Working Papers*, no. 4 (2007), 2–9, 2–5.
40 George E. Marcus, 'Ethnography in/of the world system: the emergence of multi-sited ethnography', *Annual Review of Anthropology*, no. 24 (1995), 95–117, 102.
41 David Joselit *et al.*, 'Roundtable: the global before globalization', *October*, no. 133 (2010), 3–19.
42 Kobena Mercer, 'Erase and Rewind: When Does Art History in the Black Diaspora Actually Begin?', in Mathur (ed.), *The Migrant's Time*, pp. 17–31, p. 22. Emphasis added.
43 Walter Benjamin, 'The author as producer', *New Left Review*, 1:62 (1970), 83–96, 96.
44 Hal Foster, *The Return of the Real: The Avant-Garde at the End of the Century* (Cambridge, Mass., London: The MIT Press, 1996), pp. 171–2.
45 *Ibid.*, p. 173.
46 *Ibid.*, p. 198.
47 Gunhild Borggreen, 'Asian art on display: questions of representation in the ethnographic turn', *Kontur*, no. 20 (2010), 2–7, 2.
48 Foster, *The Return of the Real*, p. 178.
49 Bourriaud, *The Radicant*, pp. 15–18, 40–4. 'Altermodern' was also the title of the 2009 Tate Triennale curated by Bourriaud.
50 *Ibid.*, pp. 37, 51.
51 Walter Benjamin, *Charles Baudelaire: A Lyric Poet in the Era of High Capitalism* (London, New York: Verso, 1989); 'The Work of Art in the Age of Mechanical Reproduction', in Walter Benjamin, *Illuminations* (London: Fontana Press, 1992), pp. 211–44.
52 Bourriaud, *The Radicant*, p. 51.
53 *Ibid.*, pp. 21–2, 51–4.
54 Drucker, 'After after'.
55 Catherine Soussloff, 'History of the Concept of the Artist', in Michael Kelly (ed.), *Encyclopedia of Aesthetics* (New York, Oxford: Oxford University Press, 1998), pp. 130–5, pp. 130–1.
56 Ciotti, 'Post-Colonial Renaissance', 641.
57 *Ibid.*, 639.
58 Zehra Jumabhoy, 'Now, voyager', *Art India*, 17:3 (2013), 32–43, 36.
59 Nicholas Baume, 'Mythologies in the Making: Anish Kapoor in Conversation with Nicholas Baume', in Nicholas Baume (ed.), *Anish Kapoor: Past, Present, Future* (Cambridge, Mass.: The MIT Press, 2008), pp. 28–54, p. 31.

60 *Ibid.*, p. 32.
61 For an illuminating, balanced and erudite reading of Kapoor's work in terms of Indian aesthetics, philosophy and heritage, with due consideration of other cultural references in his work, see Partha Mitter, 'History, Memory, and Anish Kapoor', in Baume (ed.), *Anish Kapoor*, pp. 104–18.
62 Kher's statement on the occasion of her 2012 solo exhibition 'The hot winds that blow from the West' at Hauser & Wirth in New York. See: www.hauserwirth.com/exhibitions/1243/bharti-kher-the-hotwinds-that-blow-from-the-west/view/ (accessed November 2016).
63 Stine Høholt, 'Reverse Cannibalism: Introduction to *India: Art Now*', in Gether *et al.* (eds), *India: Art Now*, pp. 13–34, p. 32.
64 Ajay J. Sinha, 'Contemporary Indian art: a question of method', *Art Journal*, 58:3 (1999), 31–9, 38.
65 *Ibid.*
66 Holland Cotter, 'Ravinder G. Reddy', *New York Times* (12 October 2001).
67 Samira Rahmatullah, 'Rina Banerjee', in *The Matter Within: New Contemporary Art of India*, p. 26.
68 Laura Steward, 'A Whole Composed of Parts That Are Wholes: An Incomplete Picture of Rina Banerjee', in Anne Leclercq (ed.), *Rina Banerjee: Guimet vis à vis* (Paris: Musée Guimet, 2011), pp. 15–21, p. 19.
69 Rahmatullah, 'Rina Banerjee', p. 26.
70 Borggreen, 'Asian art on display', 6.
71 Rina Banerjee, 'Rina Banerjee: 500 words – as told to Zehra Jumabhoy', in *Artforum* (22 June 2011).
72 Turner and Webb, *Art and Human Rights*, p. 132.
73 Høholt, 'Reverse Cannibalism', p. 33.
74 Nick Baker, 'Managing the reputations of the new British sculptors', *Sculpture Journal* (2012), 74–84, 76–7, doi:10.3828/sj.2012.18 (accessed November 2016).
75 *Ibid.*, 80.
76 Niru Ratnam, 'Chris Ofili and the limits of hybridity', *New Left Review*, 1:235 (1999), 153–9, 153.
77 Christoph Becker (ed.), *Documenta IX Kurzführer\Guide* (Stuttgart: Edition Cantz, 1992), p. 119.
78 Richard Deacon, 1997, quoted in Baker, 'Managing the reputations', 79.
79 See: www.tate.org.uk/art/artworks/kapoor-as-if-to-celebrate-i-discovered-a-mountain-blooming-with-red-flowers-t03675 (accessed November 2016).
80 Anish Kapoor, quoted in Gayatri Sinha, 'Transcultural curating of art from India', *Arken Bulletin*, special issue 'Migration – Contemporary Art from India', no. 6 (2013), 53–62, 54.
81 M. Stancati, 'Anish Kapoor's homecoming', *India Real Time* (29 November 2010).
82 Rina Banerjee, 'Possessing Heritage', in Leclercq (ed.), *Rina Banerjee*, pp. 9–12, p. 12.
83 A critical interrogation of issues of forced migration, border politics, racism and inequality in migration is found in Demos, *The Migrant Image*. I will return to these in Chapter 6.

Mining the museum in an age of migration

4

Migratory aesthetics and artists with a migrant background can have various points of entry into museums, galleries and collections. The genre of artists' interventions is one of the most important in this regard because of its critical, transformative and bridge-building potential. After a brief introduction to the practice, this chapter examines interventions by three artists, Fred Wilson, Yinka Shonibare and Rina Banerjee, who all take a critical de- and postcolonial approach to the institutional structures and spaces of Western museums. Using their potentially disruptive and transformative interventions in American and French museums as examples, this chapter seeks to explore the potential of such interventions by artists at a time when Western cultural institutions need to be developing new policies of representation which reflect the fact that the societies and populations they cater for have been profoundly changed by migration.

Recent decades have witnessed a growing recognition that new forms of bridge-building, as well as more self-investigation, are needed in museums, and particularly in the Western institutions: the museums of art, ethnography and history. Since the 1970s, the meta-discursive activities commonly described as institutional critique have established a strong tradition of detailed analysis of networks of power and systems of representation. The practice of interventions by artists has arisen from this tradition. Institutional critique often uses museological practices themselves to question the ways in which history has been rewritten through the politics of collection and display;[1] and it has proved to be capable of revealing the cultural mechanisms at play in museums and other institutions that market or display art and cultural artefacts.[2] Projects by, for example, Michael Asher, Marcel Broodthaers and Hans Haacke have illustrated how an artwork is inseparable from its context and the significance of the museum experience and environment itself, and since the 1990s an increasing number of museums have been commissioning artists to respond to their collections.[3] New forms of collaborations with museum professionals have resulted from the development of this relationship between artists and host institutions, and as a consequence, artists in the 1990s and 2000s have been grounded not so much in an ideologically driven, oppositional and confrontational critique of cultural institutions but in a more reflective analytical approach, based on co-production.[4] There is now ample evidence that one of the most efficient means of deconstructing Western museums as cultural spaces is to invite an artist to stage an intervention in the museum, thereby temporarily transforming the relatively static display of a permanent collection into a living, self-reflective archive and an innovative exhibition context. As curator Lisa G. Corrin remarks, these types of projects and installations have formed a veritable movement that could be described as 'Artists Look at Museums, Museums Look at Themselves'.[5] Claire Robins, a specialist in educational strategies in relation to art and museums, has also stressed that 'In interventions artists are invited to "speak" not against the museum but with the museum.'[6] How do such interventions operate *inside* the system; and can artists' interventions help us envision what a 'postcolonial' museum, or a more inclusive museum for the age of migration, might be? And what could it do?

According to Robins, the term 'artists' interventions' describes a genre of art 'that becomes an interlocutor within the discourse of museum collections'.[7] The term is often used quite broadly, and uncritically, about the temporary insertion of contemporary art into the permanent collection of a cultural institution, so that 'contemporary art is experienced in an environment designated for other types of objects, for example historical artworks, specimens or artefacts'.[8]Although the methods of engagement with the taxonomies and narratives of museums differ greatly, there are some common denominators. An artist's intervention is 'an interpretive technology' that relies on dialogism and seeks to disturb and thereby change the existing structures. As a result, appropriation, disruption, parody and irony recur as favoured methods and tropes.[9]

As Robins observes, interventions by artists can be both disruptive and stabilising with regard to the institutionalised knowledge production they engage with, and there have been debates about the effects and inherent contradictions. Some commentators have criticised contemporary artists and museums for alienating audiences and catering only for the elites with an interest in art, while others have emphasised the contribution that can be made to positive developments in new approaches to the visitor experience and learning.[10] Although the methods employed in many interventionist artworks are indebted to avant-garde practices with a tradition of disruptive and parodic approaches, they are not necessarily radical gestures made in opposition to an allegedly conservative institution – in most cases, the artist has been invited in by the institution. Many artists' interventions do offer an epistemological critique of museological practices,[11] and commissioning an artist to propose a counter-narrative can be used strategically by an institution to signal a shift in the way its collections, identity and purposes are understood.[12] This was the case in two of the projects discussed below.

It is important to understand that such interventions are not at odds with the educational role of the museum since the inception of museums in the Enlightenment period and their subsequent establishment as an integral part of the public sphere of nation-states. Public museums can partake in the exercising of the constitutional right to dissent and 'so are fundamental to the Western concept of democracy'.[13] Counter-hegemonic interventions by artists, which challenge dominant narratives and the institutional limits of what can be said and shown, can be seen as a continuation of this democratic tradition, because they can make visible the previously invisible and open up a space for imagining other ways of thinking. As Claire Robins and museum educator Miranda Baxter conclude:

> Artists' interventions can be seen to carry on the constitutional right to propose dissent; they often occupy museums for such purposes, not in the way that might have been envisaged in the eighteenth century, nor as forms of logical argumentation, but as disruptions, interruptions, questions and subversions. They both act as fissures in the dominant discourses of galleries and museums and stand as part of a continuum of radical discursive possibilities intended for the public sphere.[14]

Artists' interventions and the legacies of colonialism

A well-known example of an interventionist practice by an artist is the American artist Fred Wilson's groundbreaking installation *Mining the Museum* at the Maryland Historical Society in 1992–93. This was based on a collaboration that allowed the artist to interview the staff and to have open access to the collection, including the objects and histories that had been hidden away in the museum's basement. *Mining the Museum* brought to light previously untold histories of African Americans and Native Americans in Maryland; and it thus supported the Historical Society's efforts to make its collections more relevant to greater Baltimore's mainly African-American population.[15] A particular characteristic of *Mining the Museum* was that it did not involve actual artworks by the artist but a curatorial selection and reinstallation of items from the collection in a way that invited visitors to reconsider the items on display as well as the ideological function of the exhibition itself as a knowledge technology imparting particular interpretations of history, thereby invariably suppressing others. In this case, the suppressed, or 'invisible', histories were the histories of slavery and racism in America. Wilson's critical, revisionist intent was summed up succinctly in a vitrine labelled *Metalwork 1793–1880*, in which a slave's iron shackles were displayed alongside the usual display of ornate silver goblets and elegant decanters, evoking for visitors one of the darkest and cruellest chapters of immigration to the United States and the history of forced migration: the transportation of millions of enslaved Africans to the Americas and the Caribbean.

Similarly, the room entitled *Modes of Transport, 1770–1910* (see figure 4.1) revealed a Ku Klux Klan hood resting in the sheltered space of a pram, contextualised by an early twentieth-century photograph of African-American nannies with white children in their prams,[16] reminding visitors of the continued racism, violence and persecution and social oppression of black people following the abolition of slavery in America.

The British-Nigerian artist Yinka Shonibare's installation *Garden of Love* at the Musée du quai Branly in Paris in 2007 was not an intervention in a museum collection like Fred Wilson's *Mining the Museum*, yet it had a similar disruptive effect on the institution's display policies in the way that it exposed how colonial history permeates European ethnographic museums. The Quai Branly Museum features indigenous art, cultures and civilisations from Africa, Asia, Oceania and the Americas. Seventy per cent of its objects were 'acquired' between 1880 and 1939, at the height of European imperialism.[17] It is telling of the interplay between Shonibare's installation, the permanent collection and the museum environment that one critic commented

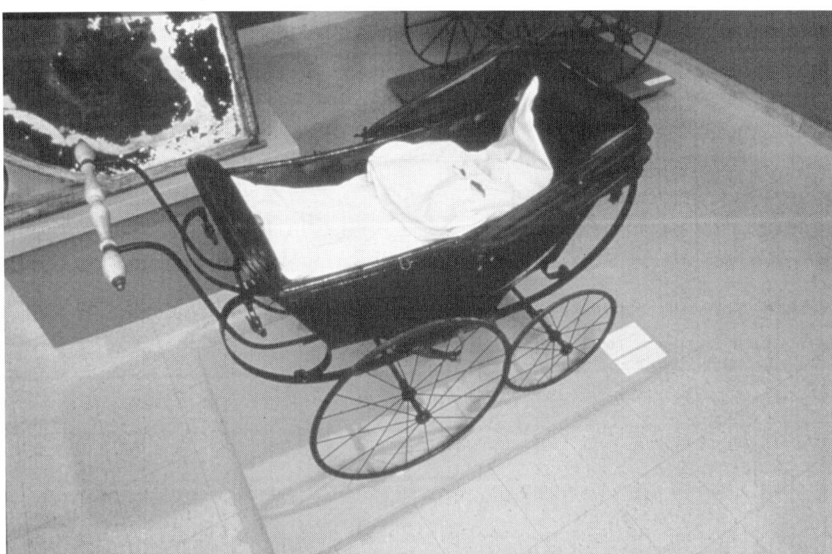

4.1 Fred Wilson, *Modes of Transport, 1770–1910*, detail, from *Mining the Museum: An Installation by Fred Wilson*, 1992–93. Baby carriage (c. 1908), hood (twentieth century), makers unknown. Installation view, the Contemporary Museum and Maryland Historical Society, Baltimore. © Fred Wilson. Image courtesy of the artist and Pace Gallery.

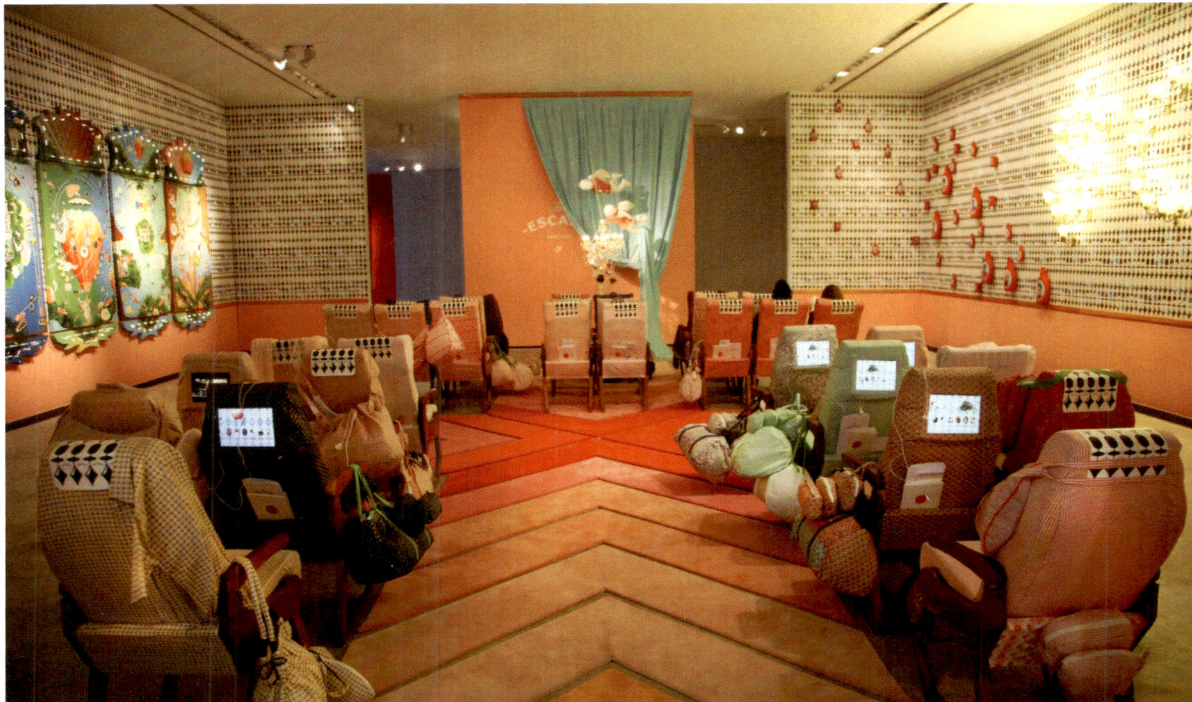

Plate 1 Thugral & Tagra, *THE ESCAPE! Resume/Reset*, 2012. Mixed media. Installation view from *India: Art Now*, Arken Museum of Modern Art, 2012. © Thugral & Tagra. Photograph courtesy of the artists.

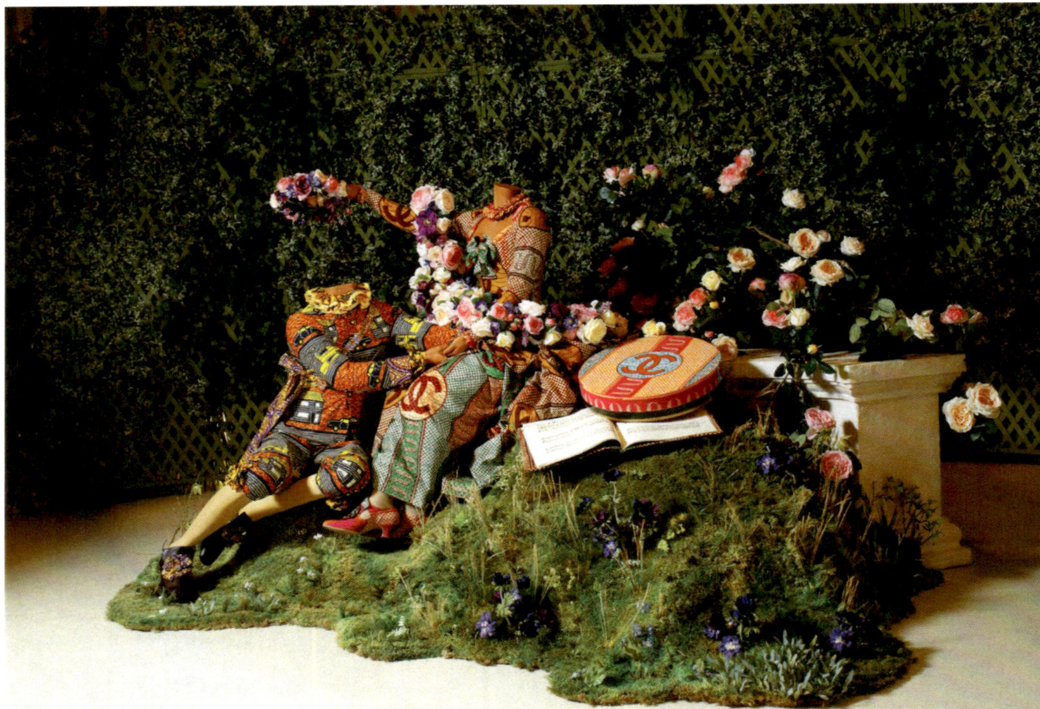

Plate 2 Yinka Shonibare, *The Crowning* from *Garden of Love*, 2007, Musée du quai Branly, Paris, 2007. Two fibreglass mannequins, Dutch wax printed cotton textile, shoes, coir matting, artificial silk flowers. 160 x 280 x 210 cm. Arts Council Collection, Southbank Centre, London. Acquired in honour of Sir Peter Bazalgette, 2017. © Yinka Shonibare. Photograph: Patrick Gries.

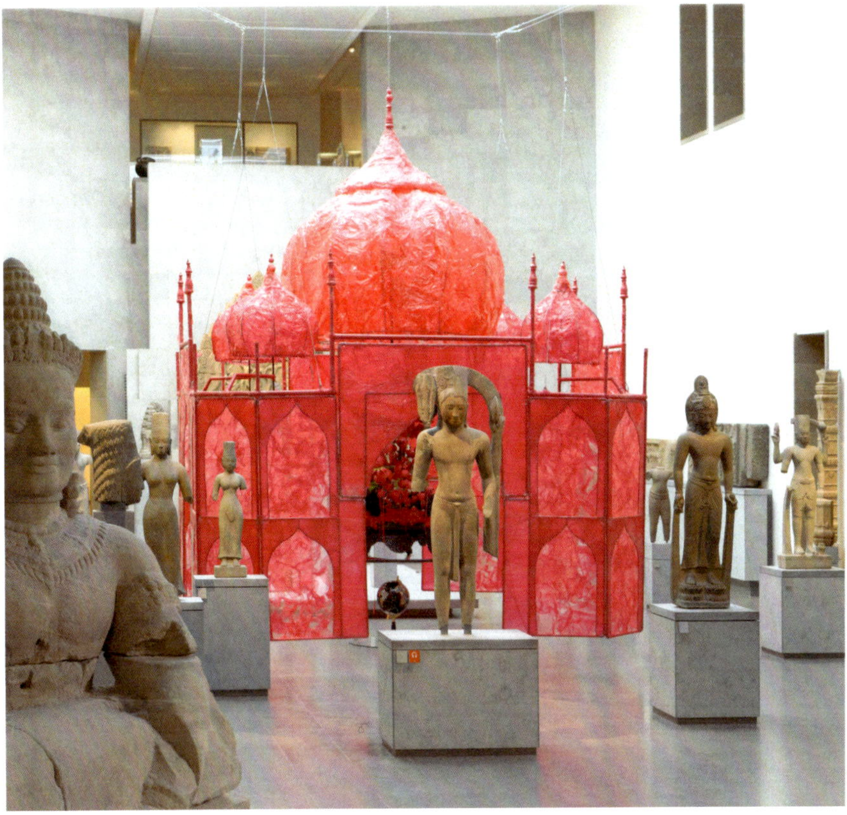

Plate 3 Rina Banerjee, *Take me, take me, take me ... to the Palace of Love*, 2003. Plastic, antique Anglo-Indian Bombay dark wood chair, steel and copper framework, floral picks, foam balls, cowrie shells, quilting pins, red-coloured moss, antique stone globe, glass, synthetic fabric, shells, fake birds. 515 x 410 x 410 cm. Installation view, *Chimeras of India and the West*, Musée Guimet, Paris, 2011. © Rina Banerjee. Photograph courtesy of the artist and Galerie Nathalie Obadia, Paris/Brussels.

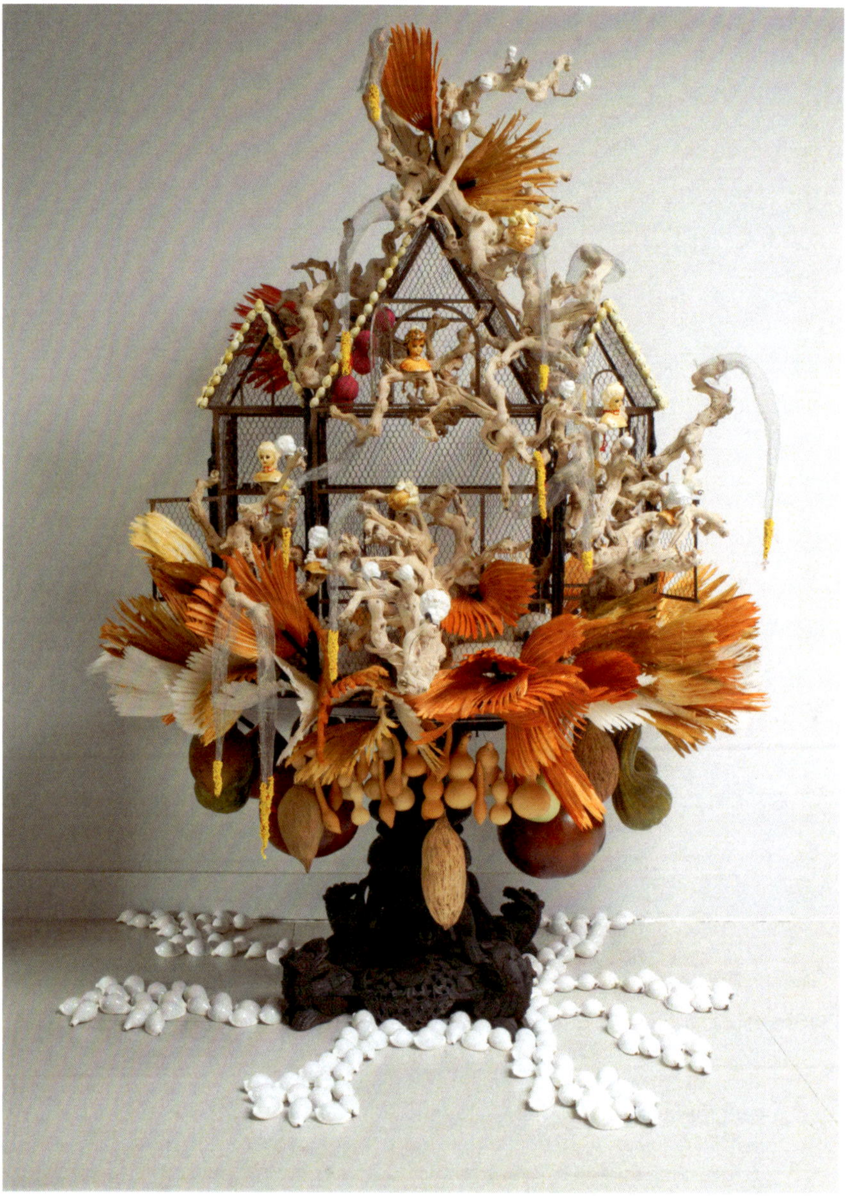

Plate 4 Rina Banerjee, *Her captivity was once someone's treasure and even pleasure but she blew and flew away took root which grew, we knew this was like no other feather, a third kind of bird that perched on vine intertwined was neither native nor her queen's daughters, a peculiar other*, 2011. Mixed media. 213 x 213 x 183 cm. Purchased with the Michel Roux Acquisitions Fund, Cornell Fine Arts Museum. © Rina Banerjee.

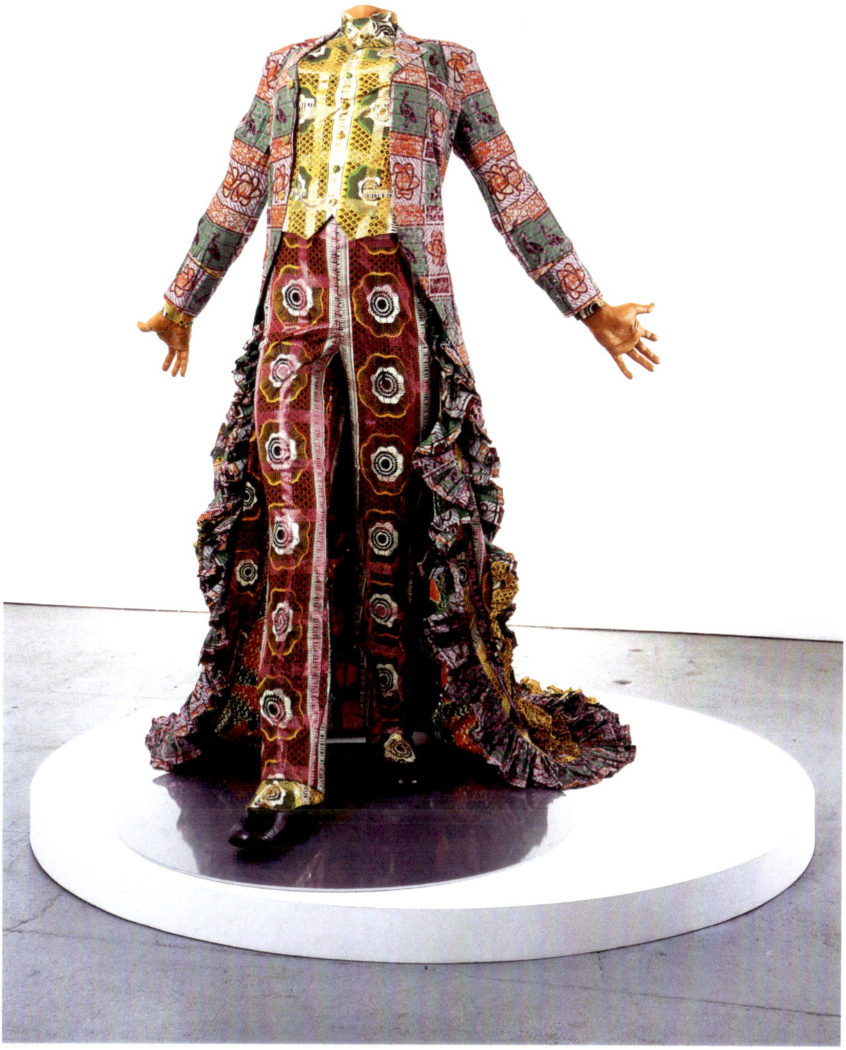

Plate 5 Yinka Shonibare, *Big Boy*, 2002. Fibreglass mannequin, Dutch wax printed cotton textile, leather and steel baseplate. Figure: 215 x 170 x 140 cm, plinth: 220 cm diameter. Art Institute of Chicago, gift of Susan and Lewis Manilow. © Yinka Shonibare. Photograph: Ahlburg Keate, courtesy of Yinka Shonibare MBE and Stephen Friedman Gallery, London.

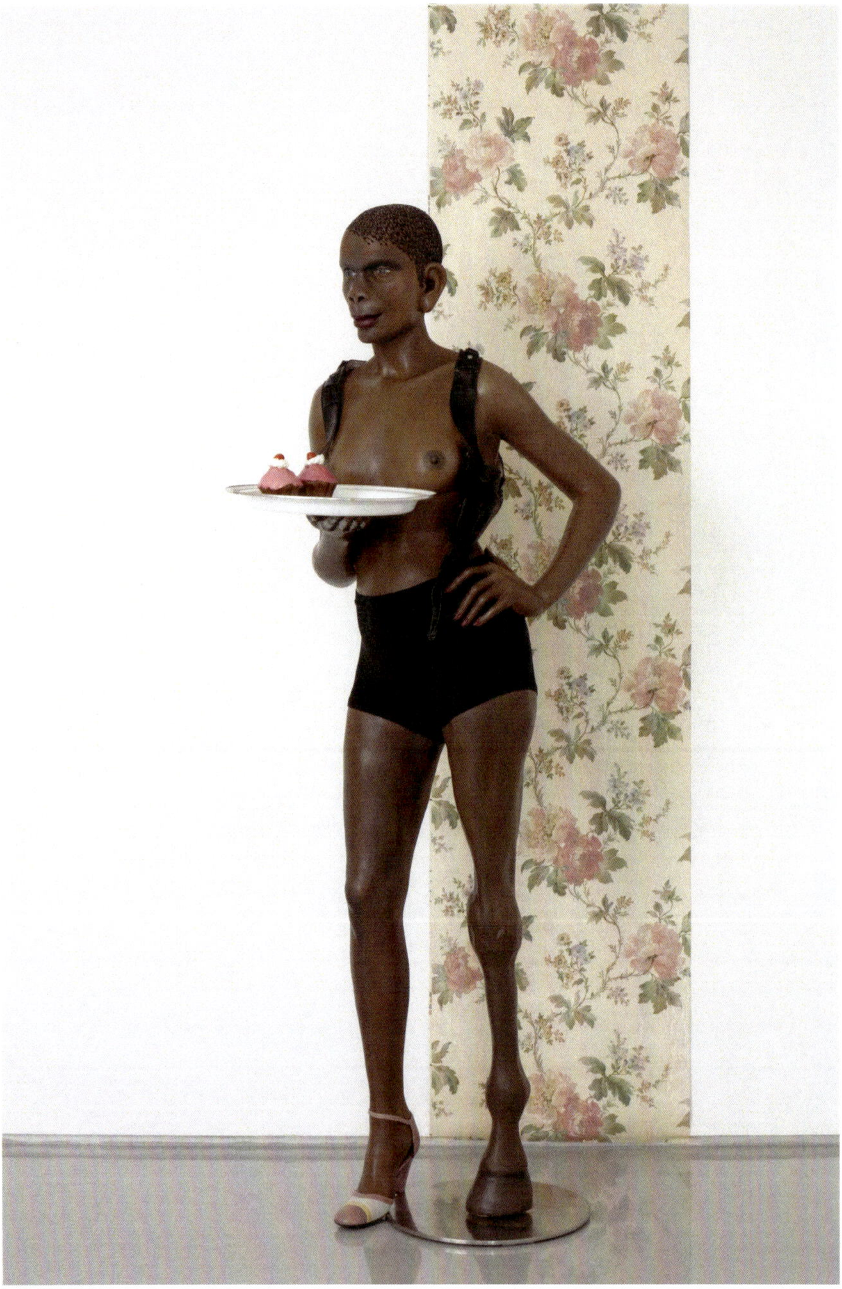

Plate 6 Bharti Kher, *Arione*, 2004. Mixed media. 180 x 50 x 50 cm. © Bharti Kher. Photograph: Shankar Natarajan, courtesy of the artist and Galerie Nature Morte, New Delhi.

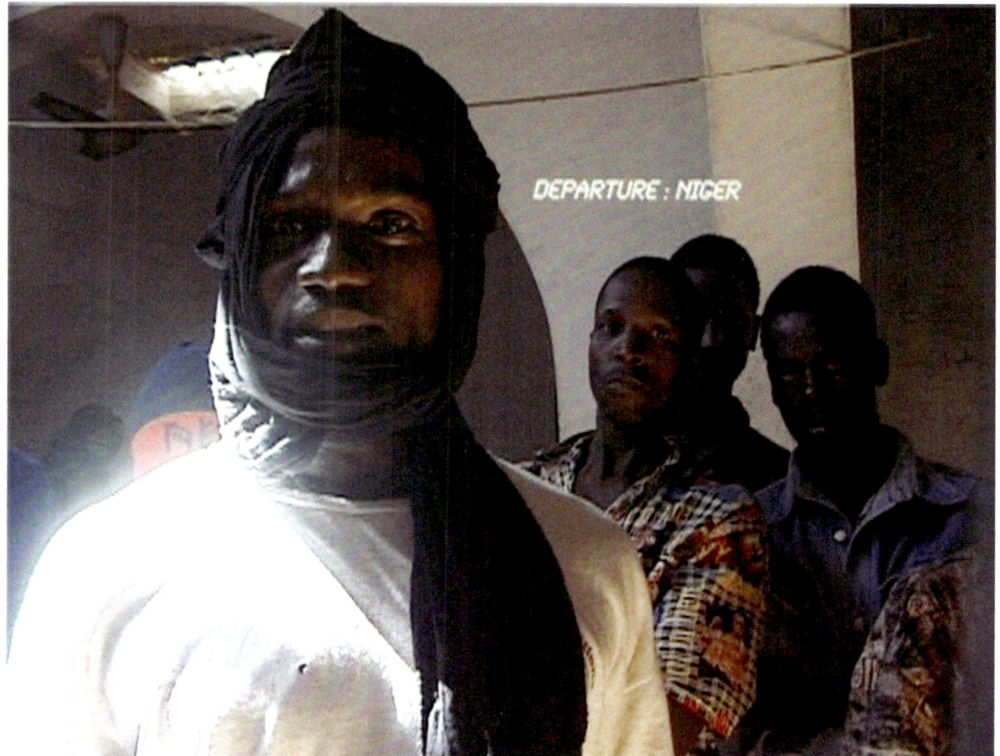

Plate 7 Ursula Biemann, still from *Sahara Chronicle*, 'Deportation Prison Laayoune' (2006–7). Video collection, 78 min. © Ursula Biemann. Image courtesy of the artist.

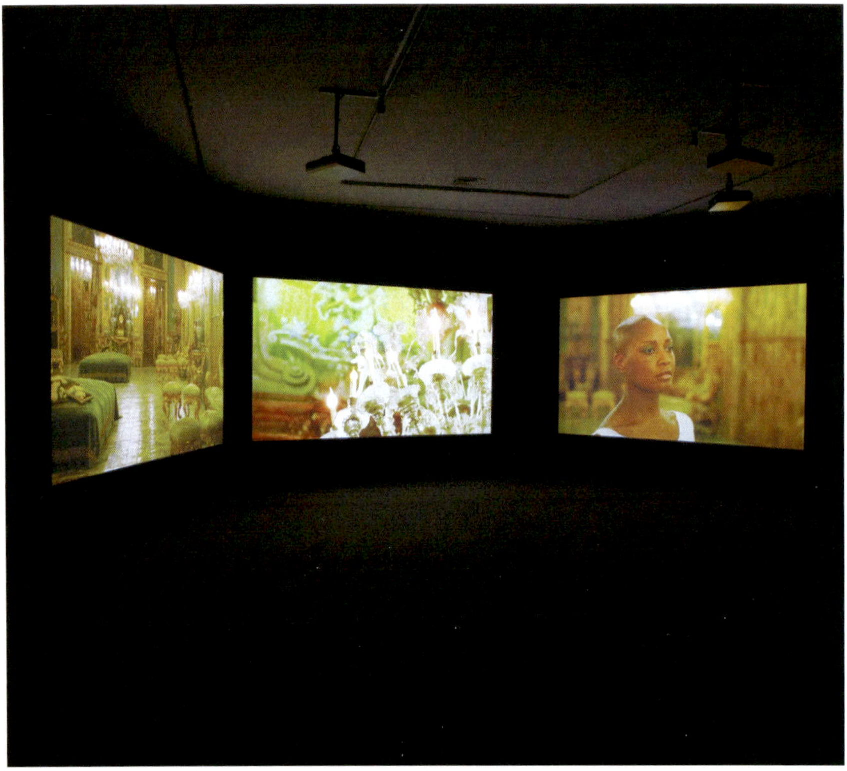

Plate 8 Isaac Julien, *Western Union: Small Boats*, 2007. Installation view, Galería Helga de Alvear Madrid, 2008. Three-screen projection. 35 mm colour film, DVD/HD transfer. 5.1 SR sound. Total running time: 18 mins 22 secs. © Isaac Julien. Photograph: Joaquin Cortes, courtesy of the artist and Galeria Helga de Alvear.

that Shonibare was 'doing a Fred Wilson'. The labyrinthine installation led the critic to take the wrong exit, thereby finding himself in the permanent collection and confronted with a maroon-red box with funerary sculptures made from richly decorated human skulls, which could be perceived as a Fred Wilson style intervention, although the sculptures were, in effect, exhibits in the section 'Nouvelle-Irlande, arts du Pacifique Sud'.[18]

Shonibare was prompted to use the French 'picturesque garden' to launch an institutional critique from the museum's garden, which contains plants not indigenous to Europe. He linked the site-specific 'garden' motif to his own fascination with the lavish lifestyle of the aristocracy in eighteenth-century Europe, when members of the ruling class lived in unimaginable luxury and enjoyed themselves in sumptuous castles and secluded gardens while revolution was brewing around them. The three tableaux entitled *The Confession*, *The Crowning* (see plate 2) and *The Pursuit*, the core elements of *Garden of Love*, staged this pre-revolutionary moment by paraphrasing images of couples in the series *The Progress of Love* painted by the quintessential Rococo painter Jean Honoré Fragonard for Madame du Barry's pavilion in Louveciennes in 1770–71. Contrary to Fragonard's silk-clad, rosy-cheeked aristocrats, Shonibare's figures wore Rococo costumes made of African-print fabrics. Originally produced by Dutch colonisers anticipating an Indonesian market, these fabrics were sold to customers in West African colonies and later became an emblem of African identity and pan-African nationalism. As a result, they are invested with both colonial and postcolonial connotations, which Shonibare exploits in his efforts to decolonise the minds of his audiences and to make viewers understand that coloniality is a constituent of modern Western societies, and not something external to them. Moreover, the heads of the mannequin figures were removed as a warning that a bloody revolution may also be imminent in the contemporary world, with its increasingly uneven distribution of wealth.

Literary scholar Madeleine Dobie has examined the longstanding silence in France surrounding colonial slavery. Such silence veils the fact that during its history as a slaving nation, France imported three times as many enslaved persons to its colonies in the Americas as the British North American colonies and the US combined. In fact, the island of Martinique alone imported more enslaved persons than the US. During the eighteenth century, French vessels are estimated to have transported over a million people from Africa to the New World. At the same time, France was also leading the trade in sugar, coffee, indigo and a number of other tropical commodities. Thus, by the mid-eighteenth century, it was France, not England, that was the world's leading producer of sugar, and it had a dominant share of the global coffee market.[19] The circulation of colonial commodities was an important source of revenue not only for individual traders and investors but also for the state. Historian

Robert Louis Stein has calculated that in the 1780s – i.e. only a decade after Fragonard painted his visions of an aristocratic life of love and luxury – a full half of France's exports to other European countries consisted of goods from the colonies, and colonial trade generated employment opportunities for many French workers.[20] Dobie contends that one of the reasons that the so-called *vieilles colonies*, which were so economically important, were not culturally visible in France is that the mercantilist principles of French colonial policy subordinated the colonies to the metropole, meaning that the colonies were not viewed as an integral part of France. Slavery was 'out of sight and out of mind in safely distant "offshore locations"'.[21] Another reason why France's involvement in slavery in her Caribbean colonies has been repressed is, Dobie explains, that the *vieilles colonies* have, for the most part, been treated as a colonial prehistory superseded by the colonial projects of the nineteenth and twentieth century with their *mission civilisatrice*. She concludes: 'Whereas French colonial rule in Africa and Asia can, at least to an extent, be dressed up in the rhetoric of assimilation and civilizing mission, France's two hundred-year participation in the Atlantic slave trade simply does not lend itself to this kind of recuperation.'[22]

Dobie's point underlines the critical cut and interruptive force of Shonibare's decision to displace Fragonard's French aristocrats to the Quai Branly Museum with its collection of indigenous art and cultures from safely distant 'offshore locations'. To associate his exhibition with the museum garden, Shonibare placed his three tableaux in a faux garden labyrinth (constructed by exhibition scenographer Régis Guignard), which visitors had to enter to see and circumnavigate the individual tableaux.[23] The artificiality of his installation enhanced the 'artful naturalness' of the exotic garden outside.[24] As Amanda Gilvin has noted, the delight of losing yourself among the trellises covered with fake ivy, and the feeling of disorientation, helped visitors re-enact the satisfaction of discovery when they stumbled on one of the couples. The labyrinth mimicked the experience of wandering in the museum's garden and among its collections. It also offered multiple perspectives on the individual tableaux through carefully placed windows from the passageways of the labyrinth into the spaces with the figures. Sometimes visitors would even find dead ends, where they could see but not enter other exhibition spaces.[25] In this way, the ethnographic museum was put into critical perspective as a system that assigns fixed places to objects-as-signs and fixed points of view to audiences-as-receivers.

Four years after Shonibare showed *Garden of Love* at the Quai Branly Museum, another museum in Paris, the Musée Guimet, invited Rina Banerjee to engage in a dialogue with their collection of art from Asia, which consists primarily of art related to the religions of Central, East and South East Asia.[26] Like Fred Wilson's *Mining the Museum*, Rina Banerjee's

2011 exhibition *Chimeras of India and the West* reflected a wish for change already formulated by people in the institution who were well aware that this might necessitate the kind of controlled transgression that artists' interventions offer. In her catalogue entry, curator Caroline Arhuero explained that the Musée Guimet invited Banerjee as part of their endeavours to 'move away from' the orientalist and Eurocentric presentation of Asian art as curiosities. As a representative of 'the society of a diaspora where the notion of heritage is perceived in a different light', Banerjee was expected to stage an intervention that would revolve around the relationship between Asian cultural heritage and diasporic experience. Arhuero hoped that this might help shift the perspective away from the binary opposition between Western and Eastern cultures that had historically shaped the museum and instead 'reveal the exchanges between and multiplicity of cultures'.[27] In *Chimeras of India and the West*, Banerjee inserted some of her own recent works into different rooms in the collection so that they would initiate a dialogue between her contemporary 'diasporic' work and the mostly ancient pieces in the collection. Visitors would not encounter them as a group, like 'a Rina Banerjee exhibition'; the works would crop up here and there as strange and colourful things that did not really 'fit in' and thus disturb the overall impression of a museum for Asian arts of the past. When visitors walked through the collection, the individual works would intrude into their field of vision like an unexpected and deviant 'activity' in the room, signalling that something else is happening here.

Museums are spaces that generate narratives, events and experiences, and, thereby, give rise to new cultural memories and other ways of remembering history. Postcolonial perspectives have effectively demonstrated the entanglement of 'us' and 'them', 'here' and 'there' by reading colonisation as part of a transnational and transcultural process that produces multiple connections and migratory forms and forces.[28] In addition, the perspectives developed in postcolonial criticism have, in many ways, become indispensable to the interrogation of discrepant global practices.[29] There is no doubt that artists' interventions such as those of Wilson, Shonibare and Banerjee are capable of disrupting the traditional narratives and order of the objects held and displayed in Western museums, and of questioning accepted understandings of history and systems of classification. Can they also help us envision a more inclusive and critically interrogative 'postcolonial' museum that is tuned to the societal conditions and historical changes resulting from intensified migration?

Postcoloniality and decoloniality

In recent years, an agonistic discourse on 'decolonial thinking' and 'decolonial aesthetics' has emerged from the broader field of postcolonial studies and theory. In his essay on Fred Wilson's *Mining the Museum*, 'Museums in the Colonial Horizon of Modernity', Walter Mignolo made a case for a clear-cut distinction between 'postcoloniality' and 'decoloniality'. According to Mignolo, Wilson's intervention in the collection of the Maryland Historical Society was a decolonial and hence political reminder of the 'underlying syntax' of coloniality and 'the hegemonic relations of power' that shape museums culturally, socially and economically.[30]

In what follows, I will use Mignolo's assertive interpretation as a bridgehead for a reconsideration of two issues central to the idea of the 'postcolonial' museum: firstly, whether it is possible to differentiate sharply between postcolonial and decolonial thinking, or should decoloniality be viewed, rather, as a faction of postcoloniality. And secondly, whether the extent to which Mignolo equates an art project with the politics of decoloniality captures the transformative potential of artists' interventions in museums in an age of migration, when the much desired diversity of audiences should also be mirrored in the chosen exhibits and modes of display –meaning, in the histories that are told and the way in which they are told. Although there is considerable overlap between the problematics of colonialism and those of racism, I will leave the categories of 'race' and 'blackness' in the background in order to focus on the critique of colonialism and the decolonising potential of Wilson's, Shonibare's and Banerjee's projects.

In Mignolo's understanding, postcolonial and decolonial thinking are two different spheres. He defines postcoloniality as an offspring of Western postmodernism. Briefly, it is a critique of European colonialism that emerged in Western Europe and the US, and which brought French post-structuralism into dialogue with Orientalism, and subaltern studies in India. Decoloniality, on the other hand, seeks to unmask the inseparability of modernity and coloniality and to 'delink' from the 'Eurocentered', post-structuralist projects of postmodernity and postcoloniality. It emerged from the critical traditions of Latin America, particularly from the writings of the Peruvian sociologist Anibal Quijano in the late 1980s. Quijano introduced the concept of 'coloniality' as the invisible and constitutive side of modernity, and it found a continuous source of inspiration in the countless social movements and uprisings of indigenous activist groups in Latin America and elsewhere.[31]

In the manifesto 'Decolonial Aesthetics (I)' (written jointly by Mignolo and a group of other thinkers, artists and activists), decoloniality is understood as a political and ideological project in which artistic practices and activism play a leading role. In addition, decolonial aesthetics is seen as a revival of the historical avant-garde's belief in the emancipatory power of its own artistic practices and as a representative of community-based and coalitional interculturalism 'from-below'; as opposed to multiculturalism, which the authors claim to be state-enforced 'from-above':

> Decolonial aesthetics, in particular, and decoloniality in general have joined the liberation of sensing and sensibilities trapped by modernity and its darker side: coloniality. Decoloniality endorses interculturality (which has been conceptualized by organized communities) and delinks from multiculturalism (which has been conceptualized and implemented by the State) … Decolonial transmodern aesthetics is intercultural, inter-epistemic, inter-political, inter-aesthetical and inter-spiritual but always from perspectives of the global south and the former-Eastern Europe.[32]

Postcolonial and decolonial thinking obviously have different intellectual pedigrees. As opposed to the deconstructive approach and dialectic perspective that characterise postcolonial theories concerning hybridity and cultural translation, the polemical proponents of decoloniality adopt a more polarising geopolitical perspective. It is founded on a dualistic view of a world divided into what often comes across as a hemisphere of Evil and a hemisphere of Good: an imperialist North dedicated to imposing on all others 'Western imperial reason'[33] and a liberating South, including post-communist Eastern Europe. Whereas the first hemisphere is demonised as purely racist, colonialist, capitalist and universalist, the latter is defined as the home of convivial 'pluriversalism' and decolonial emancipation.[34] Despite these differences in perspective, the two positions seem to share some basic assumptions and aims.

Mignolo claims that the basic premise in decolonial thinking is that 'coloniality is constitutive of modernity and there is no modernity without coloniality'.[35] However, this assumption and line of enquiry is fundamental to postcolonial thinking, too. Moreover, when reading Janet Wilson, Christina Şandru and Sarah Lawson Welsh's stocktaking of the aims and institutional position of postcolonial studies,[36] one gathers that there are more similarities than differences between the postcolonial and decolonial 'projects'. Both take as their object of study underprivileged subjectivities, marginalised political entities and the violence of colonial and imperial agendas; and both primarily articulate their critique from institutional positions in major, often Western, universities. Walter Mignolo is Professor of Literature and Director of the Center for Global Studies and the Humanities at Duke University. He co-authored the book *Learning to Unlearn: Decolonial Reflections from Eurasia and the Americas* (2012) with Madina Tlostanova, who joined the unit for Interdisciplinary Gender Studies at Linköping University in Sweden in 2015 – although at the time she was co-author, she was Professor in the History of Philosophy and Cultural Studies at the Peoples' Friendship University of Russia in Moscow.[37] In other words, decoloniality does not evade the accusations of academic privilege and lack of representativity regularly launched against the metropolitan spearheads of postcolonial studies.[38]

To conclude, Mignolo's sharp distinction between postcoloniality and decoloniality seems to be more rhetorical than actual, although Mignolo and Tlostanova claim that decolonial epistemologies 'will be constructed with their "back" toward the West', thereby also 'delinking' from westernised postcolonial studies.[39] Rather than seeing postcolonial studies and decolonial thinking as discrete fields of knowledge, I will argue that decolonial thinking could be seen as a variant of the wider field of critical engagements with coloniality understood as the structures of power, control and hegemony emerging with the era of modernity, which is also the era of colonialism; a variant that is not confined to academia but builds coalitions between the spheres of art, activism and academia. Decolonial thinking is thus a certain mode of practising critique which favours an interventionist mode of 'doing' or performing art, culture and politics, with the aim of 'mining', and thereby undermining, colonial perceptions of the world. If decoloniality is understood as a critical, interventionist and emancipatory strategy, it is of particular relevance to the revision of European museums.

I will now return to Wilson, Shonibare and Banerjee in order to substantiate my proposition that decolonial interventions can be a means of turning museums into sites of contamination that are capable of including formerly repressed histories and migrating memories. Borrowing Mignolo and Tlostanova's phrase, I wish to propose that artists' interventions can be a means of 'learning to unlearn in order to relearn'.[40] Mignolo and Tlostanova do not glean this expression from Western critical theory, but from the documents of Amawtay Wasi (The Intercultural University of the People and Nations of Ecuador). In other words, their choice of phrasing is part of a deliberate strategy that aims at introducing a canon of critical thinkers from 'the South', thereby recasting critical theory within the frame of 'an-other' geography and politics of knowledge.[41] I propose that the three artists deploy similar decolonial strategies.

As a first step, I will scrutinise Mignolo's reading of Wilson's installation. In 'Museums in the Colonial Horizon of Modernity', Mignolo opens with the question of how museums with historical roots in the logic of coloniality can contribute to the decolonisation of knowledge and become places to learn how to unlearn, in order to relearn.[42] He builds his argument on Wilson's *Mining the Museum*, which he considers to be 'an exemplary case of a decolonizing perspective' and 'an exemplar of epistemic and aesthetic disobedience'.[43] Mignolo is primarily concerned with explaining the basic tenets of decolonial thinking and how coloniality continues to be 'an underlying syntax' that affects 'the entire socio-economic system and subject formation'.[44] As Mignolo's critique is not only aimed at museums, but also at Western imperial knowledge systems in general, he only briefly introduces the three most well-known displays of *Mining the Museum* before jumping to his conclusion that its most powerful element was 'a decolonial statement in the heart of the museum which is an imperial/colonial (and of course national) institution'.[45] He then proceeds to criticise the art world's recognition of Wilson as amounting to an assimilation of the disobedient artist into 'the imperial paradigm'.[46]

To Mignolo, Wilson's art is nothing but a political statement that constitutes a decolonising reminder of the museum's underlying colonial syntax, and it is the political content that makes *Mining the Museum* 'one of the enormous contributions … to the decolonization of being and knowledge'.[47] The aesthetic aspects of Wilson's installation are no more part of Mignolo's understanding of Wilson's work than the history of slavery was a visible part of the collection of the Maryland Historical Society before Wilson so effectively mined it. Only when Wilson put the slave shackles, the Ku Klux Klan hood and the photo of the African-American nannies into his installation did the items that had formerly been stored away become part of the public displays in the museum. Since Mignolo does not explore Wilson's artistic method, he fails to answer the critical question of what it is about his installation – its strategy of display and the modes of attention it invited – that constitutes its decolonising perspective. Surely, it is not the slave shackles and the Ku Klux Klan hood in themselves. Rather than simply ignoring the connections between the postcolonial *and* the aesthetic, as Mignolo does, I will argue that in a museum context, where visual display is a primary medium of communication, it is crucial to consider the aesthetic aspects in order to grasp art's decolonising potential. If institutional interventions by artists are instances of 'politics' and emancipation from 'an underlying syntax' of colonial forms of knowledge, as Mignolo suggests, they are instances of politics performed *by means of* aesthetics.

The postcolonial and the aesthetic

The little-examined notions of 'a postcolonial aesthetic' and 'decolonial aesthetics' will serve as starting points for a consideration of how 'aesthetics' figure in postcolonial discourses. I have adopted the notion of a postcolonial aesthetic from Elleke Boehmer's essay 'A Postcolonial Aesthetic: Repeating Upon the Present', and of decolonial aesthetics from the 'Decolonial Aesthetics (I)' manifesto.[48] As Boehmer points out, postcolonial critics are generally hostile to matters 'solely aesthetic', considering this a Western, middle-class indulgence. They tend to avoid the word 'aesthetic' and to read artworks – in the widest sense – as testimonies, political critique or ideological manifestos. As a result, they often come to rely on a reductive and generally unacknowledged notion of aesthetics and aesthetic modes of attention.[49] Judging from the 'Decolonial Aesthetics (I)'manifesto and Mignolo's reading of Wilson's exhibition, this critique also applies to decolonial thinkers, too. According to

Boehmer, the unreflecting implicit notion of aesthetics in postcolonial scholarship typically invokes polyglot layering and cross-cultural mixings – like the manifesto's declaration of decolonial aesthetics as being 'inter-aesthetical' and aimed at plurality or 'pluriversalism'. Such invocations rest fundamentally on what Boehmer calls a 'mimetic aesthetic', i.e. an aesthetic of imitation in which the work is presumed to merely mirror postcolonial cultural politics or social conditions[50] rather than generate its own response and interpretation. It is, indeed, a mimetic aesthetic that underlies Mignolo's understanding of Wilson's work as a political critique of colonialism.

Although I wish to highlight the issue of aesthetics in postcolonial discourses, I hesitate to speak of postcolonial or decolonial aesthetics. Artists working with a postcolonial or decolonial perspective are often deeply entangled in the institutional and economic structures of the Western art world and draw on movements in Western mainstream art such as conceptual art, institutional critique and installation. Care should be taken therefore not to validate neo-essentialist notions of a particular postcolonial or decolonial aesthetics, and promote the illusion of the singularity and detachment of postcolonial or decolonial art. For example, Wilson's work is based on the strategies of conceptual art and institutional critique,[51] whereas Shonibare's draws heavily on Western art history and installation art. Banerjee's work is based on the techniques of assemblage and installation, and generally revolves ambiguously around the recognition and disavowal of Western Orientalism. However, this complicity with the Western economic, social, cultural and art institutional systems does not stifle these artists' critique; on the contrary, complicity is the very precondition for their decolonising infiltration of Western institutions in order to launch their critique *from within* the institution.

Despite these reservations, I use the terms in question as my starting points to emphasise the centrality of 'aesthetics' to any exploration of how postcoloniality and decoloniality are articulated in art and culture. We cannot grasp how artists such as Wilson, Shonibare and Banerjee articulate a post- or decolonial critique without analysing their respective artistic methods. Without attention to artistic forms and languages, we cannot comprehend what it is within art, or in particular works of art, that performs postcolonial or decolonial work. Only through aesthetic analysis can we discover *how* interventionist strategies can bring repressed histories and the museum's inherent power-knowledge systems to light.

As Boehmer points out, 'the postcolonial entails a definition drawn not from the *work* but from the *world*'.[52] It primarily denotes history, not aesthetic form. Thus, I will use Boehmer's definition of the term 'aesthetic' as referring to a concern with the work's generic and formal aspects and its connotative language as a critical part of a work's content. It follows that 'form' is *not* defined as something autonomous but as an element that actively shapes the work's content, and is complicit with that content and with the contexts the work is situated in. Consequently, 'aesthetic' implies attention to form as well as a concern not to relate a work of art solely to historical, social and political frames of reference. Although the topic of the work emanates from outside, from the world and its injustices, the artist has felt that this could only find adequate expression in a particular kind of work. Thus, the work must be read on its own artistic terms, insisting on its particular modes of articulation and reception.[53]

Mieke Bal's distinction between 'an art of politics' and 'an art of the political' supports this definition of the 'aesthetic'. The former is an art of didactic political statements; the latter uses aesthetics as a weapon that moves people, so that their perspectives may change.[54] The decolonising effect of Fred Wilson's *Mining the Museum* is not only explained by the installation's rather obvious antiracist and anticolonial contents – its function as 'an art of politics'. Its deconstructive disclosure of the museum's politics of exhibiting, and of its ideological role as a social institution, relies on Wilson's subtle use of artistic and curatorial means to move his audiences in *affective* ways. The sensory impact of his works stirs bodily, emotional and reflective responses, which are not so easily controlled and politically uniform as Mignolo's reading of Wilson's installation suggests. As Wilson himself has observed, his juxtaposition of objects traditionally kept apart functions as 'one way of unlocking [history] without a didactic tone – allowing the objects to speak to each other'.[55] The Maryland museum's director of education, Judy Van Dyke, also stressed the variety of reactions of some of the visitors, especially to the Klan hood: 'One black man said to me that it was almost humorous. I was blown away … And another black man said, "Well, I don't see anything funny about it. To me it's not funny at all. I've had personal experience with the Klan in Louisiana and I can hardly look at this. I am sweating right now, just looking at it."'[56] Wilson's emphatically corporeal juxtaposition of the child's pram and the adult-size hood functioned as a visual metaphor for how enslaved African Americans, and later African-American citizens, were forced to nurture the baby masters whose cruelty and violence would later make them sweat with fear.

Reading Mignolo against the grain, the most interesting points become the tiny affective cracks in his otherwise seamless political argument. Contrary to the visitor who broke out in a sweat on encountering Wilson's intervention, Mignolo 'shivered' when confronted with the juxtaposition of the pram and the Klan hood. When Mignolo saw Wilson's pairing of pedestals supporting busts of famous Westerners from the museum's collection with empty pedestals with the names of famous local Marylanders who were *not* represented in the museum collection, 'The impact was like a slap in the face.'[57] In addition, the unusual experience of seeing a bust of Napoleon placed on a pedestal so low that visitors were looking down on the emperor left Mignolo bewildered because the unfamiliar debasement produced 'some strange sensation in your body and in your brain'.[58] It could be inferred that Wilson's juxtapositions caused an aesthetic shock that stirred ambiguous sensations not easily verbalised but capable of disrupting naturalised modes of perception and producing fresh political insight. Mignolo's article is, in itself, an eloquent and thought-provoking testimony to this effect.

To substantiate my claim that artworks and artistic interventions derive a great deal of their decolonising energy from the 'aesthetic' and the way form 'shapes' content, I will turn to Shonibare's palpable use of aesthetic seduction. Like Wilson, Shonibare highlights the complexity and reciprocity of interracial and colonial relations. Not only did Shonibare's *Garden of Love* manage to smuggle artworks loaded with references to canonical masterpieces of Western art history into an ethnographic museum otherwise reserved for non-Western 'indigenous' art, but by adding his artworks to a museum of the 'Other' Shonibare also succeeded in provincialising – or *indigenising* – Europe.

The Quai Branly Museum was intended as a gesture of respect for the arts and cultures of the tribal peoples of the Americas, Africa, Asia and Oceania. However, some reasoned critiques of neo-primitivism were expressed when the Museum opened in 2006.[59] It could, therefore, be said that one outcome of Shonibare's installation was to filter European culture through the neo-primitivist aestheticisation of the museum. In the manner of an ethnographer, he made the European colonisers the objects of his curiosity, thereby reversing the gaze: 'These members of the aristocracy, as a modern African, I find in a way that they are objects of curiosity, in a kind of reverse way. So the fetish for me, as an African, is the eighteenth-century European culture, whilst their fetish is the African mask!'[60]

At the Quai Branly, the artifice of 'illusion' and the 'work of art' coexist uneasily with the realism of ethnography and history. As a result, the balance between ethnography and aesthetics has been the focus of the debate at issue, with the neo-primitivism and aestheticism of the permanent display area being the main point of criticism. As James Clifford has noted, in a critique of the museum's architecture designed by Jean Nouvel, the neo-*Naturvölker* concept of the architect's spectacular building becomes oppressive here, overpowering the curatorial attempts to claim conceptual space for the displayed objects.[61] Classification is a way of maintaining the order of a system; an object that appears 'out of place' disrupts the order. The presence of an exhibition by a big name in the global art world such as Shonibare made the distinction between fine art and ethnographic artefacts even more uncertain and enhanced the aestheticisation already present in the display of the ethnographical collection.

But what about politics? Here it is useful to recall Bal's distinction. While an art of politics risks falling into propaganda, Bal argues that an art of the political 'demonstrates that the political impact is not dependent on political statements'. On the contrary, '[the] political of art must stay aloof of politics in order to be effective'.[62] With its combination of unequivocal political messages and affective impact, Wilson's installation functioned as both. Shonibare's garden was an art of the political, seeking to move audiences politically by aesthetic means: luscious colours, titillating eroticism, suggestive decapitation and an eye-opening ethnographic recontextualisation of European culture. It is to be wondered, therefore, whether the affective impact of art may move spectators more than the immediate political statements that count for so much with Mignolo.

Mimicry in the museum

The Musée Guimet invited Rina Banerjee to make an intervention in the hope that this could help the institution get beyond the orientalist and Eurocentric outlook on which the Museum's collection was originally founded. That some visitors may experience the Guimet Museum as an alluring cabinet of Eastern curiosities, and that Banerjee was aware of this is evident from the way she describes her own impression of the place, in a talk she gave shortly after the exhibition had closed:

> I have to say this is one of the most amazing museums I've been in because of its variety of spaces and the way it has been able to handle delicate objects – textiles, embroidery, jewelry – alongside statues, simultaneously. It incorporates a myriad of spaces for discovery, and you do, finally, have a sense that you are wandering throughout Asia, if you can do that in a museum space.[63]

The first room the visitor sees after passing through the humble foyer is a large room with vertical statues. Here, Banerjee staged the grand opening of her exhibition *Chimeras of India and the West* with the installation *Take me, Take me, Take me … to the Palace of Love* (2003), a temple-like structure crowned by cupolas and spires and hovering weightlessly above the floor like a vision surrounded and guarded by the 'temple statues' of the collection (see plate 3).[64] The model for the structure was the marble mausoleum of the Taj Mahal, a cultural landmark in India. The Mughal (and therefore Muslim) mausoleum has become a generic symbol of India's greatness as well as a lasting symbol of love (Shah Jahan built the mausoleum for his beloved wife Mumtaz Mahal).[65] The luminous pink colour of Banerjee's temple, and the tantalising promise of entering a realm of sensual pleasure evoked by the title, acted as a portal to the museum and Banerjee's exhibition. As Courtney J. Martin has noted, the title of the work makes 'the mildly orgiastic euphemism

(*Take me, Take me …*) a more toned down exhortation of mobility, i.e. "Get me to the Taj Mahal!".'[66]

Claire Robins has drawn attention to the fact that, unlike science, the work of art can address serious issues without asking to be taken completely seriously. Borrowing a term from Pierre Bourdieu, she describes this as the 'charm' (in both senses of the word) of the artwork; its ability to take the visitor's attention in several directions at the same time, 'whether that is through the parallel or counter-text within parody or whether it is through a visual pun or juxtaposition of familiar and unfamiliar language'.[67] Given the beauty and the playful, yet serious, character of Banerjee's work, Robins's notion of 'charm' is a suitable opener for an analysis of her intervention. The polysemy of Banerjee's orientalised assemblage sculptures provokes multi-directional associations, and their sensuousness is designed to stimulate desire and enchant the viewer. In this, Banerjee is an heir of the poet Comte de Lautreamont's, giving his surreal and gendered vision (his encounter between a sewing machine and an umbrella on a dissection table, for example) new cross-cultural meanings. Wilson, Shonibare and Banerjee all engage critically with colonialism and its historical effects, but in different ways. Like Wilson's *Mining the Museum*, Banerjee's intervention was based on juxtapositions of familiar and unfamiliar languages – in her case, the encounter between the 'familiar' tradition-bound language of the religious sculptures in the Musée Guimet's historical collection and the 'unfamiliar' subjective idiosyncrasies of Banerjee's artworks. However, contrary to Wilson's intervention, Banerjee's exhibition did not present a critical analysis that unveiled the institutional structures and normative historical narratives underpinning the way the collection was presented. Her intervention did not interfere directly with the institutional structures by reorganising them, but, rather, enhanced and unmasked the underlying orientalist vision through mimicry.

The Musée Guimet was founded in 1889 by the industrialist Émile Guimet, who was passionately interested in philosophy and ancient religions. In 1876, he was sent on a scientific mission by the Ministry of Public Instruction to study the religions of Japan, India and China. The museum contains the thousands of artworks and artefacts collected during this expedition, as well as objects from other French expeditions and excavations in the first half of the twentieth century.[68] It is therefore closely linked to European colonialism, and the Orientalism and taste for the exotic that it fostered. Like Shonibare, Banerjee engages with the theme of consumption, and the circulation of goods and artefacts in colonial and postcolonial times; she also includes consumer goods in her range of artistic materials. As she explains: 'There is a huge history in trying to make objects that will sell and you can't dissociate with the world of migration and colonization and occupation – there is this idea of exchange that we have, one before and beyond currency.'[69] Banerjee also shares with Shonibare a deliberate play on desire, exuberance, exoticism and seduction, but while Shonibare's object of curiosity or 'fetish' is European culture, Banerjee's object is her own cultural background in India and the Indian diaspora. Therefore, her artistic practice also raises the question of self-exoticisation. Do Banerjee's works represent acts of self-exoticisation that draw on and maintain stereotyped essentialist notions of the Indian or Eastern Other? Alternatively, can their exoticism be seen as an expression of subversive acts of mimicry intended not to copy but to reveal something about Orientalism, insofar as Banerjee's exaggerated mimicry of Orientalism sets it apart from the historical forms of Orientalism complicit in colonialism?

Banerjee is no doubt acutely aware of the mechanisms of orientalised vision and representations. She often comments on Orientalism, and in a 2013 interview she also recalled the significant impact that Edward Said's seminal book *Orientalism* (1978) had on her when she read it just before enrolling in Yale School of Art for graduate studies.[70] Banerjee has given many of her works extraordinarily long titles that present themselves as short tales with metaphoric, enigmatic or dramatic content, with a protagonist who is always feminine but never named. As art critic Cédric Vincent has observed, her characters are hybrid or metamorphosing beings like the divinities of the Hindu pantheon, struggling with their identities and situated in a sensual and troubling universe where the boundaries between the human, the animal and the vegetal are indistinct.[71] Her titles metaphorically echo the voice of a hybridised diasporic culture without clearly identifiable borders. Vincent aptly likens the semi-independence between the work and its title to a diptych, in which the work activates a story from the clues in the text while the text in turn offers clues to the meaning of the work.[72] Among the other works in the Guimet exhibition were *The world as burnt fruit …* (2009), mentioned in Chapter 3, and a new piece that Banerjee refers to by using the contracted form 'Captivity' (see plate 4). It is reminiscent of a crossover between a luxurious Victorian birdcage and a cabinet of curiosities, where all the artefacts – feathers, doll heads, branches, and more – have mysteriously escaped the captivity in which they have been held and are now perching on the outside of the cage. This theme of captivity and liberation is stressed in the work's enigmatic title:

> *Her captivity was once someone's treasure and even pleasure but she blew and flew away took root which grew, we knew this was like no other feather, a third kind of bird that perched on vine intertwined was neither native nor her queen's daughters, a peculiar other*

The tale revolves around the identity formation of 'a third kind of bird'. Being neither 'native' nor British ('her queen's daughters'), she is marked by her radical alterity as 'a peculiar other'. She has come into existence through a journey that sets out from a situation of exploitation ('captivity', 'someone's treasure'), goes on to migration ('blew and flew away'), after which she re-grounds herself ('took root') in a new place of residence where cultural differences are linked and forming what Chapter 3 called a 'scene of situational laterality' ('perched on vine intertwined').

Rina Banerjee's titles are intended to add layers of meaning to the work, but they are not didactic texts that communicate a 'message'. Instead, they offer poetic starting points for associations and deeper interpretations of the work, while at the same time functioning as linguistic gestures of intervention, appropriation and rebellion:

> I am very aware that I speak the English language, because I am Indian, and that it's not mine, so I like toying with it, making it bend, stretch, reach … My corruption of the English language is not just a small rebellion but my attempt to massage it to speak for a vast number of people who use it sparingly, awkwardly, creatively under the pressures of globalization, colonization, and the commercialization of English culture. I am laying ownership to this language to make it cooperate with my vision and imagery.[73]

Laying ownership to and toying with it is also what Banerjee does with the Orient as a Western system of representation in which the East is often conceived of as the inferior, sensual and eccentric Other, displaying a feminine penetrability while passively awaiting conquest by a masculine West.[74] In a noteworthy comparison, Laura Steward has likened Banerjee's way of expressing herself to the feminist writing or *écriture féminine* ('women's writing') of Hélène Cixous and Julia Kristeva. As protagonists of a strand of feminist theory that originated in France in the 1970s, Cixous and Kristeva sought to develop a new way of writing that balances the communicative clarity of what Lacanian psychoanalysis calls the 'symbolic', which is founded in a strictly regulated relationship between words and meaning, with the more poetic, personal and connotative register of what Kristeva calls the 'semiotic'.[75] The same could be said of Banerjee's combination of wordy titles with an excess of diverse objects; there is a wealth of material and linguistic ornaments. Here, identifiable words, symbols and objects are assimilated into a poetic, connotative and feminised whole.

In the following I will turn to another of the foundational theorists of *écriture féminine*, the feminist philosopher Luce Irigaray and her claim that in patriarchal cultures, such as Western culture, in which discourses are profoundly phallogocentric and the subject thus always-already defined as masculine, it is necessary to inscribe the female body and female difference in language and text through the deployment of mimicry. I wish to use the concept of mimicry to put Banerjee's intervention into perspective and to propose that her sculptures enact mimicry on two levels: that of gender and that of culture. Irigaray's feminist concept of mimicry underpins my exploration of the first, while the concept of colonial mimicry developed by postcolonial theorist Homi Bhabha will support my examination of the latter. Although developed for different types of critique, these concepts do converge as they have common theoretical roots in Lacanian psychoanalysis and Lacan's understanding of mimicry as a technique that 'reveals something in so far as it is distinct from what might be called an *itself* that is behind'.[76] Mimicry does not aim to harmonise with its background; its effect is more akin to *camouflage*, writes Lacan, thus stressing the centrality of the visual and the gaze in mimicry and comparing the function of mimicry to the way that 'the art of painting' always makes the artist's subjectivity and gaze manifest in the composition of the work.[77]

When Irigaray applies mimicry to the phallogocentric discourses of Western thinking, such as Freudian psychoanalysis, mimicry takes the shape of an ironic 'playful repetition' of the discourses that have historically fabricated essentialised and gendered 'facts' and 'truths' about female (and male) sexuality. According to Irigaray, one has to work through essentialism in order to get beyond it. She recommends mimicry as an instrument to reach the goal of 'jamming the theoretical machinery itself, of suspending its pretension to the production of a truth and of a meaning that are excessively univocal'.[78] Due to her overtly 'sexed' way of writing, Irigaray's mimetic rewriting of Freud appears to be essentialist. However, she is, in fact, mimicking the essentialist and 'sexed' nature of Freud's assumptions about the 'facts' of female sexuality to draw attention to and expose the 'sexed' essentialism inherent in Freud's theories, and in male-dominated discourses in general, since they are normally believed to be gender-neutral and hence 'objective' and 'true'.[79] According to Irigaray, women have historically been assigned the role of mimicry, i.e. of imitating the ideas about 'woman' elaborated by a hegemonic masculine logic. By assuming the role of mimicry deliberately and strategically, it is possible, asserts Irigaray, to convert this traditional form of subordination into an instrument of critique and open a space for female difference.

There is an accentuated irrationality in Banerjee's sculptures which links them to a strong tradition of resistance to Western logocentrism (both inside and outside the West). It is perhaps most conspicuous in those works that bring the strange hybrid creatures of Max Ernst's surrealist collages to mind: the crocodile in *The world as burnt fruit*, for instance, and the 'chimeric' hybrid between a woman, a ram and the Hindu elephant-headed god Ganesha in one of the new works produced for the Guimet exhibition, which Banerjee refers to as 'Western Style' (2011, see figure 4.2). Its full title goes:

> *She was now in western style dress covered in part of Empires' ruffle and red dress, had a foreign and peculiar race, a Ganesha who had lost her head, was*

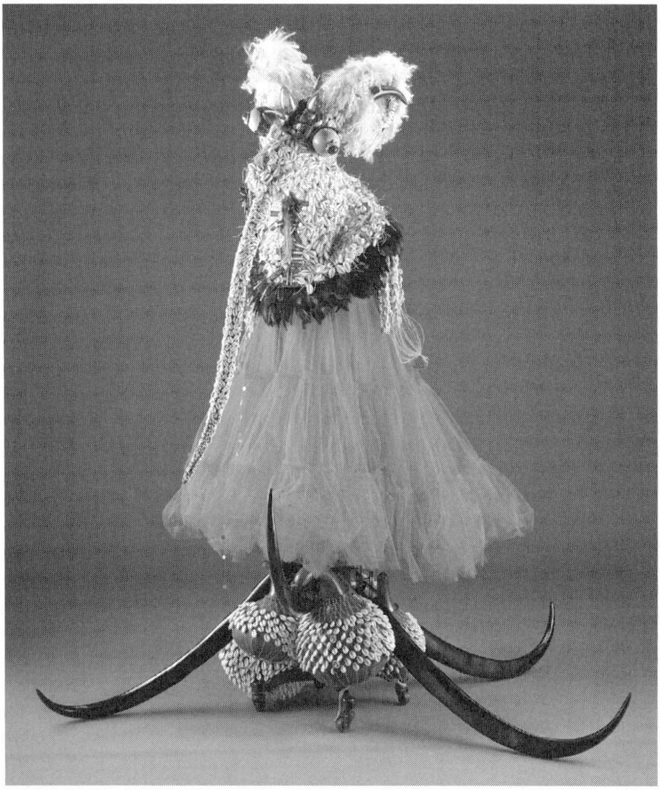

4.2 Rina Banerjee, *She was now in western style dress*, 2011. Mixed media. 180 x 160 x 109 cm. Collection of the National Taiwan Museum of Fine Arts. © Rina Banerjee. Photograph courtesy of the artist and National Taiwan Museum of Fine Arts.

> *thrown across sea until herself shipwrecked. A native of Bangladesh lost foot to root in bidesh, followed her mother full stop on forehead, trapped tongue of horn and groomed a ram – like under stress*

The title conjures up a story similar to that of 'Captivity', where migration takes place in the stressful context of colonial empire. The adjective 'peculiar' is used again to stress the strangeness of the protagonist, a migrant who has been 'thrown across sea' to 'root in bidesh' where she is perceived as 'foreign'. Vincent has suggested that the geographical aspects of the terms 'desh' and 'bidesh' can be related to the terms 'routes' and 'roots' as used in globalisation theory. In parts of north-western Bangladesh, *desh* denotes the place of community and family residence, whereas *bidesh* refers to 'elsewhere', with *bideshi* denoting foreigner.[80] Banerjee's mimic figure of 'woman' has eyes as big as saucers that emphatically return the visitor's curious gaze. Despite its cute and friendly expression and the disarmingly girlish red of its stiff underskirt, the transgender figure's 'skin' or 'mask' of cowrie shells – each of them a symbolic 'vagina dentata' *en miniature* – introduces a menacing undertone. It is mixed with a carnivalesque atmosphere of masquerade, although it is obvious that there is no self hidden behind the mask. The toothed vaginas of the mask send an overtly gendered and 'sexed' note of warning, conjuring up the bogey of woman as the castrating 'other'. However, even as she conjures up a traditional and stereotyped symbol of woman as the embodiment of male castration anxiety, Banerjee displaces the image so that it evokes more ambiguous and violent gender connotations. Not only can the sculpture be seen as covered in symbols of menacing femininity. Peeping under the hem of the skirt, the curious visitor discovers that the figure also has 'testicles' in the shape of calabashes, decorated with an ornament of cowrie shells. Moreover, from the hidden space under the skirt protrudes the phallic warning of pointed black buffalo horns (from America), aggressively returning the viewer's desiring gaze. Add to these gendered symbols the monumental womb-like structure of the 'burnt fruit' in *The world as burnt fruit ...*, the feminised embrace of the almost provocatively girlish pink plastic walls of the installation *Take me, Take me, Take me ... to the Palace of Love*, and there is enough evidence that Banerjee deliberately deploys 'playful repetition' (Irigaray) to stage humorous parodies of phallogocentric stereotypes in order to inscribe a female aesthetic and difference into her art. Moreover, the excess and ambiguity produced by Banerjee's mimicry of femininity generate an uncertainty that, it could be suggested, might also undo certain stereotypes of masculinity.

As a general critical strategy, mimicry is one response to the circulation of stereotypes and essentialised notions of the (gendered, racialised or cultural) 'other'. As a technique of resistance, it seeks to circumvent assimilation into the dominant order of representation. In both Irigaray's and Bhabha's understanding, humour, parody and irony are among its favoured tools.[81] The subject enacting mimicry pretends to adapt to the hegemonic or normative model. It appears to assimilate but 'fails' as it slyly deviates from the model, introducing instead an alienating difference that displaces and unsettles the model it was supposed to imitate. The general effect that this 'flawed' imitation creates is a disturbing resemblance, or, in Bhabha's words, '*a difference that is almost the same, but not quite*' and, in colonial and racial terms, '*Almost the same but not white*'.[82] In this articulation of cultural, historical, racial and gender differences lies the menacing effect of mimicry. In a colonial context, the effect of mimicry is therefore, according to Bhabha, capable of undermining the coloniser's apparently pre-given, exemplary identity (i.e. the fixed model of Britishness to be imitated by the colonised subjects), thereby also suggesting that there is no 'whole' presence or fixed identity behind the mask, only a 'partial' presence.[83] Mimicry thus underscores that identification in a colonial context should, rather, be understood as 'a *process* in which both the "Western subject" and the "Oriental other" are mutually implicated in each other and thus neither exists as a fully constituted entity'.[84]

Let us go back to the palace at the entrance to Banerjee's exhibition *Chimeras of India and the West*. Banerjee's pink plastic imitation of the Taj Mahal introduced an element of parody that was underscored by the title *Take me, Take me, Take me … to the Palace of Love*, words from a kitsch Hindi movie from the mid-1950s. The romantic but garish structure, deftly built of a cheap material – plastic, an ubiquitous token of today's globalised consumer culture – conjured both the romanticism and orientalism of the Western infatuation with this celebrated symbol of India's rich history. In the centre of the palace, Banerjee placed an intricately carved dark wood chair that was produced in Bombay in the 1850s. The chair alluded to late nineteenth-century Anglo-Indian relationships and interchange as, in the Victorian era, these chairs became a popular exotic souvenir.[85] The Bombay chair was surmounted by a bizarre chandelier of Styrofoam balls, decorated with cowrie shells, red-coloured moss and other bits of bright colour. Hovering between form and formlessness, this exotic, ornate apparition seemed to have taken seat in the large chair which was staged like a throne, the symbolic place of power.[86] Supported by an unobtrusive suspended frame, the throne seemed to float magically and majestically in the centre of the palace as if it reigned over the whole world – symbolised by the antique stone globe placed under the elevated throne – just as Britain once reigned over her global empire on which the sun never set. Although the parodic subversion and aesthetic excess of mimicry revolved around the Taj Mahal as a migratory icon of 'India', the targets of the artist's critique were decidedly Western: the Raj, specifically, and the absurdity of Western orientalist fantasies in general.

Defining parody as a vital instrument of artists' interventions, Claire Robins has emphasised its potential to bring into question an aspect of an institutional practice, or an object in the collection. In Banerjee's exhibition, the interrogated aspect was the naturalised perception – institutional or popular – of Asia. The 'object' was not so much the exhibits as the more encompassing and less graspable phenomenon of Orientalism as a system of thought and representation, constructed by and for the West. Robins notes that parodic intervention operates at a remove from imitation and quotation. It is best described as a process of mimicry, 'most often couched in Bakhtin's "quotation marks", implying a device that distances speaker from spoken, display cabinet from simulacrum'.[87] To explain how it operates, Robins draws a parallel between parodic intervention and the two meanings of the prefix *para* in Greek: according to Robins, one meaning is counter or against, suggesting an oppositional stance or mockery; the other is beside, as in *para*llel.

The second meaning indicates closeness rather than contrast, suggesting a critique that allows humour and absurdity,[88] as seen in Banerjee's exhibition *Chimeras of India and the West*.

Of particular relevance to the exhibition's staging of an exchange between cultural heritage and diasporic experience is the sculpture 'Captivity'. Banerjee has explained that for this work, she assembled 'things that one might find on an oriental painting': feathers, gourds, coconuts, shells, twisted branches of vine, Kenyan tourist sculptures and heads of Charlotte dolls – a type of china head doll popular in the Victorian era.[89] She adds that she deliberately painted and 'exoticised' the dolls that sit among the vines 'to have them look like what I would imagine them looking like [i]n faraway lands'.[90] The escaped, 'Indianised' dolls, some of which have a *bindi* (here, a marriage sign) on their forehead, might be read as symbols of the liberation of Indian women – in terms of national independence as well as emancipation from the dominant male subjects of their own patriarchal culture. After all, the birdcage is a frequently used symbol of sexuality and domesticity in Western painting in the age of colonialism. Inspired by Dutch seventeenth-century painting, the Victorians adopted the birdcage as a symbol for the home. While the bird in the cage can have multiple meanings, in patriarchal Victorian society it was ultimately linked to women's role as a nest-maker confined within the institution of the home, i.e. what Elaine Shefer has called 'the home-nest syndrome'.[91] Banerjee's comment on the work, quoted earlier, also suggests that she has created her three-dimensional version of an 'orientalist' still life at a remove from both the tradition of orientalist painting and the geographical Orient. It is the product of a diasporic, postcolonial imagination that seems to have been positioned both close to and distant from Western and Eastern cultures when fabricating what is basically a diasporic fantasy about a Western fantasy about the Orient.

Banerjee's playful strategy of mimicry begs the question of how one distinguishes between a subversive repetition and a loyal one. The sparkling humour and alluring beauty of her works might fulfil some viewers' expectations of aesthetic pleasure and oriental exoticism so effectively that they overlook the subversive aspects. All artworks are, in principle, exposed to all sorts of superficial readings, oversights and misinterpretations by audiences, so the question of complicity and the risk of being caught up in the stereotypes one seeks to combat is perhaps best approached from the perspective of the artist's project. For Irigaray, parodic repetition differs from mere loyal repetition because it represents, at the same time, a recognition and a disavowal of the dominant codes. In other words, mimicry can only be subversive on the condition that the naturalised codes and structures are critically reflected upon.[92] Bhabha likewise defines mimicry as a strategy of 'double articulation' that both affirms and repudiates the idealised model by problematising the signs of its priority, so that the model is no longer naturalisable.[93] The preceding analyses suggest that all the three works by Banerjee discussed at length in this chapter can achieve this effect in some visitors.

Embedded criticality

It is important to remember that artists' interventions are based on collaboration between an artist and the professionals within the host institution, not on the artist's autonomous act of protest *against* it. This means that, if an intervention is to problematise and not just stabilise the institutional framework, it is not only the artist but also the representatives of the host institution that need to reflect critically on how the institution produces and reproduces assumptions and traditions, and on how perspectives and priorities can be changed or expanded. Put differently, the host institution must have 'internalised' a self-critical perspective and developed a desire to change before taking the decision to invite an artist to make an intervention.

As Walter Mignolo has pointed out, there is no right or natural way to define what museums should do, but they should span different and contesting kinds of interpretive practice.[94] Inviting artists to stage critical interventions into museum collections and practices can help unravel the colonial syntax and logic that is still deeply ingrained in many Western museums. However, the decolonising potential of artists' interventions in those institutions may well be greater than that.

There has been a significant shift in postcolonial studies since the 1990s, leading to a broadening of the range of topics and disciplines involved as well as a refinement of the critical engagement with contemporary neo-imperial practices. The emergence of decolonial thinking and aesthetics signals this change. As the postcolonial and the decolonial have come to signify a greater variety of oppositional practices and gestures of resistance, the criticised dominant part may no longer be exclusively Western colonialism, imperialism and capitalism, as in classic postcolonial narratives. It could be expanded to include other historical and geographical contexts, bringing other types of repressed memories to light – of repressive nationalist communism, for example.[95]

Artists' interventions can question the dominant discourses of galleries and museums by deploying surprise, juxtaposition, disruption, incongruity and humour. As Claire Robins remarks, 'significant others' within the institution with whom the artist collaborates and co-produces 'are squarely implicated in any disruptions and parodic transgressions made by the artist'.[96] Thus, contemporary artists' interventions should not be defined in opposition to the institution, in the spirit of 1960s and 1970s institutional critique, not even when the artist takes a postcolonial or anti-racist stance, as is the case with Wilson, Shonibare and Banerjee. Artists' interventions result from a critical practice founded in an awareness of its own complicity with the system, that is to say, in the kind of questioning, reflective approach that Irit Rogoff has called criticality. As opposed to criticism that investigates and exposes its object from the position of the analytical outsider, criticality operates from 'an uncertain ground of actual embeddedness' in the very system that the artist investigates.[97] Consequently, the artist needs to articulate a 'difference', because it is only possible to shift the balance of power if it is possible for something to be perceived as deviating or 'other'.

Artists have practised institutional interventions for several decades now. Having a legacy does not mean that the *detournement* provided by artists has lost its poignancy. Quite the opposite; it means that artists can now draw on a range of interventionist strategies with a knowledge of which of them have achieved critical, deconstructive work and succeeded in introducing a certain instability that opened a space for negotiation – and which ended up stabilising the institutions they were intended to interrogate, meaning that the collaboration with the institution did not contribute to any change, but only to maintaining the status quo and the image of the museum as a pillar of tradition. Just as postcolonial studies have been able to renew themselves, so, too, are artists able to produce new types of critical interventions that contribute to the decolonisation of museum practices. Interventions such as those of Wilson, Shonibare and Banerjee can provide the necessary conditions for acts of disidentification that enable museum professionals, and audiences, to imagine what a more inclusive museum could be like, a museum which also produces views from the 'other' side.

Notes

1 Lisa G. Corrin, 'Mining the Museum: Artists Look at Museums, Museums Look at Themselves', in Lisa G. Corrin (ed.), *Mining the Museum: An Installation by Fred Wilson* (Baltimore: The Contemporary, 1994), pp. 1–22, pp. 4–7.
2 Jennifer A. González, *Subject to Display: Reframing Race in Contemporary Installation Art* (Cambridge, Mass.: The MIT Press, 2008), p. 67.
3 Claire Robins, *Curious Lessons in the Museum: The Pedagogic Potential of Artists' Interventions* (Farnham: Ashgate, 2013), p. 1.
4 *Ibid.*, p. 197.
5 Corrin, 'Mining the Museum: Artists', p. 1.
6 Robins, *Curious Lessons in the Museum*, p. 208.
7 *Ibid.*, p. 2.
8 *Ibid.*, p. 4.
9 Claire Robins and Miranda Baxter, 'Meaningful Encounters with Disrupted Narratives: Artists' Interventions as Interpretive Strategies', in Suzanne MacLeod,

Laura Hourston Hanks and Jonathan Hale (eds), *Museum Making: Narratives, Architectures, Exhibitions* (London, New York: Routledge, 2012), pp. 247–56, pp. 247–8.
10 Robins, *Curious Lessons in the Museum*, p. 1.
11 *Ibid.*, pp. 6, 8.
12 Robins and Baxter, 'Meaningful Encounters with Disrupted Narratives', p. 252.
13 *Ibid.*, p. 247.
14 *Ibid.*, p. 255.
15 González, *Subject to Display*, p. 83.
16 *Ibid.*, p. 88.
17 Bernard Müller, 'Le "Jardin d'Amour" de Yinka Shonibare au musée du quai Branly ou: quand l'"autre" s'y met', *CeROArt*, no. 1 (2007), http://ceroart.revues.org/386 (accessed 16 November 2016), par. 26.
18 Ronald Jones, 'Yinka Shonibare: musée du quai Branly', *Artforum International*, 46:2 (2007), unpaginated, http://search.proquest.com/docview/214339765?accountid=13607 (accessed 8 November 2012).
19 Madeleine Dobie, *Trading Places: Colonization and Slavery in Eighteenth-Century French Culture* (Ithaca, NY, London: Cornell University Press, 2010), p. 4.
20 *Ibid.*, p. 3.
21 *Ibid.*, p. 5.
22 *Ibid.*, p. 20.
23 Müller, 'Le "Jardin d'Amour"', par. 9.
24 Amanda Gilvin, 'Yinka Shonibare: Garden of Love', *Nka: Journal of Contemporary African Art*, no. 24 (2009), 168–70, 168.
25 *Ibid.*, 169–70.
26 Hélène Prigent, *Guimet: National Museum of Asian Arts: Visitor's Guide* (Paris: Guimet musée national des arts asiatiques and Artlys, 2004).
27 Caroline Arhuero, 'Divinities and Chimaeras: Toward a New Way of Looking at Art', in Leclercq (ed.), *Rina Banerjee*, pp. 25–9, p. 26.
28 Alessandra De Angelis *et al.*, 'Introduction: Disruptive Encounters – Museums, Art and Postcoloniality', in Iain Chambers *et al.* (eds), *The Postcolonial Museum: The Arts of Memory and the Pressures of History* (Farnham: Ashgate, 2014), pp. 1–21, p. 2.
29 Saloni Mathur, 'Museums and globalization', *Anthropological Quarterly*, 78:3 (2005), 697–708, 705.
30 Walter Mignolo, 'Museums in the Colonial Horizon of Modernity: Fred Wilson's *Mining the Museum* (1992)', in Harris (ed.), *Globalization and Contemporary Art*, pp. 71–85, p. 83.
31 Walter D. Mignolo, 'Delinking: the rhetoric of modernity, the logic of coloniality and the grammar of de-coloniality', *Cultural Studies*, 21:2–3 (2007), 449–514, 450–2; Mignolo, 'Introduction: coloniality of power and de-colonial thinking', *Cultural Studies*, 21:2–3 (2007), 155–67, 163–4; Mignolo, *The Darker Side of Western Modernity: Global Futures, Decolonial Options* (Durham, NC, London: Duke University Press, 2011), p. 79. For references to Quijano, see Mignolo, *The Darker Side of Western Modernity.*

32 Walter Mignolo *et al.*, 'Decolonial Aesthetics (I)', *TDI/Transnational Decolonial Institute* (2011), unpaginated, http://transnationaldecolonialinstitute.wordpress.com/decolonial-aesthetics/ (accessed 16 November 2016).
33 Walter Mignolo and Madina V. Tlostanova, *Learning to Unlearn: Decolonial Reflections from Eurasia and the Americas* (Columbus, OH: The Ohio State University Press, 2012), p. 7.
34 Mignolo *et al.*, 'Decolonial Aesthetics (I)'.
35 Mignolo and Tlostanova, *Learning to Unlearn*, p. 8; Mignolo, 'Introduction: coloniality of power and de-colonial thinking', 162.
36 Janet Wilson, Christina Şandru and Sarah Lawson Welsh, 'General Introduction', in Janet Wilson, Christina Şandru and Sarah Lawson Welsh (eds), *Rerouting the Postcolonial: New Directions for the New Millenium* (London, New York: Routledge, 2010), pp. 1–13.
37 Tlostanova's homepage: www.tema.liu.se/tema-g/medarbetare-och-kontakt/madina-tlostanova/presentation?l=en (accessed June 2016).
38 See Wilson, Şandru and Welsh, 'General Introduction', p. 8.
39 Mignolo and Tlostanova, *Learning to Unlearn*, p. 12.
40 *Ibid.*, pp. 12ff.
41 Mignolo, 'Delinking', 485.
42 Mignolo, 'Museums in the Colonial Horizon of Modernity', p. 73.
43 *Ibid.*, p. 72.
44 *Ibid.*, p. 84.
45 *Ibid.*, p. 76.
46 *Ibid.*, p. 81.
47 *Ibid.*, p. 80.
48 Mignolo *et al.*, 'Decolonial Aesthetics (I)'; Boehmer, 'A Postcolonial Aesthetic'.
49 Boehmer, 'A Postcolonial Aesthetic', pp. 170–1.
50 *Ibid.*, p. 171.
51 González, *Subject to Display*, pp. 66–7.
52 Boehmer, 'A Postcolonial Aesthetic', p. 176.
53 *Ibid.*, pp. 171, 179.
54 Mieke Bal, in discussion at the conference *India! Art on the Move: Migration and Contemporary Art*, Arken Museum of Modern Art, Ishøj, Denmark, 26 October 2012.
55 Quoted in González, *Subject to Display*, p. 87.
56 Quoted *ibid.*, p. 88.
57 Mignolo, 'Museums in the Colonial Horizon of Modernity', p. 75.
58 *Ibid.*, p. 76.
59 James Clifford, 'Quai Branly in process', *October*, no. 120 (2007), 3–23, 5–6.
60 Bernard Müller, 'Interview with Yinka Shonibare MBE', in Germain Viatte (ed.), *Yinka Shonibare, MBE: Jardin d'Amour* (Paris: Flammarion and Musée du Quai Branly, 2007), pp. 11–26, p. 21.
61 Clifford, 'Quai Branly in process', 10.
62 Mieke Bal, 'Political Art', www.miekebal.org/research/book-projects/ (accessed November 2016).

63 Rina Banerjee and Jane DeBevoise, 'Presentation by Rina Banerjee', *Asia Art Archive in America* (October 2011), unpaginated, www.aaa-a.org/programs/presentation-by-rina-banerjee/ (accessed November 2016).
64 Banerjee made this piece originally for the exhibition 'Yankee Remix' in 2003–4 at the Massachusetts Museum of Contemporary Art (MASSMoCA) in Boston, and adjusted it for the new site in Musée Guimet.
65 Courtney J. Martin, 'Mistaken for a Cloud', in *Rina Banerjee: Forever Foreign* (London: Haunch of Venison, 2010), unpaginated; Elaine W. Ng, 'Marvellous Beings: The Work of Rina Banerjee', *ibid.*, pp. 21–7, p. 16.
66 Martin, 'Mistaken for a Cloud'.
67 Robins, *Curious Lessons in the Museum*, p. 101.
68 Prigent, *Guimet*, p. 6.
69 Banerjee and DeBevoise, 'Presentation by Rina Banerjee'.
70 Hervé Mikaeloff, 'Conversation with Rina Banerjee', *Take*, no. 3 (2013), 56–8, 58.
71 Cédric Vincent, 'The Politics of the Title', in Grégoire Robinne (ed.), *Rina Banerjee 2006–2015* (Paris: Galerie Nathalie Obadia and Édition Dilecta, 2015), pp. 15–20, pp. 15–16.
72 *Ibid.*, p. 19.
73 Mathias Ussing Seeberg, 'Interview with Rina Banerjee', in Gether *et al.* (eds), *India: Art Now*, pp. 84–7, pp. 86–7.
74 Meyda Yeğenoğlu, 'Veiled Fantasies: Cultural and Sexual Difference in the Discourse of Orientalism', in Reina Lewis and Sara Mills (eds), *Feminist Postcolonial Theory: A Reader* (New York, London: Routledge, 2003), pp. 542–66, pp. 543, 554.
75 Steward, 'A Whole Composed of Parts That Are Wholes', p. 18.
76 Jacques Lacan, 'The Line and the Light', in *The Four Fundamental Concepts of Psychoanalysis* (New York, London: W.W. Norton & Company, 1981), pp. 91–104, p. 99.
77 *Ibid.*, p. 100.
78 Luce Irigaray, *This Sex Which Is Not One* (Ithaca, NY: Cornell University Press, 1977), p. 78.
79 Ping Xu, 'Irigaray's mimicry and the problem of essentialism', *Hypatia*, 10:4 (1995), 76–89, 82.
80 Vincent, 'The Politics of the Title', p. 17. L. A. Louver, 'Rina Banerjee: Western Style (2014)', 5:18 mins, www.youtube.com/watch?v=WJkocAukEno (accessed November 2016).
81 David Huddart, *Homi K. Bhabha* (New York: Routledge, 2006), p. 58; Xu, 'Irigaray's mimicry and the problem of essentialism', 83–4.
82 Bhabha, *The Location of Culture*, pp. 122, 128.
83 *Ibid.*, pp. 123–4.
84 Yeğenoğlu, 'Veiled Fantasies', p. 555.
85 Martin, 'Mistaken for a Cloud'.
86 Presentation of the exhibition 'Yankee Remix' (2003–4), for which the installation was made, on the MASSMoCA website: http://yyz.massmoca.org/event_details.php?id=45 (accessed 16 November 2016). For details of materials used, see also:

http://rinabanerjee.com/artwork/1218780_Take_me_take_me_take_me_to_the_Palace.html (accessed November 2016).
87 Robins, *Curious Lessons in the Museum*, p. 90.
88 *Ibid.*
89 http://rinabanerjee.com/artwork/3577235_Her_captivity_was_once_someone_s.html (accessed August 2016).
90 Banerjee and DeBevoise, 'Presentation by Rina Banerjee'.
91 Elaine Shefer, 'Women's mission', *Women's Art Journal*, 7:1 (1986), 8–12, 11.
92 Yeğenoğlu, 'Veiled Fantasies', p. 559.
93 Bhabha, *The Location of Culture*, pp. 122, 125.
94 Mignolo, 'Museums in the Colonial Horizon of Modernity', p. 84.
95 Wilson, Şandru and Welsh, 'General Introduction', pp. 1, 7.
96 Robins, *Curious Lessons in the Museum*, p. 213.
97 Irit Rogoff, 'Academy as Potentiality', in Angelika Nollert *et al.* (eds), *A.C.A.D.E.M.Y.* (Frankfurt am Main: Revolver, 2006), pp. 13–20, p. 16.

5 Identification, disidentification and the imaginative reconfiguration of identity

With respect to identities in flux, art can be an instrument of orientation and positioning oneself in the world. Thanks to its ability to negotiate contradictions and encompass double articulations, tensions and complexities, art can chart how identifications may shift continually and dynamically as one navigates across countries and cultures. In this chapter, I wish to approach this thematic through close readings of works by the London-based Nigerian expatriate Yinka Shonibare, Delhi-based British expatriate Bharti Kher, and Vietnamese-born Danh Vo, who grew up in Denmark, spent the early years of his professional career in Berlin and then became a resident of Mexico City. Stuart Hall's observation that 'identities are about questions of using the resources of history, language and culture in the process of becoming rather than being' is pertinent to the work of all three of these artists.[1] While there are obvious differences between their artistic practices and the geopolitical contexts in which they unfold, Kher, Shonibare and Vo all probe colonial and postcolonial archives of history, seeking to uncover 'hidden histories'. As Hall has remarked, in the context of decolonisation and postcoloniality 'the importance of the act of imaginative rediscovery' cannot be overestimated, nor should one overlook its ties to a political desire to see marginalised communities or oppressed people – the enslaved and colonised, women, LGBTQ communities, etc. – rehabilitated and recognised. Yet, it is vital to bear in mind that this 'archival' work does not entail a rediscovery, but a *production* of identity, which means that it is not grounded in archaeology but in a resourceful act of resistance and an imaginative *reconfiguration* of the past.[2] As noted in the Introduction, Hall perceives identity to be 'constituted, not outside but within representation'. In his understanding, a visual representation does not merely constitute a 'second-order mirror held up to reflect what already exits'; a visual representation can act as an imaginative reconfiguration: it is a 'form of representation which is able to constitute us as new kinds of subjects, and thereby enable us to discover places from which to speak'.[3] A visual representation thus understood becomes a political intervention into the dominant notions of what it is to be a person, i.e. *subjectivity*, and how we describe ourselves to each other, i.e. *identity*.

I will turn to Amelia Jones's book *Seeing Differently: A History and Theory of Identification and the Visual Arts* for an apposite concept of identification. As the author herself remarks, she primarily proposes 'a history and a theory' of identification as an issue in the visual arts.[4] Consequently, Jones specifically refrains from devoting herself to interrogating the relationship of identity politics to developments in *contemporary* art,[5] which is the focus of this chapter. I do not seek to cover the vast field of global contemporary art, which would have meant doing no more than skimming the surface of issues and artistic practices; nor to elaborate on the already nuanced and subtle identity theories conceived by Amelia Jones, Stuart Hall, José Esteban Muñoz and Nira Yuval-Davis, which constitute the theoretical backbone of this chapter. Instead, I wish to apply what can perhaps best be given the designation 'an intersectional approach' in a pointed examination of selected works by the three aforementioned artists. I argue that their works can be read as theoretical propositions in their own right, which means that they aspire to be artistic 'answers' to the same challenge Jones, Hall and Muñoz have sought to meet: that of fleshing out a dynamic, non-reductionist understanding of identity formation as flowing identifications that draw meanings from the discursive as well as the psychological register.

It was the black feminist Kimberlé Crenshaw who, in 1989, coined the term 'intersectionality' to describe theoretically the way multiple oppressions are experienced. Intersectionality can be described as a development of feminist standpoint theory, which holds that it is essential to account for the social position of the social agent and to challenge the positivist and masculinist idea of the all-seeing eye of objectivist positioning. Instead, feminist standpoint theory and intersectional approaches emphasise that a situated gaze, situated knowledge and situated imagination determine differently how we see and experience the world. Taking my lead from the understanding of intersectionality developed by sociologist Nira Yuval-Davis and social psychologist Ann Phoenix, I see intersectional analysis as an instrument to prioritise any facet or category of social difference and to treat them as mutually constitutive.[6]

Of particular relevance to the issue of migrant identities is Yuval-Davis's emphasis on the intimate connection between identity and belonging. It is important, however, to bear in mind that identity encompasses more than belonging, because not all the narratives, i.e. the 'stories people tell themselves and others about who they are (and who they are not)', are about belonging to particular groups or communities; they can also relate to body images, vocational aspirations and individual attributes. Nevertheless, belonging is an important component in the production of identity, because collective identity narratives often act as a resource for individual narratives, and because both individual and collective narratives provide people with 'a sense of order', explains Yuval-Davis. She adds that, since the production of identities is always 'in process', order should here be understood as a sense of continuity and agency that enables change or contestation within the identity boundaries of the individual and/or collective subject.[7]

The concept of intersectionality can thus be deployed to rebut essentialist notions of identity and belonging. It provides a conceptual language for considering the ways in which everybody is simultaneously positioned in different social categories that intersect with each other in ways that produce complex, multifaceted identities. In addition, it allows the examination of 'unmarked' positions such as 'whiteness' and 'masculinity', as well as of 'marked' positions such as 'femininity' and 'blackness'/'people of colour'.[8] Last but not least, it permits recognition that some social structures are deeply ingrained, e.g. the normative organisation of sexualities in 'the heterosexual matrix', which (re)produces sex, gender and desire,[9] but within those relatively fixed structures there is also a scope for individual agency and transformable self-identifications. If the latter is stressed, intersectionality can be used to conceptualise individual agency. As Ann Phoenix has pointed out, intersectionality is incompatible with essentialist identity politics. It 'fits better with a notion of strategic alliances, where people make temporary alliances for particular purposes'.[10] It is thus well suited for exploring how identifications and disidentifications can shift as migrant artists (and migrants in general) cross national borders, reorient themselves in new contexts and develop other attachments.

The primary focus in my analyses will be intersections between the categories of ethnicity, culture, race, gender and regional and national attachments. Following Phoenix's advice to ensure historical accuracy by making a strategic choice of the most relevant intersections for specific cases and contexts, my consideration of Shonibare's work emphasises ethnicity, culture and race, while my approach to Kher's work gives priority to ethnicity, culture and gender. Finally, my analysis of Vo's work examines how gender, sexual orientation and the feeling of belonging to national and regional collectivities can be negotiated in migration.

Identification and disidentification in art

Following up on Chapter 2, this chapter takes a further step away from conventional identity politics that are grounded in Western binary thinking. Art is always about identification, Amelia Jones reminds us. Identification evolves as a dynamic, reciprocal process that occurs between viewers, bodies, images and other kinds of visual representations and media. It is therefore rewarding and illuminating to explore questions of identity and identification through the self-reflective modes of representation characteristic of modern and contemporary art.[11] Jones emphasises that, when exploring identity formations, one should bear in mind that the notion of art as an inherently superior mode of individual human production was invented at a time when European colonisers were confronting other kinds of cultures and needed to reinforce their superiority. This means that the Western notion of art was formulated at a moment when European cultures were confronted with profound cultural differences and needed ideological formations such as 'modernity', 'individualism' and 'art' to claim cultural superiority over non-European cultures, which were perceived as inferior according to the binary structures of belief about the self and the other resulting from European colonising and industrialising processes.[12] Moreover, the conflation of the notions of individualism and artistic subjectivity has a long history that can be traced back to the early modern European experience. In effect, the modern Western notions of the 'individual' and 'art' were articulated in tandem during the Renaissance and developed with Enlightenment philosophy. Ever since, the figure of the artist has served as the very paradigm of modern subject formation:[13] 'The legacy of Renaissance to modern, nineteenth- and twentieth-century, European aesthetics was to elaborate a way of understanding a particular kind of individual expression *as* "a work of art," thereby reciprocally defining both the origin of the work (as "author"/artist) and the work itself (as the authentic expression of the artist).'[14]

As has been pointed out by Jones and others, this historical discourse on art conflates the work of art itself, understood as a superior mode of human production, with a set of identities circulating around the figure of the artist as a superior being (a genius) and her or his subjectivity and intentionality. Here, it is worth recalling Hall's insight into the split nature of self-identification: although we, so to say, speak 'in our own name', the one who speaks and the subject who is spoken of are never identical, never positioned identically.[15] Or, to borrow a distinction from literary theory: the author and the narrator of a text are not identical. The narrator of a work of fiction (or an autobiography, for that matter) is a figure created by the author, like the other characters in the text. Hence, the narrator or the 'voice' that speaks in the text is a construction, not to be mistaken for the author, although that voice may echo that of the author. This principle also applies to works of visual art. This study thus adheres to a constructivist understanding of the subject's self-identification as based on performative and discursive processes of identification that may involve several and changing points of identification. It also distinguishes between the artist's identity and the points of identification constructed in the work through aesthetic and conceptual means. This line of theoretical thought will be further developed in the analyses below, which also link the feminist concept of intersectionality to the postcolonial concept of hybridity. Moreover, the analyses follow Amelia Jones's use of the term 'queer' in a sense that transcends debates on gay, lesbian and transsexual bodies and identities, and expand the meaning of the term to denote the queering not only of sexuality and gender, but also of ethnicity, class, nationality and thus identification in general.[16] Quoting literary critic and queer theorist Eve Kosofsky Sedgwick, Jones concludes that 'a lot of the most exiting recent work around "queer" spins the term outward along dimensions that can't be subsumed under gender and sexuality at all: the ways that race, ethnicity, postcolonial nationality criss-cross with these and other identity-constituting, identity-fracturing discourses'.[17]

This expanded notion activates the term 'queer' as a marker of a *tactical disorientation* intended to frustrate static, closed and stereotyped notions of identity and to underscore embodied experience. José Esteban Muñoz's analysis of queer identities and racial minority issues from a performance studies perspective is particularly relevant to the study of migrant identities as criss-crossing, intersectional identities. Like queer identities, migrant identities are often shaped by the interlinked processes of identification and disidentification, recognition and disavowal. Processes of identification with others, and with social discourses, enable the subject to embody an illusion of wholeness.[18] Employing disidentification as an analytical concept can provide a way to deconstruct this illusion of wholeness and underscore the heterogeneous and intersectional nature of identity. In *Disidentifications: Queers of Color and the Performance of Politics* from 1999, Muñoz proposes a theory of queer disidentification which sees the act of disidentifying as a specifically *minoritarian* strategy, i.e. a survival strategy used by minority subjects to negotiate a hegemonic public sphere that either stigmatises or punishes those who do not conform to the normative models of citizenship, gender, race, heterosexuality, etc.

Muñoz demonstrates how disidentifying can function as a hermeneutic process and a mode of performance. It is 'a way of shuffling back and forth between reception and production' which seeks a third way that is neither identification nor counteridentification. Disidentification eschews affirmative assimilation as well as oppositional anti-assimilation, and it unfolds, oppositely, simultaneously within and outside the 'majoritarian' norms of dominant culture.[19] It thus works as a distancing mode of negotiating with existing cultural codes. It signals different strategies of performing, viewing, interpreting and locating 'self' within representational systems that aim to block out a minority subject.[20] As Muñoz explains, disidentification is about questioning and expanding identity and identification. It is about *recycling* and *rethinking* encoded meaning, not abandoning socially prescribed identity constituents:

> The process of disidentification scrambles and reconstructs the encoded message of a cultural text in a fashion that both exposes the encoded message's

> universalizing and exclusionary machinations and recircuits its workings to account for, include, and empower minority identities and identifications. Thus, disidentification is a step further than cracking open the code of the majority; it proceeds to use this code as raw material for representing a disempowered politics or positionality that has been rendered unthinkable by the dominant culture.[21]

Almost two decades after the publication of Muñoz's important book, the majority/minority binary has, however, become a straitjacket to identity theory instead of a vehicle of clarification and critique, because the borderlines between majority and minorities have become increasingly unclear. However, if the concept of disidentification is unhinged from the majority/minority distinction, it can be deployed in its queer sense (as defined by Jones) to address the broader issues of how the interplay between distancing and identification helps generate complex identities.[22] Stuart Hall, who has been a key figure in articulating a nuanced theory of identity as identification, has, in fact, pre-empted such a broader application of the term 'disidentification' to a wider set of questions of cultural identity, which have been brought into sharper focus with intensified migration since the 1980s. In his introduction to the anthology *Questions of Cultural Identity* from 1996, Hall develops his thoughts on identity and *différance* – a concept developed by Jacques Derrida to become the key deconstructivist descriptor of the inherently unstable nature of meaning that constantly slides away. By *différance* is meant 'difference and deferral'; it is the deconstructivist term for a marker that plays the oppositional terms of the binary off against each other (majority/minority, man/woman, white/black, us/them, self/other, Western/non-Western, etc.), thereby unsettling the hegemonic understanding of a word or concept and setting its meaning in motion towards new meanings. In his 1996 introduction, Hall expands on how the play of *différance* imposes on the process of identification an interplay between similarity and difference that never produces 'a proper fit, a totality' but instead enables the process of identification to operate 'across difference' and thus to function as a strategic *positioning*[23] which defies any notion of pure 'otherness' and a stable unitary core of self.[24]

Amelia Jones's theory of identity as identification

Chapter 3 explored how an altered experience of being in the world – globalised, migrant, precarious, hyper-networked, hybridised, and so on – has come to shape artists' practices and careers differently. This chapter traces some of the ways in which this altered experience of subjectivity has begun to shape identifications differently, so that older ways of thinking about identity in terms of binary oppositions no longer resonate in quite the same way. Nor do they possess the same explanatory power as they did at the height of identity politics from the late 1960s into the 1990s,[25] when binaries became lodged in identity theory and thus in activism, art and, eventually, also in the discourses of the art world, as explained in Chapter 2.

What comes to the fore in this chapter is neither the politicised debates on cultural and national identity, nor the identities of the artists themselves, but, rather, the question of how the recent permutations of identity politics and attempts to rethink identification have surfaced in visual art practices. In particular, I wish to explore how the insistence by the three artists (Shonibare, Kher and Vo) on circulation, movement and cultural contamination as the 'ground' of their artworks has come to determine the models of identity that their works suggest. I seek to demonstrate that their works propose a model subject that is engendered by an intricate interplay between different points of identification and disidentification, an interplay that eventually constitutes the subject's hybrid identity. In Marsha Meskimmon's formulation, this is a subject 'configured through networks *across* – translation, transcription, transliteration and transculturation'.[26] In what follows, a detour around Amelia Jones's perceptive and erudite analysis of how a Western binary model of subjectivity came to structure postmodern identity politics, and how this binary structure filtered through to the visual arts, will provide the theoretical frame for some close readings of works by Shonibare, Kher and Vo.

Post-1960 identity politics have deep roots in European history and philosophy, which have shaped the very understanding of social power as functioning through the privileging of one particular group over another within an oppressive binary power structure – which is, in turn, linked to a binary model of identity. According to Jones, this understanding of identity, which can be traced back to G. W. F. Hegel's influential master/slave dialectic, became pivotal to identity politics and activism in the 1970s and 1980s.[27] She founds her theory of identity as identification on a critical analysis of the founders of modern art theory, which pays particular attention to 'the ways in which structures of belief attach artworks to individuals while, at the same time, modern Euro-American concepts of identity, as noted, stage the self in opposition to an other (the "master" in opposition to the "slave")'.[28]

To link together the histories of the Western concept of art and the binary identity theories of self and other – usually perceived as unrelated – Jones not only subjects Hegel's influential theory of the master/slave dialectic in his *Phenomenology of Spirit* (1807) to close scrutiny; she also traces, genealogically, how the theory of subjectivity in the model of the master/slave dialectic was later developed in twentieth-century neo-Hegelian theory 'to crystallize the binary at the base of modern European thought'.[29] Hegel's thoughts were mediated through the highly influential Marxist lectures of Alexandre

Kojève in Paris in the 1930s, which were attended by protagonists of French existentialism and phenomenology such as Jean-Paul Sartre and Maurice Merleau-Ponty. Transmitted through these influential thinkers, Hegel's master/slave dialectic came to shape twentieth-century models of subjectivity and identity, asserts Jones. Coinciding with this, Simone de Beauvoir and Franz Fanon, both working in close proximity to Sartre and Merleau-Ponty, introduced a *political* codification of the master/slave dialectic as they developed it into *oppositional* models of identity. De Beauvoir highlighted gender and sexuality but mentioned class and race, while Fanon explicitly foregrounded race and nationality and only implicitly addressed gender, sexuality and class. From the 1960s onwards, the models that de Beauvoir developed in *The Second Sex* (French 1949, English 1953) and Fanon in *Black Skin, White Masks* (French 1952, English 1967) were extended into models of 'coalitional identity politics'.[30]

In Jones's reading, Hegel's theory opens subjectivity to intersubjectivity by implicitly rejecting the Cartesian idea of the subject as 'potentially full within himself' and proposing an alternative model of the subject as constituted in (power) relation to others.[31] Hegel's master/slave dialectic thus became, so Jones argues, fundamental to the understanding of subjectivity as founded in flagrant asymmetries of how subjects position themselves in and experience the world. Citing Susan Buck-Morss's article on 'Hegel and Haiti' (2000), Jones renders probable that Hegel's binary understanding of master and slave, self and other, was related to actual historical master/slave relations in the colonies, since Hegel wrote *Phenomenology of Spirit* shortly after the successful revolutions in Haiti, in which enslaved Caribbeans overthrew first the British and then the French forces.[32] In post-war Europe, Hegel's theory resonated with the historical aftermaths of two devastating world wars; with the explosive processes of decolonisation and postcolonial independence; with the collapse of the European colonial powers and the rise of the US and USSR to become super-powers; and last but not least, with the rise of female empowerment during the Second World War and the Civil Rights Movement in the US of the 1950s and 1960s. As Jones concludes: 'In such a period, a model that sketched the violent opposition – and yet also the co-dependency – of a dominant and subordinate subject, such as Hegel's, had huge explanatory power.'[33]

To Jones, the binary models of post-1960 identity politics (which also structure the discourses on institutional multiculturalism discussed in Chapter 2) are thus basically neo-Hegelian in the sense that they propagate an understanding of self and other structured by the binary model of the Hegelian master/slave dialectic. Moreover, in the first decades of identity politics, the intricate *dialectical* aspect of the relations of self and other was often downplayed to strengthen political efficacy:[34]

> The extent to which these latter models [of coalitional identity politics] are informed by the Hegelian binary structuring of Beauvoir's and Fanon's model cannot be overestimated, nor can the impact of this binary model on Freudian psychoanalysis, which largely determined structures of critical analysis in art criticism, art history, and film theory, particularly of the feminist variety, from the early 1970s into the 1980s.[35]

Jones's analysis uncovers how a specifically binary model of identity came to inform visual theory and practice by the 1970s and continued to dominate well into the 1990s. To substantiate her proposition, Jones uses as her example British artist Keith Piper's work *The Body Politic* from 1983, in which a diptych of two hinged canvases represents a naked black man on one side, and a naked white woman on the other, both of them subtitled with similar texts starting with the same phrase: 'To you I was always (just) a body … I was your best fantasy and your worst fear. Everything to you but human.' There are many other examples of similar politically engaged artworks from this period, although not all are as explicitly dichotomous as Piper's *The Body Politic*. The invocation of the gender binarism and its division of men and women into opposite and disconnected categories in some of the slogans in Barbara Kruger's posters come to mind, e.g. *Untitled (We construct the chorus of missing persons)*, in which an anonymous woman, face covered by her hair, represents the 'chorus' of women excluded by patriarchy; or the slogan 'You construct intricate rituals which allow you to touch the skin of other men' (1983) in *Untitled (You Construct Intricate Rituals)* (1981), where a group of cheerful men in evening dress are tugging an unwilling buddy by the arms. Another pointed example from the 1980s is American artist Adrian Piper's *My Calling (Card) # 1* (1982), which is addressed specifically to white people and informs recipients of the card that they have made or consented to a racist remark in the mistaken belief that their interlocutor was white, too. The text starts like this: 'Dear Friend, I am black. I am sure you did not realize this when you made/laughed at/agreed with that racist remark. In the past, I have attempted to alert white people to my racial identity in advance.'[36] Although Adrian Piper complicates the issue of race by pointing to the fact that the colour of one's skin does not tell everything, the work nevertheless revolves around an unbending division of people into 'black' and 'white', which constructs the white interlocutor as the 'other' of the speaking black 'self' and as the 'offender' of a 'victim'.

From the 1990s, Pat Ward Williams's *What You Lookin At* (1992) (see figure 5.1) is a black and white photograph of five young black men, with the confrontational title of the work tagged across the picture surface, graffiti-style. Originally made for installation in the windows of two US galleries hosting shows that Williams was participating in, this 'photo-text mural'

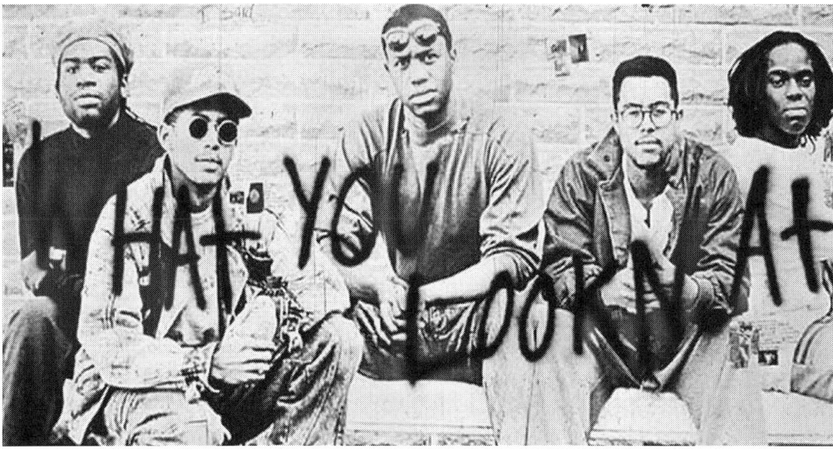

5.1 Pat Ward Williams, *What You Lookin At*, 1992. Darkroom silver photograph, attached colour Xeroxes and family photographs, texts. 213.38 x 487.68 cm. © Pat Ward Williams. Photograph courtesy of the artist.

confronts the passer-by with life-size images of black men, frontally posed and directly facing the street. Although nothing about the group suggests any particular threat, Williams is evidently setting the stage for a play on common white fears of black male youth and on the connotations of graffiti itself: often perceived as a gesture of disrespect for property and order, it suggests the presence of, and potential encounter with, anarchic and violent youth. Williams thus deliberately activates the mechanism of *projection* of individual fantasies, as well as collective stereotypes of what young black men *are* and *do*.[37] However, because the work remains stuck in the binary of black and white, it fails to deconstruct or challenge the racial and sexual stereotypes of black men in America. It tends, rather, to confirm ingrained stereotypes because it sets up the cultural and social encounter between those who look (on their way to the art gallery) and those who are looked at, within the framework of a binary view on black and white America. In the context of this chapter, these works by Barbara Kruger, Adrian Piper and Pat Ward Williams provide a foil for my attempt to trace how identity-oriented works by Yinka Shonibare, Bharti Kher and Danh Vo negotiate the shift from notions of identities as fixed categories towards a more dynamic understanding of identification that is attentive to 'an intersectional array of complex identifications'.[38]

The overarching hypothesis of my analyses is that the works in question articulate an 'intersectional' identity premised upon transcultural movement and exchange, rather than notions of fixity, origin and purity. Kher's, Shonibare's and Vo's works thus participate in a historical transformation of the concept of identity. To some degree, this change can be linked to the rise of queer theory and the concept of queering culture. As Jones has pointed out, the 1990s witnessed an 'explosive development of queer theory' in literature, cultural studies and performance studies, although not in art history. As a result, less instrumental concepts of identification were gradually adopted from the mid-1990s: 'At its best, queer theory precisely refuses the fixing of identity so common to more empirically based, strategically essentializing, or activist and coalitional oriented rights discourses (at its weakest, of course, queer theory becomes gay/lesbian politics and reverts back to binaries …).'[39]

This present study offers a situated perspective – on Kher as a British-Indian, Shonibare as a British-Nigerian, and Vo as a Vietnamese artist who has grown up in Denmark but who chooses to identify himself as a global nomad with no particular national strings, notwithstanding his persistent exploration of his Vietnamese background. I will try to be clear in each case to which culture and transnational interrelation I am referring. However, my North European outlook explains why I share with Jones, and other scholars, a strong desire to transcend the limitations of Western binary thinking, but also need to acknowledge, firstly, how profoundly this has shaped the Euro-American academic fields that this study draws on, and, secondly, that there is consequently no way to avoid including the binaries that I also seek to critically address and complicate: the structural power of binary thinking must be recognised in order for it to be challenged. In addition, with respect to transcultural relations, it is just as important to be attentive to connections and similarities as to differences and disjunction. For more than a thousand years, travel and trade, colonialism and warfare have connected European cultures to the Middle East, Africa, the Americas, Asia and beyond, so it will always be difficult, if not impossible, to make clear-cut distinctions between cultures. In addition, 'Western' liberalism and individualism, for example, were defined in relation to knowledge of 'other' systems, and notions of freedom, agency, hegemony and economic gain are, of course, not unique to 'Western' culture.[40] Moreover, Shonibare, Kher and Vo all have strong relations to Europe, so their works have also been influenced by a European outlook: Kher was born in the UK; Shonibare resides in the UK, Vo is a former resident of Denmark and Germany (and was invited to present a 'national' solo exhibition at the Danish Pavilion at the 56th Venice Bienniale in 2015).

To create art always entails a 'production of locality'[41] that reflects the artist's situatedness. I will therefore be concerned with the question of how personal as well as local geopolitical circumstances have informed the preoccupation of these three artists with identity. Although I do seek to avoid the biographical approach, which tends to consolidate the myth of the work of art as an authentic expression of the artist's inner self, I believe that knowing the artist's background can help viewers and scholars gain a deeper understanding of the artist's work. Identity-oriented works (which are not the same as autobiographical works) seem particularly able to reflect the artist's cultural and historical situatedness, because they often function as a working-through of issues of identity related to the artist's societal and historical situatedness, although abstracted, on a more general level, from the artist's own life. I will therefore begin each analysis with a brief introduction to the artist's background, bearing in mind Hall's perceptive observation that the one who speaks and the subject who is spoken of are never identical, and never positioned identically.[42] Accordingly, I will focus on the ways in which the artists speak of or articulate identifications and disidentifications in *representations* of symbolic figures or model subjects. I will draw on the artists' life stories, not only to contextualise their works, but also to challenge the conventional expectation of authenticity and unbroken continuity between a migrant artist's work and their 'roots'.

Yinka Shonibare: the fabrication of hybrid identities

Yinka Shonibare was born in London in 1962 to Nigerian parents with a Yoruba background. They moved back to Nigeria when he was three, to become part of a new Nigerian elite that was working to build up the country which had acquired its independence from the UK in 1960. Shonibare thus grew up in an upper middle-class environment in the cosmopolitan city of Lagos. He returned to the UK as a teenager to go to boarding school, continuing his education at London art schools after a serious illness in his late teens had reduced his spinal cord functions. In 1991 he graduated from Goldsmiths' College and rapidly established his career as an artist, since when he has had countless solo exhibitions around the world. He participated in *documenta X* in 2002 and was nominated for the Turner Prize in 2004. In 2005, he was awarded the MBE – an acronym for 'Member of the Most Excellent Order of the British Empire'. Ever since, Shonibare has added this title of honour to his professional name, becoming Yinka Shonibare MBE. Just as his perpetual use of the so-called Dutch wax fabric, produced in Holland and Manchester for African consumption, is a deliberately chosen signifier of 'African' identity, his appropriation of the British honour is part of a strategy aimed at stirring debates about postcolonialism – Europe's violent colonial past and its aftermath in the present. Yet it speaks of his generous sense of humour and sensibility towards ambiguities, that he brings attention to his position as part of the Establishment while insisting simultaneously on his right to criticise and deconstruct its historical and ideological structures.

Shonibare refers to himself as a postcolonial hybrid[43] and can be seen as a representative of the growing transcultural and transnational hybridisation of what were formerly often perceived as unitary national cultures – a process of hybridisation that has fundamentally altered the ways in which art and culture are produced and evaluated. From the beginning, Shonibare's works were imbued with a subtle ideological critique of European racism, colonialism and imperialism, and they were quickly drawn into the comprehensive theoretical discussions of the 1990s on postcolonialism and identity politics.[44] As a result, the sensuality, humour and frivolity that also characterise his work were often ignored or seen as subordinate to the political content. Shonibare consciously draws on both African and Western cultural spheres, and consistently emphasises their intertwinement, and thus obstructs any attempt to categorise him or his works based on simplistic notions of ethnic authenticity and 'Africanness'. An intersectional approach to his art seems highly appropriate therefore. Although the complexity with which Shonibare treats issues of race, ethnicity, culture and class is widely recognised, there has been little appreciation of how these coordinates intersect with 'gender', and what bearing the criss-crossing of identifications in his work has on the overall understanding of identity formation in postcolonial times, as communicated by this artist.

Shonibare's works are usually easy to recognise with their mix of patterned African fabrics and references to European cultural history, a colourful and peculiar crossbreed with layers upon layers of meanings. They build on such larger aesthetic issues as beauty and theatricality, as well as wider political concerns of imperialism, postcolonialism and globalism. At the same time, he interrogates issues of race and gender and the status of the excluded, especially migrants – who are personified as 'aliens' in works such as *Alien Child* (2011), a work that evokes the destiny of unaccompanied refugee minors. The alien has almost become a leitmotif in his work. 'It' emerges continually as a kind of Afro-futurist creature of fantasy in differently patterned disguises, beginning in 1998 with the installation *Alien Obsessives ..., Mum, Dad and the Kids*. I use the word 'disguises' deliberately because in works such as *Alien Obsessives, Alien Man on Flying Machine* (2011) and *Alien Woman on Flying Machine* (2011), the African-print fabrics are used to represent the skin of the figures, leaving the figures themselves virtually naked (and thus vulnerable). At the same time, the patterns suggest that they are covered by some kind of camouflage, or are heavily tattooed – i.e. visually stigmatised as hyper visible 'others' in the predominantly white societies of Europe.

Shonibare began including 'African' print cloth in his work in 1992.[45] In 1995, he used it for the first time in Victorian clothing styles in *Five Under Garments and Much More* (1995). *How Does a Girl Like You Get to be a Girl Like You?* (1995) marks the point when he began to present his Victorian costumes on tailor's dummies, which are replaced in his later works by equally headless, full-size fibreglass mannequins with a brown 'mixed race' or 'post-racial' skin tone. Shonibare finds the historical models for his costumes in periods that can function as historical mirrors of our time. These early works draw on the Victorian era when the British Empire was at its peak and the European powers were dividing Africa between them – a crucial colonialist act with immense historical repercussions, later commemorated by Shonibare in his monumental installation *Scramble for Africa* (2003). Shonibare's gesture of hanging Africanised Victorian undergarments on display in *Five Under Garments and Much More* was clearly intended to serve as a synecdoche for the artist's act of revealing the dual nature of modernity. Just as industrial growth and 'progress' in Europe have been inseparable from European colonialist repression and exploitation elsewhere, so 'African' patterns and Victorian fashion function as integrated signifiers in Shonibare's work.[46]

The patterned fabrics known today and marketed as 'African' print fabrics have a complex history involving and connecting Asia, Europe and Africa. They were modelled on Indonesian batik textiles and were first produced in Holland and Manchester in the nineteenth century, with sales to Indonesia in mind. The Indonesians were not interested in Europe's industrial imitations, but in the latter third of the nineteenth century the manufacturers found a booming market for their fabrics in West Africa. Here, the exuberant textiles gradually became symbols of authentic African identity, especially in the wake of decolonisation in the 1960s and the revival of pan-African nationalism. Already in the 1950s, as independent countries emerged in Africa, entrepreneurs in West Africa were establishing their own printing mills that began to undermine the monopolies of the European factories.[47] Thus, the history of the Dutch wax fabric is interlinked with Europe's colonial history and the processes of decolonisation. That a product of European colonialism ended up being a symbol of African identity and authenticity seems ironic, yet it is exactly the irony and ambiguity of this transcontinental history that attracted Shonibare.

In Britain's Anglo-African communities, the bright batik fabrics also became, paradoxically, an important symbol of African authenticity, and they were an essential part of the consumption of African material cultures that went hand in hand with the international Afrocentrism which spread in the black middle class in the United States and Britain during the 1980s.[48] Shonibare buys his material at Brixton Market in London, in the heart of the old British Empire, adding yet another layer to the complex meaning of these fabrics, and emphasises that his works also play with expectations and perceptions emanating from the Afrocentrism that has developed in the West. As Shonibare has put it: 'the fabrics are for me a metaphor for something that is multicultural and essentially hybrid like my own identity'.[49] The artist uses the textiles in ways that enhance their inherent tensions and paradoxes; in his hands, they are at once 'fake' and 'authentic' signifiers of 'Africanness'. He thus formulates what Anthony Downey has described as a 'politics of (in)authenticity' by simultaneously presenting the audience with an ideal of an 'authentic' identity and a sense of identity as 'fabrication'.[50] In addition, the incorporation of the fabrics into the world of art brings references to class distinctions and economic inequality into play, and with them the traditional boundary between high art and popular culture. This evidently is not a boundary of separation but one of distinctions, largely defined by differences in taste and value determined by class and the social function of the artefacts in question, as status objects and as articles for everyday use. As Shonibare himself has explained:

> As soon as you look at my work, there are issues of taste involved and issues of class. It is already quite a political move to take a 'working-class' item, for instance something from the market, and make it into 'high art' that sells for a lot of money. The people who normally buy the fabrics I use are not really into art at all. I mean, high-art galleries are visited by minority groups; it is very much a luxury middle-class thing.[51]

From his early years at Goldsmiths, Shonibare has been engaged in the discussions about identity and influenced by the feminist debates in contemporary art, notably the way that these debates paved the way for recognition of the work of women artists and the inclusion into the mainstream of the work of those artists who were adding new aspects of craft and popular culture to the vocabulary of art.[52] The spread of installation art, and in particular the development of feminist art in the early 1970s, contributed to the revaluation of the traditionally inferior standing of textiles as linked to women's domestic work and handicraft rather than the intellectual accomplishments of artists. In feminist art of the 1970s, the widespread use of such materials by artists such as Miriam Shapiro, Su Richardson and Judy Chicago was perceived as a way of articulating an essentialist notion of a feminine aesthetics. This powerful belief that the creative use of fabric and textiles embodies a specifically feminist discourse and authentic femininity has long since disintegrated. Today, artists such as Shonibare, Thomas Bang and Robert Gober also explore the sculptural potential of textiles and subject the gendered and bodily connotations of these soft materials to unexpected twists and turns.[53]

As Jean Fisher has noted, Shonibare's play with the elusive signs of cultural and ethnic identity is 'compounded by a gender-inflected cross-dressing'[54] because the very use of textiles and the artistic transformation of the gaudy fabrics into historical feminine dresses and feminised man-tailored suits point both to a traditional women's sphere and an emphatically 'feminine' aesthetics. The compound gender connotations also surface as androgyny in some of Shonibare's mannequin-based sculptures, especially in *Gay Victorians* (1999) and *Affectionate Men* (1999), which depict same-sex pairs of figures under titles that suggest same-sex relationships. Also, in his film *Un ballo in Maschera* (2004), the two leading male roles of Gustav III of Sweden and his assassin are played, or rather performed, by women dancers.[55] Sexual motifs are present too, most explicitly in the spectacular, orgy-like installation *Gallantry and Criminal Conversation*, made for *documenta 11* in 2002, and the early photographic series *Diary of a Victorian Dandy* (1998).[56]

A particularly interesting work, from a gender perspective, is the larger than life figure *Big Boy* (2002) (see plate 5) dressed in Victorian splendour and spreading his arms behind him in an apparent gesture of pride and self-confidence.[57] However, his suit has been queered, with coat-tails expanding into a multi-coloured train with frills around the edge, more reminiscent of an extravagant Victorian dress than a man's suit. As always in his mannequin-based sculptures from before the 2010s, Shonibare has left *Big Boy* headless. The missing heads are often interpreted as a gallows humour reference to the guillotining of aristocrats during the French Revolution – a reference that comes across easily in Shonibare's 2007 installation at Paris's Musée du quai Branly, *Garden of Love* (see plate 2), which paraphrases French eighteenth-century paintings by Fragonard (see Chapter 4). This allusion to the guillotine is also intended as a thinly veiled *memento mori* for the elites of contemporary affluent societies who turn a blind eye to the increasingly uneven distribution of wealth.[58] However, since Shonibare is not only interested in French eighteenth-century culture and revolutionary politics, but equally so in the Victorian era, the missing heads can also be understood more broadly as gesturing towards a view of history that sees its actors not so much as empowered rational beings but as marionettes manipulated by historical events.[59] Yet, I would argue that in *Big Boy*, the missing head seems to take on additional meaning in that the 'boy' is depicted as an anonymous man of African descent (suggested by his clothes of African-print fabric) who adopts the manners and dress of a genteel European dandy, thus revealing the larger pattern of 'cultural imperialism' and the migratory nature of people and culture by his very clothing.

As Roland Barthes has demonstrated, fashion and costume constitute a language, a system of signs and meanings.[60] Hence, the function of dress is not only to protect and to beautify the body but also to communicate and exchange information with others by advertising one's self-identifications. Manthia Diawara, an expert on black diaspora studies, perceptively reads *Big Boy* from the perspective of the traditional critique of Nigerian imitation of the English. Diawara suggests that Shonibare deliberately reiterates the stereotype of the *been-to* – those returned African migrants who imitate the English by adopting their style of dress, for example – but that Shonibare also cannibalises the stereotype in order to create something new. Diawara's understanding of the *been-to* comes close to Homi Bhabha's notion of colonial mimicry and identification as bringing about a form of difference that effects a resemblance to Britishness that is '*almost the same but not quite*':[61] '*Big Boy* is a poetics of Englishness – as they say "he is a been-to", a grotesque copy of the real thing. But seen from a post-colonial viewpoint, it is the real deal, and the existential mode of this new identity depends on creating Englishness while destroying our prior knowledge of it.'[62] Diawara elaborates on his point about destruction by adding that in the twenty-first century, identities have become so entangled that is hard to distinguish a 'real' Englishman from a 'pretender': 'Englishness has been permeated by so many different identities and hues, that it has become impossible to tell who is English and who is not, based on appearance, accent, and way of life alone. For Shonibare, the stereotype is all we have left to invoke Englishness, its different histories and futures.'[63]

I contend, therefore, that Shonibare deliberately disrupts the borders and divisions by which binarist thought defines 'self' against an excluded or inferior 'other'. His costumed sculptures represent identity as emphatically cross-cultural, intersectional, ambiguous and dynamic – that is, as a subversive process of 'fabrication' rather than an authentic 'being'. Reading Shonibare's work from the perspective of José Esteban Muñoz's theory of disidentification would suggest that disidentification is a vital aspect of his fusion of elements from African and European spheres. His works display neither an identification nor a counteridentification with either of the two spheres. Instead, Shonibare negotiates with existing cultural codes, tropes and stereotypes drawn from both spheres. He does not abandon the identity constituents of 'majoritarian' British national culture, European colonial legacies, Nigerian culture, or Afrocentrism for that matter, but he turns them all inside out by bringing them in hybridising proximity to each other.

For José Esteban Muñoz, disidentification and hybridity are closely related, as both concepts capture theories of fragmentation and can be used to characterise and analyse the composite subject formation of people whose identities travel back and forth between diverse identity vectors. In effect, Muñoz contends that 'A theory of migrancy can potentially help us better understand the negotiations of these fragmentary existences.'[64] Muñoz's theory of disidentification is founded in Jean Laplance and Jean-Bertrand Pontalis's psychoanalytic definition of identification as 'a psychological process whereby the subject assimilates an aspect, property or attribute of the other and is transformed, wholly or partially, after the model the other provides. It is by means of a series of identifications that the personality is constituted and specified.'[65] Muñoz also couples the psychoanalytic definition of identification to Marxist theorist Louis Althusser's seminal theory of ideology as *the* determining factor in subject formation. According to Althusser, ideology is the imaginary relationship of individuals to their conditions of existence. This relationship is formed when subjects are 'hailed' or placed in subject positions, a process he calls *interpellation*. Moving on from Althusser to linguist Michel Pêcheux's Althusserian understanding of disidentification, Muñoz eventually opts for an understanding of disidentification that sees the subject as constructed *inside* the purview of ideology. Thus, disidentification is defined as a critical strategy that aims neither to assimilate within a dominant ideological structure, nor to oppose it. Quite the opposite, it is 'working on and against' to transform a cultural logic from within.[66]

A disidentifying subject is unable to fully identify or to establish what Sigmund Freud described as a 'just as if' relationship, Muñoz argues. When crafting and performing the self, the disidentifying subject makes emphatic that identification does not build on unilateral mimesis and simple similitude. It involves variegated processes of *identifying with and against*. Such processes of identifying with a person, a group, an object, a history, a nation, an ideology, a religion or a lifestyle are, as Kosofsky Sedgwick has explained, 'fraught with intensities of incorporation, diminishment, inflation, threat, loss, reparation and disavowal'.[67] Identifying with, is therefore also partially counteridentifying, as well as only partially identifying, with various aspects of the social and psychic world.[68] Subjects such as migrant and minoritarian individuals who understand themselves to be outside the dominant public sphere often encounter difficulties in forming 'just as if' relationships with the 'majoritarian' culture. Muñoz's concepts of disidentification and disidentity can help account for the intersectional nature of transcultural identifications, as articulated in artworks.

Diawara identifies Shonibare's *Big Boy* as a Nigerian *been-to*, a man who partially counteridentifies with his African background and partially identifies with Victorian dandyism. His feminised coat also suggests a distancing from masculinity and a partial identification with femininity. In terms of culture as well as gender, *Big Boy* proudly and willingly presents himself as a hybrid. Furthermore, in his paraphrases of celebrated artworks of European art history, Shonibare also exposes European subjects and subject matter to a kind of enforced or critical disidentification with the ideal of white purity– for example, in the mimicry in his *Mr and Mrs Andrews Without Their Heads* (1998) of Thomas Gainsborough's painting *Mr. and Mrs. Andrews* (c. 1750); of Sir Henry Raeburn's *Reverend Robert Walker Skating* (1784) in *Reverend on Ice* (2005); and of paintings by Fragonard in *The Swing (after Fragonard)* (2001) and *Garden of Love* (see Chapter 4). In these staged disidentifications of the European 'other' from its previous self-identification as 'white', Shonibare has deployed his usual headless mannequins of a racially indefinable complexion to break open the dominant Eurocentric ideology and lay bare Europe's real hybridity and colonial entanglement with other parts of the world.

Bharti Kher: intersections of gender and ethnicity

Like Yinka Shonibare's *Big Boy*, the art of Bharti Kher raises the question of how identifications are formed in reverse migration. Kher was born in 1969 in suburban London, where she grew up, eventually enrolling at Middlesex Polytechnic to study painting, and continuing her art studies at Newcastle Polytechnic in northern England. In 1993, she made her second visit to India – her parents' country of origin. Here she met her future husband, the artist Subodh Gupta, and stayed on to become one half of New Delhi's 'No. 1 Power Art Couple'[69] and one of India's top selling women artists, exhibiting extensively in India as well as across the world.[70]

Just as African-print textiles have become Yinka Shonibare's trademark, so, too, is the name Bharti Kher associated with a particular signature: the *bindi*, the small decorative dot that Indian women often stick on to their foreheads between the eyebrows. Like Shonibare, she has transformed her signature material into her own language through acts of repetition. The texturing, layering and colour in Kher's *bindi* series suggest a sensibility to woven textiles. The story goes that Kher's fascination with *bindis* was sparked when she saw a woman wearing a sperm-shaped one, and 'the irony of an uber male symbol adorning an uber feminine accessory struck her forcefully'.[71] Such stories aside, the *bindi* is a traditional element that has taken on several meanings in the course of history. From originally signifying the fertility of married women in some parts of India, as well as being a religious marker of the invisible 'third eye' of spiritual insight beyond ordinary perception, the *bindi* has become a contemporary fashion accessory. Although it has been torn loose of its cultural moorings to enter the mix'n'match culture of globalised fashion, it is still the symbol par excellence of Indian femininity. As Indian writer and literary critic Anita Roy dryly notes, 'It says "I'm a woman" and "I'm an Indian". Straightforward sentences, and yet there are few more complex ideas than gender and nationality.'[72]

British by birth, Bharti Kher is nevertheless identified as an 'Indian' artist both in her adopted home country and abroad. It is telling that when interviewed in 2010 by one of India's leading newspapers, the *Times of India*, she was presented as 'one of India's bestselling women artists', whereas London, where she grew up, was presented as the city that 'plays host' to her first solo exhibition.[73] Correspondingly, Western galleries and art institutions continually include her works in group exhibitions of 'contemporary Indian art', thereby consolidating the clear-cut identification of the artist as 'Indian' rather than 'British Asian' or 'diasporic'. Yet Kher herself opposes national categories and the labels that are forced on people. For instance, when the reporter from the *Times of India* asked whether she was still a Brit in India with an outsider's perspective on it, she replied that she did not like to be classified, thus actively rejecting the identification as British and seeking to craft an Indian or perhaps a cosmopolitan self: 'I am not from one place or another. We all play multiple roles. Some of them are chosen and some put upon us. My sculptures, too, defy all classification of class, race, time – they could be anybody.'[74]

As someone who is part of two distinct cultures that are intimately related historically, Kher seeks to express a multifaceted understanding of identity formation that complicates essentialist notions of gender, race, class and ethnicity. The best example of this is perhaps the growing body of cast sculptures, which Kher calls her 'urban goddesses' to stress their contemporaneity as well as their status as aggrandised models of female subjectivity and bearers of myth.[75] Realising that her work is manifestly feminine, Kher has publicly declared herself to be a feminist.[76] With a father who was a textile consultant and a mother who was a seamstress and owned a fabric shop,[77] Kher shares with Shonibare an interest in textiles and fashion, particularly traditional or historical garments, which has informed many of her efforts to launch a critique of gender roles. Her critical feminist stance is, for instance, conveyed by a series of works from 2011 in which twisted saris fall dramatically down wooden stairs, suggestive of domestic violence and torment under such ominous titles as *The day they met*, *An encounter that changed their lives* and *The night she left*. The series suggests if not identification then at least a strong political solidarity with Indian women subjected to domestic violence and a brutal patriarchy.

The staircase series can be seen as a thematic continuation of three 'cubicle' works that deal with the domestic violence and claustrophobia that many Indian women struggle with. In the first one, *Confess* (2010), Kher decorated the interior of a traditional bride's chamber with vibrant and flowing streams of *bindis* reminiscent of Jackson Pollock's all-over paintings.[78] The second is an enclosure built of bricks entitled *The deaf room* (2001–12). Once inside, the visitor is subjected to the sternness of the tall structure, which evokes feelings of imprisonment and isolation. However, as Zehra Jumabhoy has pointed out, without information on the context, as regards locality, to support a cultural translation of the work's sinister depths, Western audiences are likely to overlook the 'minimalist' structure's foreboding association with danger and violence. The bricks were made of melted, dark-red glass bangles like those worn by many Indian women. These are highly personal, in the sense that each woman's movements prompt her bangles to create different sounds. The silence of *The deaf room* thus points to the absence of the body. Superstition surrounds these bangles in India – breaking one is believed to bode that the woman's husband is in danger.[79] The sense of enclosure of both *Confess* and *The deaf room* elicits a claustrophobic uneasiness that ties in with Kher's engagement with domesticity and women's roles in India. As the artist herself has explained, 'In Asia and India, the house and domestic space constitute a female domain, and this is where women are able to truly assert more 'self' within space. But a house is also fraught with social, economic and sexual excesses.'[80]

The third cubicle, *The hot winds that blow from the West* (2011) (see figure 3.1), also mentioned in Chapter 3, shifts the perspective and offers a cross-cultural view on domesticity. The monumental cube is constructed from 131 old radiators that Kher imported from and later 'exported' back to the US. Symbols of domestic comfort in the West, these displaced appliances have been dismantled both literally and metaphorically; the journey eastward has stripped them of their purpose and altered their meaning. Made for Kher's solo exhibition at Hauser & Wirth's New York gallery, *The hot winds that blow from the West* presents itself as a cheeky response to the cool industrial finish of American minimalist sculptures – an evocation, in the negative, of the sheen that radiates from Donald Judd's modular steel cubes. With its rows of pipes and peeling paint, Kher's cube resembles a decaying animal carcass with ribs exposed. Here, the familiar is transformed into something alien and uncanny, which inspires shock, perhaps even revulsion. The imposing installation is named after The Loo, the hot burning winds which sweep across North India. If radiators are necessary as protection against the cold in North America, they are – to quote Kher – 'defunct' in New Delhi and thus all the more apt as metaphors of shifting power relations and a perception that sees the third world as steadily taking over the role of the first as the global economic powerhouse.[81]

Kher's use of staircases, mirrors, furniture and the cubicle pays homage to the domestic space in which women have traditionally served as homemakers and mothers. In addition, her urban goddesses testify to a concern with female identity formation. Kher's transition from the UK to India was not easy, particularly because she found the restrictions on women in India inhibiting.[82] Yet, with time, these restrictions also triggered an interest in the life and home environment of women in India, further stimulated by her observation of the many forces at play.[83] One may wonder whether the persistent exploration of domesticity has also provided Kher – a Western artist with feminist convictions – with opportunities to perform processes of 'home-building' in India. As sociologist Avtar Brah has remarked, the very strong association of notions of diaspora (and migration, for that matter) with dislocation and displacement has pushed the experience of 'location' into the background. As a result, discourses on migration and diaspora have tended to highlight the image of the journey and downplay the significance of the processes of settling down 'elsewhere' and the 'homing desire' that fuels them.[84] In their joint introduction to the anthology *Uprootings/Regroundings: Questions of Home and Migration*, Sara Ahmed, Claudia Castañeda, Anne-Marie Fortier and Mimi Sheller seek to move beyond the ingrained opposition of stasis versus mobility and insist that the various forms and conditions of migrancy exist in relation to similarly diverse 'configurations of placement, or being "at home"'.[85] *Homing*, whether in migration or in one's country of origin, entails the (re)creation of attachments to a place:

> the affective qualities of home, and the work of memory in their making cannot be divorced from the more concrete materialities of rooms, objects, rituals, borders and forms of transport that are bound up in so many processes of uprooting and regrounding. Homing, then, depends on the reclaiming and reprocessing of habits, objects, names and histories that have been uprooted … Making home is about *creating* both pasts and futures through inhabiting the grounds of the present.[86]

A defining characteristic of Kher's urban goddesses is the unfamiliar amalgamation of signs and figures, and the contradictions and hybridity effected by her 'reclaiming and reprocessing' of these signs and figures. Most recall dark goddesses from various mythologies such as Persephone, Hecate, Lilith and Kali, who are connected to the Earth and to issues of survival, desire and death and known to unsettle the order of things.[87] However, Kher's goddesses are also *urban*. The pale, cyborg-like *Arione's Sister* (2006) is emphatically so. With hands filled with shopping bags that create a fan-like halo around her body, Arione's sister presents herself as a consumerist version of Botticelli's *Venus* emerging from the sea on a scallop shell. She is cast as an elegant and self-confident shopaholic whose proximity to the rising Indian middle class links her to Kher's fashionable-looking *Miss Hera Moon* (2006) and her environment of floral wallpaper and domestic furniture. Sculptures such as these reveal a fascination, perhaps even an identification, with the Indian middle class rather than any social critique of urban elites. But the panoply of Kher's urban goddesses also comprises *And all the while the benevolent sleep* (2008) (see figure 5.2), *Warrior with Cloak and Shield* (2008), *The Messenger* (2011) and, in particular, *Arione* (2004) (see plate 6), which all present themselves to viewers in a much more confrontational and ambiguous way. As art critic and curator Gayatri Sinha has observed, they 'completely invert their domestic role with a powerful physicality'.[88] *Arione* is a hybridised bare-breasted Amazon who wears leather hot pants, sports a holster with a gun and carries a tray of pink cupcakes. The most disturbing aspect is probably the figure's left leg, which is modelled after the leg of a horse and ends in a hoof. She is, in Ranjit Hoskote's words, 'an intimidating hybrid'.[89] At first glance, one is likely to associate her with submission in either a domestic or an orientalist setting. She could be the embodiment of a wife attending to the needs of the family patriarch, or a dark-skinned 'slave' about to serve an absent white 'master' whose substitute becomes the viewer. The next moment, however, one notices that, although she offers cakes, her stance is semi-aggressive;

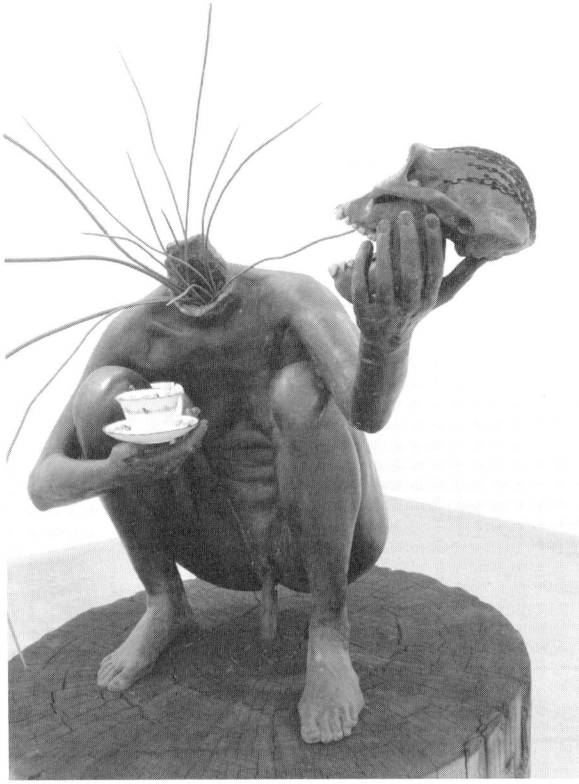

5.2 Bharti Kher, *And all the while the benevolent sleep*, 2008. Fibreglass, porcelain, plastic, pedestal in mahogany wood, copper wires, 180 x 100 x 180 cm. © Bharti Kher. Photograph: Guillaume Ziccarelli, courtesy of the artist and Galerie Perrotin.

and the gun suggests empowerment as well as a 'naked' vulnerability that may induce her to use it. Despite their association with objects and acts of domesticity, Kher bestows on her figures a different kind of agency. As Sinha has proposed, they seem to function metaphorically as extensions of Kher's refusal to accept existing social systems and her desire to interfere with their stability and hierarchies.[90]

Kher has explained how her work changed when she moved to New Delhi. If 'race' defined her in suburban England, 'sex' would define her in India in a way that made her conscious of the fact that she was identified as a 'woman'. And if she found racism potentially a restriction for her in England, the encounter with gender discrimination and sexual harassment curbed her artistically in the beginning of her career in India. *Hirsute* (1999–2000), comprising 351 small oil paintings based on photographic close-ups of moustaches, is Kher's response to the unnerving and intrusive male gaze she often encountered in the streets of New Delhi. In line with *Hirsute*, her urban goddesses can be read as a critical artistic response provoked by racial and sexual discrimination. As such, the goddesses represent a disidentification with the reductionist notions of identity that fuel discrimination in British as well as Indian society. As Kher has remarked: 'You realise that all of these things define you in a way that you do not necessarily want to be defined, and maybe that's why these women I make are not racially defined and are often sexually ambiguous. I actually don't believe that these things are important.'[91]

It is thus clear that Kher reformulated her identity into a form that both reflected her experience of living in two distinctly different socio-cultural environments *and* was compatible with her wish to position herself as an artist from India – an artist who was working with indigenous references, mining Indian mythology for the manifold manifestations and narratives of the divine feminine,[92] and seeking to create works that would resonate in India. In an Indian context, Kher can be seen as an artist who pursues, in Hoskote's words, 'the radical political purpose of turning the female body into a device of rebellion and intransigence against the etiquette of acceptable shapes, uses and duties that contemporary Indian society prescribes for it'.[93]

Kher's urban goddesses suggest that she was working to achieve what Muñoz called *disidentity*. The term does not refer to some kind of 'anti-identity' that rejects the idea of identity as such. Instead, disidentity rejects conventional binary and discriminatory notions of identity and opts for a *reconstructed* identity politics and version of self.[94] A subject who is interpellated by a dominant ideology may respond with a '*tactical misrecognition*'. Through such self-empowering acts of disavowal, the subject may be able to expose the dominant ideology and the way in which it is articulated in public space as 'discursively pre-constituted' ideology, explains Muñoz.[95] I would like to suggest that this is exactly what Kher's array of hybrid and queer urban goddesses achieve. The series proposes a model of radical intersectional identification comparable to the theoretical models of Jones and Muñoz. By hybridising her sculptures, Kher is able to propose an understanding of identity as a dynamic formation, emerging at the intersection between gender, race, ethnicity, and, in the case of *Arione*, *Arione's Sister* and *Miss Hera Moon*, also class. She pushes the limits of identifications even further than Shonibare tends to do by letting her figures transgress the borderlines between the human and the divine, as well as between humans and animals.[96] As Sinha has explained, Kher is mainly interested in the minor goddesses ranked below the great gods. They 'people the charmed world at the interface between humans and animals, the world of Aesop's fables as much as the Buddhist *Jataka* tales and Hindu *Panchatantra* animal fables'.[97] Take, for example, Kher's *And all the while the benevolent sleep* (2008) – a dark-skinned headless figure of a woman squatting on a wooden plinth (suggesting closeness to 'earth' and 'nature') and holding a skull in one hand while balancing a teacup in the other (evoking mortality and the fragility of the human body). The figure refers to the Indian goddess Chinnamasta, a severed-head deity who holds her own head on a platter. Feeding her devotees from her gaping wound, she symbolises feminine sacrifice, life and death.[98] The substitution of the goddess's traditional props with others is characteristic of the way Kher recodes mythology. Like the merging of human and bestial in *Arione* and *Arione's Sister*, the antler-like extensions of the figure in *Warrior with Cloak and Shield* and *The Messenger*'s spearing of a sari with her pitchfork suggest a magical empowerment that transgresses the closed circle of mundane domestic experience and convention-bound understandings of women and femininity.

I have argued that Kher's work could be read as answers to issues of identification and as acts of self-identification, but this interpretation leaves open the question of where the identification takes place: in the artist, the artwork, the interpreter/viewer, or the interpretive frameworks constructed by curators, critics and historians? My interpretation does not resolve this confusion but suggests that the analysis of identification *through* art, as it were, involves all these different and interconnected 'sites'. The analysis of Danh Vo's works below supports this assumption.

Danh Vo: the ready-made as a means of identification

In the Introduction, I used Danh Vo's project *We, the People (Detail)* to explore the fact that the circulation of cultural forms has become central to globalised contemporary art and culture, as both a condition and a topic. I return to Vo here to demonstrate how complicated the intersectional patterns of identification and disidentification that surface in artworks can be.

Politics of belonging are high on the political agenda almost everywhere, observes Nira Yuval-Davis.[99] Yural-Davis is one among many scholars who have questioned the hegemony of nationalist modes of belonging in the twenty-first century, and suggested that other projects of belonging are competing with nationalism. Transnational belonging is clearly one of these, as are religious and political attachments and the spectrum of 'minoritarian' identity politics. Historian Ulf Hedetoft and visual studies scholar Mette Hjort are in accord with Yuval-Davis about belonging as constitutive of identity. They use the English word 'belonging' – 'a fortuitous compound of *being* and *longing*'[100] – to stress this point: 'Today, belonging constitutes a political and cultural field of global contestation (anywhere between ascriptions of belonging and self-constructed definitions of new spaces of culture, freedom, and identity), summoning a range of pertinent issues concerning relations between individuals, groups, and communities.'[101]

Compared to Yinka Shonibare and Bharti Kher, Danh Vo's approach to identity and belonging is characterised by a stronger emphasis on national and regional attachments. Accordingly, the interplay between identification and disidentification in his works often seems to revolve around national histories and politics, but it should be emphasised that he also engages with issues of gender, sexuality and, occasionally, race. Danh Vo's artistic practice thus presents a range of interesting examples of how a migrant artist can negotiate belonging.

As collective identities are founded in attachments to particular collectivities and (imagined) communities, i.e. in a sense of belonging, I will begin by introducing Yuval-Davis's clarifying distinction between *belonging* and *the politics of belonging*. Belonging concerns emotional attachments and feeling 'at home'. It is an open-ended process entailing a sense of hope regarding the future, which can partly be ascribed to the common notion of home as a 'safe' space. Yuval-Davis reminds us that in the daily life of the early twenty-first century, in the many parts of the world stricken by war and disaster (and the ensuing forced displacement of people), the emphasis on safety gains a new poignancy. She also makes a point of stressing that 'feeling "at home" does not necessarily only generate positive and warm feelings'.[102] Its spectrum of emotional engagement encompasses anger, shame and indignation, too. As an 'unmarked' everyday experience, belonging tends to be naturalised. It only becomes articulated, formally structured and politicised when it is threatened or put under pressure in some way:

> The politics of belonging comprise of specific political projects aimed at constructing belonging to particular collectivity/ies which are themselves being constructed in these projects in very specific ways and in very specific boundaries (i.e. whether or not, according to specific political projects of belonging Jews could be considered to be German, for example, or abortion advocates can be considered Catholic).[103]

When creating their works, artists may draw on their own everyday experience and sense of belonging as well as the (mediated) study and knowledge of other people's experience. However, it is crucial to keep in mind that artworks materialise as *representations* that communicate through languages (visual, verbal, bodily, etc.). This means that they mediate and interpret experiences and observations by drawing on existing systems of representation or by proposing imaginative reconfigurations of those systems, or both. Using Yuval-Davis's distinction, I wish to posit that works of art that address the issues of belonging to and (dis)identification with particular collectivities partake in the politics of belonging. They achieve this through the construction, or deconstruction, of representations of belonging, or by expressing, directly or indirectly, their identification with a particular national, ethnic, religious, diasporic or other group. It is important to understand that the politics of belonging involve the maintenance and reproduction of the boundaries of the community of belonging by the hegemonic political powers, both within and without the community. They *also* involve the contestation of and resistance to these boundaries by other political agents who struggle for the promotion of their specific position on the construction of collectivities and their boundaries.[104] In short, the politics of belonging also include struggles around the determination of what is involved in belonging, i.e. struggles around the definition and representation of who belongs. Art has a vital role to fulfil in these negotiations of belonging. It is a powerful and sophisticated cultural means of reproducing, negotiating and contesting publicly what signals belonging, not only in terms of skin colour, ethnicity and legal citizenship but also in terms of the symbols, views, lifestyles and possessions by which subjects identify themselves as individuals and as members of communities – and by which they are also identified by others.

Quoting Stuart Hall, Yuval-Davis observes that globalisation has produced 'the multicultural question', meaning that globalisation and international mass migration has turned the question of how people can live together in difference into one of the most pressing societal issues of the twenty-first century. Yuval-Davis's point is that the contemporary politics of belonging, and contesting projects of belonging, need to be seen as taking place in this context.[105] Thomas Gammeltoft Hansen, an expert on human rights and international refugee law, has pointed out that – after years of seemingly unending war in Syria, and with an increasing number of people fleeing civil wars in places the world over where military and other power sources of the state are used against particular groups of the population – it has become clear that the world is not facing a 'global migration crisis' but 'a global refugee crisis'.[106] The memories of refugee histories fade quickly in collective consciousness and media discourses, with their rapid turnover of fleeting images and news stories. Across the global North and the global South, countries struggle to engage with and commemorate their histories of refugeedom, because these transnational histories challenge homogeneous notions of the national body, observes Veronica Tello.[107] In connection with the increased scale of forced migration, some of the early works of Danh Vo take on a particular topicality. These works are not about the horrors of forced displacement or the vulnerability of refugees. They explore, rather, what comes after the flight: how 'home-grown' notions of the West and Western ways of receiving refugees determine the newcomers' life in the receiving society, how society enables inclusion and the ways in which refugees seek to include themselves.

Danh Vo was born in 1975 in Bai Rai near Saigon (now Ho Chi Minh City), the same year the capital fell to the North Vietnamese Army, against which the US had waged a doomed military campaign since 1960. Together with

20,000 other South Vietnamese, Vo and his family were evacuated by the US military to the island of Phu Quoc off the Cambodian coast. Four years later, his father Phung Vo crammed his family and 100 other refugees in a boat he had covertly built. Their dream was to cross the Pacific Ocean to the US, but they never got that far. A Danish freighter from the Maersk shipping company intercepted them at sea, and they were taken to Copenhagen where the family were given asylum and began their new lives. Danh's parents became owners of a restaurant and takeaway, while he went to school on weekdays 'like any other young Danish citizen'[108] and to the Catholic Mass on Sundays with his tradition-bound family.[109] Vo has explained that he has no memory of his early childhood and the flight from Vietnam, nor has he been brought up with nostalgic stories about Vietnam and the cultivation of memories of a lost homeland. His interest in his country of origin came much later: 'I did not develop an interest in Vietnam before I was in my late twenties. Actually, I had travelled a lot in Thailand before I visited Vietnam. It came in a roundabout way. It was especially the US I was interested in – Vietnam's history came to me via the history of the US, and after I had been absorbed in the Vietnam War.'[110] Asked by Jeppe Villadsen to respond to the recurrent description of Vo's work as 'obsessed with his own origin' (which undoubtedly stems from a framing of the artist as a migrant 'ethnic' artist in search of his lost cultural 'roots'), Vo adds the much-needed nuances: 'I would rather say that I am obsessed with my work. Origin is a strange thing. After all, I have been educated at an institution of higher education for seven years; it is also my origin and my real expertise, not Vietnam.'[111]

The important point here is that Vo's works do not represent a migrant's obsession with, or a nostalgic attempt to recuperate, his own past. In his work, 'Vietnam' and 'migrancy' are filtered through a 'high-end form of conceptualism in which carefully arrayed objects are supplemented by a *studium* of explanatory text', as Claire Bishop has so succinctly put it in her trenchant discussion of the two exhibitions Vo was involved in on the occasion of the 2015 Venice Biennale: his solo exhibition *Mother Tongue* in the Danish Pavilion, and *Slip of the Tongue*, the group exhibition he curated (with Caroline Bourgeois) at the François Pinault Foundation's Punta della Dogana.[112] Vo often mixes personal reflection and historical allusion. Several of his works allude, for example, to American cultural imperialism and military interventions, while others hint at European colonialism, particularly the role of the Catholic Church and its Missions. These postcolonial and historical strands in his works suggest that he strives to critically address the symbiosis of modernity and coloniality, but these strands are also a part of the artist's general concern with the overall theme of worldwide circulation, exchange, translation and transition of objects, ideas and (political and religious) beliefs. As the curator Luigi Fassi has put it, Vo is 'much less a maker of things than an arranger and stager of them'.[113] His artistic practice is based on a subtle combination of appropriation and reconfiguration that inscribes itself in the complicated historical relationship between the West and other regions of the world. With migration and cultural exchange, aspects of non-Western cultures have, in various ways and to varying degrees, become internal to Western-style modernity. However, a significant number of Vo's works are also historical tokens of how, in the wake of the collapse of colonial regimes, some Western countries continued their political and military engagement with the new nation states – through the war in Vietnam, for example.

When he was nominated in 2009 for the Preis der Nationalgalerie für junge Kunst in Berlin, Vo's contribution to the exhibition at Hamburger Bahnhof, Berlin, was a chandelier with the title *08:03:51, 28.05.2009*. The title refers to the exact time when the chandelier – originally installed in the ballroom of the Majestic Hotel in Paris – was taken down to make way for a remodelling of the building. In that chandeliered ballroom, the United States, South Vietnam, North Vietnam and the Vietcong had negotiated a peace pact in 1973. Throughout the 1950s and 1960s, the Vietcong, a lightly armed South Vietnamese communist front directed by the North, had fought a guerrilla war against anti-communist forces and the Government of South Vietnam, which they regarded as a US puppet state. But despite the Paris Peace Accords signed by all parties at the Majestic Hotel in January 1973, the fighting continued. After the collapse of the South Vietnamese government, Vo's family had had to flee the country, as did an estimated one to two million other citizens in the late 1970s after the Communists' victory and the Fall of Saigon in 1975.[114] The title of Vo's work thus marks the time of the disappearance of a historical site, while the object itself – thanks to Vo's transformation of the chandelier into an artistic ready-made – seeks to preserve the memory of the broken peace pact and its devastating human consequences.

Vo's recurrent use of material objects his family acquired as part of their adaptation to European ways of living signifies the personal reflections in his works. In a perceptive analysis, H. G. Masters has rightly pointed out that the family keepsakes included in Vo's works do not only represent the particular history of his family, but also serve the broader purpose of representing the experiences and aspirations of other people with similar histories. *If You Were To Climb the Himalayas Tomorrow* (2005) consists of a commercial glass vitrine with lighting, protecting and displaying a Rolex watch, a Dupont lighter and an American military class ring. *Das Beste oder Nichts* ('The Best or Nothing') (2010) also consists of a relic of family life and social climbing: the outworn engine of his father's Mercedes-Benz, displayed on the floor. Both jewellery and car are objects that, in Vo's interpretation, represent his father's idea, or more generally the idea that immigrants from a communist country have, of European material comfort[115] – and probably also of a certain Western brand of masculinity and success. As Vo has explained about his father: 'From Vietnam, he has always dreamt of getting a Rolex watch and a Dupont lighter. It was very particular trademarks that counted. It was not because we had a lot of money, but every time he had a little, he had to have all these things. He was obsessed with it. I have always thought that it was false, in a way.'[116]

While masculinity is a marked feature of the symbols and artefacts by which Vo represents his father's, and more broadly, the male immigrant's identifications, it is domestic femininity that reigns, in contrast, in *Oma Totem* ('Grandmother's Totem') (2009) (see figure 5.3). Here, Vo has also used family possessions to invite viewers to reflect on how artefacts and commodities function in soft-power strategies of control and 'integration'.[117] The sculpture comprises objects that his grandmother, Nguyen Thi Ty, received

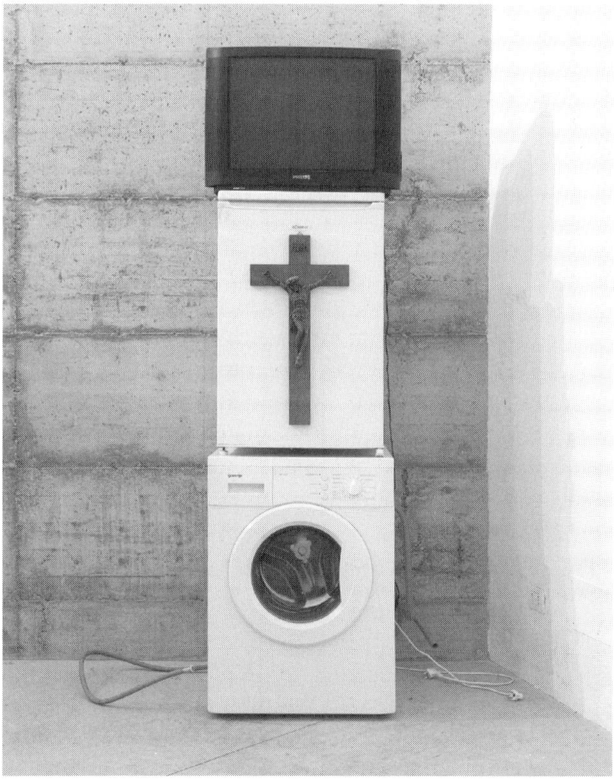

Danh Vo, *Oma Totem* ('Grandmother's Totem'), 2009. Gorenje washing machine, Bomann refrigerator, wooden crucifix, casino card, 26 in. Philips television. 220 x 60 x 60 cm. Private Collection, Turin. © Danh Vo. Photograph: Jacopo Menzani, courtesy of the artist and Galleria Zero, Milan. 5.3

from the Immigrant Relief Program and the Catholic Church when she arrived in Germany as a refugee. A half-size Bomann refrigerator is placed on top of a Gorenje washing machine. On top of this minimalist stack of home appliances sits a black 26-inch Philips television. This modern Western family altar – the TV – is symbolically elevated above the wooden crucifix that is fastened to the front of the refrigerator, seemingly serving as a centrepiece for prayer.[118] In a related flat relief sculpture from the same year, *Untitled* (2009), Vo has re-presented the stack of electronic goods in marble and granite and the crucifix in wood and bronze and placed the whole stack horizontally on the floor. Shifted from the vertical position of a standing, living body to the horizontal position of the body at rest, the stack becomes a gravestone – an actual one, in fact, to be placed on the grave of Vo's grandmother as a memorial to the deceased in her post-migration incarnation as an acculturated European citizen. Designated as a 'totem', the towering stack of *Oma Totem* is meant to be read symbolically. The blatant straightforwardness with which the state and the church sought to socialise the newly arrived in the image of urban capitalist standardisation is almost amusing. Yet, *Oma Totem* is also to be mused on in the context of the twenty-first century's significant increase in the number of people seeking refuge in Europe, and the blend of nationalistic, anti-immigrationist, humanitarian and economic anxieties which have surfaced in the conflict-ridden debates on European asylum, immigration and integration policies.

This analysis of Danh Vo's early works was written in the autumn of 2015, at a time when large groups of refugees, especially from Syria, were crossing European borders, the sheer numbers of whom were creating chaos at the borders and exploding former European asylum policies and EU consensus. It was a time when European politicians and citizens finally realised that this was not a passing humanitarian crisis that would soon be over, but a long-term state of affairs that could only be alleviated by supra-national collaboration and coordinated asylum policies; a time when the media described the situation as Europe's worst humanitarian crisis since the Second World War, and when the German Chancellor, Angela Merkel, declared that Germany would receive 800,000 refugees in 2015 – which would profoundly change German society. At that historical moment, everybody was wondering if and how European societies would receive and help refugees build new lives for themselves. How would this large and steady stream of refugees and forced migrants change European societies, cultures and self-perception as the cradle and pinnacle of Enlightenment-based humanism? It was an explosive moment, in Vo's foster country of Denmark also, where hard-hearted government policies and protectionist campaigns were attempting to enforce the nation's borders.[119]

In the context of these present-day battles and urgencies, it is important to remember that it is not the question of ethnicity that is at the heart of Danh Vo's early works, although some Western critics have seen these works as intimately linked to the artist's Vietnamese background. The issues at stake relate to class and to what Althusser would describe as the interpellation of the immigrant as a new denizen or citizen of the West – and this is why these works have not become archival documents over time and lost their topicality. Accordingly, I would like to suggest that those of Vo's works that are related to the story of his family should be read as reflections on the production of denizenship and citizenship through socialisation and the acculturating mechanisms of identification, as well as on the co-creative role of consumption in forging such new acculturated transnational identifications. Vo's early works allude to the immigrant dreams of social mobility and ownership of iconic Western commodities – emblems of 'the good life', such as the Mercedes-Benz, the Rolex watch, the fridge and the washing machine.

Within the fields of Actor-Network Theory (ANT) and new materialism, objects are often perceived as active and performative, meaning that they are 'actants' rather than purely material and mute materialities. These fields emphasise the social life of things, the entanglement between human activity and the performance of things and consequently also the interpellating effects that things have on human activity and social relationships. In other words, there is an identificatory side to the purchase, ownership and use of things.[120] However, it is important to keep in mind that the relationship between subjects and objects is interactive: 'Objects need symbolic framing, storylines and human spokespersons in order to acquire social lives; social relationships and practices in turn need to be materially grounded in order to gain temporal and spatial endurance.'[121] According to psychologist Rom Harré, it is by its 'embedment' in some kind of narrative that a material object is transformed from 'a piece of stuff' into a 'social object'. Hence, the category 'alcohol' does not define a social object, Harré explains, but the category 'communion wine' does.[122] Harré's micro-sociological constructionist perspective gives priority to symbolic, especially discursive, action over the material order in the genesis of social things. It can thus help explain how Danh Vo can assign to artefacts a powerful role as constituents and signifiers of identity. By staging significant material objects by which a refugee family have translated themselves into a European (Danish or German) context – by their own acts as well as those of agents in the receiving countries – he draws attention to the soft power of Western consumer goods and how they can become actants in a migrant's self-perception and self-identification. In other words, social objects.

Vo's early works are emblematic of the way he uses objects. By revealing the particular origins of carefully selected, one-of-a-kind objects, Vo infuses historical and political meaning into commodities and invites us to see them as vessels of history and/or as products of relations based on law (owned, inherited, borrowed or appropriated).[123] By turning objects into relics, i.e.

non-verbal equivalents of historical documents, Vo makes his works dependent on verbal mediation. Like photographs used for documentation, they do not speak by and of themselves but require explanatory captions in order to communicate to audiences the subject matter of the works and the particular provenance of the objects they include. Moreover, the captions do not always work that way, so at times 'we are uncertain what Vo wants us to see'.[124] In Claire Bishop's opinion, this introversion tends 'to keep meaning withheld from the viewer' and thus, inadvertently, to block the viewer's critical engagement with the historical events and structures that Vo seeks to question. For Bishop, Vo's work is typical of a major trend since the 1990s, in which the works of artists doing research into overlooked histories are promoted as critical historical interrogations, even though the artists often present history to audiences as 'a cut-and-paste accumulation of details' and in such an aestheticised and introverted fashion that their works are 'prone to develop into information as ornament'.[125] Choosing as her example Vo's ready-made chandelier in *08:03:51, 28.05.2009*, Bishop exemplifies the problem as follows: 'The chandelier is presented as a bystander to political history, but without Vo's caption, *08:03:51, 28.05.2009* it is just another nineteenth-century chandelier. The ready-made object is injected with history-as-readymade: Both are presented wholesale, without any further complication.'[126]

Although I agree with Bishop's points regarding Vo's introvertedness and ready-made approach to history, I cannot chime in with her opinion that his approach to research-based art is symptomatic of a general reluctance among artists who probe the archives of history 'to synthesize and organize the information in which they are trading'.[127] On the contrary, I think that Vo's reluctance to create symbolic and formal cohesion in the traditional 'compositional' sense of the word is part of a deliberate strategy. He seems to organise objects and information in a way that underscores the fragmentary nature of historical relics, and this permits him to point to the fissures and gaps which the cultural translation and transcultural circulation and scattering of artefacts and information engender. I would also suggest that, in those of Vo's works that concern issues of identification, this lack of cohesion could also be seen as an indication that the different coordinates involved in the formation of an identity do not constitute a seamless whole. But Bishop is right about the (over)dependency on captions and commentary: without them, the cultural, historical and biographical meanings of the works are lost on visitors who may not be in the know.

In her discussion of Vo's two Venice exhibitions in 2015, Claire Bishop has also identified homosocial and homosexual relationships as a leading theme in Vo's practice.[128] Time and again, Vo has used identification with friends and fellow artists to position himself as belonging to a network of (internationally renowned) gay artists. One way of understanding Vo's take on the Venice group exhibition *Slip of the Tongue* is thus, as Elisabeth Lebovici has suggested in the accompanying press release, to read it as a mapping of 'friendship',[129] or in Bishop's words, as a mapping of 'networks of affinity among previous generations of gay artists, among them Peter Hujar, Paul Thek, and Martin Wong'. As Bishop adds, 'Vo's family tree' comprises 'a group of artists who may have been marginalized in the past, but who together now constitute an impeccable artistic pedigree'.[130] If Vo were not concerned with homosexual and homosocial relationships in his artistic practice, his sexual and gender identifications would be irrelevant to our interpretation of his curatorial preferences, which, interestingly, includes his 2010 reinstallation of the retrospective *Felix Gonzalez-Torres: Specific Objects without Specific Form* at Wiels Contemporary Art Center in Brussels. On this occasion, Vo agreed to write a '1000 words' entry in *Artforum* about his reinstallation, in which he declared his fascination with the artist's works, but evaded explaining the reason for his fascination and his curatorial ideas by changing the subject. Instead, Vo gave an account of his identificatory travel in the footsteps of Gonzalez-Torres (1957–96) to the Père Lachaise Cemetery in Paris to visit the burial place of a famous same-sex couple, Gertrude Stein and her lover and life partner Alice B. Toklas, whose names have been engraved on the same tombstone, with Stein's name on the front and Toklas's name added twenty-one years later to the flip side of the stone.[131]

However, taken together, Vo's artistic and curatorial priorities form a significant pattern that he wants viewers to take notice of. His ongoing project *Vo Rasmussen Rosasco* (2002–) adds to his birth name the surnames of friends Vo has married and immediately divorced. It also amasses the legal documents relative to these acts, displaying the marriage certificates and divorce proceedings as apparent works on paper.[132] As Vo's name may potentially expand until it becomes administratively and socially unmanageable – the artist's full name now being Trung Ky Danh Vo Rasmussen Rosasco – the project invites viewers to reflect on how the artist's acts test the boundaries of socially and legally acceptable behaviour. As H. G. Masters has noted, this project drains the intimacy from the institution of marriage in a manner that is strangely taboo. It is marriage represented as a purely legal or business-like transaction. As the project enables Vo to add names of individuals he feels close to, but never intended to have as a partner, it evokes 'the supposedly liberating gay marriage' as well as the pragmatic solution of getting married to win citizenship for one's partner, a practice in many immigrant communities.[133]

Vo Rasmussen Rosasco is conceptually linked to Vo's 2007 project *Good Life*. During a residency in Los Angles, Vo developed a friendship with Joe Carrier, an American counterinsurgency specialist who had lived in Vietnam in the 1960s and early 1970s. In Vietnam, Carrier had worked first for the

RAND Corporation and, after accusations of homosexuality had cost him his job, for a foundation researching the effects of Agent Orange.[134] During these years, Carrier assembled an archive of diaries, love letters and his own photos of lovers and young Vietnamese men, walking hand in hand or assuming erotically charged body postures. Carrier granted Vo access to his personal archive, which constituted a missing history for the artist whose family had left all their mementos behind when they fled Vietnam. The two men developed both a personal and an artistic relationship, with Vo exhibiting some of these photos and crediting them to Carrier. Later, Vo would also display Carrier's last will and testament, leaving his possessions to Vo.[135] From a selection of Carrier's material, Vo thus constructed a 'proxy "self-portrait"'[136] that provided him with sexual, gendered and racialised identity components.

(Dis)identification and the artist' s self-identification

In José Esteban Muñoz's theory of disidentification as a process of self-actualisation, the concept of disidentification is linked to a cluster of related terms: hybridity, queerness, migrancy and auto-ethnography. They all refer to processes that involve (different kinds of) response to ideologies and systems that discriminate or inhibit aspects of subjectivity that 'do not conform or respond to narratives of universalization and normalization'.[137] In my analysis of Bharti Kher's urban goddesses, I concluded that she responded with a 'tactical misrecognition' to racial and gender stereotypes and called for a reconstructed, intersectional understanding of identity. Something similar happens in Vo's 'ethnographic' works about members of his family. In these works, Vo seems to pursue a dual goal: they disclose how immigrants are interpellated by the dominant ideology of European consumerist welfare states, and, through the very act of exposure, Vo also distances himself from this ideology. Here, it is worth recalling Muñoz's important point that disidentification is a process that operates *inside* the system that it criticises: 'A "disidentificatory subject" ... tactically and simultaneously works on, with, and against a cultural form.'[138] While Vo distances himself from the Western consumerist and capitalist system in works such as *Oma Totem* and *If You Were to Climb the Himalayas Tomorrow*, his whole career and the soaring prices of his works are at the same time dependent on the very same model.[139] One of the protagonists in Muñoz's study of 'queers of colour' also happens to be one of Vo's artistic role models: Felix Gonzalez-Torres. As Muñoz notes, he was 'queer, *cubano*, and a person living with AIDS'.[140] Although Gonzalez-Torres was politically committed to exploring questions of (homosexual) identities, his works never represented identity elements in any obvious manner. Rather, he refunctioned the language of minimalism 'to rethink identity and instead opt for a disidentity', meaning a reconstructed, politicised understanding of identity.[141] To some extent, Muñoz's observation also applies to Vo's work. Drawing on conceptual art rather than minimalism, Vo also uses the language of a mainstream art form to link his personal life to a larger social order and overall questions of identification.

Vo's works and statements strongly suggest that he used an ethnographic engagement with the history of his family and Vietnam to disidentify from 'Danishness' and 'Westernness' (notwithstanding his solo exhibitions at the Danish Pavilion in Venice in 2015, and at the National Gallery of Denmark in 2010). An important, but also ambiguous, component of Vo's acts of disidentification is his strong identification with his father Phung Vo, whom he has contracted to copy, in exquisite calligraphy and as long as he is able to continue, the last letter that the French missionary Jean-Théophane Vénard wrote to his father before Vénard was beheaded for evangelising in Vietnam. As Bishop has pointed out, the extent to which Vo's works rely on personal history is unusual, and it is reflected in the extent to which critics and curators rely on the story of Phung's conversion to Catholicism, the way he organised his family's flight by boat, and their subsequent settlement in Europe: 'This is admittedly an amazing story, but is has by now acquired almost Beuysian levels of myth. It's also the exegetical code that binds together the diverse elements in Vo's practice: his interest in Catholicism, Western missionaries to Vietnam, ephemera relating to the Vietnam War, and, more generally, homosocial, homosexual and father-son relationships.'[142]

Publicly, however, Vo likes to identify himself as a kind of nomad. In a long interview with the journalist Sandra Brovall, who also interviewed Vo's parents and brother, Vo has distanced himself from the idea of national identity, declaring that he has disentangled himself from such attachments to become a kind of global nomad. His account tallies closely with the statement quoted earlier that he only became interested in Vietnam through his interest in the history of the US and as part of his professional work, not as part of a personal process of exploration and identification: 'I lived in Denmark for a quarter of a century, so of course it has a certain influence. But there is also much that I would like to forget. The list of Danish monarchs. I do not need it … All those constructions of national identity are based on strange symbols. If America or Switzerland would offer me a passport, I could just as well take this as the Danish one. It has no significance to me.'[143] This remark concerns national identity, but, judging from his works and career, his perception of himself as a globally mobile, westernised citizen of the world is also relevant with respect to Vo's treatment of class and ethnicity, in terms of social mobility and of the cultural translation and adaptation required when building a new home in another part of the world.

An assemblage of other identities

I would like to return to the discussion of identity, identification and belonging with which this chapter began. Amelia Jones's theory of identity as identification provides a model for understanding identity dynamically as '"an assemblage of other identities", always in motion as identification'.[144] It is a model that focuses on the negotiating effect of identification, and remains attentive to the 'dis'-identificatory and distancing aspect of the subject's negotiation of cultural codes, as well as observant of the sexual and gendered dimensions of race and ethnicity – thereby, as it were, 'queering' ethnic identity.[145] This chapter has tested the applicability of such an understanding of identity as multiple, performative, intersectional and contingent. It has applied this understanding as a theoretical framework for an exploration of the ways in which identification and disidentification are performed 'intersectionally' in works by three rather different artists with a migrant background. These three artists all do 'archival' work, and their critical examinations of history are also acts of imaginative rediscovery of the past, leading to originative and important reconfigurations of the dominant models of identity. Among other things, this chapter has made it evident that the idea of identities set in motion by shifting identifications deviates from the notion of fluid identities, which has become a staple of the discourses on migrant identities and migrant artists. The widespread notion of fluid identities is undergirded by binaries such as uprootedness and rootedness, displacement and (re-)integration, which tend to fix attention on issues of movement and transnational identities suspended 'forever in some form of transit between two cultures'.[146] In my view, the works of Yinka Shonibare, Bharti Kher and Danh Vo represent identities as being neither fixed nor fluid, but intersectional, meaning that they stress the complexity of an identity formation that is shaped by multiple and shifting forms of identification and belonging. In fact, these artists have consistently referred to African, Indian and Vietnamese cultures, respectively, as well as to European and American cultures, so some of their coordinates are, in effect, fixed, if not for life then at least on a long-term basis.

Shonibare stages an entanglement of some of the ethnic and cultural coordinates of 'Western' and 'African', traditionally regarded as mutually exclusive opposites. He also occasionally draws attention to queer intersections between ethnicity and gender, particularly in *Big Boy* (2002). Kher's identification with India is so pronounced, and the materials and symbols she uses to advertise the 'Indianness' of her works so conspicuous that they risk reproducing a traditional politics of unilateral national belonging, even if Kher has an immigrant background herself, and her works effectively unsettle the categories of race and gender as well as question gender roles. Both Shonibare's and Kher's works include everyday materials and objects, such as textiles, and enhance their symbolic and metaphoric meaning, and thus their role as social objects. Danh Vo's approach, on the other hand, is more conceptual than those of Shonibare and Kher. He often uses historical and personal one-of-a-kind artefacts, which he transforms into ready-mades or assemblages as a means to explore, and expose, the role of artefacts as social objects and as constituents and signifiers of identifications.

As Jones has pointed out, there is no simple, conclusive answer to the questions of identification. This is particularly evident in the case of the nebulous category of ethnicity. In many ways, 'ethnicity' informs the works of Shonibare, Kher and Vo, but their central concern is, rather, the broader question of how identity is actively constructed through shifting, intersecting and imaginative identifications. As such, their works can be seen as part of a broader current of 'post-identity' art works and exhibitions that disavow simplistic notions of identity while, at the same time, recognising the legacy of identity movements.[147] In fact, they only become historically meaningful when seen in relation to the legacy of identity politics discussed in Chapter 2 and the shifts identity politics have undergone inside and outside the global art world.

Notes

1 Hall, 'Introduction: Who Needs "Identity"?', p. 4.
2 Hall, 'Cultural Identity and Diaspora', pp. 22–3.
3 *Ibid.*, p. 32.
4 Jones, *Seeing Differently*, p. 1.
5 *Ibid.*, p. 3.
6 Nira Yuval-Davis, *Power, Intersectionality and the Politics of Belonging*, Freia Working Paper Series (Aalborg: FREIA Feminist Research Center, 2011), pp. 3–4.
7 Yuval-Davis, *The Politics of Belonging*, p. 14.
8 Ann Phoenix, 'Interrogating intersectionality: productive ways of theorising multiple positioning', *Kvinder, køn & forskning*, special issue on intersectionality, no. 2–3 (2006), 21–30, 22.
9 Judith Butler, *Gender Trouble: Feminism and the Subversion of Identity* (New York, London: Routledge, 1991), pp. xxviii–xxx, 9, 36.
10 Phoenix, 'Interrogating intersectionality', 22.
11 Jones, *Seeing Differently*, pp. 1–3.
12 *Ibid.*, pp. 3, 20.
13 *Ibid.*, pp. 20–1.
14 *Ibid.*, p. 3.
15 Hall, 'Cultural Identity and Diaspora', p. 21.
16 Jones, *Seeing Differently*, p. 232.
17 Eve Kosofsky Sedgwick, *Tendencies* (Durham, NC: Duke University Press, 1993), p. 9. Quoted in Jones, *Seeing Differently*, p. 237.
18 Chris Barker, *Cultural Studies: Theory and Practice* (London: Sage Publications, 2000), p. 23.

19 Muñoz, *Disidentifications*, pp. 12, 18, 26.
20 *Ibid.*, p. 26.
21 *Ibid.*, p. 31. See also p. 29.
22 Jones, *Seeing Differently*, p. 9.
23 Hall, 'Introduction: Who Needs "Identity"?', p. 3.
24 Amelia Jones also acknowledges Stuart Hall's importance as a key source of inspiration and a scholar who 'pioneered a fluid concept of intersectional identities functioning as "points of identification … not an essence, but a positioning"'. Jones, *Seeing Differently*, pp. 8–9.
25 *Ibid.*, p. 34.
26 Meskimmon, *Contemporary Art and the Cosmopolitan Imagination*, p. 58.
27 Jones, *Seeing Differently*, p. 35.
28 *Ibid.*, p. 3.
29 *Ibid.*, p. 4.
30 *Ibid.*
31 *Ibid.*, p. 38.
32 *Ibid.*, p. 36.
33 *Ibid.*
34 *Ibid.*, p. 37.
35 *Ibid.*, p. 4.
36 Abigail Solomon-Godeau, 'Mistaken Identities', in Dan Meinwald (ed.), *Mistaken Identities* (Santa Barbara, Calif.: University Art Museum, University of California, 1993), pp. 19–63, p. 31.
37 *Ibid.*, p. 36.
38 Jones, *Seeing Differently*, p. 125.
39 *Ibid.*, p. 131.
40 *Ibid.*, p. xviii.
41 Appadurai, *Modernity at Large*, pp. 178ff.
42 Hall, 'Cultural Identity and Diaspora', p. 21.
43 Yinka Shonibare, 'Fabric, and the Irony of Authenticity', in Nikos Papastergiadis (ed.), *Mixed Belongings and Unspecified Destinations* (London: InIVA, 1996), pp. 38–41, p. 40.
44 Jean Fisher, 'In Defiance of Gravity', in Sarah Coulson and Clare Lilley (eds), *Yinka Shonibare MBE: Fabric-Ation* (Wakefield: Yorkshire Sculpture Park, 2013), pp. 129–37, p. 130.
45 Robert Hobbs, 'Yinka Shonibare MBE: The Politics of Representation', in Rachel Kent (ed.), *Yinka Shonibare MBE* (Munich, Berlin, London, New York: Prestel Verlag, 2008), pp. 24–37, p. 30.
46 *Ibid.*, p. 32.
47 *Ibid.*, pp. 28–9.
48 *Ibid.*, pp. 27–8.
49 Yinka Shonibare, 'Yoruba: in bed with Derrida' (1997), quoted from John Picton, 'Laughing at Ourselves', in Jaap Guldemond and Gabriele Mackert (eds), *Yinka Shonibare: Double Dutch* (Rotterdam: NAi Publisher, Museum Boijmans Van Beuningen and Kunsthalle Wien, 2004), pp. 45–62, p. 46.

50 Anthony Downey, 'Yinka Shonibare', *BOMB Magazine*, no. 95 (2005), unpaginated, http://bombsite.com/issues/93/articles/2777 (accessed 16 November 2016).
51 Shonibare, quoted in Jaap Guldemond and Gabriele Mackert, 'To Entertain and Provoke: Western Influences in the Work of Yinka Shonibare', in Guldemond and Mackert (eds), *Yinka Shonibare: Double Dutch*, pp. 35–44, p. 37.
52 Shonibare, quoted *ibid.*, p. 36.
53 Peter Brix Søndergaard, 'Tekstil-plastik', *Passepartout*, 17:32 (2011), 30–54, 32.
54 Fisher, 'In Defiance of Gravity', p. 131.
55 Anne Ring Petersen, 'Film som kunst: Yinka Shonibare MBE og *Black British film*', *Passepartout. Skrifter for kunsthistorie*, 18:34 (2011), 66–86.
56 Robert Stilling, 'An image of Europe: Yinka Shonibare's postcolonial decadence', *PMLA* (Publications of the Modern Language Association of America), 128:2 (2013), 299–321.
57 Lisa Dorin, 'Big Boy', *Art Institute of Chicago Museum Studies*, 32:1 (2006), 42–3 and 95, 42.
58 Rachel Kent, 'Time and Transformation in the Art of Yinka Shonibare MBE', in Kent (ed.), *Yinka Shonibare MBE*, pp. 12–23, p. 13.
59 Hobbs, 'Yinka Shonibare MBE: The Politics of Representation', *ibid.*, pp. 24–37, p. 32.
60 Roland Barthes, *The Fashion System* (New York: Hill and Wang, 1983), pp. ix ff.
61 Bhabha, *The Location of Culture*, p. 127.
62 Manthia Diawara, 'Indepencence Cha Cha: The Art of Yinka Shonibare', in Guldemond and Mackert (eds), *Yinka Shonibare: Double Dutch*, pp. 18–23, p. 21.
63 *Ibid.*
64 Muñoz, *Disidentifications*, p. 32.
65 Jean Laplance and Jean-Bertrand Pontalis, *The Language of Psychoanalysis* (New York: W. W. Norton, 1973), p. 206. Quoted in Muñoz, *Disidentifications*, p. 7.
66 Muñoz, *Disidentifications*, pp. 11–12.
67 Eve Kosofsky Sedgwick, *The Epistemology of the Closet* (Berkeley, Los Angeles: University of California Press 1990), p. 61. Quoted in Muñoz, *Disidentifications*, p. 8.
68 Muñoz, *Disidentifications*, pp. 7–8.
69 unnamed, '"Yes, I Am a Feminist"', *Times of India, The Crest Edition* (20 May 2010), unpaginated, http://timesofindia.indiatimes.com/life-style/people/Yes-I-am-a-feminist/articleshow/5731385.cms (accessed November 2016).
70 Daniel Völzke, 'Das Orakel von Delhi', *Monopol*, no. 10 (2008), 58–73, 63.
71 unnamed, '"Yes, I Am a Feminist"'.
72 Anita Roy, 'Bharti Kher "Sing to them that will listen"', *BING*, no. 9 (2008–9), 22–9, 22.
73 unnamed, '"Yes, I Am a Feminist"'.
74 *Ibid.*
75 Gayatri Sinha, 'Bharti Kher: A Bearer of Intimate Signs', in Ziba Ardalan (ed.), *Bharti Kher* (London: Parasol Unit Foundation for Contemporary Art, 2012), pp. 122–31, p. 134.
76 unnamed, '"Yes, I Am a Feminist"'.

77 Aveek Sen, 'Fragments of a Conversation: Bharti Kher with *Aveek Sen*', in Ardalan (ed.), *Bharti Kher*, pp. 52–63, pp. 58–61.
78 An expert on contemporary art from India, Zehra Jumabhoy has established the following chronology based on a conversation with the artist: 1. *Confess* (2010), 2. *The deaf room* (2001–12), 3.*The hot winds that blow from the West* (2011). Email from Zehra Jumabhoy to the author, 14 December 2013.
79 Zehra Jumabhoy, 'Bharti Kher: Parasol Unit', *Artforum*, 51:6 (2013), 255–6.
80 Kher, in Kanchi Mehta, 'Bharti Kher: the macabre and the beautifully grotesque', *Flash Art*, November/December (2012), 82–5, 84.
81 Zehra Jumabhoy, 'Me, Myself, and You', in Gether *et al.* (eds), *India: Art Now*, pp. 64–81, p. 68.
82 Minhazz Majumdar, 'Bharti Kher: transformative vision', *ArtAsiaPacific*, no. 56 (2007), 134–9, 136.
83 Ziba Ardalan, 'Second Skin That Speaks of Truth', in Ardalan (ed.), *Bharti Kher*, pp. 14–20, p. 17.
84 Brah, *Cartographies of Diaspora: Contesting Identities*, pp. 180–2, 93.
85 Ahmed *et al.*, 'Introduction: Uprootings/Regroundings', p. 1.
86 *Ibid.*, p. 9.
87 Sinha, 'Bharti Kher', p. 123.
88 *Ibid.*, p. 125.
89 Ranjit Hoskote, 'The Pursuit of Extreme Propositions: Recent Works by Bharti Kher', in *Bharti Kher* (New York: Jack Shainman Gallery, 2000), pp. 7–17, p. 10.
90 Sinha, 'Bharti Kher', p. 128.
91 Kher, in Sen, 'Fragments of a Conversation: Bharti Kher with *Aveek Sen*', p. 62.
92 Sinha, 'Bharti Kher', pp. 125–6.
93 Hoskote, 'The Pursuit of Extreme Propositions', p. 10.
94 Muñoz, *Disidentifications*, pp. 164, 170.
95 *Ibid.*, p. 168. Emphasis added.
96 In a group of works from 2012, *Revolution Kid (Calf)*, *Revolution Kid (Fox Girl)* and *Revolution Kid (Fox)*, Shonibare also mixed human and animal figures.
97 Sinha, 'Bharti Kher', p. 126.
98 *Ibid.*, pp. 125–6.
99 Yuval-Davis, *The Politics of Belonging*, p. 2.
100 Ulf Hedetoft and Mette Hjort, 'Introduction', in Ulf Hedetoft and Mette Hjort (eds), *The Postnational Self: Belonging and Identity* (Minneapolis, London: University of Minnesota Press, 2002), pp. vii–xxxii, p. ix.
101 *Ibid.*, p. x.
102 Yuval-Davis, *Power, Intersectionality and the Politics of Belonging*, p. 4.
103 *Ibid.*, pp. 4–5.
104 Yuval-Davis, *The Politics of Belonging*, p. 20.
105 *Ibid.*, p. 26.
106 Thomas Gammeltoft-Hansen in 'AMIS Roundtable: The Refugee Crisis', University of Copenhagen, 7 September 2015.
107 Tello, *Counter-Memorial Aesthetics*, p. 9.

108 H. G. Masters, 'Danh Vo: defining documents', *ArtAsiaPacific*, no. 77 (2012), 106–15, 109.
109 Sandra Brovall, 'Jagten på Danh Vo', *Politiken, Kultur-sektionen* (1 June 2013), 6–10, 9–10.
110 Jeppe Villadsen, 'Danh Vos Vietnam. "At overleve er jo praktisk"', *Udvikling*, 38:1 (2011), 52–4, 53.
111 *Ibid.*, 54.
112 Claire Bishop, 'History depletes itself', *artforum.com*, September (2015), unpaginated, https://artforum.com/inprint/issue=201507&id=54492 (accessed September 2015).
113 Luigi Fassi, 'Terra incognita: Luigi Fassi on the art of Danh Vo', *Artforum International*, 48:6 (2010), 152–9, 155.
114 Varadinis, 'Shattered freedom', 215–16; Fassi, 'Terra incognita', 154.
115 Masters, 'Danh Vo: defining documents', 110.
116 Brovall, 'Jagten på Danh Vo', 9.
117 Fassi, 'Terra Incognita', 155.
118 Masters, 'Danh Vo: defining documents', 110; Amy Zion, 'Texts for Danh Vo', in Elisabeth Lebovici (ed.), *Slip of the Tounge* (Venice: Marsilio Editori, 2015), unpaginated. In the catalogue, Zion specifies that the work includes a 'casino card', and that it has been acquired independently. Masters writes that a 'personalized entrance card for a casino' is placed on the top of the wooden crucifix (p. 11), but it is not visible in photos of the work, suggesting that the card might have been removed at some point. In any case, Masters's and Zion's descriptions of the work suggest that the artist originally wanted the crucifix to serve a double function as a centrepiece for prayer and a support for the casino entrance card, thus subtly linking the sacred and the profane.
119 In September 2015, the right wing government in Denmark lead by Prime Minister Lars Løkke Rasmussen inserted an advertisement in four Lebanese newspapers to 'inform' people smugglers and potential asylum seekers about the tightened Danish asylum laws and signal 'we don't want you here'. After investigating the case, the Parliamentary Ombudsman (elected by the Danish Parliament, the *Folketing*, to investigate complaints about the public administration) concluded in his critical report of 10 December 2015 'that the advertisement must be regarded as suitable for leaving, among others, Syrian refugees with a view of the Danish asylum system which is not true and fair'. Folketingets Ombudsmand, 'Informationsindsats i bl.a. libanesiske aviser', document no. 15/04009-26, www.ombudsmanden.dk/find/nyheder/alle/kritik_af_flygtningeannonce_/pdf1/?obvius_version=2015-12-10%2013:31:15 (accessed November 2016).
120 Dick Pels, Kevin Hetherington and Fréderic Vandenberghe, 'The status of the object: performances, mediations, and techniques', *Theory, Culture & Society*, 19:5/6 (2002), 1–21, 1–2, 7.
121 *Ibid.*, 11.
122 Rom Harré, 'Material objects in social worlds', *Theory, Culture & Society*, 19:5/6 (2002), 23–33, 24–5.
123 Masters, 'Danh Vo: defining documents', 112.

124 *Ibid.*, 113.
125 Bishop, 'History depletes itself'.
126 *Ibid.*
127 *Ibid.*
128 *Ibid.*
129 Elisabeth Lebovici, *Slip of the Tongue* (press release), www.palozzograssi.it/en/exhibitions/slip-tongue (accessed August 2015).
130 *Ibid.*
131 Tim Griffin, '1000 words: Danh Vo', *Artforum International*, 48:6 (2010), 161. The exhibition was first installed by curator Elena Filipovic and opened to the public on 16 January 2010. On 5 March 2010 Vo reinstalled the exhibition. See: www.e-flux.com/announcements/37342/felix-gonzalez-torres-specific-objects-without-specific-form/ (accessed May 2017).
132 Jennifer Piejko, 'The not-so-secret life of Danh Vo', *Performa* (2012), unpaginated, http://performamagazine.tumblr.com/post/19579863833/the-not-so-secret-life-of-danh-vo (accessed November 2016).
133 Masters, 'Danh Vo: defining documents', 110.
134 Fassi, 'Terra Incognita', 158.
135 Piejko, 'The not-so-secret life of Danh Vo'.
136 Fassi, 'Terra Incognita', 158.
137 Muñoz, *Disidentifications*, p. 161.
138 *Ibid.*, p. 12.
139 Ann Binlot, 'Artist Danh Vo to Collector Who Sued Him: "Shove It up Your Ass"', *Forbes* (18 July 2015), unpaginated, www.forbes.com/sites/abinlot/2015/07/17/artist-danh-vo-to-collector-who-sued-him-shove-it-up-your-as-you-faggot/2/ (accessed September 2015).
140 Muñoz, *Disidentifications*, p. 165.
141 *Ibid.*
142 Bishop, 'History depletes itself'.
143 Brovall, 'Jagten på Danh Vo', 8.
144 Jones is quoting from Alan Gilbert's *Another Future: Poetry and Art in a Postmodern Twilight* (Middletown, Conn.: Wesleyan University Press, 2006), p. 6. See Jones, *Seeing Differently*, pp. 148, 167.
145 Jones, *Seeing Differently*, p. 147.
146 Daniela Berghahn, 'No place like home? Or impossible homecomings in the films of Fatih Akin', *New Cinemas: Journal of Contemporary Film*, 4:3 (2006), 141–57, 156.
147 Jones, *Seeing Differently*, pp. 147–8.

6 Migrant geographies and European politics of irregular migration

Globalisation is frequently thought to cause an unbounded movement of capital, people, information, culture and goods. However, there is an often neglected flip side to this globalised mobility: the increased international collaboration on border controls aimed at restricting the movements of people who have been forced to migrate because of war, destitution, persecution or environmental reasons. This securitisation of borders constructs categories of included and excluded populations; and the media and political discourses exacerbate the popular fear of immigration and the exclusionary effect of securitisation by coupling migration with crime. As the criminologist Katja Franko Aas has observed, this discursive correlation creates a dynamic of social exclusion, which deals not simply with an 'immobilised global underclass' but an *illegalised* one.[1] Labelled 'Fortress Europe' in the critique of contemporary immigration politics, the European Union, with its advanced border and migration surveillance systems, is deeply implicated in this production of exceptions to citizenship and what has been described as *the citizenship gap*. This term refers to the legal discrepancy between citizenship rights and human rights, and it manifests itself especially at the border zones that mark the geographical and political limits of national entities.[2] Rights of citizenship refer to the individual's membership of a body politic, whereas the concept of human rights disconnects from this in anchoring them in a universal humanity. The United Nations Universal Declaration of Human Rights of 1948 defines human rights as the natural rights we have simply by virtue of being alive.[3] As the European studies scholar Uta Staiger has pointed out: 'The extra-juridical position of migrants corresponds to the extra-territorial position within which they are contained at borders. In areas such as detention centres, refugee camps or the no man's land, spaces which technically belong to the countries they guard but which are already outside their normative realm, the citizenship gap is spatially instituted.'[4]

This chapter is concerned with how art can engage with migration politics related to the categories of forced and irregular migration. These categories include refugees and asylum seekers, but neither these two groups, nor others, are singled out for special examination in this chapter, which falls into two parts. The first examines how artworks can question the citizenship gap and the social stigmatisation of irregular migrants as 'crimmigrant' bodies.[5] The centrepiece of this discussion is *Sahara Chronicle* (2006–7), a video-based work by the Swiss artist Ursula Biemann, which investigates the conditions of migration in the geopolitical space of the Sahara. The second part of the chapter focuses on the migrants' perilous journey from the coast of Africa across the Mediterranean Sea to the shores of Europe as it has been evoked in the British artist and filmmaker Isaac Julien's video installation *Western Union: Small Boats* (2007). This part of the chapter considers issues of European border politics and securitisation, along with their consequences for forced migrants. Both works illustrate some affinity with the current in contemporary art that Veronica Tello has called counter-memorial aesthetics. As mentioned in connection with Danh Vo's family-related works (see Chapter 5), nation-states often struggle, or neglect, to include refugee histories in their national memory and history. Thus, the processes of collective forgetting coupled with the fragility of refugee memories generate a need for counter-memorialisation. Like Vo, Biemann and Julien have created 'mnemonic objects' in an attempt to critically examine the possibilities and limits of recording refugee and migrant histories for posterity. In doing so, both Biemann and Julien also test the capacity of art to visualise and memorialise histories of displacement in ways that are reflective of the heterogeneity and interconnectedness of a globalised world.[6]

The politics of containment in Ursula Biemann's *Sahara Chronicle*

In what follows, an analysis of Ursula Biemann's video-essay and installation *Sahara Chronicle* (2006–7) (see plate 7 and figure 6.1) is used as a vehicle to unpack the general question of how artistic productions can respond to discourses on complex political issues such as forced migration, European border politics and the risk of reducing migrants to 'bare life'[7] in the politico-juridical order. It pursues three distinct but interrelated strands of enquiry: the first explores forced migration on a theoretical level by drawing on political theory and criminology. The second engages with *Sahara Chronicle*, one of several examples of how contemporary artists seeking to investigate the nexus of immigration control, citizenship and human rights have crossed the boundaries between theory, political activism and the visual arts. The third strand adds to the exploration of Biemann's work some reflections on methodological questions concerning the intertwinement of art and politics: firstly, there is the question of the particular ways in which *artists* translate complex issues articulated in political and philosophical discourses into visual artistic representations, with the clear intent to impact on their audience's

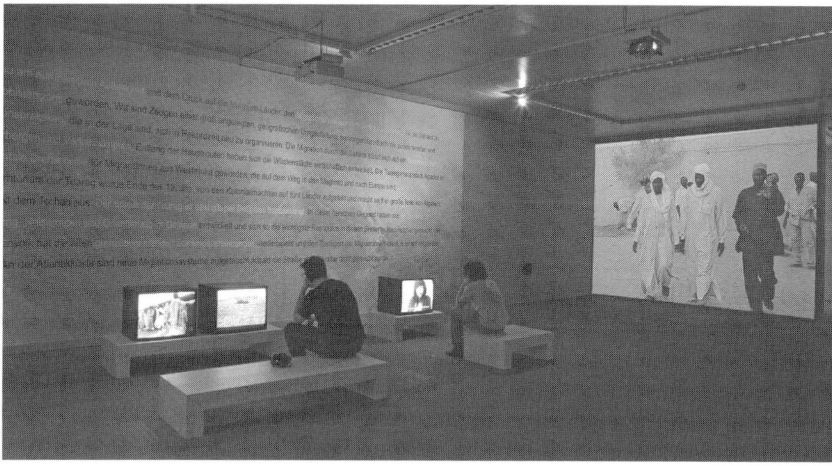

Ursula Biemann, installation view from *Sahara Chronicle* (2006–7), Kunstmuseum Bern. 6.1
Video collection, 78 min. © Ursula Biemann. Photograph: Dominique Uldry, courtesy of the artist.

political and ethical awareness. The fact that such politico-activist artworks already in themselves constitute critical comments on political and social issues has implications for *academics* who aim to theorise and analyse such works. This leads to the second methodological question: how do scholars and critics avoid becoming mimetic transcribers writing a commentary on the artist's own exemplary commentary and seeing *through* the work as if it were merely a window on the world, instead of seeing the world *in* the work and analysing how existing images of that world may be transformed or subverted *by* the work? In other words, how do we adapt our methods to the obvious need to cross disciplinary borders and substantially include insights from, for example, philosophy, anthropology and the political and social sciences in our work on art and cultural productions, while *also* ensuring that we stay firmly anchored in our own field of academic expertise: the history, theory and analysis of art and culture?

Philosopher Hannah Arendt was the first to point out that the supposedly universal and inalienable rights of an individual are only enforceable as citizenship rights. She analysed the difficulty of claiming the 'right to have rights' when one's nationality status has been lost.[8] By examining the status of stateless persons during the collapse of the nation-state system in connection with the two world wars, Arendt demonstrated that a person who loses his legal status as a citizen also loses the rights bestowed upon him by the Universal Declaration of Human Rights. As Arendt phrased it: 'It seems that a man who is nothing but a man has lost the very qualities which make it possible for other people to treat him as a fellow man.'[9]

More recently, philosopher Giorgio Agamben has developed a theory of 'bare life', which expands on Arendt's analysis of what she called the 'abstract nakedness of being human and nothing but human'.[10] Agamben's prediction about all life potentially becoming bare life remains problematic.[11] Yet his analysis of the absolute nakedness of a life that the law has seized to protect but which it still wields power over can contribute to our understanding of stateless persons such as refugees and so-called undocumented migrants.[12] Rather than the exception becoming the norm, and citizenship dissolving into bare life, as Agamben claims, citizenship is still a relevant political category – although it contains significant exceptions, predominantly directed at specific groups of 'crimmigrant' others.[13]

According to Agamben, refugees and irregular migrants disrupt the continuity between citizen and human, birth and nationality. By excluding this life from political representation in the nation-state, the nation-state affirms itself as a unitary community. It is exactly by spotlighting the difference between birth and nation that refugees put the foundations of modern nation-states in crisis, argues Agamben.[14] Turning to sociologist Willem Schinkel, Katja Franko Aas distinguishes between two forms of state control both central to citizenship: zoepolitics and biopolitics. Zoepolitics is primarily directed externally towards persons outside the state, whereas biopolitics is internally directed and concerned with the control and health of populations within the state's territory. Zoepolitics represents a move from the disciplinary normalisation characteristic of biopolitics to exclusionary types of control, with an emphasis on denying entry and thereby producing precarious life conditions.[15]

When border control is handed over to third countries, or enacted by private companies like airlines, and security companies such as G4S and Finmeccanica, legal practices become more ambiguous and the actual location of the border is blurred.[16] As Aas has pointed out, the tightening of the policing and surveillance of entire border regions has turned many borders across the world into frontiers, marked by a 'shifting terrain between legality and illegality'.[17] It is, however, important to keep in mind that the social sorting performed by the actions of border control does not simply divide people into a mobile global North and a 'mobility poor' global South. Admittance to the global community of highly mobile 'supracitizens' (including the artists discussed in this book) is not primarily based on citizenship but most often on private forms of economic, cultural and social capital.[18]

Mapping borders and boundaries in the Sahara

Philosopher Edward Casey's distinction between borders and boundaries can help us understand this development and the image of border control that surfaces in Ursula Biemann's *Sahara Chronicle*. In Casey's understanding, a border is a political and discursive entity, established by law or treatises; it is a clearly delineated edge, designed to be impervious. The border is in itself an ideal construct, although it can, of course, be realised materially as walls and checkpoints. A boundary, on the other hand, is seldom clearly demarcated in location and extent; it can be porous and thus admit the passage of various substances as well as living beings. One of Casey's points is that nation-state borders have boundary as well as border aspects, and require us to consider both[19] – as does Ursula Biemann's video-essay about clandestine migration in the Sahara.

Biemann is one of several artists working globally who have reorganised their artistic workspace across disciplinary and geographical borders. Other works that have engaged with similar territory include the Multiplicity collective's project *Solid Sea 01: The Ghost Ship* (2001), which pieced together the history of a ship sinking in the Mediterranean Sea in 1996 with hundreds of clandestine immigrants on board, and of how Italian and Maltese authorities tried to cover up the tragedy.[20] Another important work is the collaborative video project *Timescapes* (2005–6), initiated by Angela Melitopoulos, which is based on historical migration routes in south-eastern Europe at the crossroads of three major political regions (Europe, the countries of the former Soviet Union, and the Arab-Islamic world).[21] These artists, and collectives, often use ethnographic techniques and digital video for observing the everyday life of several locations in order to investigate and then represent the complexities of contemporary migration. Their artworks are research-based products of the gathering of information over the long-term, often involving collaborative processes, which aim at tracing migratory movements and uncovering transnational connections. Ursula Biemann's transdisciplinary practice is typical of this approach to art-making, also in the sense that it problematises the distinctions between art and reality, and between real and virtual spaces.

Biemann's *Sahara Chronicle* is one of several video-essays and writings of hers from the 2000s in which the artist has engaged in the geopolitical and social transformations caused by globalisation. Like her earlier video-essays *Europlex* (2003) and *Contained Mobility* (2004), *Sahara Chronicle* is what Biemann calls a 'geographic project' in the sense that it seeks to visualise complex spatial relations and is based on a notion of geography as both a social practice and an organising system. However, at the level of signification these works are, in fact, about the political, cultural and social meaning given to borders when traversed by commuters, migrants, ships, border patrols and surveillance systems. In *Sahara Chronicle*, Biemann maps the sub-Saharan exodus towards Europe as a social practice, induced by historical conditions and local destitution. She explores how smuggling, border patrolling and clandestine migration are lived out on a local level to produce transnational micro-geographies that are interwoven with international border politics.[22]

What makes *Sahara Chronicle* a distinct geographical practice, rather than a traditional documentary, is Biemann's essayist approach to video-making, which, she states, is not about documenting realities but about organising complexities.[23] In the 1980s – the decade Biemann graduated from art school – the moving-image essay became increasingly relevant, especially through works such as Chris Marker's *Sans Soleil* (1983) and John Akomfrah and the Black Audio Film Collective's anti-racist *Handsworth Songs* (1986).[24] This meant a move away from documentary film and video towards a hybrid form of engagement that included elements of fiction and lyric passages to reform realist methods and propose an 'imaginary space' where the real is treated as an effect to be produced, rather than as a pre-existing fact to be reproduced.[25] Biemann relies on documentary methods and elements – such as a hand-held camera (which mimics every-day-perception), unedited live-action footage of people and places, and captions that link specific images to named geographical and historical locations. However, she subjects her video footage to various digital postproduction procedures in order to hybridise the result, by inserting maps and appropriated footage from official sources, for example, and by using composite images, split-screen displays, stop-action functions and different types of subtitling.[26] Finally, yet importantly, she prefers to distribute her footage on several projections and monitors organised as a spatial environment, thereby creating a spatio-temporal installation of great complexity.

Empathy and the aesthetics of video installation art

Comprising twelve videos in total, *Sahara Chronicle* takes the construction of a heterotemporal and heterospatial environment to extremes. According to Biemann, this video-essay seeks to represent the structure of a transnational migration industry as 'an arrangement of pivotal sites, each of which have a particular function in the striving for migratory autonomy, as well as in the attempt made by diverse authorities to contain and manage these movements'.[27] Hence, the work includes videos featuring the transit migration hubs of Agadez and Arlit in Niger, and the traditionally nomadic Tuaregs who play a key role in the migration industry by transporting undocumented persons across the desert to Niger's northern borders. She follows military patrols along the Algerian-Moroccan border and visits the deportation prison of Laayoune in Western Sahara,[28] but she also includes aerial footage similar to that used by the Libyan military to keep the vast desert under surveillance. There is no authorial voiceover or any other narrative device to tie the scenes together as 'a story'. Biemann has shot each scene in an ethnographic documentary style, often centred on interviews with agents of the migration industry, with the border patrols or with the migrants themselves. The individual videos are presented almost like pieces of a puzzle, leaving it to the viewer to piece the multi-sited structure of the network together and tease out the causes and effects of the enforcement of borders. As T. J. Demos explains: '*Sahara Chronicle* acts as a "diagram" of the geopolitical reality of North African migration – that is, a function that joins different regimes of signs into a heterogeneous assemblage: *Sahara Chronicle* links everyday life with colonial history, legal structures with economic facts, the politics of containment with the will toward mobility.'[29]

To emphasise the hidden aspects of clandestine migration, Biemann never shows all the videos simultaneously. She usually presents them in the form of an installation in which some are projected and some displayed on monitors, to create what she has described as 'a multiperspective audiovisual environment that can be inhabited by viewers in much the same way that migration space is inhabited by the actors depicted'.[30] Viewers can choose to watch the videos in any order they like; they can skip some and return to others. Since all the videos run in loops, viewers rarely watch a video from the beginning to the end but dive into them at random points in the narratives, amplifying the feeling of disorientation and the impression that clandestine migration constitutes a system that is impenetrable to outsiders. In other words, *Sahara Chronicle* engages viewers through an aesthetic and affective interplay of closeness and distance, alienation and empathy. Biemann encourages a kind of empathic perception, but avoids stirring the kind of emotional over-identification often sparked by the reports of human suffering and victimhood which are the stock-in-trade of television news broadcasts and the imagery put out by humanitarian organisations. Again, this is a geographical project with a political agenda, but the ethical question of empathy is nevertheless vital to it and an issue to which I will return.

The video 'Desert Truck Terminal' plays a central role in *Sahara Chronicle* as it provides viewers with the overall thematic and geographical frames for reading and interpreting the work. It focuses on traffic across the Sahara as a professionally organised, clandestine migration industry, in which the city of Agadez in Niger functions as a contact zone for agents and the migrants from West African countries such as Niger, Ghana, Nigeria, Benin and Senegal who wish to travel north to Algeria or Libya, or cross the Mediterranean Sea to find work in Europe. This video consists of brief conversations with main figures such as local agents and brokers who work as intermediaries or guides. They talk about their work, their use of satellite phones, the financial transactions and picking up the rejected migrants on their way back from the Libyan border to Agadez. This montage is interspersed with footage that focuses on the daily business of the truck terminal, with an emphasis on the mixture of men in traditional African dress and wearing turbans with those in westernised clothes, communicating via phones or loading luggage and people onto large trucks before driving off into the desert. Biemann consciously draws on the genre of ethnographic documentary, but she twists colonial stereotypes, and the conventional interpretive voiceover is lacking. The interviewees are identified only by name and occupation, thus leaving interpretation open. 'Desert Radio Drone', on the other hand, focuses on the high-tech surveillance technologies used in border control. It consists of footage recorded by a drone flying over the Libyan border areas, which captures sand, some water and vegetation, traces of the trajectories of seasonal nomadic journeys, a tiny cluster of buildings or shelters, a road, and tyre tracks in the sand. It is footage that can barely be described as figurative; the overall impression is of a strangely poetic abstract landscape created by the interaction of people, nature and surveillance technology. The steady movement of the camera is accompanied by a soundtrack consisting of a muddled mix of snatches from Saharan and Middle Eastern radio and TV stations, electronic sounds and the wind.[31] It is just as impossible to 'make sense' of the soundtrack as it is to extract 'information' about the locations and traces of human activity from the video footage. However, superimposed on the footage are commentaries that tell viewers about the dangers of the landscape and the risk of death:

> In this geography/orientation makes all the difference/between drifting and travelling/between fate and destination.[32]

'Deportation Prison Laayoune' focuses on some of the *exodés*, the many young men from West Africa on the move for a better life in the Maghreb or Europe. It takes us to an overcrowded reception centre in a former colonial prison in Laayoune in Western Sahara and propels the audience two hundred years back into a brutal past. The prison/reception centre is packed with clandestine migrants picked up by the Moroccan police or military in the desert. After an official has explained that the migrants are held in the prison until they can be repatriated, the camera cuts to the detainees themselves to hear their stories. The main light source is a barred skylight. Through this hole the harsh sunlight hits the sweaty bodies of the detainees and reveals the signs of starvation and weakness.[33] Their stories bear witness to hope as well as desperation. All the interviewees emphasise that they consider Morocco a transit country, a territory they need to cross to find work in Europe, so the Moroccan authorities should have no interest in detaining them. A man from Gambia relays that he is on his way to Europe to find work because there is none where he comes from, and he has to feed his family. A man from Niger, aged thirty, explains that he has no choice but to migrate because without a job and money he cannot marry and start a family. Each statement is moving, but kept short so that viewers are not so much invited to feel compassion for individuals as they are encouraged to reflect on the underlying structures of poverty that force such destitute people to leave West Africa.

'Fishery in Eez' adds a geopolitical perspective to the personal storytelling: we learn how the large quotas of octopus caught by the European Union's industrial trawlers off the coast of Mauritania starve the impoverished country's fishing industry of resources and put local people out of work. 'Coumba's Boat Passage' is a longer interview with Coumba Sow Mbour, a returning young female migrant from Senegal. The camera focuses steadily on her face as she gives an account of her journey to the Canary Islands and of how she was repatriated to Senegal by the Spanish authorities. As the oldest child, Coumba is the breadwinner in her family who must help her parents provide for her younger siblings. As she tells of her motives for spending her savings as the only woman among men on the perilous boat journey, and why she now sells fish in the harbour and works hard to help her mother, viewers get to know her as a courageous and caring individual with a strong sense of responsibility to her family. The staging of Coumba, so that we 'meet' her as an interlocutor in a mediated but nonetheless intimate face-to-face encounter also strengthens the video's affective impact.

The genre of the video-essay functions as a *formal* tool enabling Biemann to assemble her footage and appropriated material *thematically* into a multiperspectival and ever-changing whole. *Sahara Chronicle* maps clandestine transnational movements by weaving a web of connections between different places and spheres. Its *affective* and *political* impact is thus founded in what Demos has called 'her video-essays' organisational power'.[34] *Sahara Chronicle* offers the viewers who are willing to make the considerable effort needed to piece the elements together a revisionist representation of irregular migration that runs counter to the media and official representations of undocumented African migrants as either powerless victims or lawless threats to European nation-state security. The political significance of *Sahara Chronicle* lies in its assertive counter-representation of migrants as definers of their own destiny, and as agents capable of circumventing the border control systems of sovereign states with the paid help of well-organised migration brokers who provide the infrastructure that conditions their mobility. Biemann's installation immerses viewers in a complex montage of moving images and scattered information. It therefore depends on the viewers' capacity to (learn to) be with multiplicity; to stay immersed in the work's messy image of an entangled world, rather than to expect the satisfaction of arriving at a conclusion after considering *Sahara Chronicle*'s multiple temporalities and its spatial, thematic and historical markers, many of which remain impenetrable or easily missed.

If one accepts my interpretation of *Sahara Chronicle* as a counter-representation with political implications, the question of the activist effect of art is reopened: how can an artwork such as *Sahara Chronicle* influence public opinion? How does it intervene in hegemonic media discourses? With its sophisticated emphasis on the partly hidden and impenetrable nature of clandestine migration, the video-essay clearly does not present anything like a coherent, persuasive argument in the manner of a political theory or speech. How, then, may it influence the way its audience thinks and feels about migration?

One way of approaching an answer would be to look at the conjunction of affective and critical operations in the viewer's response to the work. Jill Bennett has distinguished between three types of empathy in the viewer. Over-identification with a victim can lead viewers to abstract from the specifics of the other's suffering and become caught up in their own emotions, thinking 'I wonder what I would be like if that happened to me.'[35] Under other conditions, a lack of identification may occur. Subjected to the incessant bombardment by the news media, viewers may become unable to absorb violently disturbing images of human disaster and experience a kind of compassion fatigue.[36] However, Bennett suggests that visual imagery may also produce a critical and self-reflective kind of empathy. Turning to Dominick LaCapra's trauma studies, she proposes the concept of *empathic unsettlement* to describe the aesthetic experience of simultaneous 'feeling for another' and becoming aware of the fundamental difference between one's own perceptions and the experience of the other. Bennett argues that some signs are felt rather than recognised or perceived through cognition. Borrowing a term from Deleuze, she calls them *encountered signs*. Many artworks function as encountered signs rather than transparent communicative signs. Generated through art, the affective and emotional response these encountered signs engender is not an end in itself. Bennett argues, however, that, on the contrary, art acts in a performative way as 'a catalyst for critical enquiry or deep thought'.[37]

The dissociative structure of *Sahara Chronicle* prevents the audience from developing an identificatory relationship with the African migrants, which would blot out the differences between the migrants' experience and the audience's perception of it in the safe environment of an art exhibition.[38] The brutal realities of the migrants' conditions, and an interview-style that reveals their side of the story, may certainly touch the viewers and trigger a kind of emotional empathy. Yet, Biemann's conscious use of alienation effects works towards a conjunction of empathy and critical reflection that may lead to empathic unsettlement. This empathic unsettlement operates as a dynamic process of approaching the other without forgetting to reflect on where one is coming from. Hence, it also has an ethical potential to transform ingrained perceptions.[39] The complex network of interconnected times and places in

Sahara Chronicle generates what Marsha Meskimmon has called 'precarious ecologies', i.e. sustainable and continually evolving systems of relations premised upon the cohabitation of people and their openness to difference and negotiation with others, often across significant inequalities; a relationality that calls upon the privileged to mobilise 'response-ability and responsibility'.[40] In *Sahara Chronicle*, Biemann creates a space of encounter in which empathy is partly an effect of being touched by others, and partly the product of critical reflection on the nature of European democracies and the way European policies have contributed to producing the sub-Saharan exodus. *Sahara Chronicle* thematises what Staiger has described as the nakedness of humanity in the gap between a universal human rights regime and a territorially inscribed enforcement of it. Consequently, it also uncovers 'the constitutive discrepancies that are at the heart, if invisibly so, of Europe's liberal democracies'.[41]

These considerations answer my first methodological question, how the artist can translate a complex political issue into an artwork that stimulates political reflection. It thus leads to my second question: does the fact that a work like *Sahara Chronicle* in itself presents a self-reflective and theoretically informed interpretation of a socio-political issue pose a challenge for scholars seeking to theorise and analyse it? What can scholars do to avoid merely writing a commentary on the artist's own exemplary commentary, thus serving as a mouthpiece for the artist (as is often seen in exhibition reviews)? There is no doubt that such works as *Sahara Chronicle* require scholars from visual studies and art history to develop interdisciplinary approaches. It is necessary to integrate insights from disciplines such as political science, philosophy and anthropology, yet it is also vital that we continue to bring our skills in analysing the aesthetic and affective capacities of images and the arts to bear on such works when we choose an approach more akin to interdisciplinary and theoretically-oriented cultural studies than traditional art history. If not, we risk reducing artworks to vague political statements or ethnographic projects – vague, precisely because artworks are seldom intended to deliver hard facts or unequivocal political messages about the real world. I am *not* advocating a return to formalism, but it is paramount that our work is not considered to be done once the political meaning has been deduced from an artwork. Ideally, we should also aspire to produce answers to the question of *how* art intervenes in and seeks to reconfigure existing systems of knowledge, and *how* artists can exploit aesthetic and affective means to transform existing images of the world into a subversive politics of images.

Migratory aesthetics in Isaac Julien's *Western Union: Small Boats*

As a result of the burgeoning migratory movements to, from and within Europe, the borders of its nation-states have been increasingly fortified across the continent. Irregular migrants and refugees from the war zones and destitute areas of the world are trying to gain entry to what they imagine to be a Promised Land, only to discover that the practical and legal measures of border control, which have been described as the securitisation of migration,[42] have in many ways turned Europe into a pan-national fortress under the constant surveillance of the guards from Frontex, the European Union's agency for external border control.

At a historical moment when more people than ever before have fled or been forced from their homes, with the war in Syria one of the major causes of these rising figures, a misleading conclusion could be drawn from the desperate governmental decisions and acts that securitisation is only about the fortification of geographical borders. Such an assumption would find support, for example, in the Hungarian government's decision to build, in August 2015, a 175 km-long security fence along its border with Serbia to keep out the thousands of refugees seeking to cross the country to reach Western Europe, where almost 429,000 Syrians sought refuge between April 2011 and August 2015. About half of these were granted asylum in Germany and Sweden.[43] However, securitisation is a much more pervasive political and discursive process, by which the language and practices of security become the organising principle of social relations. In Europe, as well as elsewhere, cross-border surveillance systems have become vital instruments of an emergent system of transnational governance shaping a global polity increasingly regulated through a combination of crime control and immigration control, also known as 'crimmigration control'.[44] As Aas has noted, in recent decades the securitisation of borders has become not only one of the defining traits of migratory movements but also a defining feature of contemporary governance, and has framed issues of refugeedom, asylum and irregular immigration as threats to national security rather than humanitarian problems.[45]

The pressure of immigration, caused by forced migration and the resulting escalation of surveillance and control, has been especially intense in the Mediterranean region. In 2006 – the year before Isaac Julien made his video installation *Western Union: Small Boats* (2007) (see plate 8 and figure 6.2)[46] – almost 30,000 Africans tried to reach the shores of the Spanish Canary Islands in dilapidated boats, and 2,000 were estimated to have died on the islands' shores.[47] In the same year, about 22,000 people reached Italy by boat.[48] The urgency of Isaac Julien's installation has not diminished with time, since it is made in and reflects on a situation of 'limited solidarity and internationalism between Europe and the population of Africa'.[49] As is well known the numbers have increased dramatically since 2007. The UNHCR's annual report, 'Global Trends: Forced Displacement in 2015', released on 20 June 2016, recorded the highest level of worldwide displacement ever. Although most of these were internally displaced people or refugees staying in neighbouring countries, the huge number of migrants has also increased the pressure on Europe. In 2015, the UNHCR estimated that by the end of 2014, the forced displacement numbers in Europe had increased by 51 per cent.[50] During the second half of 2015, there was a dramatic increase in the number of refugees and migrants trying to reach Europe by sea. Overall, more than one million people arrived by sea in 2015, a more than fourfold increase compared to the 216,000 arrivals the year before.[51] Years of tragic drowning accidents in the Mediterranean culminated on 18 April 2015 when 800 people on board one single ship lost their lives at sea.[52]

Although innumerable migrants pay with their lives each year, the political discussions and media discourses envision irregular immigration almost exclusively as a security threat to Western nations. As Aas has pointed out, one of the inadequacies of the traditional nation-state framing of migration develops from the disparity between humanist ideas of security and concepts of state security. The concept of human security aims at the protection of individuals, not states. Irregular migrants are vulnerable precisely because they are excluded from concepts of security for the nation-state.[53] The fortification of borders thus functions as a boundary-defining mechanism, which excludes some people as non-members in relation to the nation-state. Sometimes it even jeopardises 'the right to have rights'[54] granted by the human rights discourse to all individuals by virtue of their being human, regardless of their particular citizenship.[55]

Considering the so-called 'political turn' in contemporary art since the 1990s, it is not surprising that a number of artists have committed themselves to spotlighting the geopolitical issue of the securitisation of borders and its recurrent fatal consequences for unwanted immigrants. Thus, the second part of this chapter focuses on this issue as part of the overall phenomenon of international migration. It examines how the enforcement of the European borders surfaces in the artistic-cinematic imaginary in an analysis of Isaac Julien's video installation *Western Union: Small Boats*, and its theme of African migrants crossing the Mediterranean Sea to reach the coasts of southern Italy. Although the analysis focuses on a video installation that has pronounced cinematographic features, it draws more on a reading of the work through the prism of cultural studies than on a specifically cinematographical or art historical analysis.

Isaac Julien's works have often been labelled 'queer', as many of his films have addressed issues of homosexuality; or they have been labelled 'postcolonial', because they deal with racism and interracial relations as well as the colonial legacy and the complicated postcolonial relationship between Africa, the Caribbean and Europe. However, merely naming Julien's position tends to miss the point that diagonal moves and connective procedures are at the core of his *modus operandi*.[56] In his multi-screen video installations, he weaves together dance, music, poetry, painting, film, documentary and fiction to create a visual and artistic translation of the concept *créolité*. By allowing hybridised and complex spaces of representation to develop through movement between different geographical sites and different temporalities, he creates a moment of re-seeing the European world from different points from within its expanded geographies. As Kobena Mercer has observed, viewing Isaac Julien's work in film, video and installation intertwines dreaming and critical awakening:

> the experience is one in which the dream-like quality of the image flow induces a luxurious mood of 'drift'. In this *condition of critical reverie*, which feels at once '*transgressive and hallucinatory*', thoughts and sensations are directed by a poetic touch that loosens the stream of semiotic material from rigid adherence to sedimented conventions. Amid the flow, there are sharp moments felt as a piercing of the commonplace which create a '*punctum*' – a moment of surprise offset by the holding environment of the surrounding pictorial narrative.[57]

Kobena Mercer is acutely aware that Julien may be addressing politically sensitive issues such as migration and homosexuality, but the artist's sophisticated use of aesthetics (including the 'piercing', affective effect of the detail that Roland Barthes has named *punctum*) to move his audiences across boundaries would make it problematic to reduce his works to political statements. Hence, rather than simply reading *Western Union: Small Boats* as a critical comment on European immigration policies, I wish to explore the tensional interpenetration of politics, ethics and aesthetics in Julien's installation. The sheer beauty of his cinematic representation of the misery of migrants makes it necessary to move beyond the question of aesthetics and consider the issue of aestheticisation and the artist's ethical relation to his subject matter. For theoretical support, I turn to Mieke Bal's concept of migratory aesthetics and Jacques Rancière's distinction between ethics and politics. I also refer to Iain Chambers' thoughts on migration and modernity in the Mediterranean region, as well as anthropologists Didier Fassin and Richard Rechtman's analysis of a paradigmatic change in the Western relationship to history, from looping back on and celebrating historical victories to looping back on the history of the wrongs of genocide, colonisation, the trade in enslaved people, etc. Fassin and Rechtman argue that one outcome of this shift is that the victim has become a central figure, in the Western common sense understandings of history and its bearing on the present. Taking my lead from Fassin and Rechtman, I examine therefore how Julien interprets the cultural trope of the migrant as victim.

Western Union: Small Boats was shot in Sicily, and it is the third film in an ongoing exploration of sea passage and transnational crossings that Julien calls his *Expedition* series. The series also includes *True North* (2004), a tale set against a spectacular snowy landscape and based on the story of the explorer Matthew Henderson who was believed to be the first person to reach the

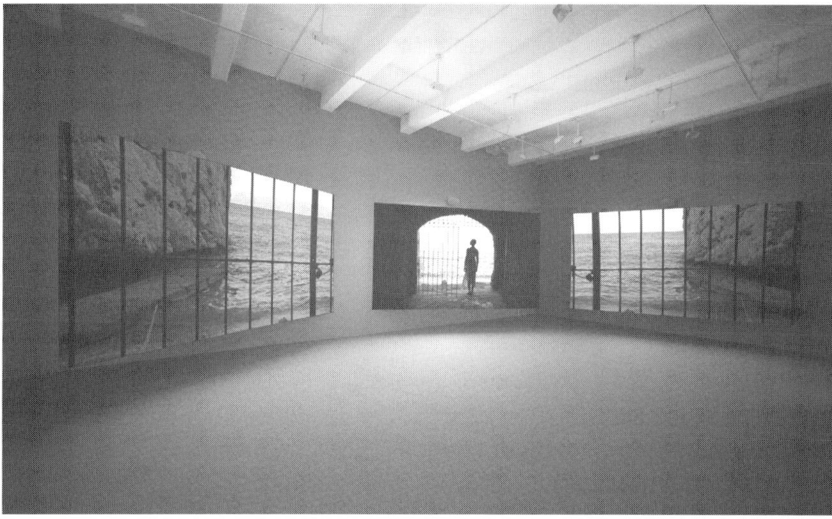

Isaac Julien, *Western Union: Small Boats*, 2007. Installation view, Metro Pictures Gallery, 2007. Three-screen projection. 35 mm colour film, DVD/HD transfer. 5.1 SR sound. Total running time: 18 mins 22 secs. © Isaac Julien. Courtesy of the artist and Metro Pictures Gallery. 6.2

North Pole in 1909; *Fantôme Afrique* (2005), which weaves together urban and rural landscapes of Burkina Faso in a meditation on the denationalised, de-territorialised spaces born of the encounters between local and global cultures; and *Ten Thousand Waves* (2010), based on Chinese migration to England and which explores the movement of people across continents and meditates on unfinished journeys.[58] When considering *Western Union: Small Boats*, and especially the way it seeks to engage viewers, it is important to understand that Julien does not attempt to speak on behalf of migrants and lend a voice to refugees but tries to reflect on the human aspect of migration: 'One thing I always try to avoid is "behalf-ism." Although my parents came to England from the Caribbean, they were asked to come and work. They were never refugees. Nor am I an immigrant – I'm a black European. In *Western Union: Small Boats*, I'm showing human qualities, individual elements that get lost in all the official rhetoric.'[59]

The work is structured as a tripartite video installation with five large-scale projections.[60] An antechamber with a single screen projection functions as an 'overture'. It shows a graveyard of rickety wooden boats painted with Arabic script. Solemnly, the camera pans along the mass of abandoned boats, seemingly without beginning and end, thereby silently setting the stage for a human drama and introducing a note of tragedy from the beginning. The antechamber precedes a central room with a display of three projections, followed by an exit with a single projection, which mirrors that of the antechamber and closes the sequence. There is no authoritative narrator (or voiceover), only carefully selected juxtapositions of footage which create multiple layers of meanings, suggestively enhanced by a soundscape of electronic music, *a cappella* singing and barely decipherable fragments of information about imperilled refugees on a scratchy radio frequency. *Western Union: Small Boats* thus follows a loose narrative in which documentary elements provide a more realistic and sobering framework for the wondrous and perturbing interpretive gestures of the lyric passages.[61]

The combination of a partly documentary, partly fictive rendering of the current fates of unwanted immigrants on the doorstep of Europe with almost hallucinogenic images of Europe's former aristocratic wealth is in keeping with Julien's interdisciplinary method and the general complexity of his videographic language. According to Mieke Bal, 'the migratory' is a feature of cultures at large in today's globalised world where it has become a condition of life, and as such also a condition of art and aesthetics. Unpacking the concept of *migratory aesthetics*, Bal defines 'aesthetics' and the 'migratory' in broad terms:

> I use 'aesthetics' here not so much as a philosophical domain, but rather, according to its traditional meaning, as a term to refer to an experience of sensate binding, a connectivity based on the senses, and the '-s' at the end of the word is meant to indicate the plural form, not the 'science of' or meta-meaning. 'Migratory' does not claim to account for the actual experience of migrants, but instead refers to the traces, equally sensate, of the movements of migration that characterize contemporary culture. Both terms are programmatic: different aesthetic experiences are offered through the encounter with such traces.[62]

Bal also claims that there are important politico-epistemological connections between video, as an influential medium of our time, and migration, as a situation characteristic of the contemporary world – or better, between the 'videographic' and the 'migratory'. It is because video is a temporal medium based on moving images that it shares with migratory life 'a complex and confusing, challenging multi-temporality'.[63] Bal also suggests that video art involving the migratory does 'political work',[64] and that video-making is always a political act in the sense that it involves an act of 'making visible' by which 'it opens perception up to others'.[65] Although her claims concerning video's potential *vis-à-vis* migration remain politically vague and metaphorical, and although they sometimes come close to the notion of the multicultural, Bal's concept of migratory aesthetics has proven to be able to focus the current discourse effectively on the nexus of art and migration, and strengthen the efforts to balance reflections on art's political content with a consideration of its aesthetic dimensions (see Chapter 1).

Thus, migratory aesthetics denote an inclusive understanding of contemporary culture at large as profoundly transformed by migration and the confluence of people. It is not undergirded by a minority studies perspective that reserves the qualifier 'migrant' for separable minority cultures. Moreover, it entails a perspective that prioritises the aesthetic and lets topical concerns – such as refugee issues, racism, cultural diversity and citizenship, as well as matters of contention like structural discrimination and democratic participation – come to the fore *through* the aesthetic analysis.[66] It is my opinion that Isaac Julien's *Western Union: Small Boats* could be conceived of as an instance of migratory aesthetics. Taking my cue from Bal's observation that temporal heterogeneity is an important link between videographic moving images and migratory mobility,[67] I will argue that the complex temporal structure of Julien's work shapes the way it engages its audience in the problematics of irregular migration and European immigration policies.

Tourist and migrant gazes

The narrative of *Western Union: Small Boats* unfolds in the triptych projection of the central room. The opening shot presents a view of the open sea and blue sky through a gloomy gated archway. Accompanied by the voice of singer Oumou Sangaré, the graceful figure of actor Vanessa Myrie steps out of the darkness and into light and freedom (see figure 6.2). Myrie is a recurrent figure in Julien's video installations from the 2000s. She is not a conventional protagonist but appears as witness as well as actor on the margins of historical events: as the one who enacts, or the one who observes, reveals and reflects. Thus, the first scene triggers associations ranging from the Atlantic Middle Passage, through incarcerations past and present to perilous sea passages of contemporary African migrants across the Mediterranean Sea.[68] In other words, it evokes a history of wrongs.

Next, the video jumps to a harbour with small boats and Italian fishermen arranging their fishing tackle on a quiet, sunny morning. From the harbour with its implicit metaphor of the ocean as sustaining human life, the video cuts to a contrasting location: the graveyard for boats abandoned by their owners on the coast of Italy and gathered by the authorities into heaps of broken vessels, still scattered with things left behind by the people who sailed them – empty water bottles, discarded life vests, as well as shoes and clothes bleached by the sun and saltwater. After establishing the maritime setting, Julien shifts from the suggestive realism of documentary footage to a lyrical interpretation of the migrant's journey.[69] It begins with a moment of relief and aesthetic pleasure. The close-ups on the ghostly remains from precarious sea journeys is succeeded by a panoramic view of the Scala dei Turchi, or the Turkish Steps, at Agrigento in Sicily, stretching horizontally over all three screens. The white rocks become a spectacular backdrop for a group of five dancers walking in a line towards the coastline, where Myrie, the witness, reappears and lifts a red t-shirt out of the surf as a remnant of a life lost. From the beauty of the barren rocks the camera cuts abruptly to a group of exhausted African men sailing in a small boat under an unforgiving sun against a burning orange sky. As one man falls asleep, the roaring of the sea ceases, and we enter the silence of a dream. Cross-cutting to the rich decor of the Palazzo Valguarnera-Gangi in Palermo, Julien leads us through the dreamscape of the migrant subject, a space of desire and fantasies of wealth (see plate 8). As Jennifer González remarks, 'The shimmering palace is the wished-for haven from hardship and strife, but also a mirage of luxury that is, finally, a site of refusal and unyielding power.'[70]

Borrowing a term used by film scholars Dina Iordanova and Yosefa Loshitzky, it could be said that *Western Union: Small Boats* revolves around the mechanism of 'projective identification',[71] whereby the primary intent is not to represent African migrants but to project concerns about Europe itself. As demonstrated by the first eight minutes of the video installation's eighteen-minute loop, which I have just summarised, the mechanism of 'projective identification' is triggered by Julien's careful staging of a dialectic that puts attentive viewers in an ambiguous viewing position that conflates insider and outsider positions. He thereby invites viewers to reconsider European policies of irregular migration and asylum in particular and Europe's mainly negative perception of immigration in general. The dialectic of the work is played out on two different levels: that of the gaze and that of temporality. I will discuss them in proper order.

The camera alternately identifies with the migrant's gaze and the tourist's gaze. It invites the spectator to oscillate between the two and reflect on the tensions that link them together, as well as the gaps that separate them.[72] As the narrative evolves from the theme of the journey, it has the potential of activating a tourist gaze by positioning the audience as virtual tourists enjoying the magnificent Sicilian landscapes and the palace. The sunlit panoramas and the camera's lingering on Palazzo Valguarnera-Gangi's sumptuous gilded ballroom, illuminated by shining chandeliers, deliberately stimulate such scopophilic desire. However, 'touristic' pleasure is awakened only to be withdrawn the next time the camera cuts to a contrasting scene, where the audience is invited to identify with another gaze: that of the migrant. To the clandestine migrant, the sea and the coast are not picturesque spectacles, but inhospitable spaces that have to be traversed and penetrated. While the tourist's gaze seeks aesthetic stimulation and is driven by the pleasure principle, the migrant's gaze seeks survival and is driven by the dream of a better life, here represented by the dreamscape of the gilded ballroom. The image of the ballroom is, in effect, doubly coded as an object, and as a metaphor of the desire that connects the two unequally positioned types of travellers. As Loshitzky has demonstrated, such an oscillation between tourism and 'poorism' can create a distanciation effect, resulting in a Brechtian alienation.[73] The dialectic oscillation between gazes thus establishes the *ethical* thematic of *Western Union: Small Boats*: is an artist entitled to use and represent the migrant's misery for artistic ends? Is a spectator entitled to derive pleasure from a sensually gripping representation of a migrant's suffering?

There are two important points here. Firstly, staging a dialectic of contrastive gazes enables Julien to offer his audience a critical viewing position reminiscent of the double perspective of migrants that Salman Rushdie dubbed the 'stereoscopic vision' to denote the ability to combine an insider and an outsider perspective on society.[74] Secondly, the critical reflection on the ethical dilemma of aesthetics is not just something that viewers bring to Julien's work. It is already built into the thematic of the work by the way the camera is used and the editing of the video footage. Ultimately, the dialectic of gazes alerts the viewer to the inequalities and differences between the social positions of the tourist and the migrant, and their points of view. Oscillating between such contrastive perspectives, the audience is displaced from the tourist's secure, distanced position to one of immersion into and tensional identification with the contradictory perceptions of the world presented by the installation. In addition, the introduction of theatrical dance and the shifts between realist and lyrical filming intensify the unsettling of the spectators' habits of seeing by causing uncertainties about how to read the work in terms of genre.

A temporal dialectic

As mentioned above, *Western Union: Small Boats* also stages a dialectic of temporalities. This is established by the alternation between a realist and a lyric mode of representation and by cross-cutting from various moments and places 'in the present' (e.g. the opening scene, the graveyard of 'small boats', the fishermen at the Italian harbour) to various moments and places 'in the past' (e.g. the palace, flashbacks to/memories of landscapes and townscapes in Africa). Moreover, Julien has also included moments of fiction, like the dancers at the Scala dei Turchi and, as we shall see, a minimalist but highly symbolic social drama acted out with the Palazzo Valguarnera-Gangi as a historical backdrop.

Mieke Bal has proposed that video and migration are linked by the experience of time as multiple and heterogeneous, and that video – because of the moving camera and the cutting of the footage – is eminently suited to represent what movement and multi-temporality means, and how it feels in the body. As Bal puts it, 'Both video and migratory culture intensify the experience of heterochrony.'[75] Bal distinguishes between the term *multi-temporality*, which she uses to denominate the way heterogeneous time is structured as a 'phenomenon', and *heterochrony*, which refers to the 'experience' of multi-temporality. How 'representation' enters the equation is not exactly clear in Bal's definition. As my object of study is a work of art, I will use the term 'multi-temporality' about the work of art as a phenomenon that presents itself to us as a representation (rather than an object or an event), in order to unpack the dialectic structure of time in Julien's work. In brief, I will argue that it is the alternation between realist and lyric temporalities and the complex interweaving of different moments in time which produce the work's multi-temporality. The term 'heterochrony', on the other hand, will refer to the experience of multi-temporality, primarily the audience's experience.[76] One more note on Bal's terminology: too sharp a distinction should not be made between the videographic and the cinematic. Julien has made films as well as video installations, and he draws freely on techniques, genres and stylistic features from both video and cinema.[77] This practice reflects a general trend in contemporary video art with its increasing assimilation of cinematic features and techniques. My point is not that this development limits the usefulness of Bal's concepts, but, rather, that her concepts are sufficiently generalised to be of use in the study of both the videographic and the cinematic as they pertain to all kinds of moving images.

To make a multi-temporal representation effective, i.e. to enable it – heterochrony, Julien uses what Mieke Bal calls 'temporal foreshortening'. Like the spatial foreshortening known from linear perspective, a temporal foreshortening distorts the image or, in film, the flow and sequence of images. Time is slowed-down, sped-up; or a scene cross-cut with another scene; in order for time to be condensed. Temporal foreshortening undoes the ontological temporal cut between past and present.[78] Foreshortening remains an illusionistic device, but foreshortened time is not only enchantingly unreal, it is also irresistible, especially when deployed in video and film. Although it does not offer us a real passage to the past, foreshortening makes the past feel compellingly 'present'.[79] In *Western Union: Small Boats* temporal foreshortening condenses time and blurs the boundaries between past, present and future as the camera jumps between Sicily and Africa, boats at sea and in the harbour, cliffs and ballroom. As opposed to a conventional diegetic compression of a story, Julien's temporal foreshortening is non-linear and non-logical. As a result, the different scenes and their locales enter into a dialectic relationship that suggests to the viewer that past and present, near and far, North and South are interconnected. Last, but not least, the cross-cutting between discrepant moments in time may also produce an acute feeling of heterochrony in attentive viewers, thereby not only suggesting that this experience is intrinsic to the experience of migration but also offering viewers unsettling empathic insight into it.

Heterochrony is perhaps most urgently felt when Julien cuts from the sleeping African migrant in the boat to the ballroom, thus staging a temporal dialectic between past, present and a yearned-for future. Temporally, we are displaced from a realist to a lyric temporality or 'dream time', but also from 'our time' to 'historical time'. The ballroom of the Palazzo Valguarnera-Gangi was also used as the location for a famous scene in Luchino Visconti's *The Leopard* (1963), the eponymous film adaptation of the 1958 novel by Prince Guiseppe Tomasi di Lampedusa. Visconti's film is set in the 1860s and examines the unification between the Sicilian society in the south and the Italian society in the north, as well as the decline of the Sicilian aristocracy and the rise of a bourgeois class. It portrays the Prince of Salina's struggle to accept these transformations and his own role in a modern society. The cinematic reference enables Julien to relocate the issues raised in Visconti's historical costume epic to the present day, which is also a time of transition due to the mobility of people, both geographically and socially. In the ballroom scene in *The Leopard*, the prince broods on how aristocratic privilege may lead to decadence, while beautiful silk-clad women frolic in the very same hall of mirrors, some gracefully circumnavigating the ballroom, others resting on luxurious divans and entertaining each other with polite conversation.[80] *The Leopard* is ambiguous about class relations in bourgeois modernity, although it makes it clear that the gap between rich and poor will remain. In Julien's reinterpretation of Visconti's ballroom scene, the room is not crowded but empty, but into the image steps *la principessa* Carine Vanni Mantegna di Gangi, the current descendant of the Prince and Princess Pietro and Marianna Valguarnera, who occupied the palace in the eighteenth century. The whiteness of her skin and the way her smile stiffens somehow transform her into an uncanny 'sentinel of aristocratic privilege'.[81] Cutting away from the princess, the camera focuses on Myrie who strolls around the ballroom, confidently fanning herself like the young women at Visconti's ball as if she were a protagonist of the social ambitions and mobility of people of colour. What her relaxed presence in this fortress of wealth might mean to the migrant dreamer is left to the imagination. Next, the camera jumps back to the Scala dei Turchi, where a man is carrying another man across his shoulder. The latter sags like a corpse, and we are thus returned to the theme of the perilous journey and the migrant as victim, but the politics of race have been further complicated because the rescuer is a man of African descent while the man we are led to believe has drowned, or who is perhaps being rescued, is white. By using multi-temporality to suggest causal relations between and the deep entanglement of seemingly unrelated people, places and incidents across time, Julien is, in fact, using *aesthetic* means to open up the ethical and political perspectives of his work.

Europe as geopolitical borderlands

Skin colour is also used as a signifier in a sequence near the end of *Western Union: Small Boats*. The video intercuts from the African boat people to documentary footage of light-skinned tourists bathing on the Italian shore, before Julien zooms in on the tragic signs of death at the margins of carefree beach life: five corpses wrapped in silver mylar lined up along the water's edge. The dead bodies represent a *punctum*, a perturbing cut of the flow of idyllic images, because the camera suggests that tourists and the fatalities of migration are united in a continuous space-time. Julien's critical montage of tourists, migrants and dead bodies – all of them travellers – takes the viewer by surprise by establishing an unexpected proximity between what is usually separated and held apart, thereby enabling another telling.[82]

Although Julien has staged the line-up of the anonymous drowned bodies, it has a disturbing air of realism. The reality effect derives from the scene's intertextual references to prototypical mass mediated images. As part of his research for new works, Julien mines the media for images. When *Western Union: Small Boats* was shown in Warsaw in 2009, Julien used the accompanying exhibition catalogue to reprint a newspaper article with a similar press photo, published the year before Julien completed the work, to emphasise the work's status as an intervention into current debates on irregular immigration to Europe.[83] However, the work also operates on another level of meaning. With its specific references to African migrants, it contributes to widening our notion of Europe and 'the Mediterranean' as geopolitical territories expanding well beyond their present borders.

Iain Chambers and Lidia Curti have made the case for a reconfigured and more fluid and multicultural understanding of the Mediterranean as 'aesthetic and cultural, as well as geographic borderlands'. This conception of the Mediterranean as an intricate site of encounters and migratory flows is based on the centrality of seaborne communication, connecting Europe, Asia and Africa in a historical net that stretches over centuries:[84] 'This would be a critical space in which it becomes possible to recognize Cairo as a Mediterranean city, Islam as a European religion … and Turkey as a part of the formation of Europe for at least six centuries.'[85] One outcome of the historical and cultural clashes and exchanges across the Mediterranean Sea is that borders have been both transitory and zones of transit. In the twenty-first century, the European Union has established a complex system of filters and channels that stretch outward into extraterritorial space, both on the Mediterranean and into the Maghreb, in an attempt to stem the tide of migration from beyond its borders.[86]

However, border control has also become a tool for intensifying the integration of the European Union and building supranational structures in the field of justice and surveillance. For example, policing agencies such as Frontex are supported by the surveillance resources of countries outside the EU, especially in Eastern Europe and Northern Africa. Katja Franko Aas has drawn attention to the mixture of a language of help and a language of control which characterises Frontex's account of their own activities, in which lives diverted back are presented as lives that have been saved. In addition, Aas has demonstrated how the language of human security also permeates the language used to legitimate EU security and immigration policies, and how immigration and crime are linked closely together in the discourse on security. She finds a poignant example in a press release from the European Commission on the European Border Surveillance System known as Eurosur. Here the loss of lives resulting from 'illegal immigration' on 'overcrowded boats' is declared 'unacceptable' and therefore to be 'significantly reduced … through a comprehensive strategy that includes cooperation with third countries, also on border surveillance'. The press release also states that the objective of Eurosur is not only to prevent unauthorised border crossings, but also 'to counter cross-border crime such as the prevention of terrorism, trafficking in human beings, drugs smuggling, illicit arms trafficking etc'.[87] This conflation of immigration and crime control with humanitarian concerns also characterises the public presentation of Eurosur. On Frontex's website, Eurosur is described under 'Intelligence' as an 'information-exchange framework' aiming to 'support Member States by increasing their situational awareness and reaction capability in combating cross-border crime, tackling irregular migration and preventing loss of migrant lives at sea'.[88] As cultural studies scholar Roger Bromley has emphasised, refugees and asylum seekers are irritants to the national imaginary with its narratives of citizenry, nationhood and the territorial state.[89] Despite the fact-oriented wording, Eurosur's self-presentation thus reflects the tensions between, on the one hand, the humanitarian self-perception of European member states and EU agencies and, on the other, EU border and immigration policies, which directly and indirectly contribute to endangering lives. These two sides are interrelated, as humanitarian discourses and forms of solidarity are at work in the policing of European borders and of what Aas and Gundhus term 'humanitarian borderlands', i.e. conflict-ridden environments in which the objectives of protecting state security collide with the needs of people in precarious life situations.[90]

Despite transnational measures of securitisation and surveillance, European borders, like all borders, remain permeable. The thousands of Africans who try to fulfil their dream of a better life by embarking on the risky journey across the sea testify to this porosity of borders as well as to the notorious European fear of the South. As Chambers has pointed out, most immigrants to Western Europe have actually come from the east, either Eastern Europe or Asia. Yet, this fact is often ignored because the signs of race and religion stir 'a spiralling moral panic obsessively staring south toward Africa and Islam' and activate the fear of a continent reduced in the world media to the home of 'the wretched of the earth'.[91] For Julien, as for Chambers, 'the Mediterranean' thus becomes a site of experimenting with different ways of representing history and contemporaneity. Redefining 'the Mediterranean' enables them to engage with the 'outside' of the history of Western modernity and its repressed colonial pasts, thereby connecting Europe with the more extensive elsewhere that it has always been part of.

Western Union: Small Boats foregrounds contemporary migration. In an interview, Julien has explained that this work is about the thousands of irregular immigrants coming to places such as Sicily and Lampedusa.[92] However, the work is also about the history inherent to the actual location of Sicily. Julien re-examines historical buildings and sites like the Palazzo Valguernera-Gangi, frequently highlighting the scars and traces of time as metaphors for traumatic memories and the violence of history. He also includes the Scala dei Turchi, where the Ottoman colonisers disembarked on the hillside's natural steps of white rock, and the coast at Scopello on Sicily as the emblem of today's invasion by tourists. Julien thus constructs a complex image of the Mediterranean as a multi-temporal meeting point between East and West, North and South – a genuine multicultural and transcultural 'contact-zone'.

The language of humanitarianism

Let us return to the cultural trope of the migrant as victim. In recent years, a strong emphasis on screening migrants to sort the 'good' and desirable migrants from the 'bad', undesired migrants has transformed the politics of immigration in Europe.[93] Anthropologists Didier Fassin and Richard Rechtman have demonstrated that this transformation has also caused a shift in the European conception of asylum since the 1990s, leading to a weakening of the legitimacy of asylum for victims of political violence, while a new criterion based on humanitarianism has been developed for sick migrants with no access to proper treatment in their home countries. Moreover, if refugees applying for asylum are exposed as so-called economic immigrants, rather than political refugees, their chances of obtaining asylum are in jeopardy.[94]

As Fassin notes, administrations and police officers have come to view asylum seekers with 'systematic suspicion'. Until it is proven otherwise, anyone seeking refugee status is now considered an undocumented immigrant 'seeking to take advantage of the generosity of the European nations'. As a result, the use of the term 'false refugees' as a reference to 'economic immigrants' who claim political asylum has become central to immigration control.[95] Fassin points to the fact that refugees and irregular immigrants occupy an important place in the biopolitics of Europe.[96] As the suffering body becomes an important legal resource for undocumented immigrants seeking a residence permit in Europe, the political increasingly integrates humanitarianism and is thereby also redefined by the latter. As Fassin observes, repression and compassion have become profoundly linked.[97] We would thus be missing the point if compassion is seen as merely emotional and outside the sphere of politics, while it is, in fact, developing into a mode of governance that concerns populations and groups in situations of precariousness. Moreover, it is a form of governance that does not draw on discourses of injustice and rights but mobilises moral sentiments of compassion and assistance.[98]

Of particular relevance to *Western Union: Small Boats* is the change in attitude to irregular immigrants caused by this shift in emphasis from political asylum to humanitarianism in European immigration policies. In political and media discourses, as well as the public imagination shaped by these discourses, asylum seekers and irregular immigrants are often bracketed together, by which both groups are typecast as victims.[99] Alternatively, they are separated into two categories: 'refugees', who are recognised as 'authentic' victims with the right to asylum; and 'migrants', as a shorthand for economic immigrants, who are to be forcibly and quickly repatriated. This distinction was, for instance, mobilised in the Danish media and governmental politics in September 2015 when the public debates on what was called a European refugee crisis came to a head and events shifted the meaning of the neutral word *tilrejsende* (visitor), so that it became a euphemism for asylum seeker, while the term 'migrant' came to connote a bogus refugee – suggesting that the migrant's claim was not real or genuine but, rather, fake or false.[100] Prior to and in tandem with this change, the use of the term 'illegal' about migrants became widespread. Ninna Nyberg Sørensen, Senior Researcher at the Danish Institute for International Studies, rightly pointed out that 'the word "illegal migrant" suggests some kind of voluntariness that legitimises our doubt and right to decline entry, residence and work. The more and more frequent use of the word "illegal" among political spokespersons and in the press contributes to confirming the general opinion about abuse of our systems.'[101] Fassin concludes that Europe increasingly bases the management of immigrants from poor countries on the recognition of rights in the name of the suffering body, or what he terms *biolegitimacy*. This goes hand in hand with a turn in Europe's moral economy towards 'a compassionate attention to individual suffering in which the search for a common humanity resides in the recognition of bare life, that of the physical alteration of the body'.[102] The question is, does *Western Union: Small Boats* challenge Europe's consensual immigration policy with its conflation of legal repression and humanitarian compassion? Or does Julien affirm it by monumentalising it?

Here, one must bear in mind the complexity of the work. It does not communicate an unequivocal political message, but what does catch the eye is the representation of African boat people as purely passive figures, lost at sea, dreaming in vain, suffering or drowning and, thus, literally becoming victims of the sea. But the ballroom scene complicates this representation of the migrant as victim. This is partly because of the self-confident presence of Myrie as an embodiment of migrant agency and potentiality in the stronghold of declining European power, and partly because the artificiality of the scene could also be taken as an invitation to read it as a metaphor of the European fear of immigration.[103] Yet, it is the trope of the migrant as victim that dominates Julien's piece with its appeal to the viewer's ethical consciousness.

Aestheticisation after the ethical turn

Having identified the migrant victim and the language of humanitarianism as central to *Western Union: Small Boats*, it is time to address the question of aestheticisation and the ethical relation of the artist to his topic. As Jennifer A. González has phrased it, 'Is it unethical to build a body of expensive, lush, and sensually gripping work around the real-life tragedies of immigrants?'[104]

In his critique of the so-called 'ethical turn' in contemporary political discourses, Jacques Rancière warned against a new regime of humanitarian consensus which may endanger the political dissensus at the very core of democratic societies and lead to a de-politicisation of the political community.[105] Of particular relevance to Julien's work is Rancière's claim that the disappearance of political dissensus and the political struggle for rights in 'the indistinctness of ethics' has its counterpart in the arts. The artist's political engagement in society tends to be redistributed between, on the one hand, a vision of art as a remedy to strengthen social bonds (as in relational aesthetics and social outreach projects), and, on the other, a vision of aesthetics transformed into ethics. To Rancière, this amounts to an evacuation of art's political agency and a reduction of art to an ethical witnessing of historical wrongs, interminably looking back to memorialise the victims instead of calling for political change in the present.[106] While *Western Union: Small Boats* is surely an ethical commemoration of the fatalities of migration, it is not only that. It also poses political questions of globalisation and economic inequality. By inviting its audiences to engage in a projective identification with the dispossessed, without forgetting their own privileged position, it opens up a critical perspective on European immigration policies and economic policies. As T. J. Demos has argued, art becomes political not simply by communicating a political message but by intervening in the very forms of communication. Quoting Rancière, Demos insists on the paradox of political art: it must maintain the 'readability of a political signification' for its political claims to be taken seriously, while simultaneously producing an aesthetic shock by avoiding a fully transparent, and hence purely political, signification.[107] It is exactly the emphasis on the unsettling effect of aesthetics that enables *Western Union: Small Boats* to transport spectators out of the narrow politico-historical context of contemporary Europe and make them see migration in a broader, transhistorical perspective and recognise that they are themselves historical subjects of migratory movements. Isaac Julien is highly conscious of the potentially politically awakening effect of aestheticisation. His words are worth quoting as a conclusion not only to this chapter but also to this book's overall engagement with the question of why multifarious and unsettling stories of migration have found their way into contemporary art:

> I've been asked many times how I can represent such ugly facts in such beautiful ways. To me, the question isn't why but why not? Why not apply the most aristocratic of styles to important stories?[108]

Notes

1 Katja Franko Aas, '"Crimmigrant" bodies and bona fide travelers: surveillance, citizenship and global governance', *Theoretical Criminology*, 15:3 (2011), 331–46, 337.
2 Uta Staiger, 'Visualizing the Citizen Gap: EU Borders and Migration in Cultural Production', in Ursula Biemann and Jan-Erik Lundström (eds), *Ursula Biemann. Mission Reports: Artistic Practice in the Field: Video Works 1998–2008* (Umeå: Bildmuseet, Bristol: Arnolfini, 2008), pp. 142–54, p. 142.
3 Turner and Webb, *Art and Human Rights*, pp. 8–9.
4 Staiger, 'Visualizing the Citizen Gap', p. 149.
5 The term 'irregular' is used here to avoid the commonly used dehumanising and incriminating term 'illegal'. See Koser, *International Migration*, pp. 54–7.
6 Tello, *Counter-Memorial Aesthetics*, p. 9.
7 Agamben, *Homo Sacer*.
8 Hannah Arendt, *The Origins of Totalitarianism* (San Diego: Harcourt, 1976), pp. 297–8.
9 *Ibid.*, p. 300.
10 *Ibid.*, p. 297.
11 Agamben, *Homo Sacer*, p. 20.
12 *Ibid.*, pp. 17–18, 28–9.
13 Aas, '"Crimmigrant" bodies and bona bide travelers', 342.
14 Agamben, *Homo Sacer*, p. 131.
15 Aas, '"Crimmigrant" bodies and bona fide travelers', 339–40. Schinkel draws on Giorgio Agamben's distinction between two forms of life, *zoē*, which denotes the simple fact of living, and *bios*, the biological life of human beings in a society. It is based on a distinction between those who belong to society, and thus to *bios*, and

those who are excluded and reduced to *zoē* or 'bare life'. See Agamben, *Homo Sacer*, pp. 9, 12–13; Willem Schinkel, 'From zoēpolitics to biopolitics: citizenship and the construction of "society"', *European Journal of Social Theory*, 13:2 (2010), 155–72, 156–7, 160–8.

16 Martin Lemberg-Pedersen, 'Private Security Companies and the European Borderscapes', in Thomas Gammeltoft-Hansen and Ninna Nyberg Sørensen (eds), *The Migration Industry and the Commercialization of International Migration* (London, New York: Routledge, 2013), pp. 152–72; Thomas Gammeltoft-Hansen, 'The Rise of the Private Border Guard: Accountablility and Responsibility in the Migration Control Industry', *ibid.*, pp. 128–51.

17 Katja Franko Aas, 'A Borderless World? Cosmopolitanism, Boundaries and Frontiers', in Cecilia Baillet and Katja Franko Aas (eds), *Cosmopolitan Justice and its Discontents* (London, New York: Routledge, 2011), pp. 134–50, p. 141.

18 Aas, '"Crimmigrant" bodies and bona fide travelers', 337, 341.

19 Edward Casey, 'A Matter of Edge: Border vs. Boundary at *La Frontera*', in Moslund, Petersen, and Schramm (eds), *The Culture of Migration: Politics, Aesthetics and Histories*, pp. 27–39, pp. 28, 32–4.

20 Demos, *The Migrant Image*, pp. 15–16; Anna Schneider, 'Die maritime Wende. Die Abkehr von territorialen Perspektiven als Chance für die Globalisierung', *Springerin*, no. 16 (2010), 54–7, 57.

21 See Anselm Franke (ed.), *B-Zone: Becoming Europe and Beyond* (Berlin: Kunstwerke, 2006).

22 Ursula Biemann, 'Counter-Geographies in the Sahara', in Michael Dear *et al.* (eds), *Geohumanities: Art, History, Text at the Edge of Place* (London, New York: Routledge, 2011), pp. 162–72, pp. 162–4.

23 *Ibid.*, p. 171.

24 T. J. Demos, 'Sahara Chronicle: Video's Migrant Geography', in Biemann and Lundström (eds), *Ursula Biemann*, pp. 178–90, p. 184.

25 Angela Dimitrakaki, 'Materialist Feminism for the Twenty-First Century: The Video Essays of Ursula Biemann', *ibid.*, pp. 115–27, p. 125; Demos, 'Sahara Chronicle', p. 184.

26 Demos,'Sahara Chronicle', pp. 182–3.

27 Biemann, 'Counter-Geographies in the Sahara', p. 164.

28 *Ibid.*, pp. 164–5.

29 Demos, 'Sahara Chronicle', p. 180.

30 Biemann, 'Counter-Geographies in the Sahara', p. 166.

31 *Ibid.*, pp. 168–9.

32 'Sahara Chronicle: A Collection of Videos on Mobility and the Politics of Containment in the Sahara' (DVD 78 min., www.geobodies.org, 2009), 17:09–17:17 min.

33 Biemann, 'Counter-Geographies in the Sahara', p. 169.

34 Demos, 'Sahara Chronicle', p. 187.

35 Jill Bennett, *Empathic Vision: Affect, Trauma and Contemporary Art* (Stanford: Stanford University Press, 2005), p. 111.

36 *Ibid.*, p. 64.
37 *Ibid.*, p. 7.
38 *Ibid.*, p. 111.
39 *Ibid.*, p. 10.
40 Marsha Meskimmon, 'The precarious ecologies of cosmopolitanism', *Humanities Research*, special issue 'The World and World-Making in Art', 19:2 (2013), 27–46, 37; Meskimmon, 'Making worlds, making subjects', 193.
41 Staiger, 'Visualizing the Citizen Gap', p. 154.
42 Katja Franko Aas, *Globalization and Crime: Key Approaches to Criminology* (London: Sage, 2007), p. 32.
43 UNHCR statistics of Syrian Asylum Applications in EU Countries (including Switzerland and Norway) on 1 October 2015, http://data.unhcr.org/syrianrefugees/asylum.php (accessed October 2015).
44 Aas, '"Crimmigrant" bodies and bona fide travelers', 332.
45 Aas, *Globalization and Crime*, pp. 77, 112.
46 David Frankel (ed.), *Isaac Julien: Riot* (New York: Museum of Modern Art, 2013), p. 234.
47 Aas, *Globalization and Crime*, pp. 32, 185. For historical reasons, I have chosen to refer in this chapter primarily to figures, debates and media coverage from the years leading up to the presentation of *Western Union: Small Boats* in 2007, but also to add numbers from the latest statistics to stress the continued urgency around forced displacement.
48 Jennifer A. González, 'Sea Dreams: Isaac Julien's *Western Union: Small Boats*', in Mathur (ed.), *The Migrant's Time*, pp. 115–29, p. 115.
49 Ranjana Khanna, 'Isaac Julien, or the Southern Question in Art History', in Casid and D'Souza (eds), *Art History in the Wake of the Global Turn*, pp. 176–96, p. 179.
50 UNHCR, 'Worldwide Displacement'.
51 UNHCR, 'Global Trends: Forced Displacement in 2015', 7.
52 Nauja Kleist and Ninna Nyberg Sørensen, 'Drukneulykker på Middelhavet. EU's løsning på Europas flygtningekrise er utilstrækkelig', in *DIIS Impact April 2015* (DIIS Danish Institute for International Studies, 12 April 2015), unpaginated, http://pure.diis.dk/ws/files/118718/diis_impact_drukneulykker_paa_middelhavet_WEB.pdf (accessed November 2016).
53 Aas, *Globalization and Crime*, p. 185.
54 Arendt, *The Origins of Totalitarianism*, p. 298.
55 Aas, *Globalization and Crime*, pp. 198–9.
56 Kobena Mercer, 'Avid Iconographies', in Kobena Mercer, Chris Darke and Isaac Julien (eds), *Isaac Julien: With Essays by Kobena Mercer and Chris Darke* (London: Ellipsis, 2001), pp. 7–21, p. 11.
57 *Ibid.*, p. 8. Emphasis added.
58 For a reading of *Ten Thousand Waves* as a meditation on refugeedom, see Tello, *Counter-Memorial Aesthetics*, pp. 162–70.
59 Isaac Julien (with Barbara Rose), 'Planet', in Frankel (ed.), *Isaac Julien: Riot*, pp. 164–76, p. 175.

60 The following analysis is based on the installation of the work at the exhibition *Border Crossing*, Kunsthallen Brandts, Odense, 2012.
61 González, 'Sea Dreams', p. 117.
62 Mieke Bal, 'Double Movement', in Mieke Bal and Miguel Hernández-Navarro (eds), *2 Move: Video Art Migration* (Murcia: Cendeac, 2008), pp. 13–80, p. 19.
63 *Ibid.*, p. 36.
64 Bal, 'Heterochrony in the Act', p. 229.
65 'Double Movement' (2008), p. 16.
66 Bennett, 'Migratory Aesthetics', p. 120.
67 Bal, 'Double Movement' (2008), p. 35.
68 González, 'Sea Dreams', pp. 115–17.
69 *Ibid.*, p. 119.
70 *Ibid.*
71 Yosefa Loshitzky, *Screening Strangers: Migration and Diaspora in Contemporary European Cinema* (Bloomington, Ind.: Indiana University Press, 2010), p. 37.
72 My analysis of the dialectic of gazes is indebted to Yosefa Loshitzky's illuminating analysis of Michael Winterbottom's *In This World*, *ibid.*, pp. 27–30.
73 *Ibid.*, p. 29.
74 Rushdie, 'Imaginary Homelands', p. 19.
75 Bal, 'Double Movement' (2008), p. 35.
76 Bal's analysis of Mona Hatoum's video work *Measures of Distance* (1988) actually leaves it open to interpretation whether the term refers to the work's representation of an experience or the experience that the video engenders in viewers. It may even refer to both, thus obliterating the distinction between representation and reception. 'Heterochrony in the Act', p. 217.
77 On Julien's use of digital video in combination with film equipment, see Martina Kudláček, 'Interview with Isaac Julien by Martina Kudláček', in Julien (ed.), *Isaac Julien – Western Union: Small Boats*, pp. 100–5, p. 105.
78 Bal, 'Heterochrony in the Act', p. 224.
79 Bal, 'Double Movement' (2008), p. 48.
80 González, 'Sea Dreams', p. 121.
81 *Ibid.*, p. 122.
82 *Ibid.*, p. 123.
83 Feature in *El Pais* (6 May 2006), 6. See Julien (ed.), *Isaac Julien – Western Union: Small Boats*, p. 76.
84 Iain Chambers and Lidia Curti, 'Migrating modernities in the Mediterranean', *Postcolonial Studies*, 11:4 (2008), 387–99, 387, 392.
85 *Ibid.*, 390.
86 Iain Chambers, *Mediterranean Crossings: The Politics of an Interrupted Modernity* (Durham, NC, London: Duke University Press, 2008), pp. 4–5; Katja Franko Aas and Helene O.I. Gundhus, 'Policing humanitarian borderlands: Frontex, human rights and the precariousness of life', *British Journal of Criminology*, 55:1 (2015), 1–18, 1–2.

87 Press release by the European Commission, 13 February 2008, quoted in Aas, 'A Borderless World?', p. 145. See also Aas and Gundhus, 'Policing humanitarian borderlands', 10–11.
88 See: http://frontex.europa.eu/intelligence/eurosur/ (accessed October 2015).
89 Roger Bromley, 'Displacement, Asylum and Narratives of Nation: Giving Voice to Refugees in the Film *La Forteresse*', in Moslund, Petersen and Schramm (eds), *The Culture of Migration: Politics, Aesthetics and Histories*, pp. 41–58, p. 43.
90 Aas and Gundhus, 'Policing humanitarian borderlands', 1–2.
91 Chambers, *Mediterranean Crossings*, p. 9.
92 Kudláček, 'Interview with Isaac Julien by Martina Kudláček', p. 102.
93 Loshitzky, *Screening Strangers*, p. 3.
94 González, 'Sea Dreams', p. 116.
95 Didier Fassin, 'Compassion and repression: the moral econnomy of immigration policies in France', *Cultural Anthropology*, 20:3 (2005), 362–87, 369.
96 *Ibid.*, 368.
97 *Ibid.*, 370, 381–2.
98 Aas and Gundhus, 'Policing humanitarian borderlands', 13.
99 For an example of how television coverage showing suffering 'illegal migrants' can stir public compassion and provoke political reactions from human rights associations and the public, see Fassin, 'Compassion and repression', 373.
100 Lotte Thorsen, 'Flygtningekrise ændrer danske ords betydning', *Politiken* (21 September 2015).
101 Ninna Nyberg Sørensen, 'Begrebsforvirring i migrationsdebatten. DIIS Comment' (2015), unpaginated, www.diis.dk/en/node/4699 (accessed November 2016).
102 Fassin, 'Compassion and repression', 372.
103 *Ibid.*, 380–1.
104 González defends Julien's approach, firstly by referring to the artistic and cinematic tradition of depicting human suffering; secondly, by stressing that Julien's work distances itself from today's media culture where 'all kinds of violence appear aestheticised and normalised'; and thirdly, by claiming that the work's real significance does not reside in its depiction of the migrant as a victim of historical, structural and bodily violence, but in the lyric filming which enables Julien to address the politics of migration from the psychological state of the migrant. González, 'Sea Dreams', p. 127.
105 Jacques Rancière, *Dissensus: On Politics and Aesthetics* (London, New York: Continuum, 2010), pp. 188–91.
106 *Ibid.*, pp. 193, 200–1.
107 Demos, *The Migrant Image*, p. 92.
108 Julien, 'Planet', p. 176.

Conclusion

As Isaac Julien has noted, 'there is freedom in choosing to shift one's gaze'.[1] His remark on the liberating effect of shifting one's gaze or perspective captures an essential quality of art, especially critical art: it inspires us to see, experience and conceive the world differently, and this might, potentially, contribute to political change in the world. Art's ability to spur new perspectives springs from what Marsha Meskimmon has described as 'the power to articulate against the grain, materialise ideas as yet unthought'.[2] The best works of art articulate ideas in an open and suggestive way that invites multiple interpretations, and, unlike theory, they do not unpack an issue through rigorous arguments but 'operate most powerfully in the registers of affect, imagination and resonance'.[3] This brings me back to Julien's remark on freedom and the way he elaborates on it by giving an account of his ongoing engagement with theory as a source of insight and empowerment: 'When I was reading psychoanalysis or film theory, or reading around postcolonial thought, that experience was personally empowering. Sometimes you really need to make sense out of the world, of how you are treated in it and how you are viewed by it. But maybe you're unable to articulate all those things you want to say. For me, people involved in theory have helped.'[4]

People involved in theory – understood in the broad sense of developing an understanding of the general principles, workings or conceptual basis of something – also need such eye-opening and empowering resources to help them make sense of the world. So do people involved in history. I hope this study has convincingly demonstrated that contemporary art is one of those resources, and an important and profound one, which is why I began this book by invoking Marsha Meskimmon's idea of writing *with* art instead of about art. I have sought to develop an understanding of the problematics and transformative workings of migration and globalisation through contemporary art. This has required a two-tier argumentation, with one level addressing the question of what the work (or the artist) can tell us about the historical, social and cultural effects of migration and globalisation, and the other seeking to explain how the work (or the artist) engages with these effects in an aesthetic, visual and conceptual register.

The Introduction presented the three interwoven concerns pursued throughout this book: visibility and recognition, identity and belonging, and aesthetics and politics. Chapter 1 outlined how intensified globalisation and mobility have profoundly changed the discourses on art. I argued that the discourse on art and globalisation has primarily revolved around issues concerning globalisation-from-above, whereas the discourse on art and migration has mainly addressed problematics related to globalisation-from-below, whose prime actors are the many different types of migrants. Taken together, these two interrelated discourses have made non-Western contemporary art an integral and thus visible and officially recognised part of the international discourses on global contemporary art. Chapter 2 developed this line of enquiry further by tracing how, in tandem with globalisation, the critical debates on identity politics and multiculturalism in the Western art world gradually paved the way, in the 1990s and 2000s, for greater institutional recognition and visibility of artists with a migrant or minority background. This was, in part, due to the critiques that were voiced, especially by contributors to *Third Text* and the British debate on New Internationalism in the 1990s, and which were backed by actual changes in exhibition-making and a growing recognition of artists with a migrant or minority background.

Using Indian contemporary artists as a test case, Chapter 3 explored another side of the increasing visibility of non-Western artists on the world's art scenes: the transnational career patterns and practices that many artists have had to develop in response to globalisation, and which have, in effect, transformed them into often highly respected and institutionally celebrated migrant workers. The proposed notion of the artist as a migrant worker delinks art from the conventional national frame for understanding the cultural 'location' of the artist and departs from the idea of the artist as an autonomous individual empowered by a free will. It turns away from an understanding of the artist as an independent, relatively solitary and sedentary figure, to an understanding of the artist as a networked and migratory one who adapts pragmatically to the predicaments and opportunities of a globalised art world and tactically navigates its transnational institutional and economic power structures.

As Chapter 4 demonstrated, artists' interventions can be used as a critical tactic to navigate institutional structures. It can be powerfully transformative, too, as it can help us envision what a more inclusive museum for the age of migration could be like. Postcolonial perspectives and critiques have played a vital role in the transformation of institutional practices and contributed to generating a desire to change within the institutions themselves; the increasing number of artists' interventions carried out in collaboration with institutions in a spirit of dialogism is also a token of this. As postcolonial scholars Alessandra De Angelis, Celeste Ianniciello, Mariangela Orabona and Michaela Quadraro underscore in their introduction to the anthology *The Postcolonial Museum: The Arts of Memory and the Pressures of History*, it is in the museums' own interests to change:

> How do museums 'de-colonise' themselves, not so much to ingenuously get rid of the burden of the past and the stereotypes of 'First-Worldism', but rather to undo and radically interrogate the more subtle and widespread mono-cultural perspectives of culture and the encompassing *épistémè* which imbues their language, self-perception and discourses? How will European museums succeed in 'marginalising' themselves, not merely to offer space to the 'periphery', or to tacitly 'host' and acculturate the others that come from the 'margins', but rather to recover creativity and new energy? [5]

It is with a view to these present changes, and the changes yet to come, that I express a certain optimism of my own about the development of a multifaceted understanding and recognition of art emerging from migrancy and the numerous and highly diverse art scenes outside the major metropolitan centres of the West. This optimism is expressed with the reservation that the critical and highly politicised discourses on identity and recognition have also had questionable effects. In my opinion, they have actually perpetuated and strengthened binary ways of thinking, leaving the discourse on identity and recognition in relation to contemporary art full of the kind of dichotomies and segregations that the protagonists of these discourses originally set out to deconstruct. This is the reason why Chapter 5 sought to move away from conventional identity politics, or what Amelia Jones has termed 'coalitional identity politics', by turning to Jones's theory of identity as identification and by taking an intersectional approach to works of art concerned with transnational and migrant identity formation and belonging. Analysing 'archival' works by Bharti Kher, Yinka Shonibare and Danh Vo, I substantiated the claim that their critical examinations of history function as imaginative rediscoveries of the past which lead to important reconfigurations of the dominant models of identity. These reconfigurations emphasise that identity is not 'given' but is actively constructed and continually re-constructed through shifting, intersecting and imaginative identifications.

While I am fairly optimistic about the prospect of expanding recognition geographically and culturally in the art world, the global increase in forced migration does give reason for serious concern about the growing stigmatisation of irregular migrants and refugees as 'crimmigrant' others (Aas), and about the ways in which the securitisation and fortification of borders increase the citizenship gap and jeopardise migrants' lives by forcing them to undertake perilous journeys. Such concerns gave impetus to Chapter 6, which examined the nexus of forced migration, border control, securitisation and humanitarianism through the lens of some contemporary works of art that address the problematics of clandestine migration from Africa across the Mediterranean Sea to Europe. The chapter also extended the discussion of the invariably politicised, artistic representation of unwanted immigrants to the overall issue of the relations between aesthetics and politics. It addressed the question of how the aesthetic and affective qualities and the visual 'organisational power' (Demos) of artworks can encourage, in responsive viewers, the kind of empathic perception that can trigger the 'empathic unsettlement' (Bennett) needed to stimulate reflection on these difficult political and humanitarian issues. These issues will undoubtedly continue to preoccupy the minds of Europeans as well as people in the Middle East, Africa and beyond for many years to come. Engaging with them will yet again transform the ways in which new, and older, Europeans perceive and relate to immigrants, as well as the way Europeans understand themselves, as a foreseeable effect of the always profoundly unsettling and transformative impact of migration on culture and society.

Notes

1 Julien, 'Planet', p. 176. Julien paraphrases an observation made by Jacques Rancières in *The Night of Labor: The Workers' Dream in Nineteenth-Century France* (Philadelphia: Temple University Press, 1989).
2 Meskimmon, *Contemporary Art and the Cosmopolitan Imagination*, p. 92.
3 *Ibid.*, p. 92.
4 Julien, 'Planet', p. 176.
5 De Angelis *et al.*, 'Introduction: Disruptive Encounters – Museums, Art and Postcoloniality', p. 11.

Select bibliography

Aas, Katja Franko, *Globalization and Crime: Key Approaches to Criminology* (London: Sage, 2007).

——, 'A Borderless World? Cosmopolitanism, Boundaries and Frontiers', in Cecilia Baillet and Katja Franko Aas (eds), *Cosmopolitan Justice and its Discontents* (London, New York: Routledge, 2011), pp. 134–50.

——, '"Crimmigrant" bodies and bona fide travelers: surveillance, citizenship and global governance', *Theoretical Criminology*, 15:3 (2011), 331–46.

Aas, Katja Franko, and Helene O. I. Gundhus, 'Policing humanitarian borderlands: Frontex, human rights and the precariousness of life', *British Journal of Criminology*, 55:1 (2015), 1–18.

Agamben, Giorgio, *Homo Sacer: Sovereign Power and Bare Life* (Stanford: Stanford University Press, 1998).

Ahmed, Sara, Claudia Castañeda, Anne-Marie Fortier and Mimi Sheller, 'Introduction: Uprootings/Regroundings: Questions of Home and Migration', in Sara Ahmed, Claudia Castañeda, Anne-Marie Fortier and Mimi Sheller (eds), *Uprootings/Regroundings: Questions of Home and Migration* (Oxford, New York: Berg, 2003), pp. 1–22.

Ang, Ien, *On Not Speaking Chinese: Living between Asia and the West* (London, New York: Routledge, 2001).

——, 'Unsettling the National: Heritage and Diaspora', in Helmut Anheier and Yudhishthir Raj Isar (eds), *Heritage, Memory and Identity* (London, Thousand Oaks, Calif., Singapore: Sage, 2011), pp. 82–94.

Appadurai, Arjun, *Modernity at Large: Cultural Dimensions of Globalisation* (Minneapolis, London: University of Minnesota Press, 2000).

——, 'How histories make geographies: circulation and context in a global perspective', *Transcultural Studies*, 1:1 (2010), 4–13, https://journals.ub.uni-heidelberg.de/index.php/transcultural/article/view/6129/1760 (accessed 16 November 2016).

Araeen, Rasheed, Why Third Text?', *Third Text*, 1:1 (1987), 3–5.

——, 'Our Bauhaus others' mudhouse', *Third Text*, 3:6 (1989), 3–16.

——, 'The other immigrant: the experience and achievements of Afroasian artists in the metropolis', *Third Text*, 5:15 (1991), 17–28.

——, 'A new beginning: beyond postcolonial cultural theory and identity politics', *Third Text*, 14:50 (2000), 3–20.

——, 'Re-thinking history and some other things', *Third Text,* 15:54 (2001), 93–100.
Araeen, Rasheed, Sean Cubitt and Ziauddin Sardar (eds), *The Third Text Reader on Art, Culture and Theory* (London, New York: Continuum, 2005 (2002)).
Arendt, Hannah, *The Origins of Totalitarianism* (San Diego: Harcourt, 1976).
Badiou, Alain, *Ethics: An Essay on the Understanding of Evil* (London, New York: Verso, 2001).
Bal, Mieke, 'Double Movement', in Mieke Bal and Miguel Hernández-Navarro (eds), *2 Move: Double Movement, Migratory Aesthetics* (Murcia: Bancaja, Enkhuizen: Zuiderzeemuseum, 2007), CD-ROM, unpaginated.
——, 'Lost in Space, Lost in the Library', in Sam Durrant and Catherine M. Lord (eds), *Essays in Migratory Aesthetics: Cultural Practices between Migration and Art-making* (Amsterdam, New York: Rodopi, 2007), pp. 23–36.
——, 'Double Movement', in Mieke Bal and Miguel Hernández-Navarro (eds), *2 Move: Video Art Migration* (Murcia: Cendeac, 2008), pp. 13–80.
——, 'Heterochrony in the Act: The Migratory Politics of Time', in Mieke Bal and Miguel Hernández-Navarro (eds), *Art and Visibility in Migratory Culture: Conflict, Resistance and Agency* (Amsterdam: Rodopi, 2012), pp. 211–38.
Bal, Mieke, and Miguel Hernández-Navarro (eds), *2 Move: Double Movement, Migratory Aesthetics* (Murcia: Bancaja, Eikhuizen: Zuiderzeemuseum, 2007).
—— (eds), *Art and Visibility in Migratory Culture: Conflict, Resistance and Agency* (Amsterdam: Rodopi, 2012).
Barron, Stephanie and Sabine Eckmann (eds), *Exiles + Emigrés: The Flight of European Artists from Hitler* (Los Angeles: Los Angeles County Museum of Art; Montreal: Montreal Museum of Fine Arts; Berlin: Neue Nationalgalerie, 1997).
Belting, Hans, 'Contemporary Art and the Museum in the Global Age', in Peter Weibel and Andrea Buddensieg (eds), *Contemporary Art and the Museum: A Global Perspective* (Ostfildern: Hatje Cantz Verlag in association with ZKM, Karlsruhe, 2007), pp. 16–38.
——, 'The Art Market: Hans Belting in Conversation with Clare McAndrew', in Hans Belting, Andrea Buddensieg and Peter Weibel (eds), *The Global Contemporary and the Rise of New Art Worlds* (Karlsruhe: ZKM Center for Art and Media Karlsruhe, 2013), pp. 261–5.
——, 'From World Art to Global Art: View on a New Panorama', in Hans Belting, Andrea Buddensieg and Peter Weibel (eds), *The Global Contemporary and the Rise of New Art Worlds* (Karlsruhe: ZKM Center for Art and Media Karlsruhe, 2013), pp. 178–85.
Belting, Hans, and Andrea Buddensieg, 'From Art World to Art Worlds', in Hans Belting, Andrea Buddensieg and Peter Weibel (eds), *The Global Contemporary and the Rise of New Art Worlds* (Karlsruhe: ZKM Center for Art and Media Karlsruhe, 2013), pp. 28–31.
—— (eds), *The Global Artworld: Audiences, Markets and Museums* (Ostfildern: Hatje Cantz Verlag, 2009).
Belting, Hans, Jacob Birken, Andrea Buddensieg and Peter Weibel (eds), *Global Studies: Mapping Contemporary Art and Culture* (Ostfildern: Hatje Cantz Verlag, 2011).

Belting, Hans, Andrea Buddensieg and Peter Weibel (eds), *The Global Contemporary and the Rise of New Art Worlds* (Karlsruhe: ZKM Center for Art and Media Karlsruhe, 2013).

Benjamin, Walter, 'The author as producer', *New Left Review*, 162 (1970), 83–96.

Bennett, Jill, *Empathic Vision: Affect, Trauma and Contemporary Art* (Stanford: Stanford University Press, 2005).

———, 'Migratory Aesthetics: Art and Politics Beyond Identity', in Mieke Bal and Miguel Hernández-Navarro (eds), *Art and Visibility in Migratory Culture: Conflict, Resistance and Agency* (Amsterdam: Rodopi, 2012), pp. 109–26.

Beshty, Walead, 'Introduction: Toward an Aesthetic of Ethics', in Walead Beshty (ed.), *Ethics* (London, New York: Whitechapel Gallery and The MIT Press, 2015), pp. 12–23.

Bhabha, Homi K., *The Location of Culture* (London, New York: Routledge, 1994).

Bishop, Claire, 'History depletes itself', *artforum.com*, September (2015), unpaginated, https://artforum.com/inprint/issue=201507&id=54492.

Boehmer, Elleke, 'A Postcolonial Aesthetic: Repeating Upon the Present', in Janet Wilson, Christina Sandru and Sarah Lawson Welsh (eds), *Rerouting the Postcolonial* (London, New York: Routledge, 2010), pp. 170–81.

Borggreen, Gunhild, 'Asian art on display: questions of representation in the ethnographic turn', *Kontur*, no. 20 (2010), 2–7.

Bourriaud, Nicolas, 'Altermodern', in Nicolas Bourriaud (ed.), *Altermodern: Tate Triennial* (London: Tate Publishing, 2009), pp. 11–24.

———, *The Radicant* (New York: Lukas & Sternberg, 2009).

Brah, Avtar, *Cartographies of Diaspora: Contesting Identities* (London, New York: Routledge, 1996).

Brickell, Katherine, and Ayona Datta, 'Introduction: Translocal Geographies', in Katherine Brickell and Ayona Datta (eds), *Translocal Geographies: Spaces, Places, Connections* (Farnham: Ashgate, 2011), pp. 3–20.

Butler, Judith, *Gender Trouble: Feminism and the Subversion of Identity* (New York, London: Routledge, 1991).

Bydler, Charlotte, *The Global Art World, Inc.: On the Globalisation of Contemporary Art* (Uppsala: Acta Universitatis Upsaliensis, 2004).

Carroll, Noël, 'Art and globalization: then and now', *Journal of Aesthetics & Art Criticism*, 65:1 (2007), 131–43.

Casey, Edward, 'A Matter of Edge: Border vs. Boundary at *La Frontera*', in Sten Pultz Moslund, Anne Ring Petersen and Moritz Schramm (eds), *The Culture of Migration: Politics, Aesthetics and Histories* (London, New York: I.B. Tauris, 2015), pp. 27–39.

Casid, Jill H., and Aruna D'Souza (eds), *Art History in the Wake of the Global Turn* (Williamstown, Mass.: Sterling and Francine Clark Art Institute, 2014).

Castles, Stephen, and Mark Miller, *The Age of Migration: International Population Movements in the Modern World*. 4th Edition (Basingstoke: Palgrave Macmillan, 2009).

Chambers, Iain, *Mediterranean Crossings: The Politics of an Interrupted Modernity* (Durham, N.C., London: Duke University Press, 2008).

——, 'Adrift and Exposed', in Isaac Julien (ed.), *Isaac Julien – Western Union: Small Boats* (Warszawa: Centre for Contemporary Art Ujazdowski Castle, 2009), pp. 8–13.
——, 'Adrift and Exposed', in Lene Burkard (ed.), *Border Crossing* (Odense: Kunsthallen Brandts, 2012), pp. 72–7.
Chambers, Iain, and Lidia Curti, 'Migrating modernities in the Mediterranean', *Postcolonial Studies*, 11:4 (2008), 387–99.
Chen, Nancy N., '"Speaking Nearby": a conversation with Trinh T. Minh-Ha', *Visual Anthropology Review*, 8:1 (1992), 82–91.
Chui, Melissa, and Benjamin Genocchio, 'What Is Asian Contemporary Art? Mapping an Evolving Discourse', in Melissa Chiu and Benjamin Genocchio (eds), *Contemporary Art in Asia: A Critical Reader* (Cambridge, Mass., London: The MIT Press, 2011), pp. 1–14.
Clark, Kenneth, *Landscape into Art* (London: John Murray, 1976).
Cubitt, Sean, 'Citizens, Consumers and Migrants', in Scott McQuire and Nikos Papastergiadis (eds), *Empires, Ruins + Networks: The Transcultural Agenda in Art* (London, Chicago: Rivers Oram Press, 2005), pp. 304–17.
——, 'In the Beginning: Third Text and the Politics of Art', in Rasheed Araeen, Sean Cubitt and Ziauddin Sardar (eds), *The Third Text Reader on Art, Culture and Theory* (London, New York: Continuum, 2005 (2002)), pp. 1–7.
Damme, Wilfried van, 'Introducing World Art Studies', in Kitty Zijlmans and Wilfried van Damme (eds), *World Art Studies: Exploring Concepts and Approaches* (Amsterdam: Valiz, 2008), pp. 23–61.
De Angelis, Alessandra, Celeste Ianniciello, Mariangela Orabona and Michaela Quadraro, 'Introduction: Disruptive Encounters – Museums, Art and Postcoloniality', in Iain Chambers *et al.* (eds), *The Postcolonial Museum: The Arts of Memory and the Pressures of History*(Farnham: Ashgate, 2014), pp. 1–21.
Demos, T. J., 'Desire in diaspora: Emily Jacir', *Art Journal*, 62:4 (2003), 68–78.
——, 'On the Diasporic Public Sphere', in Hans-Jörg Heussert and Kornelia Imesch (eds), *Visions of a Future: Art and Art History in Changing Contexts* (Zürich: Swiss Institute for Art Research, 2004), pp. 103–16.
——, *The Exiles of Marcel Duchamp* (Cambridge, Mass., London: The MIT Press, 2007).
——, 'Sahara Chronicle: Video's Migrant Geography', in Ursula Biemann and Jan-Erik Lundström (eds), *Ursula Biemann. Mission Reports: Artistic Practice in the Field. Video Works 1998–2008* (Umeå: Bildmuseet, Bristol: Arnolfini, 2008), pp. 178–90.
——, 'The Ends of Exile: Towards a Coming Universality?', in Nicolas Bourriaud (ed.), *Altermodern: Tate Triennial* (London: Tate Publishing, 2009), pp. 73–88.
——, *The Migrant Image: The Art and Politics of Documentary during Global Crisis* (Durham, N.C., London: Duke University Press, 2013).
Dogramaci, Burcu, *Migration und künstlerische Produktion. Aktuelle Perspektiven* (Bielefeld: transcript, 2013).
Drucker, Johanna, 'After after', *The White Review*, no. 12 (2014), unpaginated, www.thewhitereview.org/art/after-after-2/.

Durrant, Sam, and Catherine M. Lord, 'Introduction: Essays in Migratory Aesthetics', in Sam Durrant and Catherine M. Lord (eds), *Essays in Migratory Aesthetics: Cultural Practices between Migration and Art-making* (Amsterdam, New York: Rodopi, 2007), pp. 11–19.

—— (eds), *Essays in Migratory Aesthetics: Cultural Practices between Migration and Art-making* (Amsterdam, New York: Rodopi, 2007).

Edelman, Murray, *From Art to Politics: How Artistic Creations Shape Political Conceptions* (Chicago, London: The University of Chicago Press, 1995).

Elkins, James, 'Art History as a Global Discipline', in James Elkins (ed.), *Is Art History Global?* (New York, London: Routledge, 2007), pp. 3–23.

——, 'Can We Invent a World Art Studies?', in Kitty Zijlmans and Wilfried van Damme (eds), *World Art Studies: Exploring Concepts and Approaches* (Amsterdam: Valiz, 2008), pp. 107–18.

—— (ed.), *Is Art History Global?* (New York, London: Routledge, 2007).

Enwezor, Okwui, 'Modernity and Postcolonial Ambivalence', in Nicolas Bourriaud (ed.), *Altermodern: Tate Triennial* (London: Tate Publishing, 2009), pp. 27–40.

Fassin, Didier, 'Compassion and repression: the moral economy of immigration policies in France', *Cultural Anthropology*, 20:3 (2005), 362–87.

Fassin, Didier, and Richard Rechtman, *The Empire of Trauma: An Inquiry into the Condition of Victimhood* (Princeton, Oxford: Princeton University Press, 2009).

Fisher, Jean, 'Editor's Note', in Jean Fisher (ed.), *Global Visions: Towards a New Internationalism in the Visual Arts* (London: Kala Press and The Institute of International Visual Arts, 1994), pp. x–xiv.

Foster, Hal, *The Return of the Real: The Avant-Garde at the End of the Century* (Cambridge, Mass., London: The MIT Press, 1996).

Frankel, David (ed.), *Isaac Julien: Riot* (New York: Museum of Modern Art, 2013).

Gether, Christian *et al.* (eds), *India: Art Now* (Ostfildern: Arken Museum of Modern Art and Hatje Cantz, 2012).

Gilroy, Paul, *The Black Atlantic: Modernity and Double-Consciousness* (Cambridge, Mass.: Harvard University Press, 1993).

González, Jennifer A., *Subject to Display: Reframing Race in Contemporary Installation Art* (Cambridge, Mass.: The MIT Press, 2008).

Hall, Stuart, 'Introduction: Who Needs "Identity"?', in Stuart Hall and Paul du Gay (eds), *Questions of Cultural Identity* (London, Thousand Oaks, Calif., New Delhi: Sage Publications, 1996), pp. 1–17.

——, 'Conclusion: The Multi-Cultural Question', in Barnor Hesse (ed.), *Un/Settled Multiculturalisms: Diaspora, Entanglements, 'Transruptions'* (London, New York: Zed Books, 2000), pp. 209–41.

——, 'Cultural Identity and Diaspora', in Nicholas Mirzoeff (ed.), *Diaspora and Visual Culture* (London, New York: Routledge, 2000), pp. 21–33.

——, 'Creolization, Diaspora, and Hybridity in the Context of Globalisation', in Okwui Enwezor (ed.), *Créolité and Creolization* (Ostfildern-Ruit: Hatje Cantz, 2003), pp. 185–98.

Harris, Jonathan, 'Introduction. Globalization and Contemporary Art: A Convergence of Peoples and Ideas', in Jonathan Harris (ed.), *Globalization and Contemporary Art* (Chichester: Wiley-Blackwell, 2011), pp. 1–15.

Hedetoft, Ulf, and Mette Hjort, 'Introduction', in Ulf Hedetoft and Mette Hjort (eds), *The Postnational Self: Belonging and Identity* (Minneapolis, London: University of Minnesota Press, 2002), pp. vii–xxxii.

Honneth, Axel, *The Struggle for Recognition: The Moral Grammar of Social Conflicts* (Cambridge: Polity Press, 1995).

Huggan, Graham, 'Unsettled Settlers: Postcolonialism, Travelling Theory and the New Migrant Aesthetics', in Sam Durrant and Catherine M. Lord (eds), *Essays in Migratory Aesthetics: Cultural Practices between Migration and Art-making* (Amsterdam, New York: Rodopi, 2007), pp. 129–44.

Irigaray, Luce, *This Sex Which Is Not One* (Ithaca, N.Y.: Cornell University Press, 1977).

Jones, Amelia, *Seeing Differently: A History and Theory of Identification and the Visual Arts* (Abingdon, New York: Routledge, 2012).

Jones, Caroline A., 'Is International Modernism National? Is Global Postmodernism Local? Questions for Art History', in Hans-Jörg Heussert and Kornelia Imesch (eds), *Visions of a Future: Art and Art History in Changing Contexts* (Zürich: Swiss Institute for Art Research, 2004), pp. 117–28.

Julien, Isaac (with Barbara Rose), 'Planet', in David Frankel (ed.), *Isaac Julien: Riot* (New York: Museum of Modern Art, 2013), pp. 164–76.

——— (ed.), *Isaac Julien – Western Union: Small Boats* (Warszawa: Centre for Contemporary Art Ujazdowski Castle, 2009).

Juneja, Monica, and Michael Falser, 'Kulturerbe – Denkmalpflege: transkulturell. Eine Einleitung', in Monica Juneja and Michael Falser (eds), *Kulturerbe und Denkmalpflege transkulturell. Grenzgänge zwischen Theorie und Praxis* (Bielefeld: transcript, 2013), pp. 17–34.

Koser, Khalid, *International Migration: A Very Short Introduction* (Oxford, New York: Oxford University Press, 2007).

Lacan, Jacques, 'The Line and the Light',*The Four Fundamental Concepts of Psychoanalysis* (New York, London: W.W. Norton & Company, 1981), pp. 91–104.

Leclercq, Anne (ed.), *Rina Banerjee: Guimet vis à vis* (Paris: Musée Guimet, 2011).

Lee, Benjamin, 'The Subjects of Circulation', in Ulf Hedetoft and Mette Hjort (eds), *The Postnational Self: Belonging and Identity* (Minneapolis, London: University of Minnesota Press, 2002), pp. 233–49.

Lee, Pamela M., *Forgetting the Art World* (Cambridge, Mass., London: The MIT Press, 2012).

Lister, Ruth, *Citizenship: Feminist Perspectives.* Second Edition (New York: Palgrave Macmillan, 2003).

Loshitzky, Yosefa, *Screening Strangers: Migration and Diaspora in Contemporary European Cinema* (Bloomington, Ind.: Indiana University Press, 2010).

Marchart, Oliver, 'The globalization of art and the "biennials of resistance": a history of the biennials from the periphery', *World Art*, 4:2 (2014), 263–76.

Marcus, George E., 'Ethnography in/of the world system: the emergence of multi-sited ethnography', *Annual Review of Anthropology*, 24 (1995), 95–117.

Mathur, Saloni, 'Museums and globalization', *Anthropological Quarterly*, 78:3 (2005), 697–708.

——, 'Introduction', in Saloni Mathur (ed.), *The Migrant's Time: Rethinking Art History and Diaspora* (Williamstown, Mass.: Sterling and Francine Clark Art Institute, 2011), pp. vii–xix.

—— (ed.), *The Migrant's Time: Rethinking Art History and Diaspora* (Williamstown, Mass.: Sterling and Francine Clark Art Institute, 2011).

The Matter Within: New Contemporary Art of India (San Francisco: Yerba Buena Center for the Arts, 2012).

Mercer, Kobena, *Welcome to the Jungle: New Positions in Black Cultural Studies* (London, New York: Routledge, 1994).

——, 'Avid Iconographies', in Kobena Mercer, Chris Darke and Isaac Julien (eds), *Isaac Julien: With Essays by Kobena Mercer and Chris Darke* (London: Ellipsis, 2001), pp. 7–21.

——, '"Diaspora Didn't Happen in a Day": Reflections on Aesthetics and Time', in R. Victoria Arana (ed.), *'Black' British Aesthetics Today* (Newcastle: Cambridge Scholars Publishing, 2007), pp. 66–78.

——, 'Introduction', in Kobena Mercer (ed.), *Exiles, Diasporas and Strangers*, Annotating Art's Histories (Cambridge, Mass., London: inIVA and The MIT Press, 2008), pp. 6–27.

——, 'Erase and Rewind: When Does Art History in the Black Diaspora Actually Begin?', in Saloni Mathur (ed.), *The Migrant's Time: Rethinking Art History and Diaspora* (Williamstown, Mass.: Sterling and Francine Clark Art Institute, 2011), pp. 17–31.

—— (ed.), *Cosmopolitan Modernisms*, Annotating Art's Histories (Cambridge, Mass., London: inIVA and The MIT Press, 2005).

—— (ed.), *Discrepant Abstraction*, Annotating Art's Histories (Cambridge, Mass., London: inIVA and The MIT Press, 2006).

—— (ed.), *Pop Art and Vernacular Cultures*, Annotating Art's Histories (Cambridge, Mass., London: inIVA and The MIT Press, 2007).

—— (ed.), *Exiles, Diasporas and Strangers*, Annotating Art's Histories (Cambridge, Mass., London: inIVA and The MIT Press, 2008).

Meskimmon, Marsha, *Contemporary Art and the Cosmopolitan Imagination* (London, New York: Routledge, 2011).

——, 'Making worlds, making subjects: contemporary art and the affective dimension of global ethics', *World Art*, 1:2 (2011), 189–96.

——, 'The precarious ecologies of cosmopolitanism', *Humanities Research*, special issue 'The World and World-Making in Art', 19:2 (2013), 27–46.

——, 'As a Woman, My Country Is … : On Imag(in)ed Communities and the Heresy of the Becoming-Denizen', in Marsha Meskimmon and Marion Arnold (eds), *Home/Land: Women, Citizenship, Photographies* (Liverpool: Liverpool University Press, 2016), pp. 253–68.

Meskimmon, Marsha, and Dorothy Rowe, 'Editorial Introduction: Ec/centric Affinities:

Locations, Aesthetics, Experiences', in Marsha Meskimmon and Dorothy Rowe (eds), *Women, the Arts and Globalization: Eccentric Experience* (Manchester, New York: Manchester University Press, 2013), pp. 1–14.
Mignolo, Walter, 'Delinking: the rhetoric of modernity, the logic of coloniality and the grammar of de-coloniality', *Cultural Studies*, 21:2–3 (2007), 449–514.
———, 'Introduction: coloniality of power and de-colonial thinking', *Cultural Studies*, 21:2–3 (2007), 155–67.
———, *The Darker Side of Western Modernity: Global Futures, Decolonial Options* (Durham, N.C., London: Duke University Press, 2011).
———, 'Museums in the Colonial Horizon of Modernity: Fred Wilson's *Mining the Museum* (1992)', in Jonathan Harris (ed.), *Globalization and Contemporary Art* (Chichester: Wiley-Blackwell, 2011), pp. 71–85.
Mignolo, Walter, and Madina V. Tlostanova, *Learning to Unlearn: Decolonial Reflections from Eurasia and the Americas* (Columbus, OH: The Ohio State University Press, 2012).
Mignolo, Walter *et al.*, 'Decolonial Aesthetics (I)', *TDI/Transnational Decolonial Institute* (2011), unpaginated, http://transnationaldecolonialinstitute.wordpress.com/decolonial-aesthetics/.
Mirzoeff, Nicholas (ed.), *Diaspora and Visual Culture: Representing Africans and Jews* (London, New York: Routledge, 2000).
Mishra, Sudesh, *Diaspora Criticsm* (Edinburgh: Edinburgh University Press, 2006).
Mitchell, W. J. T., 'Migrating Images: Totemism, Fetishism, Idolatry', in Petra Stegmann and Peter C. Seel (eds), *Migrating Images: Producing … Reading … Transporting … Translating* (Berlin: House of World Cultures, 2004), pp. 14–23.
———, *Seeing through Race* (Boston, Mass.: Harvard University Press, 2012).
Mitter, Partha, *The Triumph of Modernism: India's Artists and the Avant-Garde, 1922–47* (London: Reaction Books, 2007).
———, 'History, Memory, and Anish Kapoor', in Nicholas Baume (ed.), *Anish Kapoor: Past, Present, Future* (Cambridge, Mass.: The MIT Press, 2008), pp. 104–18.
Moslund, Sten Pultz, 'A Migrant Aesthetics through the Phenomenality of Place', in Sten Pultz Moslund, Anne Ring Petersen and Moritz Schramm (eds), *The Culture of Migration: Politics, Aesthetics and Histories* (London, New York: I.B. Tauris, 2015), pp. 223–39.
Moslund, Sten Pultz, Anne Ring Petersen and Moritz Schramm (eds), *The Culture of Migration: Politics, Aesthetics and Histories* (London, New York: I.B. Tauris, 2015).
Mosquera, Gerardo, and Jean Fisher (eds), *Over Here: International Perspectives on Art and Culture* (Cambridge, Mass.: The MIT Press, 2004).
Mouffe, Chantal, 'Artistic activism and agonistic spaces', *Art & Research: A Journal of Ideas, Contexts and Methods*, 1:2 (2007), 1–5.
Muñoz, José Esteban, *Disidentifications: Queers of Color and the Performance of Politics* (Minneapolis, London: University of Minnesota Press, 1999).
Papastergiadis, Nikos, 'The South in the North', *Third Text*, 5:14 (1991), 43–52.
———, 'From the Edges of Exile to the Limits of Translation', in Diana Nemiroff (ed.), *Crossings* (Ottawa: National Gallery of Canada, 1998).

——, *The Turbulence of Migration: Globalization, Deterritorialization and Hybridity* (Cambridge: Polity Press, 2000).

——, 'Hybridity and ambivalence: places and flows in contemporary art and culture', *Theory, Culture & Society*, 22:4 (2005), 39–64.

——, 'Restless Hybrids', in Rasheed Araeen, Sean Cubitt and Ziauddin Sardar (eds), *The Third Text Reader on Art, Culture and Theory* (London, New York: Continuum, 2005 (2002)), pp. 166–75.

——, *Spatial Aesthetics: Art, Place and the Everyday* (London, Sydney, Chicago: River Oram Press, 2006).

——, *Cosmopolitanism and Culture* (Cambridge, Malden: Polity Press, 2012).

Petersen, Anne Ring, 'Film som kunst: Yinka Shonibare MBE og *Black British film*', *Passepartout. Skrifter for kunsthistorie*,18:34 (2011), 66–86.

——, 'Identity politics, institutional multiculturalism, and the global artworld', *Third Text*, 26:2 (2012), 195–204.

——, 'The artist as migrant worker? Framing art in an age of intensified globalisation and migration', *Arken Bulletin*, special issue 'Migration – Contemporary Art from India', no. 6 (2013), 42–9.

——,'Mining the Museum in an Age of Migration' in Iain Chambers *et al.* (eds), *The Postcolonial Museum: The Arts of Memory and the Pressures of History* (Farnham: Ashgate, 2014), pp. 125–36.

——, 'American connections: the early works of Thomas Bang', *RIHA Journal*, article no. 0128 (2015), www.riha-journal.org/articles/2015/-jul-sep/ring-american-connections.

——, 'Global art history: a view from the North', *Journal of Aesthetics & Culture*, 7 (2015), www.aestheticsandculture.net/index.php/jac/article/view/28154.

——, 'Migratory Aesthetics and the Politics of Irregular Migration: A Case Study of Isaac Julien's *Western Union: Small Boats*', in Sten Pultz Moslund, Anne Ring Petersen and Moritz Schramm (eds), *The Culture of Migration: Politics, Aesthetics and Histories* (London, New York: I.B. Tauris, 2015), pp. 205–22.

——, 'Identity Politics in "the Global Art World"', in Peter Madsen (ed.), *Challenging Identities: Individual – Collective – Politics*. Routledge Advances in Sociology (New York, London: Routledge, 2017), pp. 222–38.

Philipsen, Lotte, 'The Globalisation of Contemporary Art: Interests, Articulations, and Impact of the Discourse of New Internationalism in the Visual Arts' (PhD dissertation, Aarhus University, 2008).

——, *Globalizing Contemporary Art: The Art World's New Internationalism* (Aarhus: Aarhus University Press, 2010).

Phoenix, Ann, 'Interrogating intersectionality: productive ways of theorising multiple positioning', *Kvinder, køn & forskning*, special issue on intersectionality, no. 2–3 (2006), 21–30.

Pieterse, Jan Nederveen, 'Globalisation as hybridisation', *International Sociology*, 9:2 (1994), 161–84.

——, 'Changing definitions', *Third Text*, 14:53 (2001), 91–2.

Pollock, Griselda, *Migratory Aesthetics* (Leeds: AHRC CentreCATH, University of Leeds, 2006).

Rancière, Jacques, *The Politics of Aesthetics: The Distribution of the Sensible* (London, New York: Continuum, 2004).
———, *Dissensus: On Politics and Aesthetics* (London, New York: Continuum, 2010).
Robins, Claire, *Curious Lessons in the Museum: The Pedagogic Potential of Artists' Interventions* (Farnham: Ashgate, 2013).
Robins, Claire, and Miranda Baxter, 'Meaningful Encounters with Disrupted Narratives: Artists' Interventions as Interpretive Strategies', in Suzanne MacLeod, Laura Hourston Hanks and Jonathan Hale (eds), *Museum Making: Narratives, Architectures, Exhibitions* (London, New York: Routledge, 2012), pp. 247–56.
Rogoff, Irit, 'Academy as Potentiality', in Angelika Nollert *et al.* (eds), *A.C.A.D.E.M.Y.* (Frankfurt am Main: Revolver, 2006), pp. 13–20.
Rushdie, Salman, 'Imaginary Homelands', in Salman Rushdie (ed.), *Imaginary Homelands: Essays and Criticism 1981–1991* (London: Granta Books, 1991).
Said, Edward, *Orientalism* (London: Routledge, 1978).
———, *Reflections on Exile and Other Literary and Cultural Essays* (London: Granta Books, 2001).
Salt, John, 'Current Trends in International Migration in Europe' (The Council of Europe, 2006), www.coe.int/t/dg3/migration/archives/documentation/Migration%20management/2005_Salt_report_en.pdf.
Schinkel, Willem, 'From zoēpolitics to biopolitics: citizenship and the construction of "society"', *European Journal of Social Theory*, 13:2 (2010), 155–72.
Sheller, Mimi, and John Urry, 'The new mobilities paradigm', *Environment and Planning A*, 38 (2006), 207–26.
Shilton, Siobhán, *Transcultural Encounters: Gender and Genre in Franco-Maghrebi Art* (Manchester, New York: Manchester University Press, 2013).
Smith, Terry, *Contemporary Art: World Currents* (London: Laurence King, 2011).
———, 'Rethinking modernism and modernity now', *Filozofski vestnik*, 35:2 (2014), 271–319.
Soussloff, Catherine, 'History of the Concept of the Artist', in Michael Kelly (ed.), *Encyclopedia of Aesthetics* (New York, Oxford: Oxford University Press, 1998), pp. 130–5.
Stavrakakis, Yannis, 'Challenges of re-politicisation: Mouffe's agonism and artistic practices', *Third Text*, 26:5 (2012), 551–65.
Tello, Veronica, *Counter-Memorial Aesthetics: Refugee Histories and the Politics of Contemporary Art* (London: Bloomsbury Academic, 2016).
Turner, Caroline, and Jen Webb, *Art and Human Rights: Contemporary Asian Contexts* (Manchester: Manchester University Press, 2016).
Ulmer, Brigitte, 'Late Arrival: An Exhibition Chronology of Contemporary Indian Art', in Kunstmuseum Bern (ed.), *Horn Please: Narratives in Contemporary Indian Art* (Ostfildern: Hatje Cantz Verlag, 2008), pp. 59–77.
UNHCR, 'Global Trends: Forced Displacement in 2015' (20 June 2016), www.unhcr.org/global-trends-2015.html.
UNHCR, 'Worldwide Displacement Hits All-Time High as War and Persecution Increase' (18 June 2015), unpaginated, www.unhcr.org/558193896.html.

Varadinis, Mirjam, 'Shattered freedom', *Parkett*, no. 90 (2012), 210–16.

Vertovec, Stephen, 'Circular migration: the way forward in global policy?', *International Migration Institute. Working Papers*, no. 4 (2007), 2–9.

Wainwright, Leon, *Timed Out: Art and the Transnational Caribbean* (Manchester, New York: Manchester University Press, 2011).

Weibel, Peter, 'Jenseits des weissen Würfels. Kunst zwischen Kolonialismus und Kosmopolitismus', in Peter Weibel (ed.), *Inklusion: Eksklusion. Versuch einer neuen Kartografie der Kunst im Zeitalter von Postkolonialismus und globaler Migration* (Köln: DuMont, 1997), pp. 8–36.

———, 'Preface', in Jens Lutz *et al.* (eds), *The Global Contemporary: Art Worlds after 1989*. Exhibition Brochure (Karlsruhe: ZKM Museum of Contemporary Art, 2011), pp. 4–5.

Welsch, Wolfgang, 'Transculturality: The Puzzling Form of Cultures Today', in Mike Featherstone and Scott Lash (eds), *Spaces of Culture: City, Nation, World* (London: Sage, 1999), pp. 194–213.

Wilson, Janet, Christina Şandru and Sarah Lawson Welsh, 'General Introduction', in Janet Wilson, Christina Şandru and Sarah Lawson Welsh (eds), *Rerouting the Postcolonial: New Directions for the New Millenium* (London, New York: Routledge, 2010), pp. 1–13.

Wu, Chin-Tao, 'Occupation by absence, preoccupation with presence: a worm's-eye view of art biennals', *Journal of Visual Culture*, 6:3 (2007), 379–86.

———, 'Biennials without borders?', *New Left Review*, no. 57 (2009), 107–15.

Xu, Ping, 'Irigaray's mimicry and the problem of essentialism', *Hypatia*, 10:4 (1995), 76–89.

Yuval-Davis, Nira, *The Politics of Belonging: Intersectional Contestations* (London: Sage, 2011).

———, *Power, Intersectionality and the Politics of Belonging*, Freia Working Paper Series (Aalborg: FREIA Feminist Research Center, 2011).

Zylinska, Joanna, *The Ethics of Cultural Studies* (London, New York: Continuum, 2005).

Index

Note: 'n.' after a page number indicates the number of a note on that page. Page numbers in *italics* refer to illustrations.